Richard Attiyeh
University of California, San Diego

George Leland Bach
Stanford University

Keith Lumsden
Stanford University

BASIC ECONOMICS:

Theory and Cases

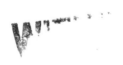

UNIVERSITY LIBRARY
GOVERNORS STATE UNIVERSITY
PARK FOREST SOUTH, ILL.

PRENTICE-HALL, INC. Englewood Cliffs, New Jersey

Library of Congress Cataloging in Publication Data

ATTIYEH, RICHARD.
  Basic economics.

    1. Economics. I. Lumsden, Keith G., joint author.
II. Bach, George Leland, joint author.
III. Title.
HB171.5.A837   330   72-8698
ISBN 0-13-059121-1

10 9 8 7 6 5 4 3 2 1

Printed in the United States of America.

Prentice-Hall International, Inc., *London*
Prentice-Hall of Australia, Pty. Ltd., *Sydney*
Prentice-Hall of Canada, Ltd., *Toronto*
Prentice-Hall of India Private, Ltd., *New Delhi*
Prentice-Hall of Japan, Inc., *Tokyo*

Contents

Preface

This dramatically different book is designed to teach basic economics to students as efficiently as possible. Its novel approach combines three different, interacting parts:

1. Programmed learning chapters, which systematically develop fundamental concepts. The student is asked to make written responses at each step of the analysis which encourages his continuous participation and involvement. Since the correct response appears at the bottom of the page, the student can see immediately whether he is understanding the material.

2. Special analytical exam questions at the end of each chapter, with the correct answer given and explained in each case. Each question highlights a key concept in an applied context. Again, the student can check for himself whether he has understood the main points.

3. Major, real-world cases to be analyzed by the student which require the concepts and theory developed in the preceding chapters. At the end of each case suggestions for analysis are presented so students can check for themselves how well they have applied the theory they are learning to real-world situations. Two of the cases are entire chapters on "Poverty" and "Does American Capitalism Need Radical Change?", which provide a concluding opportunity for students to apply what they have learned.

This integrated approach is based on the extensive research we have done, and on enthusiastic responses of hundreds of students who have tried programmed learning and have then had the opportunity to apply economic concepts and theory to real-world problems. Not only does this approach work in teaching basic economics, but it does so efficiently by concentrating on the essentials and their application. The book is strikingly shorter than most economics texts, permitting more time for related readings and student experience in applying economic analysis for themselves.

We know from research results that the approach is highly efficient when students are conscientious in filling in the programmed blanks and checking themselves through the end-of-chapter questions. Perhaps more important, the cases are both fun and intellectually satisfying, and students learn most when they enjoy what they are doing.

R.A. / G.L.B. / K.G.L.

1

Introduction: The Nature of Economic Problems

1.1 Suppose your father, wishing to encourage you to study more, made the following proposition: For every point of your grade point average (GPA) this term he will pay you $4 per day. If your GPA is 2.0, you will receive $8 per day. If an A is equivalent to 4 points, a B, 3 points, a C, 2 points, and a D, 1 point, an A average would be worth $_____ per day. Two B's and two C's would be a _(2.5/2.0/1.5)_ GPA and, therefore, would be worth only $_____ per day.

1.2 You realize immediately that the higher your grades, the _(higher/lower)_ your income from your father. Because more time devoted to studying means higher grades, the way to increase your income from your father is to spend _(more/less)_ time studying.

1.3 The more time you spend studying, however, the _____ time you have left for other income-earning pursuits, such as waiting on tables, babysitting, or pumping gas.

1.4 Your father surmised that the reason your GPA fell last semester was that you took outside jobs to earn income. He realized that in order to earn such income, you were devoting _____ to outside jobs that could otherwise have been spent studying.

1.5 Thus, your father's proposition is really an attempt to encourage you to spend_____ time studying and _____ time on outside jobs.

ANSWERS

1. 16 . 2.5 . 10
2. higher . more
3. less

4. time
5. more . less

1

1.6   The more time spent on outside employment, the _____ your income from outside sources. However, the more time spent on outside employment, the less time available for

study, and the _____ your GPA. Therefore, the more time spent on outside employment, the _____ your income from your father.

1.7   Suppose each day, on the average, you have six hours that are uncommitted to sleeping, eating, going to class, and pure entertainment. You have _____ hours per day that may be used to earn _____ by studying or from outside employment.

1.8   You know that income from your father depends upon your _____ , which in turn depends upon the _____ you spend studying.

1.9   Income from outside employment depends upon the hourly wage paid and the number of _____ you are employed.

1.10   Because you have six hours to allocate each day, your total daily _____ will be composed of GPA income from your father and/or wage income from outside employment. The more hours per day you devote to outside employment, the _____ your income from that source, but the _____ the number of hours available for study.

1.11   The smaller the number of hours devoted to study, the _____ your GPA, and the _____ your income from your father.

1.12   Thus, an increase in income from outside employment means a(n) _____ in income from your father.

1.13   In other words, there is a cost associated with earning income from an outside job that is over and above the work effort involved. This cost is the income that you could have earned by spending that time _____ . Economists call this *opportunity cost.*

1.14   When you are forced to choose from alternatives, you must give up one thing to get another. What you give up is the _____ cost of what you get. There is an opportunity _____ in taking an outside job because it is necessary to take time away from

ANSWERS

6. higher . lower . lower
7. six . income
8. GPA . time
9. hours
10. income . greater . smaller

11. lower . lower
12. decrease
13. studying
14. opportunity . cost . decreasing

something else. It is impossible, given that you have only six hours to study and/or work, to increase time spent working without _____ the time spent studying.

1.15 Likewise, in this example, it is impossible to increase income from outside employment without _____ income from your father. This loss of income from your father is the _____ cost of the outside income you earn.

1.16 What your father hopes to accomplish from his proposal is a(n) _____ in hours devoted to studying and a(n) _____ in hours devoted to outside jobs. He hopes to do this by raising the _____ _____ of the outside income you can earn.

1.17 Suppose your aim is to earn as high a daily income as possible, either from studying or outside employment or a combination of both. What would you do?

    a. Spend six hours studying
    b. Spend six hours working
    c. I do not have enough information to answer the question *(a/b/c)*

1.18 Quite correct, you do not yet have enough information. Some of the information necessary to answer the question is how your GPA changes as you vary the time spent studying. Suppose we agree on the relationship shown in Table 1.1:

Table 1.1
STUDY TIME AND GPA

Average hours spent studying per day	GPA
6	4.00
5	3.75
4	3.33
3	2.75
2	2.00
1	1.08
0	0.00

If you devoted all your uncommitted hours to studying, you would, on the average, study six hours per day; your resultant GPA would be 4.00, and at $4 per point your father would pay you $ _____ per day. In this case, your income from outside employment would

be $ _____ . Your total daily income therefore would be $ _____ .

1.19   Remember, your goal is to earn the highest possible daily _____ from both
sources combined. Do you now have enough information to decide how to allocate your six
hours to achieve this end? _(yes/no)_

1.20   If you devoted five hours to studying, your GPA would be _____ . Because your
father pays you $4 per point, your income from him would be $ _____ .

1.21   Now, five hours devoted to studying leaves _____ hour(s) free for outside employment. If you can earn only $0.50 per hour on outside employment, your five hours study-

ing plus one hour on the outside will give you a total income of $ _____ +

$_____ , which equals $ _____ .

1.22   This solution is clearly _(less/more)_ satisfactory to you, compared with studying six hours

per day, because your total income is now _____ than before.

1.23   If, however, your outside employment paid $2 per hour, your five hours studying plus one hour

working outside would yield a total income of $ _____ , which is higher than the

$ _____ from studying six hours per day.

1.24   Thus, given that your aim is to maximize (make as large as possible) your daily income, there
are several things you must know before deciding how to allocate your six hours per day. First,

you must know how much _____ you can earn from your father by studying for

different amounts of _____ . Second, you must know how much _____
you can earn by spending different amounts of time working at outside jobs.

1.25   The same kind of calculation is made, consciously or subconsciously, when you decide to spend
the evening studying in the library or going out on a date. You cannot easily quantify in
dollars "the library" versus "a date," but somehow you make the decision. When you feel
studying in the library is worth more to you (in "psychic income") than going out on a date,
you go to the library. Similarly, in this example, where you are trying to maximize

_____ , when you can earn more income by switching a study hour to outside employment, you _(should/should not)_ make that switch.

ANSWERS

19. income . no
20. 3.75 . 15
21. 1 . 15 . .50 . 15.50
22. less . lower

23. 17 . 16
24. income . time . income
25. income . should

1.26 This simple problem, concerned with the best way to allocate your six hours, is really an economic problem. Economics is concerned with the best way to allocate *scarce resources* among various alternative uses to make some individual or group as well off as possible. In our simple example, the scarce resource to be allocated is __(time/income)__ . The alternative uses of your time are outside work and _____ , and you are as well off as possible when your daily _____ is maximized.

1.27 When economists think about the economy as a whole, the scarce resources are all those things that help produce the goods and services we want. Roads, machine tools, schoolteachers, and farmland are examples of _____ resources.

1.28 Some of the alternatives society faces are more schools or more hospitals, more butter or more guns, more pop records or more classical records. Just as in our simple example income from outside work has an opportunity cost of income from your father, so in the real world there are

_____ costs. In order to produce more of one good, let us say, spaghetti, it is necessary to give up some amount of other goods. This latter amount, of course, is the

_____ _____ of the extra spaghetti.

1.29 We do not have enough _____ to produce all the goods and services everyone wants. It is for this reason that we must choose what to produce, and it is for this same reason that we say the economy's resources are _____ .

1.30 Because resources are _____ , we cannot have everything we want. Consequently, as a nation, we are faced with the economic problem of deciding how to use our _____

_____ .

1.31 Before we try to use economic analysis to understand our complex economy, let us try to master our simple example. That is, before you try to comprehend how society can use its

_____ _____ to its best advantage, let us solve the economic problem of how to use your scarce resource, which is _____ , to maximize your daily

_____ .

1.32 From the information you already have, it is possible to construct a table of figures that will permit you to see the best allocation of working time. This is the allocation that __(minimizes/maximizes)__ your daily income. Assume the hourly wage from outside employment is $2 per hour.

ANSWERS

26. time . studying . income
27. scarce
28. opportunity . opportunity cost
29. resources . scarce

30. scarce . scarce resources
31. scarce resources . time . income
32. maximizes

1.33   Table 1.2 showing the relevant information, is incomplete. Fill in the blanks. To do so you will need to remember that your father is willing to pay you $ _____ daily per each point of your GPA.

Table 1.2

TIME ALLOCATION AND INCOME

Hours spent in			Daily income		
Employment (1)	*Studying* (2)	*GPA* (3)	*Employment* (4)	*Father* (5)	*Total* (6)
0	6	4.00	$ 0	$16	$16
1	5	3.75	2	15	17
2	4	3.33	4	a) _____	b) _____
3	3	2.75	6	c) _____	d) _____
4	2	2.00	8	8	16
5	1	1.08	10	4.32	14.32
6	0	0.00	12	0	12

1.34   From Table 1.2, it is possible to determine the allocation of time that maximizes your income. This allocation is _____ hours spent studying and _____ hours in employment. In this way, you can earn a total of _____ per day.

1.35   By looking at this allocation problem in a slightly different way, it is possible to develop an analytical tool that is very useful in dealing with more difficult economic problems. As we saw above, an allocation problem concerns the use of some _____ resource so as to _____ something.

1.36   For the economy as a whole, we would be concerned about how to use the nation's _____ supply of land, labor, and capital (its resources) to _____ social welfare. In our simple example, you must decide how to use your limited _____ to maximize your daily _____ .

1.37   We solved your allocation problem by calculating for every possible allocation of six hours the resulting total income and by choosing the allocation with the _____ total income.

ANSWERS

33. 4.00
    Table 1.2 a) 13.32 . b) 17.32
    c) 11 . d) 17
34. 4 . 2 . 17.32

35. scarce . maximize
36. scarce . maximize . time
    . income
37. maximum

1.38   An alternative way to look at the problem is to start with a particular allocation, say five hours studying and one hour working, and to determine how total income changes as you change the allocation of time. If there is some way to change the allocation to increase total income, then you _(should/should not)_ make the change. If there is no change that will increase total income, then you must already have the _____ of time that gives the _____ total income.

1.39   Let us find out what happens when you reallocate one hour of your study time to outside employment. Beginning with a five hour study-one hour work combination, from Table 1.2 you can see that an increase in one hour of study time would raise your GPA from _____ to _____ . Correspondingly, the income you receive from your father would rise from $ _____ to $ _____ .

1.40   That is, starting from a level of study of five hours per day, an increase in studying of one hour per day adds $ _____ in income from your father. This, of course, is the difference between an income of $16 per day associated with a GPA of _____ and an income of $ _____ associated with a GPA of 3.75.

1.41   The increase in studying time must come from an equal _____ in time spent working. Consequently, your income from outside employment would fall from $2 to $_____ . Your new total income in this case would be $ _____ , which would be _____ than its initial level.

1.42   Carefully trace what is happening. Adding one study hour from five to six hours per day would increase your GPA; it also would _____ the daily income from your father by $ _____ . The accompanying decrease of one working hour would reduce daily income from outside employment by $ _____ . This latter amount is the opportunity _____ of the extra income from your father.

1.43   Would you increase your total income by making this change? _(yes/no)_ Essentially, you would give up $ _____ of income from working in return for $ _____ of income from studying, which is a net _(gain/loss)_ of $1. In other words your total income would _(increase/decrease)_ by the amount of $ _____ .

ANSWERS

38. should . allocation . maximum
39. 3.75 . 4.00 . 15 . 16
40. 1 . 4.00 . 15

41. decrease . 0 . 16 . lower
42. increase . 1 . 2 . cost
43. no . 2 . 1 . loss . decrease . 1

For your convenience, Table 1.2 is reproduced here.

Table 1.2

TIME ALLOCATION AND INCOME

Hours spent in			Daily income		
Employment (1)	Studying (2)	GPA (3)	Employment (4)	Father (5)	Total (6)
0	6	4.00	$ 0	$16	$16
1	5	3.75	2	15	17
2	4	3.33	4	13.32	17.32
3	3	2.75	6	11	17
4	2	2.00	8	8	16
5	1	1.08	10	4.32	14.32
6	0	0.00	12	0	12

1.44 Clearly, it __(would/would not)__ pay to change a 5-1 study-work combination to 6-0. But what about a change in the other direction? From Table 1.2, you can see that a decrease in study time to four hours would mean a _____ in your GPA from 3.75 to 3.33 and a decrease in income from your father of $ _____ .

1.45 Even though this change reduces income from your father by $1.68, it would still be worth making if the hour saved from studying could be used to earn more than $ _____ from outside employment. Because you can earn $2 per hour by working, the change from a 5-1 study-work allocation to 4-2 would _____ your total income by

$ _____ .

1.46 In this case, the $ _____ you lose from your father by studying one hour less is more than made up for by the $ _____ you can earn by using that hour working on an outside job.

1.47 Thus, it is clear that the change from 5-1 study-work allocation to 4-2 is worth making. Does this, by itself, necessarily mean that the 4-2 combination is best? __(yes/no)__ In principle, it is possible that further changes in the direction of less study and more work would lead to further increase in total _____ .

ANSWERS

44. would not . decrease . 1.68
45. 1.68 . increase . 0.32
46. 1.68 . 2
47. no . income

1.48 Consider the possibility of changing to a 3-3 study-work combination. The decline in study from four to three hours would lead to a __*(gain/loss)*__ in income from your father amounting to $ _____ , while the extra hour worked would increase your outside income by

_____ .

1.49 In this case, because the __*(gain/loss)*__ in income from your father is not matched by the _____ in outside income, the change __*(is/is not)*__ worth making.

1.50 You have seen that a change from the 4-2 study-work combination to either 5-1 or 3-3 _____ your total income. Therefore, the 4-2 study-work combination must yield the _____ total income.

1.51 What we have seen is that whether you consider this problem by looking at the total income earned from alternative allocations or by considering changes in income from _____ in allocation you arrive at the same solution. This is true because at a point of maximum income a change in any direction will _____ income.

1.52 Economists call the approach that concentrates on changes in allocations *marginal analysis.* When using _____ analysis you consider things at the margin rather than looking at the total.

1.53 In our example, we could say that a shift from 3-3 study-work combination to 4-2 would yield an increase in income from your father of $ _____ , which is the *marginal benefit* of this change. We could say that the accompanying loss in outside income of $ _____ is the *marginal cost* of the change.

1.54 In shifting from a 3-3 study-work combination to 4-2, because the _____ benefit exceeds the _____ cost, the change __*(is/is not)*__ worth making.

1.55 When you increase your study time, there are both benefits and costs because your time is scarce. Because time is scarce, you cannot increase study time without taking _____ away from some other use. As a result, you not only receive the marginal _____ of increased income from your father by studying more but you also must bear the marginal _____ of decreased income from outside employment.

ANSWERS

48. loss . 2.32 . 2
49. loss . gain . is not
50. decreases . maximum
51. changes . reduce

52. marginal
53. 2.32 . 2
54. marginal . marginal . is
55. time . benefit . cost

1.56   Generalizing from this example, we can establish several important economic principles: First, it is necessary to make choices, whenever resources (for example, time) are _____ .

1.57   Second, whenever a choice must be made there is an opportunity _____ involved. When you choose an apple over an orange, the orange is the _____ _____ of the apple.

1.58   Third, however your resources are allocated to begin with, when you consider a change in that allocation there are both a marginal _____ and a marginal _____ .

1.59   Finally, a change is worth making only when the _____ _____ is greater than the _____ _____ .

1.60   These facts of economic life hold true whether we consider your simple problem of allocating your time or the complex problem of allocating the economy's many _____ resources.

1.61   The war in Vietnam provides a case in point. To carry out this war, it was necessary to use substantial quantities of the nation's _____ _____ . Sadly, one great cost incurred was the substantial loss of human life—a loss that cannot be measured solely in economic terms.

1.62   Over and above this tragic loss of life, there was also an additional enormous opportunity cost. In 1971, it was estimated that up until then the cost of the war to the United States, excluding human casualties, had exceeded $100 billion. If the war had been avoided, the resources used to carry out the war *(could/could not)* have been used to produce civilian commodities that American families and businesses could have put to good use. If there had been no war, the land, labor, and capital used to produce jet fighters, napalm, and mortars *(could/could not)* have been used to produce new schools, better health services, and more clothing. Some facts will illustrate the _____ cost of the war; that is, alternatives foregone when scarce resources were devoted to the war effort.

1.63   Roughly half of all U.S. families could now have a private swimming pool or another automobile if the scarce _____ used to carry out the war had been diverted to the swimming pool or automobile industries over the span of the war.

ANSWERS

56. scarce
57. cost . opportunity cost
58. benefit (cost) . cost (benefit)
59. marginal benefit . marginal cost

60. scarce
61. scarce resources
62. could . could . opportunity
63. resources

1.64   In fiscal year 1969, the year of peak expenditures for Vietnam, it was estimated that of the $28.8 billion of military expenditures in Vietnam, $7.3 billion would have been spent for

defense in the absence of that war. Thus, the difference of $ _____ billion represents the extra (or marginal) cost of the war itself for that year. If this amount were given to the 10 million poorest families instead of being spent in Vietnam, these families could have received additional income of over $2,000 per family in 1969. Doing without a significant lessening of poverty in the U.S., therefore, can be considered one measure of the

_____ cost of the war. As you will see later in the text, exact definitions of the extent of poverty, its causes and cures, pose many problems for our society. What is obvious,

however, given limited resources, is that more of one type of good means _____ of some other goods.

1.65   The Vietnam war versus no Vietnam war is the classic choice between "guns and butter." In deciding to expand the war, the government chose to reallocate resources to produce

_____ guns and _____ butter. The political and strategic gain re-

sulting from more "guns" is the marginal _____ from this reallocation. The lower

living standards resulting from less "butter" is the marginal _____ .

1.66   Those who supported the government's Vietnam policy obviously believed that the war's mar-

ginal _____ outweighed its marginal _____ .

1.67   Those who opposed the war held the opposite view. To them, reallocating resources from fighting, let us say, poverty in the United States to fighting communism in Vietnam _(increased/decreased)_ the welfare of the American people.

1.68   Another example in which the concepts of scarcity, opportunity cost, and marginal analysis are useful is the battle over the California redwood forests. Redwood trees make both beautiful forests and handsome lumber. Unfortunately, if you cut a forest for lumber, it is _(just as/no longer)_ beautiful to look at. Furthermore, there are not enough redwoods to fully satisfy people's desires for both beautiful forests and handsome lumber. If society chooses to preserve a forest rather than use the wood for lumber, the foregone lumber is the

_____ _____ of the beautiful forest.

1.69   In economic terms, then, we have said that redwoods are a natural resource that is

_____ and for which there are alternative uses. Consequently, for every grove of redwoods, we _(have no/must make a)_ choice.

ANSWERS

64. 21.5 . opportunity . less
65. more . less . benefit . cost
66. benefit . cost

67. decreased
68. no longer . opportunity cost
69. scarce . must make a

1.70   Whichever choice is made, we must give up one of the alternatives. That is, we will have to accept the _____ cost. If we choose to cut a grove, we must face up to the loss of a beautiful forest.

1.71   It will pay to cut the grove, however, only if the marginal _____ of the extra lumber outweighs the marginal _____ of one less redwood grove.

1.72   In these examples, we have shown how an economist analyzes social problems. But one rather obvious point should have been made explicit. Before you can compare the marginal benefit and marginal cost of any change, you must know what the marginal _____ and marginal _____ are. In both of the policy problems discussed, it was necessary to make subjective value judgments before you could make any decision. That is, you had to subjectively weigh the _____ benefits of the war, for instance, against the marginal costs. Much bitter strife on college campuses and in cities over the war issue is evidence that different groups of people hold widely different value judgments on these benefits and costs.

1.73   In all economic problems, you must know people's preferences as well as their alternatives before you can make a rational decision. Economics __*(can/cannot)*__ determine value judgments, but once society's preferences and available resources are known, the application of economic principles will lead to rational decision-making.

REVIEW QUESTIONS

Below each question is a suggested explanation of the correct answer. Before reading the explanation, circle the response you believe is correct.

Make sure you read through all the responses and know why one is correct and the others are incorrect before making your decision.

1.1   This question is based on the following statement:
"The question facing our government is whether to build a new highway system or establish public libraries throughout the country during the next three years. Resources for both projects are not available. It must be one or the other."
The opportunity cost of the new highway system mentioned in the paragraph above is

a. greater than the economy can afford.   c. the money required to pay for it.
b. national libraries.   d. the resources required to build it.

If the government were to build the new highway system, it would have to raise the money to pay for it and resources would be required to build it. But neither of these costs is the oppor-

ANSWERS

70. marginal
71. benefit . cost

72. benefit . cost . marginal
73. cannot

tunity cost of the highway system. Whether the government builds a highway system or establishes public libraries, the money will be spent and the resources used. The opportunity cost of a good is the alternative that must be given up to obtain that good. Whether the opportunity cost of the new highway system is greater than the economy can afford depends on whether it will yield lower benefits than the library system. If it does, the opportunity cost is too high and the highway system should not be built. The correct response is b.

1.2   What is meant by the assertion that every economic system, be it communist, socialist or capitalist, faces the fundamental fact of scarcity?

a. As a country starts to develop, many commodities that were scarce become more plentiful, and people become better off on the average.

b. When jobs are unavailable, many low-skilled, poorly paid workers, including a disproportionate number of minority workers, become poverty stricken.

c. Insufficient resources exist to satisfy all the wants in any given society.

d. All economies allocate too many resources to private consumption and too few to public goods.

Although a, b, and d are all true and although they are all concerned with scarcity, none of them explains the fundamental fact of scarcity faced by each and every nation in the world today. This scarcity arises because no matter what the resources any nation in the world has today, they are insufficient to satisfy all the wants of the people of that nation. The correct response is c.

1.3   Economic resources are termed *scarce resources* because they

a. are not available in sufficient quantities to meet all orders for them.

b. are not available in sufficient quantities to meet all orders for them.

c. cannot be increased in quantity to any significant extent.

d. are of primary importance in satisfying the needs of society.

A resource is scarce whenever having more of it would make someone better off. It is possible for a resource to be scarce even though enough is available to fill all orders (people might like to have more cars but cannot afford to buy more). A resource that cannot be increased in quantity may be scarce, but so may resources that can be. Whenever there are unsatisfied wants, resources are scarce.

1.4   "Because resources are scarce, it is necessary for our society to economize." Which, if any, of the following does this statement imply should be done?

1. Consumers should save more.
2. The government should reduce its expenditure for goods and services.
3. The production of luxuries should be reduced.

a. 1 and 2 only

b. 2 and 3 only

c. 1 and 3 only

d. None of the above

The basic economic problem facing each nation is how to make the best possible use of its scarce productive resources. Neither consumers saving more, reducing government expenditure, nor reducing the production of luxuries implies economizing in this sense. The most efficient use of resources could, in some circumstances, involve less saving, increasing government expenditure, or increasing the production of luxuries. The best use of resources will involve the production of the combination of resources that satisfies people's wants as fully as possible. The correct response is   d.

Case 1

PUBLIC VS. PRIVATE EXPENDITURE

In 1958, a well-known economist and public figure, John Kenneth Galbraith, wrote a book entitled *The Affluent Society*. In it, he strongly argued for an increase in public (that is, government) expenditure and a cutback in private expenditure. Since then, his analysis has been hotly debated. The main argument of the book, freely interpreted, is paraphrased below:

American economic society has reached a level of affluence such that it is no longer important to expand the level of national output beyond what might be needed to keep pace with growth in population. This is not to say that the United States is not beset with economic problems, but just that these problems do not arise out of scarcity of resources, but rather are due to imbalances in the way those resources are used. Owing to the capitalist structure of American society and the persuasive power of advertising, we spend so much of our income on private goods (autos, clothing, liquor, television, and so on) that the public sector remains starved for financial resources. If you look at the problems of America, you see that the great needs are not more consumer goods, but more public goods, such as hospitals, schools, recreational facilities, and public transportation. If you evaluate the contributions to economic well-being of more television sets and more hospitals, there is no question that you would decide in favor of hospitals. What compounds the problem is that the typical consumer is so mesmerized by the advertising messages of Madison Avenue, he cannot see his needs clearly enough to make the right political choice. Consequently, the social imbalance will be perpetuated unless a more persuasive lobby for public needs is formed.

To help you assess the validity of this argument,

the following tables are provided to show how total income was spent by consumers and government in 1970.

What do you think of the preceding argument? What would be the costs of expanding government expenditure? Would you favor expanding the public sector, even if it meant less income for you to spend privately? Why or why not?

SUGGESTIONS FOR ANALYSIS

Although Galbraith's book obviously raised issues that are still highly relevant, part of his argument is more in the form of value judgment than economic analysis, and there are no economic tools that could ever resolve differences in such personal opinions. On the analytical side, however, the notion that scarcity is no longer a problem and the idea that there is a misallocation of resources between the public and private sectors are logically inconsistent. If resources were not scarce, it would mean we had all that we wanted and it would not matter how resources were allocated. Problems of resource allocation arise only in a world of scarcity, and to suggest that we have an allocation problem is to admit that our resources are scarce.

By focusing on the image of the upper middle class materialistic boor, Galbraith suggests that we clearly do not need more material goods. But the average American just is not that well off. If, in 1970, total disposable personal income had been divided evenly among all persons, each person would have had but $64 per week to spend. Although this puts the average American way ahead

Table 1.a

PRIVATE CONSUMPTION EXPENDITURE FOR GOODS AND SERVICES, 1970

	Expenditure (billions of dollars)	*Percent of national expenditure*
Total	617	63
Automobiles and parts	37	4
Furniture and household equipment	39	4
Food and beverages	132	14
Clothing and shoes	52	5
Gasoline and oil	23	2
Housing	92	9
Household operation	36	4
Transportation	18	2
Medical care	22	2
Other	166	17

Table 1.b

GOVERNMENT EXPENDITURE FOR GOODS AND SERVICES, 1970

	Expenditure (billions of dollars)	*Percent of national expenditure*
Total	180	18.3
National defense	73	7.5
Space research and technology	5	0.5
Education	40	4.1
Health	9	0.9
Transportation	16	1.6
Police, fire, and correction	6	0.6
Agricultural and natural resources	6	0.6
Government administration	10	1.0
Other	15	1.5

of most non-Americans, it does not provide all that much for frivolous playthings. But what is more, although the average was $64 per week, many Americans had much less than that to spend, and for them more of the good things of life that could be bought with higher incomes—better housing, higher quality food, more entertainment—would

seem well worth having even if none of them were advertised.

But Galbraith stresses fundamental economics when he emphasizes that higher levels of private consumption have a very real cost, namely, the public goods that must be foregone. Although everyone would like to have more consumer goods if they came absolutely free, Galbraith clearly implies that they can never come free because (in a world of scarcity) they will always have an opportunity cost. In this case, the opportunity cost of private consumption is public consumption foregone. But although most people will admit that there are pressing public needs, the opportunity cost argument cuts both ways. We cannot have expanded public consumption without having less private consumption.

What is clear in this, as in most resource allocation problems, is that the issue cannot be decided without making value judgments. Economic analysis cannot tell you whether you will benefit more from public parks or private entertainment. But it can help you and others in society make sure that you take into account all the benefits and costs and make your decision, given your value judgments, on a rational basis.

2

Marginal Analysis

2.1 In Chapter 1, you learned that whenever resources are _____ a choice must be made among the alternative uses of those resources. Because resources are scarce, whenever they are put to one use there will be the _____ cost of the benefit that would have resulted had they been put to an alternative use.

2.2 For example, as was discussed in Chapter 1, to carry out the Vietnam war it was necessary to use _____ that could have been used to satisfy domestic wants. That is, the civilian commodities that could have been produced with the resources used to fight the Vietnam war were the _____ cost of the war.

2.3 This can be seen in terms of Table 2.1 and Figure 2.1, which illustrate in terms of "guns" and "butter" the alternative combinations of military and civilian output that could have been produced with society's _____ in some given time period.

The curve shown in Figure 2.1 shows the production of guns and butter from all possible resource allocations. For this reason, it is called a _____ _____ curve.

2.4 If all resources were devoted to the production of guns, we would be able to produce _____ guns and nothing else. We would be at point _____ on the production possibilities curve.

ANSWERS

1. scarce . opportunity
2. resources . opportunity

3. resources . production possibilities
4. 800 . k

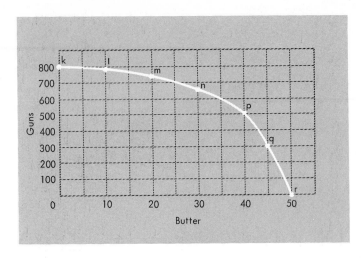

Figure 2.1
Production possibilities curve

Table 2.1

PRODUCTION ALTERNATIVES

Guns	Butter (Tons)
800	0
780	10
730	20
660	30
500	40
300	45
0	50

2.5 Now, if a small amount of resources were devoted to the production of butter, as at the point l, we would be giving up _____ guns to obtain _____ tons of butter.

2.6 The point q represents _____ guns and _____ tons of butter. By moving from k to q, therefore, we would be giving up _____ guns to obtain _____ tons of butter.

2.7 Is it worth moving from k to q? *(yes/no/don't know)*

ANSWERS

5. 20 . 10   7. don't know
6. 300 . 45 . 500 . 45

2.8   The reason we do not know if it is worth moving from k to q is because we do not know how society values guns versus butter. We do not know, for this society, in moving from k to q, whether the benefit of _____ more tons of butter is worth the cost of _____ fewer guns.

2.9   This example is similar to all resource allocation problems in economics. What proportion of resources should be allocated to the production of different goods? The _____ _____ curve tells what outputs of each good will be associated with different resource allocations. The economic problem is: Which of the different combinations of goods that can be produced with society's limited _____ should be produced?

2.10   How to allocate scarce resources to make society as well off as possible is the _____ problem.

2.11   To understand the economic problem of choice from among alternative resource allocations let us consider again our simple work-study example from Chapter 1. You will recall that the objective was to maximize the _____ you could earn by allocating your time between work and study. In this example, your scarce resource was _____.

2.12   The alternative feasible combinations of work and study time can be seen in Table 2.2 and Figure 2.2.

Table 2.2

INCOME ALTERNATIVES

	Study		Outside Work
Hrs.	In-come	Hrs.	In-come
6	$16	0	$ 0
5	15	1	2
4	13.32	2	4
3	11	3	6
2	8	4	8
1	4.32	5	10
0	0	6	12

ANSWERS

8. 45 . 500
9. production possibilities . resources
10. economic

11. income . time
12. 6

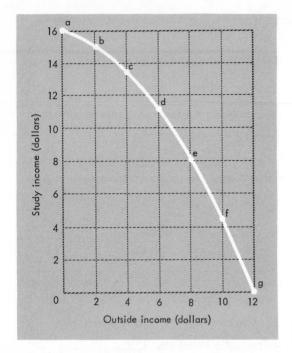

Figure 2.2
Income possibilities curve

The points a, b, c, d, e, f, and g represent the different combinations of study income plus out-

side income obtainable by using the _____ hours available, that is, by using the

amount of the scarce resource available.

2.13   Point a, for instance, represents study income of $ _____ and outside income of

$ _____ . This combination of income is obtained from _____ hours

of studying and _____ hours of outside work.

2.14   Point d represents study income of $ _____ and work income of $ _____ .

This point corresponds to _____ hours of studying and _____ hours
of outside work.

2.15   If we took all possible study-work combinations, we would obtain a smooth curve connecting
points a through g, as in Figure 2.2. For instance, 5½ hours of outside work would yield an

outside income of $ _____ and ½ hour of studying would yield a study income

greater than zero but less than the $ _____ that could be obtained from one hour
of studying. The point so derived would lie on the curve in Figure 2.2 between the points

_____ and _____ .

ANSWERS

13. 16 . 0 . 6 . 0   15. 11 . 4.32 . f . g
14. 11 . 6 . 3 . 3

2.16   The curve in Figure 2.2, then, is the income possibilities curve that gives all the alternative combinations of work and study _____ that are possible to attain with the six hours available to you. The economic problem, of course, is to pick the allocation of time that yields the _____ income.

2.17   In this simple case, it is possible to find the best allocation of time by considering all possible allocations of time. In more complex situations, for example allocating resources for the entire economy, such a straightforward approach is not possible. For that reason, it will be useful to consider in detail the marginal approach that was developed in Chapter 1. You will recall that given any initial situation you can imagine allocating one unit more of your resources to some particular use. This change will involve a benefit, which is called the _(total/marginal)_ benefit, and a cost, which is the _____ cost.

2.18   In our example, we can imagine allocating one more unit of time (an hour) to studying. The extra income from your father as a reward for the ensuing higher grade point average is the _____ _____ of studying. But because you can study more only by working less there is an opportunity cost involved. The income you give up by working one hour less is the marginal _____ of studying.

2.19   It is helpful to analyze these concepts with the help of diagrams. Look at Figure 2.3. Along the horizontal axis we measure the hours worked in outside employment and along the vertical axis we measure the hourly _____ _____ that can be earned from outside employment.

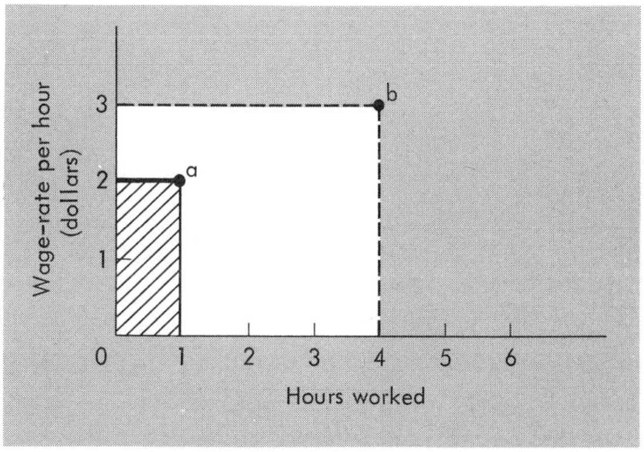

Figure 2.3
Income from outside employment depending on hours worked and the wage rate

2.20   Two points are plotted in Figure 2.3. Each point represents a particular combination of hours worked and wage rate. Point a stands for one hour worked at a wage rate of $_____

ANSWERS

16. income . maximum
17. marginal . marginal
18. marginal benefit . cost

19. wage rate
20. 2 . 4 . 3

per hour. Point b represents _____ hours worked at a wage rate of $_____
per hour.

2.21   If you worked one hour per day at a wage rate of $2 per hour, your daily income would be

$_____ . In Figure 2.3 this is represented by the area of the smaller rectangle,
which is found by multiplying length by height. The length is the same as hours worked and

the height is the same as the _____ _____ . Therefore, the area of the
rectangle and dollars of daily income will be *(equal/unequal)* . They will both be equal to

the number of _____ _____ times the hourly _____

_____ .

2.22   If you worked four hours at a wage rate of $3 per hour, you would earn $_____ .
In Figure 2.3 this is represented by the _____ of the larger rectangle.

2.23

Table 2.3

WORK INCOME, TOTAL AND MARGINAL

Hours spent working	Total income	Marginal income
0	$ 0	
		$2
1	2	
		2
2	4	
		2
3	6	
		2
4	8	
		2
5	10	
		2
6	12	

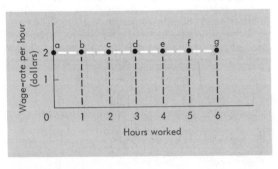

Figure 2.4
Wage rate and hours worked

In Figure 2.4, derived from Table 2.3, the points a, b, c, d, e, f, and g are all associated with the same wage rate of $ _____ per hour but with different numbers of _____ worked. The point b, for instance, is associated with one hour worked at $2 per hour. With what number of hours worked are a, d, and f associated? a) _____ d) _____ f) _____ .

2.24 As in Figure 2.3, the _____ of the various rectangles in Figure 2.4 will represent daily income from different numbers of _____ worked at a wage rate of $2 per hour.

2.25 The rectangle, for instance, whose corners are 0, 5, f, and a will have an area of _____ units, representing an income of $ _____ . The area is calculated by multiplying the length, _____ units, by the height, _____ units. Daily income is calculated by multiplying _____ _____ (on the horizontal axis) by a _____ _____ on the vertical axis.

2.26 What does the constant height of line ag indicate? It shows you for any number of hours worked the income you would gain or lose by working one hour more or one hour _____ . Thus, it shows you the _(marginal/total)_ income gained by working more or lost by working less. Because the height is constant, the _____ income from working is constant.

2.27 Let us now consider how to represent the marginal benefits from studying. Table 2.4 repeats data from Chapter 1.

Table 2.4
STUDY INCOME, TOTAL AND MARGINAL

Hours spent studying	Income from your father	Marginal income
0	$ 0	
		$4.32
1	4.32	
		3.68
2	8	
		3
3	11	
		2.32
4	13.32	
		1.68
5	15	
		1
6	16	

ANSWERS

24. areas . hours
25. 10 . 10 . 5 . 2 . hours worked . wage rate

26. less . marginal . marginal
27. marginal . less

The third column gives your _____ income, that is, the income gained from one extra hour of studying (or the income lost from one hour _____ of studying).

2.28   If, instead of studying for one hour, you decide to study for two hours, your total income from your father will increase from $ _____ to $ _____ , that is, by

$ _____ .

2.29   This increase in income is due to the additional hour of study or, in other words, the _____ income in this example is $ _____ .

2.30   Proceeding in the opposite direction: If you were originally studying for two hours per day, your daily income from your father would be $ _____ . If you now decided to study one hour less, the daily income would fall to $ _____ or decrease by

$ _____

2.31   Whether an increase from 1 to 2 in time spent studying or a decrease from 2 to 1, the marginal _____ gained or lost would be $ _____ .

2.32   In Figure 2.5, where we have plotted data from Table 2.4, we show the relationship between hours spent studying and marginal income.

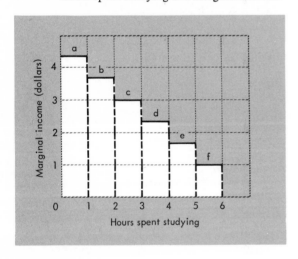

Figure 2.5
Marginal income from studying—I

In going from zero to one hour studying, total study income increases from zero to

$ _____ . This _____ income is represented in Figure 2.5 by the

rectangle a. The area of rectangle a is _____ units.

2.33 Adding another hour of studying (that is, bringing the total study time up to two hours) adds

$ _____ to study income. This marginal _____ is represented by

rectangle _____ , whose area is _____ units.

2.34 Thus, total study income from two hours of studying will be the increase in income from the

first hour of studying plus the _____ in income from the second hour of studying.
In Figure 2.5, this will be the area of rectangle a plus the area of rectangle b, or

_____ units plus _____ units, giving a total of _____ units.

2.35 Similarly, the sum of the areas of rectangles a, b, c, d, e, and f is the total _____

from six hours of study. This total is $ _____ .

2.36 For simplicity, we have considered the marginal income associated with one-hour changes in
time spent studying. This has resulted in the step graph of Figure 2.5. If we consider smaller
time increments, for instance quarter hours, we shall still have a step graph, but the steps will

be _(smaller/larger)_ , each hour now having _____ steps.

2.37 As we continue to take smaller and smaller time intervals on the horizontal axis, the number
of steps in the graph will _(increase/decrease)_ , each succeeding step becoming
 (smaller/larger) and _(smaller/larger)_ .

2.38 As the steps become smaller, the graph comes closer to being a straight line. If we divided the
first hour, for instance, into minutes instead of quarter hours, we would have _____

rectangles instead of 4, and if we divided it into seconds, we would have 3,600. As we imagine
subdividing the horizontal axis into more and more, smaller and smaller units, for example

milliseconds, the graph will become closer and closer to being a _____ line as in
Figure 2.6.

2.39 In Figure 2.6, the line jk results from taking smaller and smaller intervals of the horizontal axis.

The _____ under the line jk will represent study _____ from
studying six hours.

ANSWERS

33. 3.68 . income . b . 3.68
34. increase . 4.32 . 3.68 . 8
35. income . 16
36. smaller . four

37. increase . smaller . smaller
38. 60 . straight
39. area . income

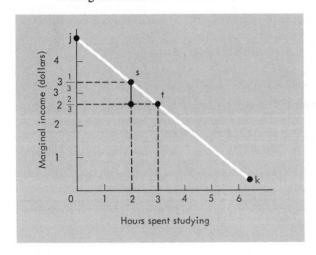

Figure 2.6
Marginal income from studying—II

2.40   This area will equal the _____ of the six rectangles a, b, c, d, e, and f. The un-shaded areas now included by the line jk will equal the unshaded portions of each of the rectangles left outside by the line jk.

2.41   In Figure 2.7, the point s on line jk is associated with 2 hours of studying and a marginal income

of _____ . The point t is associated with _____ hours of studying and

a marginal income of _____ .

Figure 2.7
Marginal income from studying

ANSWERS

40. areas

41. 3 1/3 . 3 . 2 2/3

2.42 A movement from s to t occurs when you increase study time from _____ to _____ with a corresponding decrease in marginal income from _____ to _____ .

2.43 As you increase hours studying, even though your marginal _____ decreases (that is, the line jk is negatively sloped), your total income _____ , that is, the area under the marginal income line, *(increases/decreases)* from 0js2 to 0jt3.

2.44 Now reconsider Figure 2.4 (repeated here as Figure 2.8), which shows the marginal gain from outside working or, because every hour of outside work means one less hour studying, the marginal *(gain/cost)* of studying.

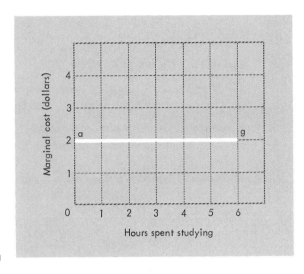

Figure 2.8
Marginal cost of studying

Each additional hour spent studying means an hour _____ spent working. Thus, the cost of an additional hour spent studying, that is, the marginal cost of *(studying/working)* , is the _____ forgone by not working that hour. In this example, that cost is constant per hour and equal to $ _____ . The area of the large rectangle 0ag6, which represents the income forgone by not working at all, equals $ _____ . The area of any of the smaller rectangles equals _____ forgone by not working that extra hour, that is, the _____ _____ of studying.

ANSWERS

42. 2 . 3 . 3 1/3 . 2 2/3
43. income . increases . increases

44. cost . less . studying . income . 2
   . 12 . income . marginal cost

2.45   In order for any activity to be worth undertaking, its benefit must exceed the opportunity cost. As you will recall from Chapter 1, the benefit that could be derived from the best alternative activity is the _____ cost. In deciding whether to study one hour, you must take into account the income forgone by not working that hour. The income forgone by not working is the _____ cost of studying.

2.46   For example, if you were to study one hour, your study income would be $4.32, but you would also lose $ _____ by not working that hour. The benefit from studying one hour is $ _____ , while the _____ cost is $2. Because the benefit from studying one hour is _(greater/smaller)_ than the _____ _____ of studying one hour, it _(will/will not)_   pay you to study at least one hour.

2.47   With this in mind, consider Figure 2.9, which is a combination of the figures with which you are familiar. The line jk shows the _____ income from studying, and line ag shows the _____ income forgone by not working. The marginal income from studying is, of course, the marginal _(benefit/cost)_   of studying, and the marginal income forgone by not working is the marginal _____ of studying. At two hours spent studying, the marginal benefit of studying is _(greater/less)_   than the marginal cost.

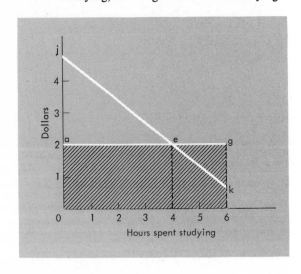

Figure 2.9
Study and work income

2.48   At point e, lines jk and ag intersect. This point e corresponds to _____ hours of studying.

45. opportunity . opportunity
46. 2 . 4.32 . opportunity . greater
    . opportunity cost . will

47. marginal . marginal . benefit . cost
    . greater
48. four

2.49 To the left of e, that is, up to four hours of studying, the line jk lies *(above/below)*   the

line ag, showing that the _____ income from studying is *(greater/less)*   than
the marginal income forgone by not working.

2.50 Thus, at any point less than four hours of studying, your income will increase if you spend

more time _____ and less time _____ .

2.51 Above four hours of studying, however, the _____ benefit from studying is
 (greater/less)   than the marginal cost of studying. At any point above four hours of studying,
it would pay you to *(increase/decrease)*   time spent studying. Only at four hours spent

studying, where the _____ benefit and cost are equal, will there be no incentive to
change the amount of time spent studying. Thus, the point where total income from both

studying and working is a maximum must be _____ hours studying and

_____ hours working.

2.52 We have seen that the optimum, or best, position is where the _____ benefit

and _____ cost are _____ . Only at such a position will it be
impossible to improve your position by making a change.

2.53 Whenever the marginal benefit of some activity exceeds the marginal cost, it will pay to
 (increase/decrease)   that activity. And, whenever the marginal benefit falls short of the
marginal cost, the activity should be *(increased/decreased)* .

2.54 This principle applies to any situation where a choice of different combinations is involved.
Taking more of one always involves giving up more of the other. As a result, there will always

be an opportunity _____ that must be compared to the benefit of taking more of

one. And the best combination will be that for which the marginal _____ and

marginal _____ are equal.

ANSWERS

49. above . marginal . greater
50. studying . working
51. marginal . less . decrease . marginal
    . four . two

52. marginal . marginal . equal
53. increase . decreased
54. cost . benefit . cost

REVIEW QUESTIONS

Questions 1 and 2 are based on the following diagram:

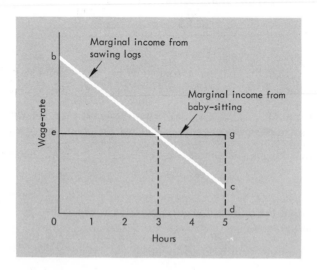

2.1   You have five hours to spend working. Which of the following statements are true?

a. The more time you spend sawing up logs, the less income you earn per hour of sawing.

b. The hourly wage rate you can earn baby-sitting is oe.

c. To maximize daily income, you would have to both saw logs and baby-sit.

d. All of the above.

2.2   You have five hours to spend working. Which of the following statements are true?

a. Daily income would be maximized by spending three hours sawing logs and two hours baby-sitting.

b. The maximum daily income you can earn is obfgd.

c. After three hours of log sawing, the marginal income from log sawing is less than the marginal income from baby-sitting.

d. All of the above.

Because the line bc is negatively inclined to the wage-rate axis, marginal income from log sawing decreases as time spent sawing increases. However, because the line eg is horizontal, marginal income from baby-sitting is constant and equal to oe per hour. The significance of those lines intersecting at f is that, after three hours of log sawing, additional time spent in the activity yields a lower marginal income compared with baby-sitting. Thus, to maximize income, you would spend three hours sawing logs (yielding an income of obf3) and two hours baby-sitting (yielding an income of 3fgd). The maximum daily income you can earn, therefore, is represented by the area obfgd. The correct response to both questions is d.

2.3   The government is considering an increase in expenditure for medical services. It should undertake this expenditure

a. if the total benefit derived from all medical services still exceeds the total cost.

b. if the total benefit derived from all medical services still exceeds that of any other good.

c. if the benefit from the extra medical services outweighs the cost of doing with less of other goods.

d. only if all of the above are true.

The real or opportunity cost of any good is what is given up to have that good. Efficiency in resource allocation is achieved when no resource, by being reallocated, could yield a greater benefit than it does in its current occupation. Thus, the government should increase medical services expenditure if and only if the benefit from the goods that must be given up does not outweigh the benefit from the additional medical services that have to be considered. (Note that only when the last dollar spent by the government on each possible service yields the same benefit will the total benefit from government expenditure not be increased by any reallocation.) The correct response is c.

2.4   A government has completed a cost-benefit study showing that the annual value of the services from an additional 100 miles of highway would be $4 million and the annual value of the services from an additional airport would be $3 million.
To achieve the most efficient use of resources the government should

a. construct only 75 miles of highway (that is, 3/4 of 100).

b. construct only the 100 miles of highway.

c. construct both the 100 miles of highway and the airport.

d. not necessarily construct either any additional highway or the airport.

To maximize society's welfare, the government should allocate expenditure so that the marginal benefit from the last dollar spent on each good equals the marginal cost. If this condition did not hold, the government could increase welfare by reallocating its expenditure. Because no information is given about the costs of constructing highways or airports, it is impossible to tell whether carrying out either project, or both projects, would achieve an efficient use of resources. The correct response is   d.

Case 2

MARGINAL ANALYSIS AND NOISE POLLUTION

There are certain sounds or noises that give certain people pleasure—the discotheque in full swing or a grand opera chorus. There are other noises, equally loud, that yield displeasure—motorcycles with no mufflers or jet aircraft. Many freeways that pass through residential areas cause noise levels that make the residents complain, and often action is taken to reduce such noise levels to tolerable proportions.

How can marginal analysis help a society make sensible decisions in reducing noise pollution? Noise can be measured on a dB(A) (decibel) scale.

For noise levels below 68 on the scale, people seldom complain, whereas permanent ear damage can result at dB (A) levels above 90 if an individual is exposed to such a level over a protracted period of time. You might think about this if you are a rock music fan and you might also note the ear muffs worn by ground personnel at airports.

Let us imagine that the residents of some community decide to reduce the noise level from the freeway passing through their community. The average noise level measures 85 on a dB (A) scale. The following four options are available to the community to reduce the freeway noise. The community can choose one or more.

Action	Marginal change in noise level	Annual cost
(1) Build concrete wall 6 feet high	−10 dB(A)'s	$ 160,000*
Or build concrete wall 8 feet high	−12 dB(A)'s	$ 190,000*
Or build concrete wall 10 feet high	−13 dB(A)'s	$ 230,000*
(2) Reduce speed limit and enforce limit through police control (−10 mph)	− 3 dB(A)'s	90,000
(3) Resurface road	− 2 dB(A)'s	70,000*
(4) Rebuild and sink the road 12 feet	−10 dB(A)'s	2,500,000*

*Total cost divided by estimated number of years of useful life.

The community voted that it is prepared to pay $31,000 annually for each dB(A) that noise is reduced. The local mayor argues for a 10-foot wall because annual costs will be only $230,000 and annual benefits will be $403,000 ($31,000 × 13). Do you agree with the mayor?

SUGGESTIONS FOR ANALYSIS

Although the mayor is correct in asserting that the total benefits from building the 10-foot wall exceed the total cost, his lack of understanding of the marginal principle has led him to propose an inefficient solution to the problem. The 6-foot wall is worth $310,000 ($31,000 × 10) to the community and costs only $160,000. The marginal gain to the community of building that wall exceeds the marginal cost; it is clearly worth building. By adding 2 more feet to the wall, the marginal gain is $62,000 ($31,000 × 2) and the marginal cost is $30,000 ($190,000 − $160,000);

the extra 2 feet are clearly worth adding. By adding yet an additional 2 feet, that is, building a 10-foot wall, the marginal benefit is $31,000 [that is, −1 dB(A)], whereas the marginal cost is $40,000 ($230,000 − $190,000). Thus, the additional benefit in going from an 8-foot wall to a 10-foot wall is not worth the additional cost. The 8-foot wall should be built, therefore, but not the 10-foot wall.

By similar reasoning, the additional benefit from reducing the speed limit by 10 mph and 3 dB(A)'s is $93,000, and the marginal cost is less, namely $90,000; thus, the speed limit should also be reduced.

However, for the remaining two options, resurfacing the road and rebuilding the road, the marginal cost exceeds the marginal benefit.

The community should therefore build the 8-foot wall and reduce the speed limit. Marginal analysis is essential in making the correct decision.

3

The Theory of Consumer Choice

3.1   In Chapters 1 and 2, we studied the principles of optimal resource allocation that apply whenever you must choose among alternative uses for scarce resources. In this chapter, we shall study how an individual allocates income to make himself as well off as possible. For most individuals, income is a scarce _____ to be allocated among many alternatives. In economic jargon, we say that the individual attempts to maximize *utility* (or satisfaction) subject to a *budget constraint.*

3.2   If, between the next two pages of this book, you found a dollar bill that was a gift from me to you (this is purely hypothetical, you realize), how would you spend it? The answer is fairly obvious; if you were a rational person, you would spend it in such a way that you would receive maximum _____ (or satisfaction) from the dollar.

3.3   There exist many ways to spend the dollar. You have many wants you would like to satisfy, and manufacturers have produced many commodities they would like you to purchase. But you cannot buy them all; you cannot satisfy all your _____ because you have a _____ constraint.

3.4   You will use your limited income, in this example $1, to purchase those commodities that will satisfy you as completely as possible in such a situation. That is, you will attempt to _____ your _____ subject to your _____ constraint.

ANSWERS

1. resource
2. utility

3. wants . budget
4. maximize . utility . budget

3.5   You know better than anyone else what you like. Subject to legal considerations, most people in this country are free to spend or allocate their _____ as they wish. As we shall see, it is the way that consumers like yourself allocate their _____ that encourages manufacturers to produce the commodities people want most.

3.6   Manufacturers respond to consumers' preferences as expressed through their spending habits. An economy operating in such fashion is said to allocate its scarce _____ through a *free market,* or *free enterprise* system.

3.7   Some people argue that consumers do not always know their best interests, and there should be limits on the way resources are allocated through a _____ _____ system to reflect _____ wants. For instance, it is argued that horror comics should be banned because they are not "good" for people. The same arguments are used in regard to alcohol, cigarettes, and large automobiles. But in a free enterprise economy like the United States, people __*(do/do not)*__ allocate part of their income to the purchase of horror comics, alcohol, cigarettes, and large automobiles, and, in response to consumers' spending, manufacturers __*(do/do not)*__ produce these goods.

3.8   Advocates of a completely free _____ system do not believe consumers should be told what to buy or not to buy but believe that individual _____ know their own interests best. We shall study how consumers signal with dollar votes to indicate their *preferences* to manufacturers. Manufacturers in turn hire scarce _____ and produce the goods and services consumers want if profits are sufficient in those fields of production. Manufacturers, we assume, are motivated by a profit incentive, __*(or/not)*__ by their judgments as to what people should buy. Consequently, in a free enterprise system, they will produce according to consumers' _____ , only to the extent that this is consistent with maximum profits for producers.

3.9   It is important to remember that manufacturers are concerned with people's preferences only to the extent that those wants are backed by dollar votes. You may prefer an expensive sports car to a standard four door sedan, but manufacturers will not be overly impressed by this preference unless you use your _____ votes to express your preferences by actively bidding in the market. In later chapters, we shall show under what circumstances in a free enterprise system resources will be allocated in accordance with consumer _____ as expressed by dollar votes.

ANSWERS

5. income . incomes
6. resources
7. free enterprise . consumers' . do . do

8. enterprise . consumers . resources . not . preferences
9. dollar . wants

3.10   Despite having many _____ , most consumers, for all practical purposes, have limited means of satisfying them. Limited means for most people take the form of limited incomes or limited budgets available for expenditure on consumer goods and services. In any time period, we normally assume, therefore, that each consumer (a consumer can be thought of as a family unit as well as one individual) has a *budget constraint*. That is, we assume the consumer is limited by his _____ from purchasing all the goods and services he desires.

3.11   Within the limits of the budget constraint, however, the consumer attempts to make his satisfaction or utility from consuming goods and services as large as possible. Expressed more rigorously, we say that the rational consumer in any time period attempts to maximize his utility subject to a _____ _____ .

3.12   Thus, a consumer will change his expenditure pattern if the change yields him a higher level of _____ . He will continue to change his expenditure patterns until he cannot _____ his total utility by a reallocation of his expenditure. Only then will the consumer _____ his total utility. And only then will the consumer be in equilibrium, that is, have no incentive to alter his expenditure patterns.

3.13   When will the consumer be in equilibrium? As we shall see, he will be in _____ when the utility he receives from the last dollar spent on any good or service just equals the utility received from the last dollar spent on any other good or service. Then and only then will he _____ his total utility.

3.14   After a certain point has been reached, the utility received from consuming additional units of a good decreases for an individual. The extra utility derived from consuming an additional unit of a good is known as the *marginal utility* of that good. Thus, after a certain point has been reached in the consumption of a good, the _____ _____ of that good decreases as consumption increases.

3.15   Suppose, for instance, that after you have consumed a few beers in the local bar one evening, the utility you derive from, let us say, your fourth beer is less than that derived from your third. That is, as your consumption of beer increases from three to four, your _____ utility decreases. Suppose that the _____ derived from the fifth beer is even less than that from the fourth, and so on. It might be that a sixth beer may give you no utility or satisfaction at all and a seventh could give you pain rather than pleasure by making you sick. (You choose the numbers according to your capacity—it is the principle that is important!)

ANSWERS

10. wants . budget
11. budget constraint
12. utility . increase . maximize

13. equilibrium . maximize
14. marginal utility
15. marginal . utility . maximize

This would be an example of negative utility from the seventh beer. You presumably would not consume a seventh beer even if it were free, because you normally would want to

_____ your total utility.

3.16   In this example, six beers would yield __*(more/less)*__ utility than seven beers and when seven

beers are consumed the _____ _____ becomes negative. This means that total utility decreases when a seventh beer is consumed; it does not mean that total utility is negative. __*(true/false)*__

3.17   In some given time period, how many beers will you consume if you have to pay for them? Given your income, we know that every beer you consume has an opportunity cost, namely the

_____ you give up by not using your income to buy other goods that you want. In deciding how much beer to buy, you will want to buy more beer as long as the marginal benefit is greater than the marginal cost of buying beer. That is, you will consume additional beers

until the last dollar spent on beer gives no more _____ than the last dollar spent on any other good.

3.18   To understand this point, consider the following example. If the last dollar spent on a beer

gives you less _____ than the last dollar spent on a hamburger, then your total

_____ will be higher if you consume the hamburger rather than the beer. In general, you obviously __*(will/will not)*__ spend another dollar on good A if the utility received from that additional consumption is less than the utility you would have received from the additional consumption of an extra dollar's worth of some other good B.

3.19   It is only when the last dollar spent on each good yields the same utility that __*(total/marginal)*__ utility will be maximum.

3.20   In order to be in equilibrium consuming both hamburgers at fifty cents each and beer at twenty-five cents a glass, the last hamburger consumed will have to yield you *(half the/the same/ twice the)* satisfaction of the last beer consumed. If fifty cents spent on a hamburger gives

you the same utility as twenty-five cents on a beer, you should buy more _____

and fewer _____ . You will maximize utility when the last dollar's worth of each

yields the same _____ , or expressing this another way, when the marginal utility

of beer divided by the price of beer equals the _____ _____ of hamburgers divided by the price of hamburgers. In this example,

ANSWERS

16. more . marginal utility . true   19. total
17. utility . utility   20. twice the . beer . hamburgers . utility
18. utility . utility . will not   . marginal utility . twice

$$\frac{MU\ beer}{25\cancel{c}} = \frac{MU\ hamburgers}{50\cancel{c}}.$$

For the ratio to be equal, the marginal utility of your last hamburger must be __(twice/half)__ the marginal utility of your last beer.

3.21 How should you divide your income between any two goods A and B? As in the hamburger-beer example, if you want to maximize utility, you should consume two goods in such amounts that the last dollar spent on each good yields the same _____ . Any different allocation of income will yield a __(smaller/larger)__ total utility.

3.22 Let us now suppose you were given additional income but were restricted still to spending all of it on goods A and B. With more income than before, you could now purchase more of each good, and, because you would be better off, total _____ would be greater than before.

3.23 However, as you saw in the beer example, the _____ _____ of each good falls the more you buy. Consequently, when you regain a position of equilibrium with your higher income buying _____ of each good, the marginal utilities of each good will be _____ than before. In your new equilibrium position, however, it must still be true that

$$\frac{MU_A}{P_A} = \underline{\quad\quad} .$$

3.24 Thus, given that you are restricted to only two commodities, and given that marginal utilities are positive, an increase in income will lead to an increase in _____ utility; _____ utilities, however, will decline. You will maximize _____ _____ when the last dollar's worth (or cent's worth) of expenditure on A yields the same satisfaction as the last dollar's worth of expenditure on B—in other words, when

$$\frac{MU_A}{\underline{\quad}} = \frac{\underline{\quad\quad}}{P_B} .$$

3.25   Assume you are in equilibrium in this two-commodity world, so

$$\frac{MU_A}{P_A} = \frac{MU_B}{P_B}.$$

Now assume the price of commodity A falls; this will cause $\frac{MU_A}{P_A}$ to become *(less/greater)*

than $\frac{MU_B}{P_B}$. To restore equality, that is, to make

$$\frac{MU_A}{P_A} = \frac{MU_B}{P_B}$$

you will reallocate your income between A and B, buying more _____ and less

_____ than before.

3.26   As you consume more A, however, the marginal utility of each additional unit consumed will

_____ and thus the ratio $\frac{MU_A}{P_A}$ will _____ . As you consume less of

B, conversely, the ratio $\frac{MU_B}{P_B}$ will _____ .

3.27   You will cease reallocating income when equality is restored; that is, when

$$\frac{MU_A}{P_A} = \text{_____} .$$

Then and only then will total _____ be a maximum.

3.28   The last three frames have shown why the quantity that people would like to buy of a good
tends to be *(greater/lower)*   at a lower price. This condition holds for most goods. Variables other than price, however, affect the quantity of any commodity purchased, and to
fully understand, we must take into account all factors affecting consumers' purchases. Price,
however, is one of the most important variables, and we would expect people to buy

_____ steak at $1 per pound than at $5 per pound.

3.29   Let us arbitrarily choose a time period of one week, and, given that you are a steak consumer,
let us consider the factors that might influence the amount of steak you would purchase. The
price of steak, one would expect, would certainly influence how much you purchase. And we

would further expect that the lower the price of steak, the _____ the amount of
steak you would purchase.

ANSWERS

25. greater . A . B   28. greater . more
26. decrease . decrease . increase   29. greater

27. $\frac{MU_B}{P_B}$. utility

3.30   One might also find, however, that if in a given week the local supermarket had lobster, chicken, and lamb at greatly reduced prices, you might buy no steak during that week. Consequently, we would expect that the _____ of goods you might substitute for steak would affect the amount of steak you would buy.

3.31   Perhaps the only way you like your steak is barbecued outdoors over an oak chip fire. You also do not like to barbecue outdoors unless the weather is pleasant. Consequently, we would expect that if we chose a week in which the weather was predicted to be inclement, you would, in all probability, buy no steak that week. Thus, we can see that in this specific example the amount of steak you might buy would depend upon the _____ . Pound for pound, sausage and hamburger tend to be cheaper than steak, and if indeed your income is very low, you might not be able to afford steak. Thus, we would expect that _____ would be another factor that would influence the amount of steak you would buy.

3.32   We could expand the list of items that would affect the amount of steak you would buy in any given week, and we can see that the amount of steak demanded in any week depends not only on the price of steak but also on many other factors. To the extent that those other factors are important in the determination of the amount of steak demanded, we cannot neglect all factors except _____ when considering demand for steak.

3.33   Suppose we wished to explore the relationship between your demand for steak and the number of your guests. If you plan to serve each person half a pound of steak, then the relationship is simple.

Table 3.1

NUMBER OF GUESTS AND QUANTITY OF STEAK DEMANDED

Quantity of steak that would be bought (lbs)	Number of guests
½	0
1	1
1½	2
2	3
2½	4
3	5

Even if you have no guests, we are assuming you have a steak yourself. From Table 3.1, we see that the quantity of steak that would be bought _____ as the number of guests increases.

ANSWERS

30. prices
31. weather . income

32. price
33. increases

3.34   Because we are concerned only with the relationship between your _____ for steak and the number of guests, we assume that anything else that could affect your demand for steak does not change during the time period under consideration. For instance, we assume the price of steak is fixed, because if steak were to increase in price to $20 per pound after you bought one pound for $2 you would probably buy chicken rather than steak for your guests.

3.35   On the assumption that everything else remains unchanged, Figure 3.1 shows what quantity of _____ you would buy today for different numbers of _____ .

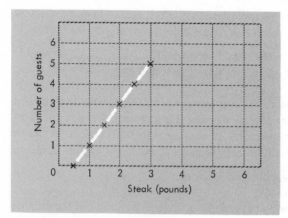

Figure 3.1
Demand for steak depending on number of guests

3.36   We could repeat this process with all the items that affect your demand for steak. If we were to draw graphs similar to Figure 3.1, we would have lines that sloped upwards to the right, as in Figure 3.1, whenever the quantity of steak demanded _(increased/decreased)_ along with the variable being considered. In Figure 3.1, for instance, the quantity of steak demanded

_____ as the number of guests increases.

3.37   If we choose an item for which the reverse relationship exists, for instance the price of steak, we would have a graph that would be _(downward/upward)_ sloping to the _(left/right)_ because at higher prices smaller quantities of steak would typically be demanded, other things remaining unchanged.

3.38   Let us hold everything except the price and quantity of steak constant for now. By *everything* we mean all items we have considered and all items we have not considered that might affect the quantity of steak you would purchase in any given week. We wish to see the amount of steak you would purchase at different prices during a given week. If you look at Table 3.2,

ANSWERS

34. demand
35. steak . guests
36. increased . increases

37. downward . right
38. 5 . 4 . lower

you will see that if the price of steak were $ _____ per pound or $ _____ per pound, you would not purchase any steak during the week. You will also see that if the

price of steak were _____ , you would purchase more steak during that week.

Table 3.2

INDIVIDUAL DEMAND FOR STEAK

Prices per pound	Pounds of steak that would be purchased per week
$5	0
4	0
3	1
2	2
1.50	3
1	5
.79	9
.50	15

3.39   In Figure 3.2, we have plotted the points from Table 3.2 and joined the points by a smooth curve. Points lying on the curve between any given points are approximations as to what you would buy if prices lay in between any of the quoted prices. We make this approximation in converting Table 3.2 into Figure 3.2 for the sake of simplicity.

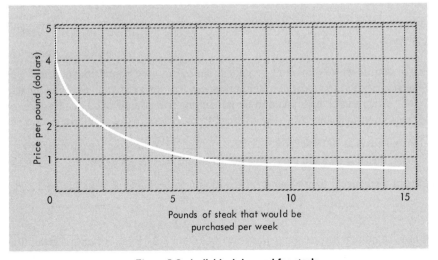

Figure 3.2   Individual demand for steak

ANSWERS

39. demand . quantity

What we have produced in Figure 3.2 is your individual _____ curve for steak for the specified week. And we can further see that at no two different prices below $4 would the

_____ of steak demanded by you be the same.

3.40 Let us look carefully at Figure 3.2 because much more lies behind your simple _____

_____ for steak than would appear. First, there is a time period involved, which in this case happens to be one week. However, if the time period became ten weeks instead of one week, we would expect that the quantities of steak you would purchase at each of the various

prices in Table 3.2 would be _____ than the existing quantities when the time period is one week. Consequently, the demand curve in Figure 3.2 *(does/does not)* reflect the situation in which the time period is ten weeks.

3.41 Figure 3.2 says that holding everything else constant, you would in a given week buy

_____ pounds of steak if the price were $2 per pound, whereas you would buy

_____ pounds of steak if the price were $.79 per pound. If the price were $2.50

per pound, you would buy between _____ and _____ pounds of steak.

3.42 Thus, if we hold everything else constant, we can tell from your _____

_____ how much steak you _____ buy at given prices.

3.43 Your demand curve for steak, therefore, is really a hypothetical curve showing the quantities of

steak you _____ buy at different prices _____ everything else were held constant.

3.44 One day in your local supermarket, you are about to buy two pounds of steak at $2 per pound when the attendant at the meat counter announces that he is reducing the price of steak to $1 per pound. When this occurs, you end up purchasing five pounds of steak. Has the meat attendant's decision to change the price of steak from $2 per pound to $1 per pound changed

your demand curve? The answer is _____ . What you have done is moved from one position on your demand curve to a new position on the same demand curve. If everything

else remains unchanged, then neither the position nor the shape of your _____

_____ in Figure 3.2 will change.

3.45 Let us now be more rigorous about the curve in Figure 3.2. First, we have a given time period. Second, there are certain factors, such as your income, number of guests, weather, and so on,

ANSWERS

40. demand curve . greater . does not
41. two . nine . one . two
42. demand curve . would

43. would . if
44. no . demand curve
45. can . parameters

that __(can/cannot)__ affect the amount of steak you will buy in any week. Those factors, other than price, that influence the amount of steak you buy are parameters. In Figure 3.2, we assume that those _____ are fixed and do not change.

3.46 Thus, in Figure 3.2, we see that movements along this demand curve tell us that the quantities that would be purchased _____ as price falls. Because prices and quantities change or vary, they are known as variables. Given that the parameters are fixed, we know that the quantity of steak you will buy will depend upon the _____ of steak. For this reason, we say that quantity is the dependent variable because the quantity taken will _____ on the price of steak.

3.47 It is highly unlikely, however, that the price of steak in the area in which you live will depend upon the quantity of steak you buy. And for this reason, __(price/quantity)__ is known as the independent variable. __(Price/Quantity)__ is known as the dependent variable.

3.48 The position and shape of the demand curve in Figure 3.2 will depend upon the _____, and if changes occur in any of the _____, the position and shape of the demand curve will change. Because we will ultimately show how resource allocation in a price system responds to _____ preferences, it is important to know that some of the parameters determining the position of your demand curve in Figure 3.2 are your tastes and preferences.

3.49 Now, it is highly likely that parameters will change over time. For instance, it would be highly unusual if your tastes, income, and prices of all other goods were to remain unchanged over time. Consequently, it is highly unlikely that the position and the shape of your _____ _____ for steak will remain unchanged over time. But this change in the position and shape of your demand curve for steak over time must be carefully distinguished from a movement along your demand curve for steak in a given time period.

3.50 A demand curve is actually a hypothetical situation. It shows what would happen, given the parameters, if the _____ of steak were to change. That is, it tells us what _____ of steak you would buy at various hypothetical prices, given no change in any of the _____ .

3.51 Let us consider a change in one of the _____ that will cause your demand curve to shift. A change in the price per pound of steak, all other things remaining unchanged, will cause your demand curve for steak to shift. __(true/false)__

ANSWERS

46. increase . price . depend
47. price . Quantity
48. parameters . parameters . consumer
49. demand curve
50. price . quantity . parameters
51. parameters . false

3.52   If you look at your new demand schedule for steak alongside your original one (Figure 3.3), we can see there has been a(n) *(downward/upward)* shift of your demand curve, to the *(left/right)*. This has occurred because there has been a change in some of the parameters, for example a lowering of lamb and chicken prices that determine the position of the

_____ _____, not because the price of steak has changed.

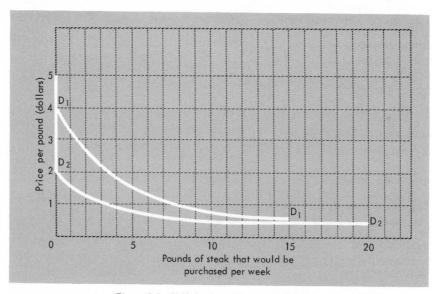

Figure 3.3 Shift in demand curve for steak

3.53   Let us now imagine that your income increases substantially. In considering your demand curve for steak, income is treated as a *(variable/parameter)*. With a higher income, you can now afford to buy more steak as well as more of many other goods. But if indeed you do buy more steak at the going price than you did with your original income, we would say there had been a *(shift of/movement along)* your demand curve.

3.54   With your increase in income, you would now have a new _____ _____ for steak because one of the _____, which determine the position and shape of your demand curve, had changed. We would expect this new demand curve to be to the *(right/left)* of your old demand curve.

3.55   In the blanks after each question, put the most appropriate statement concerning your demand curve for steak. *(shifts to the right/shifts to the left/does not change)*

ANSWERS

52. downward . left . demand curve
53. parameter . shift of
54. demand curve . parameters . right

55. a. shifts to the left
     b. does not change
     c. does not change
     d. does not change
     e. shifts to the right
     f. shifts to the left
     g. does not change

    a. The price of lamb is drastically reduced, and you enjoy consuming lamb. _____

    _____

    b. The price of lamb is drastically reduced, but you would buy lamb under no circumstances

       because you dislike it. _____

    c. Farmers are bringing fewer animals to the market, and consequently there is less steak

       in the stores. _____

    d. The government imposes a $.20 per pound tax on the price of steak. _____

    _____

    e. You are given a new barbecue as a gift and barbecuing weather is perfect. _____

    _____

    f. A friend of yours, who is a hunter, gives you a side of venison, and you have no freezer.

    _____

    g. The supermarket has a special discount sale on steak. _____

3.56   In Figures 3.2 and 3.3, we see that demand curves slope downward from _____ to

_____ . Or, in other words, the higher the price of a good, other things remaining

equal, the _____ the quantity normally bought. Let us see why this should be so.
The first and most obvious reason is that at a lower price, given your income, you can afford to

buy _____ of that good because each unit costs less. If, for instance, you have
only $5, and the price of steak is $5 per pound, you could buy only one pound of steak; where-

as, if steak were $2.50 per pound, you could buy _____ pounds of steak.

3.57   Second, at lower prices you tend to buy _____ of a good because this good now
becomes relatively more appealing when compared to substitutes. Let us imagine that lamb
and steak both sell for $1 per pound, and at those prices you buy one pound of each. Let us
now imagine that the price of lamb does not change, but the price of steak falls to $.50 per
pound. You may well decide to buy more steak for the first reason, that is, steak is now

cheaper and you can afford to buy more. But also, you may now decide to buy _____

instead of lamb because the price of steak has _____ whereas the price of lamb has
remained unchanged.

3.58   Another example would be the housewife who would prefer to cook with butter rather than
oleomargarine, but who cannot afford to do so at existing prices. If the price of butter falls,

she can afford to buy _____ butter because of the price reduction. But she may
also decide to cook now with butter, not because butter is even cheaper than oleomargarine at
the reduced price, but because the relative difference in prices may be so small that she substitutes butter for oleomargarine in cooking.

ANSWERS

    56. left . right . smaller . more . two   58. more
    57. more . steak . fallen

3.59   There is still a third way we can look at our downward sloping demand curve, as we saw earlier in the chapter. In any given time period, the more of a good consumed, the _____ the total utility, but the _____ the marginal utility.

3.60   The tendency to associate diminishing satisfaction or utility with each additional unit of a good consumed in a given time period is known as the *law of diminishing marginal utility*. The law of diminishing marginal utility essentially states that each additional unit of a good consumed within a given time period yields diminishing _____ . This being the case, you _(will/will not)_ be prepared to pay some fixed price per unit for additional units of this good.

Consequently, we would expect that you will buy additional units only at a _____ price.

3.61   You will recall that earlier in this chapter you learned that you would be maximizing total _____ if you allocated your budget in a two-commodity world so that

$$\frac{MU_A}{P_A} = \frac{MU_B}{P_B}.$$

3.62   Let us make clear the connection between utility theory and the demand curve. Imagine your daily budget is allocated between beer and hamburgers, the price of beer being twenty-five cents per glass and the price of each hamburger being fifty cents. In equilibrium, your utility will be _____ when

$$\frac{MU_B}{P_B} = \frac{MU_H}{P_H}.$$

3.63   Suppose that at the given prices

$$\frac{MU_B}{P_B} = \frac{MU_H}{P_H} = \frac{3}{1}.$$

That is,

$$\frac{MU_B}{P_B} = \frac{3}{1}$$

and

$$\frac{MU_H}{P_H} = \text{_____} .$$

ANSWERS

59. greater . smaller
60. utility . will not . lower
61. utility

62. maximized

63. $\dfrac{3}{1}$

3.64   If the price of hamburgers is suddenly reduced to twenty-five cents each, then your $\frac{MU_H}{P_H}$

would become ___*(3/2 / 3/½)*___ .

3.65   The correct answer is $\frac{3}{½}$ or $\frac{6}{1}$; that is, the last fifty cents spent on hamburgers will now yield

approximately twice as much satisfaction as before because you can now buy _____
hamburgers with fifty cents instead of one.

3.66   Thus, with the price reduction in hamburgers,

$$\frac{MU_H}{P_H} = \frac{6}{1}$$

and $\frac{MU_B}{P_B}$ will equal only _____ .

3.67   If you now spend twenty-five cents less on beer, your utility will fall by ___*(3/6)*___ . If you
spend twenty-five cents on another hamburger, your utility from the extra hamburger will be
___*(3/6)*___ . Thus, there will be a net gain in utility of 3 (+6–3) if you reduce your expenditure on

_____ and increase your expenditure on _____ .

3.68   As you consume more hamburgers, however, $\frac{MU_H}{P_H}$ will _____ because of the *law*

of diminishing marginal _____ . Simultaneously, as you decrease your expenditure

on beer, $\frac{MU_B}{P_B}$ will _____ .

3.69   You will continue to reallocate your expenditures until equilibrium is once more attained. This
will occur when

$$\frac{MU_H}{P_H} = \frac{MU_B}{P_B} .$$

Thus, you can see why your demand curve for hamburgers is negatively inclined; that is why

you will buy _____ hamburgers the lower the price. The same reasoning applies
to beer or any other good.

ANSWERS

64. $\frac{3}{½}$

65. 2

66. $\frac{3}{1}$

67. 3 . 6 . beer . hamburgers
68. decrease . utility . increase
69. more

3.70   So far, we have been concerned only with your demand curve for a product. It is unlikely that a manufacturer will be overly concerned with your demand curve for his product because sales to you are probably so _____ as to appear negligible. One would *(expect/not expect)* the owners of the local supermarket to be concerned with whether or not in any given day you purchase a loaf of bread, because the sale of one loaf of bread *(will/will not)* substantially affect the sales or profits of the supermarket. This is an important assumption, but as you can well see a very reasonable one in a freely competitive economic system. In such a system, we assume that no individual can make any significant difference to the price of a good by purchasing or not purchasing in any given market. The influence of any individual in a market in a freely competitive economic system is *(negligible/substantial)*.

3.71   However, when we consider the total demand in any given market, we are summing up all the individual demands in this market, and we *(would expect/would not expect)* manufacturers to be concerned with total demand. Total or market demand will be subject of Chapter 4.

REVIEW QUESTIONS

3.1   When the prices of goods change, a consumer alters the quantities of goods he buys. As a result, an individual discovers that in the new situation marginal utilities are all lower than they were in the old situation. Which of the following is correct?

a. The individual is better off, prices must have fallen on average.

b. The individual is worse off, but prices could have fallen or risen on average.

c. The individual is worse off, prices must have risen on average.

d. Insufficient information is given to determine whether the individual is better off or worse off.

The principle of diminishing marginal utility states that, in a given time period, as an individual consumes more of a good, he derives less and less satisfaction from each extra unit consumed. Thus, in comparing the two situations, the lower marginal utilities, the greater the quantities that have been consumed. That is, lower marginal utilities mean greater total utility, i.e., that the consumer is better off. The correct response is a.

3.2   A consumer buys only wine and cheese, and the more of any one he buys, the lower the marginal utility of that good. In spending all his income, his marginal utility of a bottle of wine is three and his marginal utility of a pound of cheese is one. The price of wine is $4 and the price of cheese is $2. If the consumer wants to maximize his utility, which of the following should he buy?

a. More wine and less cheese

b. Less wine and more cheese

c. More wine and more cheese

d. Less wine and less cheese

ANSWERS

70. small . not expect . will not . negligible   71. would expect

In allocating his income between any two commodities, for example cheese (C) and wine (W), the consumer will be maximizing his total utility when

$$\frac{MU_C}{P_C} = \frac{MU_W}{P_W}.$$

When this situation is reached, any reallocation of expenditure will make him worse off. However, in our example

$$\frac{MU_C}{P_C} = \frac{1}{2} \ \left(\text{or } \frac{2}{4}\right) \text{ and } \frac{MU_W}{P_W} = \frac{3}{4}.$$

Because the ratios are unequal, he can become better off by reallocating his expenditures. If he spends $4 less on cheese, utility will decrease by two; if the $4 is now spent on wine, utility will increase by three, that is, net gain of one. As cheese purchases decrease, MU_C will rise, and as wine purchases increase, MU_W will fall. He should continue reallocating his income until the ratios are equal. The correct response is   a.

3.3   A consumer's demand curve typically is downward sloping to the price axis for which of the following reasons?

1. At lower prices, the good in question is substituted for other goods which are now relatively more expensive.
2. At lower prices, the consumer can buy all he bought at the higher prices and with the money left over buy still more.

    a. 1 only   c. Both 1 and 2
    b. 2 only   d. Neither 1 nor 2

To the extent that goods are substitutes, consumers will substitute cheaper for more expensive goods in order to maximize utility. Starting from an equilibrium position where

$$\frac{MU_A}{P_A} = \frac{MU_B}{P_B},$$

if the price of A falls, then

$$\frac{MU_A}{P_A} > \frac{MU_B}{P_B}.$$

To restore equilibrium, less of B and more of A must be purchased.
If the price of A falls, the consumer also experiences an increase in real income; he can now buy more of all goods, including the cheaper A. Marginal utilities will, of course, decrease as more of all goods are purchased, the consumer becoming better off. The correct response is c.

3.4   Which of the following is true with respect to a consumer's demand curve?

    a. The more inelastic, the greater the marginal utility of the good.   c. It will shift to the right if the price of the good falls.
    b. Prices of all other goods are assumed to be constant.   d. It indicates what the going price of the good is.

The demand curve of a consumer for a commodity shows, for some given time period with everything else remaining constant, what quantities of the good the consumer would buy at different prices. It tells nothing about the going price of the good nor the marginal utility of the good. The correct response is b. .

Case 3

FOOD STAMPS OR CASH

Between 1960 and 1971, the number of people annually receiving government welfare payments soared from 6 to 14 million, and the dollar costs, from $4 billion to $13 billion. Recipients include mothers and children (about two-thirds of the total), the aged, blind, and disabled, and others who are poor because they hold low paying jobs or because they cannot or will not work. These totals represent less than one-third of total government income security payments, which include, in addition, social security payments, unemployment insurance benefits, and a variety of other programs, totaling about $60 billion in 1971.

One controversial part of the government's overall programs to aid the poor has been the food-stamp program, which cost nearly $2 billion in 1971. Under this program, a poor family of four could receive up to $106 monthly in free food stamps, usable as money to buy food at grocery stores. Less needy families or individuals could receive food stamps by paying part of their value, for example, thirty-five cents for each dollar stamp. The government then redeems the stamps from the grocers.

The purpose of the program is to assure that poor families, especially those with children, receive a reasonably adequate diet. By giving the poor food stamps instead of money, proponents argue, we can be sure the aid will be used for food rather than liquor, gasoline, drugs, paying off old debts, or other less urgent needs. But others, including some of the poor themselves, disagree. It is insulting and inefficient, they say, to give food stamps rather than money, restricting the recipients' freedom to judge themselves what is best for them. It is inefficient, this counterargument runs, because if the government gave the poor the

same amount of money, the poor could not possibly be worse off, and might well be better off. The poor recipient could buy the food if that is what he wants and needs most, or he could use the funds for something else if other needs are more urgent. The plan is insulting because it implies that the poor cannot be trusted to know and do what is best for themselves and their children.

Who is right? Is it better to aid the poor by giving them cash to spend as they like or by giving them essentially free or subsidized food in the form of food stamps? The question is an important one because the same basic issue arises with many other types of government assistance—for example, rent supplements to help obtain better housing, free public education, and subsidized public health benefits.

SUGGESTIONS FOR ANALYSIS

The main economics issue is in which form is aid more efficient. Is a poor person better off with $106 of food stamps or $106 in cash? Economic analysis cannot decide the issue of whether the poor should be given aid or whether those giving the aid should have the right to determine the form in which aid is given. Economic analysis can, however, help us understand the consequences of helping the poor in different ways and, consequently, can help us decide what course of action should be taken.

In deciding whether cash or stamps is a better form of aid, let us assume that the purpose of the aid is to make poor families better off and that each family is rational in the sense that each family puts its resources to their best use according to that family's preferences. Thus, if a family were given cash, we can presume that it would spend the income along with its other income to maximize its satisfaction by allocating its total income so that the last dollar spent on each good would yield the same marginal utility. If, instead, the family received food stamps, how would it spend its income? Here there are two cases to consider. If the value of the food stamps were less than the amount that would have been spent on food if the family had been given cash, then the gift of food stamps would be equivalent to giving cash because the household would be able to spend the money saved on food for anything it wanted (including more food) and it would pay market prices for those purchases. If, however, the value of food stamps it was given were greater than the amount the family would spend on food if it had been given cash, then, since food stamps can be used only for food, the family would consume more food and fewer other goods under the food stamp program than with a cash subsidy. Clearly, if the pattern of consumption under the food stamp plan differed from the pattern under the cash payment plan, then, in terms of its own preferences, the family would not be as well off under the food stamp plan.

Thus, the family may be prevented by the government's food stamp program from freely allocating all its income (including government assistance) and, thereby, may be prevented from maximizing the total satisfaction potentially obtainable from allocating that income. If the family received the aid in cash, it could be no worse off than with food stamps and it might well be better off in terms of its own preferences. On the grounds of economic efficiency, cash is likely to be the better bet than food stamps.

But many people do not believe that economic efficiency in terms of poor families' own preferences is the most important consideration in this case. Some believe that Congress does know better than some poor what is best for them. Others simply are not interested in maximizing the satisfaction of the poor, but just want to see the poor well fed. Still others doubt that many poor parents will be able to resist the temptation of wasting the money on nonessentials instead of adequately feeding their children. These are matters of ethics, however, not economics. Chapter 3 does not have much to say about ethics, but it is important to clearly separate the ethical arguments from the economic arguments. The ethical issue is whose preferences are to be satisfied. The economics issue is, for given preferences, how resources can be allocated efficiently. In making the actual decision about food stamps Congress must decide on both issues.

Make up your own mind. Then ask yourself whether your arguments hold equally for cash aid versus subsidized public education and public health services.

4

Market Demand

4.1 Aggregate demand schedules and curves are simply found by adding together individual

_____ schedules and curves.

4.2 Table 4.1 and Figure 4.1 show family A's demand for steak in some given time period for a given set of parameters.

Table 4.1

FAMILY A'S DEMAND FOR STEAK

Price per pound	Pounds of steak that would be purchased
$5	0
4	2
3	4
2.50	5
2	6
1	8
0	10

As might be expected, the higher the price, the _____ the quantity that would be purchased.

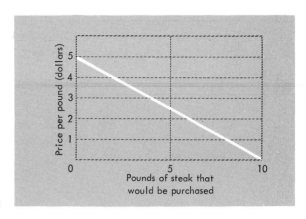

Figure 4.1
Family A's Demand for Steak

4.3 Table 4.2 and Figure 4.2 show family B's demand for steak, again for some given

_____ period and given set of _____ , such as income and prices of other goods.

Table 4.2

FAMILY B's DEMAND FOR STEAK

Price per pound	Pounds of steak that would be purchased
$5	0
2	5
1.50	7½
1	10
0	15

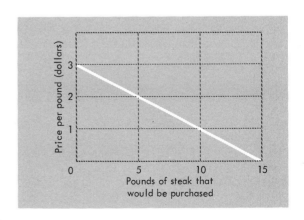

Figure 4.2
Family B's Demand for Steak

ANSWERS
3. time . parameters

4.4   Family B's demand curve for steak __*(is/is not)*__ identical to family A's demand curve. Although the slope of the curve is different, it remains true that the __*(greater/smaller)*__ the price, the greater the quantity demanded.

4.5   Let us now combine the two demand schedules. At $1 per pound, family A's purchases would be eight pounds of steak, and at $1 per pound, family B's purchases would be ten pounds.

Therefore, taken together, both families would purchase _____ pounds at $1 per pound. From Table 4.1 and 4.2, compute the quantities of steak that would be purchased by both families at the following prices.

Prices	Quantities (Pounds)
$5	_____
3	_____
2	_____
1	_____18_____
0	_____

4.6   Figure 4.3 is derived in the same manner in which Figure 4.1 and 4.2 were derived; the relevant prices and quantities from your answers (the correct answers!) in frame 5 are plotted.

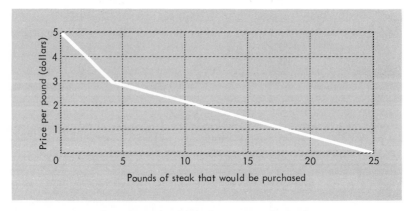

Figure 4.3 A's and B's demand curve for steak

The combined curve exhibits the same properties as the individual curves; the higher the

_____ , the smaller the quantity that would be purchased, or, for A and B to be

willing to purchase larger quantities, there must be _____ prices.

4.7   We could repeat the whole procedure for all steak buyers in some town and arrive at the

aggregate _____ schedule for steak for this community. This is the schedule
that meat suppliers would be interested in.

4.8   In each demand curve we have considered so far, we have seen that at different prices,

_____ quantities are demanded. The concept that measures the responsiveness
of the quantity demanded to price changes is known as *price elasticity of demand*. *Price
elasticity of demand* is defined in the following way: price elasticity of demand = - percentage
change in quantity/percentage change in price, which written symbolically is:

$$E_d \text{ (Price)} = -\frac{\Delta Q}{Q} / \frac{\Delta P}{P},$$

where Δ means "change in."

Because there is an inverse relationship between price and quantity demanded, the ratio
$\frac{\Delta Q}{Q} / \frac{\Delta P}{P}$ would be _(positive/negative)_ . In order to make elasticity a postive amount,
elasticity is defined as follows:

$$E_d \text{ (price)} = \underline{\quad\quad / \quad\quad}.$$

4.9   With price elasticity of demand, we are considering percentage change in quantity and

percentage change in _____ . If we wish to consider *income* elasticity, we would
measure the responsiveness of quantity taken to income change. The identity would read:

_____ elasticity of demand = percentage change in quantity/percentage change in
income or:

$$E_d \text{ (income)} = \frac{\Delta Q}{Q} / \frac{\Delta Y}{Y},$$

where Y represents _____ . Here the sign may be positive or negative. The ratio
is positive when increases in income are accompanied by increases in the quantity purchased

and when decreases in income are accompanied by _____ in the quantity purchased.
When an inverse relationship exists, for example, income increases accompanied by quantity

purchased decreases, income elasticity of demand will be _____ . Goods with
such a property are called inferior goods. For many families, cheap cuts of meat, low quality

wine, and tenement housing are examples of _____ goods.

ANSWERS

7. demand
8. different . negative . $-\frac{\Delta Q}{Q} / \frac{\Delta P}{P}$

9. price . income . income . decreases .
negative . inferior

4.10   Unless we state otherwise, however, when we speak of elasticity of demand, we shall mean

price elasticity of demand. Price elasticity of demand = – _____ /

_____ .

4.11   The reason we are concerned with elasticity of demand is that we wish to know, given a set of

_____ determining the position of the demand curve for a good, how the quantity

demanded will change as _____ changes. Let us consider a good such as salt. Let us imagine that the typical housewife purchases one pound of salt every month and that one pound of salt costs ten cents. Let us further imagine that the price of salt rises to twenty

cents per pound, that is, a _____ percent increase in the price of salt. What do you think will happen to the amount of salt purchased by the typical housewife in any month at the new price? Because salt is an essential purchase of the housewife for everyday cooking and is a trivial portion of her budget, in all probability the amount of salt purchased per month
(will/will not) change a great deal.

4.12   Let us look at this in economic terms. If every housewife did not alter her purchase of salt at all, even though the price of salt doubles, we know that if we look at an aggregate demand

curve for salt, we shall discover that the same _____ would be purchased at the price of ten cents per pound as at the price of twenty cents per pound. Or, saying the same thing, the amount of salt demanded at a price of ten cents per pound _(is/is not)_ the same as the amount demanded at twenty cents per pound.

4.13   Let us put the values from this example into the formula for price elasticity of demand (–percentage change in quantity/percentage change in price). In this example, the percentage

change in quantity obviously equals _____ , and the percentage change in price

equals _____ . Thus, the price elasticity of demand for salt in going from a price of ten cents per pound to a price of twenty cents per pound equals –percentage change in quantity/percentage change in price = _____ .

4.14   When we have a value for price elasticity of demand that is less than one, we say we have *inelastic demand* over that range of prices. When we get a value equal to one, we say we have *unitary elasticity of demand* over that price range, and when we get a value greater than one, we say we have *elastic demand* over that range of prices. Thus, in the example in the previous frame comparing price of salt at ten cents per pound and at twenty cents per pound and the corresponding quantities purchased, we would say that demand over this range is
(inelastic/of unitary elasticity/elastic) .

ANSWERS

10. percentage change in quantity/percentage change in price $(\dfrac{\Delta Q}{Q} / \dfrac{\Delta P}{P})$
11. parameters . price . 100 . will not
12. quantity . is
13. 0 . 100 . 0
14. inelastic

4.15 What elasticity of demand really tells us is the responsiveness of quantities that would be bought to changes in price. In our salt example, the responsiveness of the quantity of salt that would be bought given the change of price we considered was _____ , and consequently in this price range demand was _____ .

4.16 As you might guess, at the other end of the spectrum, if a relatively small change in price brings about a relatively large change in the quantity that would be demanded, we would say that demand was _____ in that range of prices.

4.17 Our third case would occur when a 1 percent increase in price would bring about a 1 percent *(increase/decrease)* in the quantity that would be demanded. We would say that in this case elasticity of demand is _____ .

4.18 Let us choose a couple of examples to see whether the demand is elastic or inelastic over given price ranges. Imagine that the makers of a popular brand of cigarettes, such as Kansers, were to increase the price of Kansers cigarettes by ten cents per pack, and further assume that the price of all other cigarettes did not alter. Now, because many people believe that any one brand of cigarettes has several close substitutes, we would expect smokers to switch from Kansers to some other brand of cigarettes. If this were to occur, then sales of Kansers cigarettes would _____ because of the price increase, which would cause people to switch to close _____ .

4.19 If the observed percentage decrease in the quantity of Kansers cigarettes demanded were greater than the percentage increase in price, we would say that the demand for Kansers cigarettes was _____ over this price range.

4.20 Let us imagine the reverse situation. Imagine Kansers are reduced by a few cents per pack, and this causes many people who normally smoke other brands to switch to Kansers. In this case, the percentage *(increase/decrease)* in quantity bought would be large, whereas the percentage *(increase/decrease)* in price would be small. Over this price range, we would again say that the demand for Kansers cigarettes was _____ .

4.21 If a 1 percent decrease in the price of Kansers cigarettes led to only a 1 percent _____ in the quantity of Kansers bought, the demand for Kansers cigarettes over this price range would be of unitary elasticity.

ANSWERS

15. zero . inelastic
16. elastic
17. decrease . unitary (one)
18. decrease . substitutes

19. elastic
20. increase . decrease . elastic
21. increase

4.22   Consider the following, however. If a small increase in the price of all cigarettes had a negligible effect on the quantity of cigarettes demanded, *ceteris paribus* (with other things remaining equal), the demand for cigarettes would be _____ over this price range, even though the demand for any particular brand were elastic over the same price range.

4.23   Although economists cannot tell why some people prefer good A over good B and why other people prefer good B over good A, general statements can be made about when demand for a product is likely to be elastic over some price range and when demand is likely to be inelastic over a price range. When we discussed salt, we argued that the demand for salt over moderate price changes was likely to be _____ , one reason being that salt normally consumes a negligible portion of a family's income. This means that a small change in price _(would/would not)_ significantly alter the amount of salt the typical housewife purchased.

4.24   For most people, salt is also a necessity, and there are very few items one can substitute for salt in the kitchen. We can take our salt example and generalize it by saying the demand for a good is likely to be _____ when expenditure on that good consumes a very small portion of the weekly income or weekly budget and demand is also likely to be _____ when the good in question has no close substitute.

4.25   An example of a necessity would be your urgent need of the services of a dentist or surgeon. If you required an appendectomy, and if a hospital attendant were to tell you that the surgeon's fee for performing the appendectomy was $200, you would in all probability agree to have the operation performed. If, however, the hospital attendant then told you that he had made an error and the surgeon's fee was $225, it is highly unlikely that you would change your mind about the operation. In this example, therefore, the demand for a surgeon's services is _____ , implying that for a given moderate price change, the amount of a surgeon's services demanded _(will/will not)_ vary significantly with the prices charged.

4.26   Goods that are consumed together are known as complementary goods. Left shoes and right shoes are examples of _____ goods, whereas yellow pencils and blue pencils are _____ goods. As we might expect, the demand for many complementary goods is inelastic. One requires gasoline before one can drive an automobile; because one is consuming gasoline as one consumes an automobile's services, automobiles and gasoline are _____ goods.

ANSWERS

22. inelastic
23. inelastic . would not
24. inelastic . inelastic

25. inelastic . will not
26. complementary . substitute . complementary

4.27 If the price of gasoline were to increase a few cents per gallon, one _(would/would not)_ expect sales of gasoline to fall significantly. If this were to be the case, the demand for gasoline would be _____ . However, one brand of gasoline is a very close _____ for another brand of gasoline. And if indeed the price of one brand of gasoline were to increase but all others were to remain unaltered, we would expect sales of the higher-priced brand to _____ significantly. Thus, a good that has very close substitutes tends to be characterized by an _____ demand.

4.28 From the previous frames, we can draw important inferences. If we are dealing with one good for which there is no close substitute, demand is likely to be _____ , but if we are dealing with a brand of good for which there are very close substitutes, demand for that brand is likely to be _____ .

4.29 Demand is likely to be _____ where
   a. the amount of money involved is very small
   b. no close substitutes are available
   c. the buying of this good cannot be postponed
   d. there is a large variety of possible uses for this good
It should be remembered in discussing elasticity of demand that we are considering relatively _____ price changes.

4.30 How would you classify the following goods—as complements or substitutes?

   a. Automobile tires and automobiles minus tires _____

   b. Black and white films and color films _____

   c. A film and a camera _____

   d. Two $5 bills and a $10 bill _____

   e. Coca Cola and Pepsi Cola _____

   f. Shirts and trousers _____

4.31 Let us now explore the importance of elasticity and inelasticity. Let us consider the case of one good: light bulbs. Because light bulbs have very few close substitutes, we would expect the demand for them to be _____ . Let us now imagine that all manufacturers of light bulbs got together (colluded) and decided to increase the price of all light bulbs by 10 percent.

ANSWERS

27. would not . inelastic . substitute . decrease . elastic
28. inelastic . elastic
29. inelastic . small

30. complements . substitutes . complements . substitutes . substitutes . complements
31. inelastic

4.32   Because the demand for light bulbs is relatively _____ , we would not expect there to be a significant _____ in the quantity of light bulbs purchased; and consequently we would expect that the total income manufacturers of light bulbs would receive after they started charging the higher price would be _____ than it was before. This would occur because the price had risen, whereas the quantity purchased had changed _(more than/less than)_ proportionately. Consequently, the total revenue (price X quantity) received from the sale of light bulbs would _____ .

4.33   *Total revenue* is a technical term used by economists to describe, in this example, the total income received from the sale of light bulbs, and, as you might expect, we calculate total revenue by multiplying the number of light bulbs sold by the _____ of light bulbs.

4.34   Thus, we see that in situations where demand is inelastic, total revenue will move in the same direction as price. If price is increased, total revenue will _____ , whereas if price is decreased, total revenue will _____ .

4.35   Let us choose another example that shows the importance of the concept of price elasticity in a policy setting. As you probably know, the price airlines can charge for tickets between any two cities is set by the Civil Aeronautics Board (C.A.B.). Recently, in response to low passenger loads and falling profits the airlines sought a fare increase. Now, if the demand for airline travel by prospective passengers were *inelastic,* the percentage increase in fares would be _____ than the percentage decrease in passengers.

4.36   This was obviously the assumption the airlines were making. Why? The total money or revenue an airline receives for a flight equals the number of passengers times the price of an airline ticket. There are several ways for a flight's revenue to increase: more passengers with a constant price; more passengers with a higher price; and fewer passengers with a higher price if, and only if, the proportional decrease in the number of passengers is _____ than the proportional increase in price. But, of course, this is the definition of _____ demand, which the airlines had to be assuming in seeking a price increase.

4.37   As an example, suppose the existing round trip fare between two cities is $100 and at this price an airline flies 200 passengers per day on this route. Total revenue, which is found by multiplying the price, or fare, by the _____ of _____ equals $ _____ .

ANSWERS

32. inelastic . reduction . greater .
    less than . increase
33. price
34. increase . decrease

35. greater
36. less . inelastic
37. number . passengers . 20,000

4.38 If, in response to the airline's request for a fare increase, the C.A.B. allows a 10 percent rise to $110 and the airline discovers that although fewer passengers now fly, total fare revenue rises, for example, 190 passengers at $110 equals $20,900, then, other things remaining unchanged, we would conclude that the demand for airline travel within the range of prices on the route was _____ . Thus, though _____ passengers now fly, total fare revenue has risen because the proportional increase in fare is _____ than the proportional _____ in the number of passengers.

4.39 On the other hand, if the increase in fare to $110 led to only 150 passengers per day, total fare revenue would decrease to $16,500. Demand would therefore be _____ because the proportional increase in fare is _____ than the proportional decrease in passengers.

4.40 The third possibility would occur when the fare increase was matched proportionately by a passenger decrease. In this case, the demand would be of _____ _____ , and total _____ _____ would remain unchanged.

4.41 Thus, if the airline wishes to maximize total fare revenue, it should seek a fare _____ if it believes the demand to be inelastic. By similar reasoning, it should seek a fare _____ if it believes the demand to be elastic.

4.42 It may well be that regularly scheduled airlines today find themselves in a quandary. Many private clubs and organizations charter airplanes to fly members to, say, Europe. They tend to charge each member the cost of chartering the plane divided by the number of passengers. If the plane is full, the round-trip price to London from the West Coast for a passenger is around $200 to $250. This is much less than the $838 fare set by international agreement for regularly scheduled flights (passengers, of course, on regularly scheduled flights have a wide choice of flight times, airlines, and routes compared with charter flights). Now, if demand for such travel is price elastic, and if regular airlines wish to increase total fare revenue, they should seek a fare _____ . The problem arises because it is highly probable that for other passengers—many businessmen, for example—the demand is inelastic and consequently a fare decrease would reduce total _____ _____ for this group.

ANSWERS

38. inelastic . fewer . greater . decrease   41. increase . decrease
39. elastic . less   42. decrease . fare revenue
40. unitary elasticity . fare revenue

4.43   Diagrammatically, the problem can be seen in Figure 4.4,

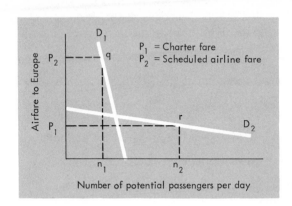

Figure 4.4
Demands for airline services

where D_1 is the demand of businessmen for regularly scheduled international airlines and D_2 the demand of vacationers. Total daily fare revenue for international airlines equals area op_2qn_1, that is, fare times the number of passengers. If, at prices aroung p_2, demand is price inelastic, the area representing total fare revenue would _____ if fares were raised.

4.44   Area op_1rn_2 represents charter fare revenue and is found by multiplying the fare of _____ by the number of passengers _____ . If, at prices around p_1 demand is price elastic, area op_1rn_2 would increase if fares were _____ .

4.45   What should the airline policy be? Many airlines are flying planes less than one-half full on several routes. They would like to fill those empty seats with fare-paying passengers to _____ total fare revenue. They do not want a decreased fare for passengers whose demand is price _____ ; they would undoubtedly want a decrease in fare for passengers whose demand is _____ because, if both groups could be isolated and not allowed to trade tickets, total fare revenue would _____ .

4.46   Do students and servicemen have price elastic demands for airline travel? The answer would appear to be *(yes/no)* if you consider the airline's policy of encouraging the C.A.B. to have special reduced fares for both groups. Similarly, the airline seeking lower fares for special summer flights to Europe is an indication that they believe the demands of many summer travelers are price _____ .

ANSWERS

43. increase
44. op_1 . on_2 . lowered

45. increase . inelastic . elastic . increase
46. yes . elastic

4.47 For most businessmen going to Europe, there is no close substitute to flying. Traveling by sea takes up too much time—the opportunity _____ is too high. Consequently, we would expect the demand for airline travel for this group to be price _____ .

4.48 For the summer traveler, however, there are many ways to spend a vacation without going to Europe. Camping in the mountains, traveling across country by car, and trips to the beach are _____ to vacationing in Europe, and, as we discussed previously, the demand for substitutes is likely to be price _____ .

4.49 To the extent that people taking a vaction can arrange a convenient charter flight, the method of traveling becomes a close _____ for commercial flights. Because there exists a large price differential between the charter and commercial flight, the opportunity to buy charter flight tickets encourages _(more/fewer)_ people to fly and also causes a switch from commercial flights to charter flights.

4.50 The demand curves we have considered so far we would describe as normal demand curves. Those curves slope downwards from _____ to _____ , indicating that at higher prices a _____ quantity would be purchased.

4.51 Just as there are exceptions to most rules, so there are exceptions to our normal demand curves. Some people believe (often for good reasons) that "you only get what you pay for," and if they see a good priced lower than what they expect it to be, they may have some doubts as to the quality of this good, whereas if this good were priced higher, they might be prepared to buy it. Thus, this could lead to a situation that would be the reverse of our normal demand curve situation. At a higher price, people would actually buy _____ of the good than they would at a lower price, and consequently, the demand curve for this good for the group of people who think in this fashion _(would/would not)_ slope downwards from left to right.

4.52 Similar to this type of situation is the situation involving prestige goods. Prestige goods, such as mink coats, may be bought by some people simply because the price of mink coats tends to be relatively _____ . If the price of mink coats were very low and many people had them, mink coats would no longer be a _____ good, and consequently, those people who buy them for prestige reasons would not purchase them at lower prices. Again, we would have an example of a demand curve for mink coats by this group of people that

ANSWERS

47. cost . inelastic
48. substitutes . elastic
49. substitute . more

50. left . right . smaller
51. more . would not
52. high . prestige . downwards . positively

would not slope _____ from left to right. In such examples, you might want to argue that other things are not being held constant and thus we are really not discussing only one demand curve in each case. This would be a legitimate objection; it would remain true,

however, that plotting of points on a graph could yield a _____ inclined curve.

4.53   There is another famous case of a nonnormal sloping demand curve, involving an inferior good, which refers to the demand for potatoes by Irish peasants.   You should recall that an inferior good is a good whose income elasticity of demand is _(negative/positive)_ , that is, where increases in income (+) are associated with decreases in quantities purchased (–). Irish peasants were very poor people who could only afford to buy very cheap food, and potatoes comprised a substantial portion of their normal diet. In good times, however, when Irish farmers had bumper crops of potatoes, the price of potatoes tended to fall. Because potatoes consumed a large portion of the Irish income or budget for the typical peasant family, a fall in the price of potatoes would mean that each family could buy the same quantity of potatoes

as they normally did at the higher price for _____ money. Consequently, they would have _(some/no)_ income left to spend on other goods after their purchase of potatoes.

4.54   With this income, the Irish peasant could now afford to buy other goods such as meat, milk, and cheese. But because families could now enjoy meat, milk, and cheese, they did not require as many potatoes, and consequently the peasants would buy fewer potatoes. Here we

have an example that shows that through a _____ in the price of potatoes, Irish peasants could afford to buy some expensive foods, and consequently, would eat

_____ potatoes. In terms of the demand curve for potatoes, we can see that at a

lower price, _____ potatoes were purchased than previously, at the higher price. Again, we have an exception to the rule where the demand curve, for potatoes in this instance, _(does/does not)_ slope downwards from left to right. From demand let us now turn our attention to supply.

REVIEW QUESTIONS

4.1   This question is based on the following hypothetical statement:
"An electrical power utility requests that the Federal Power Commission (FPC) approve an increase in rates for electricity in order to increase its revenues to overcome falling profits. The FPC disapproves the increase and suggests that the utility would do better if it reduced its rates."
On the basis of the above statement, which of the following is true?

ANSWERS

53. negative . less . some   54. fall . fewer . fewer . does not

a. The utility will not be able to increase its revenues, because it cannot raise its rates.

b. The utility believes the demand for power is inelastic; the FPC believes demand is elastic.

c. The utility believes the demand for power is elastic; the FPC believes demand is inelastic.

d. On the basis of this statement none of the above can be true.

When demand is inelastic an increase in price leads to an increase in revenue. When demand is elastic, a decrease in price leads to an increase in revenue. Because the utility wants a price increase, it presumably believes demand is inelastic. And as the FPC suggests a price decrease, it presumably believes demand is elastic. The correct response is b.

4.2 Which of the following statements would be correct if the demand for the good in question were inelastic?

1. Government sponsored agricultural research that increased acreage yields would lead to a decline in farmers' incomes.
2. Burning part of the coffee crop by the Brazilian government in years of large supply would keep export earnings from falling.

a. 1 only
b. 2 only

c. both 1 and 2
d. neither 1 nor 2

When demand is inelastic, it means that as you move along the demand curve, the precentage change in price is greater in absolute value than the percentage change in quantity. When demand is inelastic, an increase in quantity will result in a decline in total revenue (price times quantity) because the rise in quantity will be more than offset by the decline in price. If government agricultural research increases farm productivity, farm output would rise and farm prices would fall. With an inelastic demand, total revenue would fall. If revenue fell more than costs, farmers would suffer a loss in income. Similarly, if demand is inelastic, the burning of coffee when output of coffee increases would prevent revenue from falling. The correct response is c.

4.3 In traveling about a city, most people use either subway or bus. Suppose all subway fares were doubled, but bus fares remained unchanged. How would the subway fare increase affect the total fare revenue?

a. It would increase for buses but might increase or decrease for subways.

b. It would increase for subways but might increase or decrease for buses.

c. It would increase for both subways and buses.

d. It would increase for subways and remain unchanged for buses.

As subway fares increase, some people will switch to substitute goods, in this case, buses. Thus, total bus revenue will increase. Total subway fare revenue will increase if the percentage fare increase exceeds the percentage subway passenger loss, that is, if the demand for subway services in the relevant price range is inelastic. If the demand is price elastic (or of unitary elasticity), subway fare revenue will not increase as subway fares increase. The stem of the question attempts to point out that buses and subways are substitutes. Were they complements, for example, if passengers used buses to reach subway stations, then, assuming the demand for subway services is not perfectly inelastic, bus revenue would fall as subway fares increased, because traveling on both would be reduced. Again, subway revenue would rise or, fall depending on the price elasticity of demand. The correct response is a.

4.4   Several baseball teams are considering allowing persons sixty-five years of age or older to attend games for $1 instead of the usual $3.

If the gate receipts were to rise with the adoption of the proposed policy, which of the following statements must be true?

1. As a group, older people would have as a result more income to spend on all other commodities.
2. The quantity of tickets bought by older persons is more responsive to changes in price than the quantity bought by younger persons.
3. The resulting increase in revenue from new fans would exceed the resulting loss in revenue from existing fans who would pay $1 instead of $3.

    a. 1 and 2 only   c. 3 only
    b. 2 and 3 only   d. 1, 2, and 3

One would expect that, other things being equal, a lower price for tickets for older persons would mean a larger quantity bought by older persons. If, at the lower price, gate receipts are higher, it means that the proportionate decrease in price is less than the proportionate increase in tickets sold; that is, the revenue gained from the new fans exceeds the revenue lost from old fans who now pay less for their tickets. Technically, in the relevant price range, older persons' demand for tickets is price elastic. Because the question refers to price reductions only for older people, the increase in revenue to the team will come only from older people. Because as a group they now spend more on baseball, they will have less to spend on all other commodities but will, of course, experience an increase in real income. Nothing is known about the price elasticity of demand for tickets of younger persons, and, consequently, no comparison can be made. The correct response is c.

Case 4

ADVERTISING AND MARKET DEMAND

In 1971, American businesses spent $18 billion on advertising. This was just less than 2 percent of the $1 trillion gross national product—the total amount spent on all goods and services by households, businesses, and governments.
What were the main effects of this large advertising expenditure? Who benefited and who paid the costs? Would the American public have been better off with more, or less, advertising?

Complete answers to these questions will have to wait until later in the course, after we have studied the behavior of markets, competition, and monopoly. But the concepts already in hand are adequate to throw a good deal of light on the effects of advertising on consumer behavior and market demand, which is a first step toward answering the questions above.

Figure 4.a summarizes some of the main facts about advertising in the American economy over the past decade. Two main facts stand out.

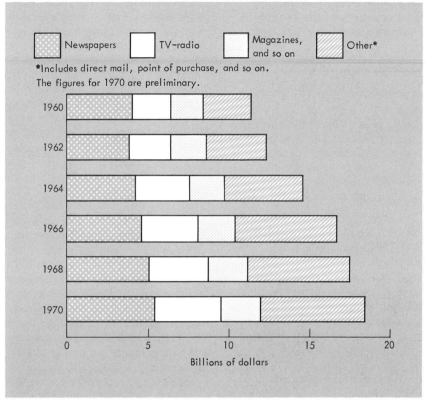

Figure 4.a   Advertising by media, 1960-1970

First, total expenditures on advertising have been growing over the decade. Indeed, this is a continuation of a trend since the great Depression, when advertising expenditures averaged less than $2 billion (though with a good deal lower price level and smaller economy than now). Second, advertising dollars go into many different channels. Nearly one-third of the total goes for newspaper advertising, substantially less for TV and radio advertising, which we often think of as the biggest component. Magazines, direct mail, in-store advertising, and the like account for a surprisingly large part of the total. One obvious question about advertising is how useful is it to consumers—how much useful information does it provide? On this, views differ widely. A lot of newspaper advertising contains directly valuable information—prices, brand availabilities, and the like. On the other hand, much TV and radio advertising is "institutional"—it mainly tells people that they ought to want a Chevrolet, Prudential insurance, Miller beer, or Right Guard deodorant, rather than specific information about the products. Other forms of advertising vary widely on the information scale.

We have no reliable, detailed information on advertising expenditure for individual products. Auto advertising, sometimes cited as a leading example of advertising designed to brainwash us into wanting something we do not really need, spends a large number of dollars, but auto makers' advertising budgets are less than 1 percent of total auto sales. On the other hand, soap, cosmetics, patent medicines, and similar "small ticket" brand items have advertising budgets reaching 5 or even 10 percent of sales. Proctor and Gamble, not General Motors, is the world's largest TV advertiser. But just about every seller spends something on advertising, ranging all the way from the want ads in the local newspaper to the fanciest TV programs.

SUGGESTIONS FOR ANALYSIS

The analytical concepts in Chapters 1 to 4 can help you in thinking through what the effects of advertising actually are, who benefits and who pays, and, in general, whether we would be better off with more or less advertising, even though they cannot give you a simple answer to the last question. Consider the questions in the order asked in the first paragraph.

What Are The Main Effects of Advertising? When TWA takes a full page newspaper ad to extoll the luxuries of its new coach lounge on its 747's, it is trying to increase the demand for its product (travel services) by (a) convincing more people they ought to fly and (b) convincing those who do fly that they ought to fly on TWA instead of American, United, or some other line. In technical terms, it is trying to raise its demand curve (move it to the right), and make its slope steeper, that is, make the demand for its product more inelastic. If its advertising is successful, TWA will achieve both. More people will buy tickets on TWA. They will believe that TWA is somehow superior to American, United, and its other competitors—that is, TWA will be differentiated in their minds, and they will be willing to pay more for its product than for the competitive services offered by other airlines with virtually identical airplanes, flight times, and the like. Whether TWA accomplishes this by actually providing useful information to potential consumers to show that its service is better, or just by convincing them that TWA is better although in fact its service is substantially identical to that of its major competitors, is an arguable issue. But if TWA convinces people either way, its demand curve shifts to the right and becomes less elastic.

Now, suppose that American and United, seeing this ad and losing customers to TWA, take comparable ads themselves in the following day's papers. One result may be a big increase in total air travel—the demand curves for American, TWA, and United all move out to the right. People decide to go more places, to fly instead of driving. But another result may be that American's and United's ads just neutralize TWA's. A 747 is about the same airplane, no matter which airline flies it. You get there just about as fast on one as on another; the prices are the same, set by government regulation; and it is pretty hard to make your coach lounge a lot plusher than your competitors'. If the various ads just offset each other, the net result is that nobody's demand curve is much different after all the advertising than it was before. The effect of TWA's advertising is to shift its demand curve to the right and its competitors' to the left. The effect of TWA's competitors' counter-advertising is to push TWA's demand curve back to the left; while it moves their curves to the right. The demand curve for the entire airline industry may not, however, change very much as a result of the industry's advertising. In competitive advertising situations, therefore, the effects can be analyzed by looking at the movements of the various demand curves for the product concerned.

Radical critics of today's scene, and some not so radical, argue that in effect the American consumer has no real freedom of choice—that his choices are controlled by advertising and by Madison Avenue. Stated in this extreme form, this is pretty obviously nonsense. Something under 2 percent of the total gross national product hardly seems adequate to govern the entire pattern of "wants" of every consumer in America. Moreover, there is a long history of business firms gone broke trying to convince consumers through advertising and other selling campaigns to buy products that consumers stubbornly refuse to purchase. The classic case is Ford's Edsel in the 1950s, which flopped colossally in spite of an enormous advertising campaign to convince the American public that it was the car of tomorrow. Only two of the ten largest industrial firms in the United States as of 1900 are still in the top ten, in spite of massive advertising by most of them. Less than a dozen of the fifty best-known automobile brands of the past half century are still with us, in spite of the best advertising assistance Madison Avenue has been able to provide.

On the other hand, it would be ridiculous to argue that advertising has no effect on how consumers spend their incomes. TV is indeed pervasive in American life, and it is full of "beautiful people" and beautiful things to want. Just how far advertising goes to influence the expenditures of the American public is a much-argued issue. Alas, there is no evidence that can give a simple, clear-cut answer.

Who Pays For Advertising?   Clearly, somebody has to pay. We have not looked at business costs yet, but you do not have to be much of an economist to see that in the long run someone is going to have to pay the total cost of running the airline, including advertising, or the company will go broke. Part of the advertising may come out of potential profits, but not most, as we shall see later. In the long run, prices for air travel are going to have to be enough higher to cover the advertising costs along with other airline expenses.

If the resources of the American economy are limited, as they are, and if we are operating near full employment, as we are a fair share of the time, clearly resources devoted to advertising must be diverted from some other use. Eighteen billion dollars worth of ink, billboards, TV entertainers, and the like are a lot of information, entertainment, and (to some) irritation. But the resources used that way cannot be used to produce beer, hair dryers, textbooks, health services, or other goods and services that consumers might like to have. Resources devoted to advertising mean fewer resources available for producing other goods and services that people want. When resources are scarce, we must economize—we must choose what we most want them to produce for us.

Do We Spend Too Much On Advertising? Would the American public be better off with more, or less advertising? Who benefits from, who pays the cost of, our $18 billion of advertising?

Each household maximizes its utility from the income it receives when it allocates that income among all the things it wants so as to equate the utility received from the last dollar spent on each

good and service bought. To make this allocation most effectively, the household needs the best possible information on the alternatives open to it. Thus, insofar as advertising provides information on the alternative goods and services available (as to price, quality, or other relevant characteristics), it helps households to maximize the utility obtainable from their incomes. Insofar as advertising provides erroneous information, of course, it has the opposite effect. If advertising simply alters consumer wants, rather than providing better information by which an optimum allocation of income can be made, it is hard to say whether that advertising increases or decreases consumer satisfaction. This is a tough ethical question.

At any given time, if the economy is substantially fully employed, we must choose among alternative uses for our resources. If, therefore, we spend $18 billion on advertising, this means that those resources cannot be used to produce other things that consumers want. Thus, when it comes to advertising, we cannot escape the fundamental need to economize—that is, to choose wisely among alternative uses of resources. If Joe Smith sells newspaper advertising, he cannot work as a bank clerk. If steel is used to make printing presses for papers, it cannot be used to make automobiles. If musicians make TV commercials, they cannot devote that same time to playing in symphony orchestras.

But, you may ask, doesn't advertising increase the *total* demand for all products and hence avoid the limitation of existing resources. The answer, if the economy's resources are already fully employed, is no. In that case, you may increase the demand for goods and services by advertising, but you cannot increase the volume of resources available to produce things. If people spend more in such cases, the result is higher prices (inflation), not more output. Given the stock of resources, we must choose between alternative uses, of which advertising is one. If there are unemployed resources (for example, in a recession), more advertising might increase demand and consequently the amount of goods produced, but even if it could, there are other ways, as you will see later, to increase demand that do not use up resources.

With advertising, as with almost everything else, the principle of marginalism applies. It would be surprising indeed if we were to come to the conclusion that advertising is completely bad or completely good, that we should completely eliminate advertising or increase it to some very high amount. From a social point of view, the decision as to whether we want more or less advertising is a marginal decision. We need to weigh the gains from the last dollar spent on advertising against alternative possibilities for that dollar devoted to other uses. Clearly, some advertising has high social value—for example, if it tells consumers about a new, highly desirable product. Conversely, the marginal value of the last dollar spent on some types of advertising may seem to you very low, particularly where the effect is simply to offset someone else's advertising. As to how much advertising we ought to have in our society, marginalism is clearly the principle to follow.

5

Productivity and Costs

5.1   In many ways, a supply curve is similar to a demand curve. Each describes a relationship between the quantity and the price of a commodity. However, whereas a demand curve tells the quantities of a good that would be _____ in any time period in any given market at different prices, a supply curve tells the quantities of a good that would be supplied in any given time period in any given market at various _____ .

5.2   A supply curve is similar to a demand curve in that it represents a set of hypothetical situations. It shows how much of a good suppliers would offer for sale in a given market in a given _____ _____ in response to various _____ .

5.3   As in the case of the demand curve, the position of the supply curve is fixed by a set of _____ , which are factors that influence supply but which are assumed to be _(variable/constant)_ . The two variables are again price and quantity, price being the independent variable and quantity that would be supplied being the _____ variable.

5.4   We saw in discussing demand curves that normally the higher the price, the _____ the quantity that will be demanded, and, consequently, most demand curves slope _____ from left to right.

ANSWERS

1. demanded . prices
2. time period . prices

3. parameters . constant . dependent
4. smaller . downward

71

5.5 In the case of a supply curve, the reverse is true. Normally, in a given time period, suppliers will be willing to supply more of a good only at a _____ price, *ceteris paribus*. Typically, therefore, supply curves slope _____ from left to right.

5.6 The suppliers of goods and services (output) in our economy face three basic problems:
a. How much output should they produce per time period?
b. What price should they charge for each unit of output?
c. What is the most efficient way to produce that output?
To fully understand the behavior of suppliers (and why supply curves typically slope

_____ from left to right), we must study productivity and costs. More simply expressed, we must study how much output will result from different amounts and combinations of inputs—this is the study of productivity—and also how much it will cost to produce such outputs.

5.7 Consider Table 5.1, which shows data on what would happen if, *ceteris paribus*, a farmer were

Table 5.1

WHEAT OUTPUT—ONE FIELD WITH VARYING LABOR INPUT

Units of labor input (man-days)	Total product (bushels)	Average product per unit of labor input (bushels)	Marginal product of labor input (bushels)
0	0	–	
1	40	40	40
2	140	70	100
3	300	100	160
4	480	120	180
5	650	130	170
6	810	135	160
7	960	137	150
8	1,080	135	120
9	1,170	130	90
10	1,200	120	30
11	1,190	108	-10
12	1,140	95	-50
13	910	70	-230

ANSWERS

5. higher . upward
6. upward

7. man-days . production . constant

to vary the amounts of labor input, which we are measuring in _____ , in one of his wheat fields. Labor is not the only factor of production involved in the production of wheat,

but here we are holding all other inputs, or factors of _____ , constant, and we are asking what happens when we vary only one input, in this case labor. That is, we are

holding _____ such things as the amount of fertilizer and the amount of mechanical aids a farmer might use.

5.8   Consider only the first two columns. We can see that as we add successive inputs of labor,

total output (product) rises until we add the _____ unit of labor. Beyond that

point, total output _____ and continues to do so, the more labor input we use.

5.9   If the farmer were to employ more than ten units of labor input, total output would be
(more/less) than total output with ten units of labor input. We could imagine workers getting in each other's way. Consequently, it _(would/would not)_ be profitable for the farmer to hire this eleventh unit of labor input as long as he has to pay a positive price for each unit of labor input.

5.10   In our example, therefore, maximum total output can be obtained when the farmer uses

_____ units of labor input. This maximum is _____ bushels of wheat.

5.11   Column 3 is derived by dividing the figures in column _____ by the corresponding

figures in column _____ . Column 3, which is also in bushels, is a measure of the

_____ _____ per unit of labor input.

5.12   In column 3, we can see that the average product per unit of labor input increases up to the

_____ unit of labor input, whereafter it _____ .

5.13   Column 4 measures the marginal product of labor input, also in bushels. This column tells us what the incremental, or additional, or marginal output will be if we add one more unit of labor input. For instance, if we consider the first two lines, total output from zero units of labor

input is _____ bushels. Total output from one unit of labor input is

_____ bushels. Thus, we can see that the increase in output in going from zero units of labor input to one unit of labor input (that is, the additional or marginal product) is

_____ bushels.

ANSWERS

8. eleventh . decreases
9. less . would not
10. ten . 1,200

11. 2 . 1 . average product
12. seventh . decreases
13. 0 . 40 . 40

5.14   We see also that the total output from employing three units of labor input is _____ bushels, and total output from employing four units of labor input is _____ bushels. Thus, the difference between those totals, in this case _____ bushels of wheat, is due to the addition of the _____ unit of labor input. Consequently, we would say that the _____ _____ of the fourth unit of labor input is _____ bushels.

5.15   Now consider the output from nine units of labor input; it is _____ bushels. Adding one more unit, the tenth unit, gives us only a very small increase in total output—an increase in total output of _____ units of wheat. Thus, we see that the _____ _____ of the tenth unit of labor input is, in this case, _____ bushels.

5.16   When we add an eleventh unit of labor input, we see that total output actually _____ from _____ bushels to _____ bushels.

5.17   Thus, the output attributable to the eleventh unit of labor input, that is, the _____ _____ of the eleventh unit, is negative in the amount of _____ bushels.

5.18   After the eleventh unit of labor input, as more labor is added, total product continues to _____ . The marginal product of each successive unit added remains _____ and becomes smaller and smaller.

5.19   The data in Table 5.1 on the marginal product of labor provide an example of the widely observed phenomenon of *diminishing returns*. After some point has been reached, the amount of *additional* output obtained through adding more units of one factor input to a fixed supply of other factors will decrease. We saw this to be true in Table 5.1. We held constant all factors of production except _____ , and we observed as we added successive units of labor that, after a point was reached, the additional output, or _____ _____ , of each successive unit of labor input _____ .

5.20   Thus, we would say that this is an example of _____ _____ because as the proportion of one factor input to other fixed factor inputs is increased, the _____ product of this factor input will, after a certain point has been reached, decrease and continue to decrease.

ANSWERS

14. 300 . 480 . 180 . fourth .
    marginal product . 180
15. 1,170 . 30 . marginal product . 30
16. decreases . 1,200 . 1,190

17. marginal product . 10
18. decrease . negative
19. labor . marginal product . decreased
20. diminishing returns . marginal

5.21 The decrease in the marginal product will ultimately result in a decrease in the

_____ product of the factor input that is being added. While the marginal product is above the average product, the average product will _(increase/decrease)_ . When the marginal product is below the average product, the average product will _(increase/ decrease)_ . The marginal product will equal the average product when the average product is at a maximum.

5.22 It should be obvious that under normal circumstances we would never expect an entrepreneur, paying positive prices for his factor inputs, to hire an additional unit of some specific input

whose marginal product was zero or _____ . Is the following statement true or false? We would, therefore, never expect an entrepreneur to hire an additional unit of any input if the marginal product of this unit were less than the marginal product of all other hired

units. _____

5.23 Do we know how many units of labor input the farmer should hire if he wishes to maximize his wheat output? _(yes/no)_ . Do we know how many units of labor input the farmer

should hire to make as high a profit as possible? _(yes/no)_ .

5.24 Consider the following piece of information, however. Imagine that you are told that the farmer has to pay each man thirty bushels of wheat for a day's work. That is, the extra cost

to the farmer of each additional man-day hired equals _____ bushels. What is the marginal benefit to the farmer of each additional man-day hired? The marginal benefit is the

additional output produced or the _____ _____ of labor input.

5.25 As you will recall from Chapter 2, we saw that when the marginal benefit of some activity

exceeded the _____ _____ , it paid to increase that activity. In the

example, therefore, as long as the marginal benefit to the farmer (the _____

_____ of labor input) exceeds the marginal cost to the farmer (the marginal wage rate), it will pay the farmer to continue hiring labor inputs.

5.26 Because the wage rate is constant and equal to thirty bushels, the farmer will not hire additional labor input whose marginal product is _(less/more)_ than thirty bushels. That is, if the marginal benefit to the farmer of an additional unit of labor input (its marginal product)

is less than the _____ _____ (the wage rate), that labor unit will not be hired.

ANSWERS

21. average . increase . decrease
22. negative . false
23. yes . no

24. thirty . marginal product
25. marginal cost . marginal product
26. less . marginal cost

5.27 Consider Figure 5.1, which is drawn from columns 1 and 4 in Table 5.1. It is very similar to the figures in Chapter 2. We can see that the first unit of labor input adds _____ bushels to total output and the second unit, _____ bushels. How much does the fifth unit add? _____ bushels. You can see that after 4 units of labor input, _____ returns set in.

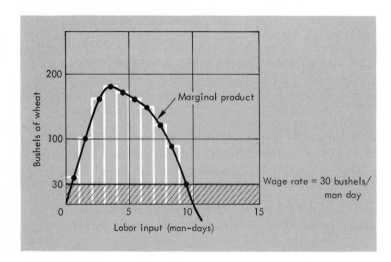

Figure 5.1
Marginal product of labor

5.28 Now, one way we could find out how much output five man-days would produce would be to add the output from the first man-day to the output from the second man-day, plus the third, fourth, and fifth. In terms of the rectangles in Figure 5.1, we would add the _____ of the first five rectangles from the origin 0.

5.29 The sum of the areas of the first five rectangles, of course, is an approximation of the area under the _____ _____ curve from zero to five on the horizontal axis.

5.30 Similarly, the area under the _____ _____ curve between zero and nine units of labor input is total output (or total benefits to the farmer) from using nine units of labor input.

5.31 Now, consider the labor costs of producing output. Each man-day costs _____ bushels and is shown by the horizontal wage line. The line is horizontal because the cost of hiring an additional man does not change as the amount of labor input changes. In other words, the marginal _____ of labor input is constant.

ANSWERS

27. 40 . 100 . 170 . diminishing   30. marginal product
28. areas   31. thirty . cost
29. marginal product

5.32 The area under the _____ _____ curve from zero to fifteen on the horizontal axis represents the total _____ of labor to the wheat farmer of employing fifteen man-days; that is, this area represents _____ bushels of wheat.

5.33 We can obtain, therefore, much useful information from Figure 5.1 because the area under the _____ _____ of labor curve represents total output (or total benefit) from hiring some given number of labor inputs and because the area under the wage line represents the total _____ of hiring some given number of labor inputs.

5.34 As long as the marginal product curve lies _(above/below)_ the wage line, the last unit of labor hired will be yielding a return greater than its cost; that is, the marginal benefit to the farmer of hiring that unit of labor will exceed the _____ _____ .

5.35 If we continue to assume our farmer is a profit maximizer, he will not hire an additional unit of labor input when the _____ benefit is less than $30. Why? The benefit to the farmer in selling an additional bushel of wheat is the extra money or marginal revenue he receives. Because the marginal revenue of selling an additional bushel of wheat is $1, the marginal benefit the farmer receives by hiring one additional unit of labor equals the marginal revenue of wheat ($1) times the _____ _____ of labor. Thus, the farmer will only hire additional labor if the marginal revenue times the marginal product, that is, the marginal revenue product of labor, exceeds its _____ _____ .

5.36 We can generalize this simple example to include any factor input. Profit maximization requires that factor inputs are hired up to the point at which the marginal _____ product of each factor input equals its marginal _____ . In Figure 5.1, this means hiring up to 9½ man-days because at that level of labor input the marginal revenue product of labor equals its _____ _____ equals $30.

5.37 Let us now assume, more realistically, that there are costs in addition to labor costs. If the farmer rents a ten-acre field for one year at $10 per acre, then, independent of how much wheat the farmer produces, he will have to pay $ _____ in rent. This is a fixed cost of production because it _(will/will not)_ vary with the annual wheat output from this field.

ANSWERS

32. marginal cost . cost . 450
33. marginal product . cost
34. above . marginal cost
35. marginal . marginal product . marginal cost
36. revenue . cost . marginal cost
37. 100 . will not

5.38   If the farmer has to pay $30, however, for each man-day of labor employed, the amount of wages he must pay _(will/will not)_ vary with the number of units of labor input hired. These costs are known as variable costs. In this example they vary with the number of units of

_____ _____ hired, and hence with the output of wheat.

5.39   We see from Table 5.1 that, up to the point of negative marginal product of labor input, in order to obtain more wheat, we had to hire _____ units of labor input, and because this hiring necessarily involves paying more wages, variable costs will indeed vary with total

_____ of wheat. Variable costs _(decrease/increase)_ as total _____

increases up to the maximum of 1,200 bushels when _____ units of labor input are hired.

5.40   Turn now to Table 5.2, derived from data in Table 5.1. If we compare the first two columns, we can see that _____ _____ _____ are independent of the annual output of wheat. This is what we would expect because if the farmer commits himself to rent a ten-acre field at $10 per acre, this cost will be the same, regardless of his

output of wheat, consequently, we regard it as a _____ cost.

Table 5.2

FIXED, VARIABLE, AND TOTAL COSTS IN THE PRODUCTION OF WHEAT

(1) Annual output of wheat	(2) Total fixed costs	(3) Units of labor input (man-days)	(4) Total variable costs	(5) Total costs
0	$100	0	0	$100
40	100	1	30	130
140	100	2	60	160
300	100	3	90	190
480	100	4	120	220
650	100	5	150	250
810	100	6	180	280
960	100	7	210	310
1,080	100	8	240	340
1,170	100	9	270	370
1,200	100	10	300	400

ANSWERS

38. will . labor input   40. total fixed costs . fixed
39. more . output . increase . output .
    ten

5.41 The figures in columns 1 and 3 indicate how many units of labor input are required to produce the various quantities of wheat. We also see that in order to produce more wheat, we have to hire _(more/fewer)_ units of labor input.

5.42 Because labor is our only variable input under our simplifying assumptions the only factor input that will vary in quantity with total output will be _____ input. Because we know the price or wage the farmer must pay for one man-day, we can calculate the labor costs corresponding to any given level of output. For instance, we see that in order to produce 650 bushels of wheat, we require _____ units of labor input. Thus, the cost to the farmer of this labor input will be $ _____ .

5.43 Similarly, the labor costs to the farmer of producing 1,080 bushels of wheat would be $ _____ , because this requires _____ units of labor input at $30 per man-day.

5.44 Thus, we can see how we derive the figures in column 4, which is headed *Total variable costs.* We derive those figures by multiplying the figures in column _____ by $30–the cost of one unit of _____ input. Because the cost per unit of labor is constant and because a _____ quantity of labor input is required to produce a larger quantity of output, we would expect total variable costs to vary in the _(same/opposite)_ direction as total output.

5.45 We derive total cost by adding total fixed cost and _____ _____ _____ , and we find, as you would expect, that total cost varies in the _____ direction as output.

5.46 In Figure 5.2, we have plotted the data in Table 5.2, and, as you would expect, the total fixed costs are represented by a horizontal line, because they do not _____ with the level of output. The total cost curve is derived by adding the _____ _____ _____ curve to the _____ _____ _____ curve.

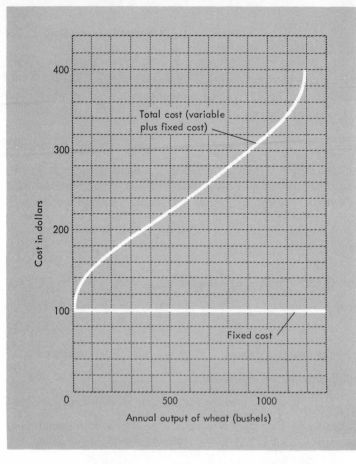

Figure 5.2
Fixed, variable, and total costs of
production

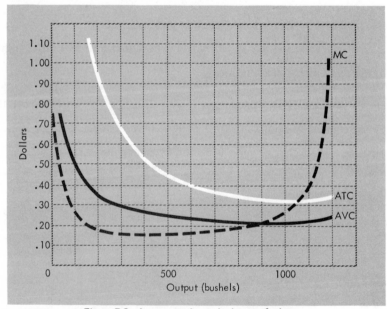

Figure 5.3 Average and marginal cost of wheat

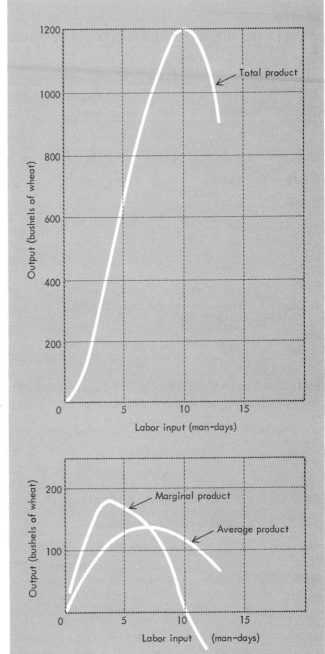

Figure 5.4
Total product of labor

Figure 5.5
Marginal and average product of labor

82   *Productivity and Costs*

Table 5.3

TOTAL, AVERAGE, AND MARGINAL COSTS OF WHEAT PRODUCTION

(1) Output	(2) Total fixed costs	(3) Average fixed costs	(5) Total variable costs	(5) Average variable costs	(6) Total costs	(7) Average total costs	(8) Marginal cost
0	100	—	0	—	100	—	
40	100	$2.50	30	$0.75	130	$3.25	$0.75
140	100	.71	60	.43	160	1.14	.30
300	100	.33	90	.30	190	.63	.19
480	100	.21	120	.25	220	.46	.17
650	100	.15	150	.23	250	.38	.18
810	100	.12	180	.22	280	.35	.19
960	100	.10	210	.219	310	.32	.20
1,080	100	.09	240	.22	340	.31	.25
1,170	100	.085	270	.23	370	.32	.33
1,200	100	.083	300	.25	400	.33	1.00

5.47 In Table 5.3, data from Table 5.2 are repeated with some additional calculations. Average fixed costs are found by dividing total fixed costs by output; similarly, average variable costs are calculated by dividing _____ _____ _____ by _____ and average total costs, by dividing _____ _____ by output.

5.48 Because total costs equal total fixed costs plus total _____ _____ , average total costs will equal average _____ _____ plus _____ variable costs.

5.49 The calculation of marginal cost is slightly more complex. Ideally, we want to know the cost of producing one additional unit of output. We know, for instance, that the total cost of producing 40 bushels of wheat is $130 and the total cost of producing 140 bushels is $160.

Thus, the differenee in cost of $ _____ is the marginal cost of producing an additional 100 bushels (that is, 140 – 40 bushels). If we treat each of those extra 100 bushels equally, we would calculate the marginal cost of one bushel as $30/100 = $ _____ .

ANSWERS
47. total variable costs . output . total costs   49. 30 . .30
48. variable costs . fixed costs . average

5.50   The problem we are encountering here is the same one we discussed earlier in the book. We are not making continuous changes but rather discrete changes; not plotting the marginal and average curves for every atom of output but rather considering output in "lumps." The smooth curves are drawn through those lumps as though we had considered continuous changes. O.K.?

_____

5.51   We have plotted the average and marginal curves from Table 5.3 in Figure 5.3. To avoid having too messy a figure, we have omitted the average fixed cost curve that, if included, would be a line of   *(constant/increasing/decreasing)*   height and that would measure the distance between

the average total cost curve and the _____ _____ _____
curve.

5.52   Although we derive the marginal cost curve in Table 5.3 from total cost figures, we could also

derive the marginal cost from total _____ cost figures, because the marginal cost of

producing additional wheat will be independent of the _____ _____ .

5.53   Note two significant points in Figure 5.3. These are where the marginal cost curve intersects the average variable cost curve and the average total cost curve. In both instances, the marginal cost curve intersects each curve at its   *(minimum/maximum)*   point. This is no accident but is necessarily true. We can see from Figure 5.3 that as the marginal cost of producing additional wheat equals the average total cost, the marginal cost curve must inter-

sect the average total cost curve at its _____ point, because once it has intersected the average cost curve (and once marginal costs exceed average costs), it will cause average total

cost to _____ .

5.54   Think about a basketball squad. If the height of a sixth player is greater than the average height of the other five, then the addition of this sixth man will cause the average height to

_____ .

5.55   To show in our example the exact relationships between the productivity of labor input and the cost of wheat output, we shall pull together the tables and figures we have analyzed in this chapter. From Table 5.1, we have drawn total average and marginal product curves and alongside have reproduced the corresponding cost table and curves. You should work through some numbers from each table and make sure you understand how each curve is derived. For example, when marginal product becomes negative at 10 man-days, you know that adding one

more man-day will cause _____ _____ to fall. As can be seen, the total product curve is at a maximum at 10 man-days.

ANSWERS

50. O.K.
51. decreasing . average variable cost
52. variable . fixed costs

53. minimum . minimum . rise
54. rise
55. total product

5.56   By juxtaposing those figures into Figure 5.4, we see the relationship between product and cost curves. The average variable cost curve will be inversely related to the average product of labor curve, remembering that the wage per man-day is set in the market and is constant. Thus,

when the average product per man-day is rising, average variable cost will be _____ , and when average product per man-day is falling, average variable cost per unit of output will

be _____ .

5.57   Another way to express the same idea would be to say that the greater the average product of each man-day of labor, the _(higher/lower)_ the average variable cost of each bushel of wheat produced. And, conversely, the less wheat a man-day of labor can produce, the _(higher/lower_, the average variable cost of each unit of wheat will be.

5.58   In Figure 5.6, a broken line traces the points we have discussed. We have shown how the

maximum _____ _____ point is reflected at the _____ average variable cost point.

5.59   Just as the maximum value of the average product of labor yields the minimum

_____ _____ _____ , so the maximum value of the

marginal product of labor yields the _____ _____ _____ , as you can see from the other connecting lines in Figure 5.6.

5.60   We have just seen how the profit-maximizing farmer in our simple example hired labor up to the point at which the marginal benefit to him, that is, the marginal revenue product of labor,

just equalled the _____ _____ to him, that is, the wage or price of the last unit of labor hired.

5.61   There are important implications in this statement not only for the competitive firm, which we shall study in Chapter 6, but also for the returns to factors of production, particularly labor (or people), which we shall study in Chapter 12. If each worker is paid the value of his

_____ _____ , and for most people the primary source of income is derived from the sale of their labor services, how well off a person is will depend upon what his contribution is to total output. Individuals whose marginal products are low—the unskilled—tend to have very low incomes. As we shall see, understanding the reasons for those different marginal productivities helps to explain the reason for widely different levels of income and standards of living within the U.S. and among different peoples of the world.

ANSWERS

56. falling . rising
57. lower . higher
58. average product . minimum

59. average variable cost . minimum marginal cost
60. marginal cost
61. marginal product

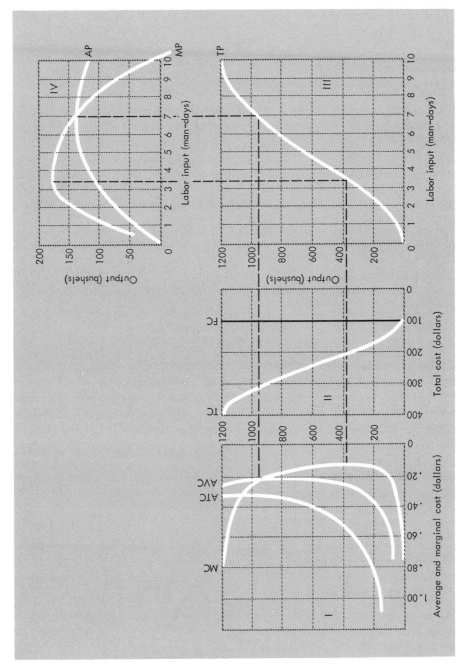

Figure 5.6   The relationship between productivity and cost

REVIEW QUESTIONS

5.1   Which of the following cannot increase, other things being equal, as output increases?

a. average total cost
b. average variable cost

c. average fixed cost
d. marginal cost

Fixed cost is independent of the level of output. If a farmer rents a field for $500 for a year, he must pay this cost whether he produces any output or not. Average fixed cost for the farmer will equal $500 divided by output and, consequently, the larger the output, the smaller the average fixed cost. Average total cost, average variable cost, and marginal cost typically decrease and, after some level of output, increase. The correct response is c.

5.2   If a firm is producing output at a point where diminishing returns have set in, which of the following is correct?

1. Each additional unit of output will be more expensive to produce.
2. Each additional unit of output will require increasing amounts of the factor of production being increased.
3. The marginal product of the variable factor of production decreases as the quantity used increases.

a. 1 only
b. 1 and 2 only

c. 2 and 3 only
d. 1, 2, and 3

Diminishing returns means that the amount of additional output obtained through adding an extra unit of one factor input, holding the amount of other factors fixed, will decrease as the, level of output increases. That is, the marginal product of the variable factor input must be falling. This means that to produce one more unit of output, the higher the level of output, the greater the additional amount required to make an extra unit of output. Consequently, each additional unit of output will be more expensive to produce. The correct response is d.

5.3   Questions 5.3 and 5.4 are based on the following data, which are for a tomato farmer who can hire tomato pickers at $12 per day:

The profit maximizing farmer should hire only

a. One tomato picker because his contribution to output is greatest.
b. Three tomato pickers because the fourth costs more than he earns.

c. Eight tomato pickers because costs will equal revenue.
d. Nine tomato pickers because the value of the marginal product of the tenth picker is zero.

The rule for profit maximization is that factor inputs be hired up to the point at which the value of the marginal product equals the price of the factor input. In the example, the price of the factor input, the tomato picker, is $12. We can calculate the value of the marginal product of each tomato picker by simple subtraction in column 2. For example, the value of the marginal product of the first picker is $30. The second picker increases the value of output by $18 ($48 - $30), and the third, by $14 ($62 - $48). The fourth, however, adds only $10 to the value of output ($72 - $62), and because he costs $12, the farmer would lose $2 by hiring him. Thus, he will not hire a fourth picker. The correct response is b.

Number of pickers	Tomato output
1	$30
2	48
3	62
4	72
5	80
6	87
7	93
8	96
9	98
10	98

5.4   The local authorities, in an attempt to make the tomato pickers better off, legislate that tomato pickers must be paid a wage no less than $16 per day. If our profit-maximizing farmer complies, which of the following will be correct.

1. Each of the three tomato pickers our farmer had previously hired will become better off.
2. The value of the average product of labor will fall.
3. The quantity of tomato output will fall.

    a. 1 only   c. 3 only
    b. 2 and 3 only   d. 1, 2, and 3

Again, our profit-maximizing farmer will hire labor to the point where the value of the marginal product of labor equals the price of labor. However, because the price of labor, or wage, has risen to $16, he will no longer hire the third picker whose marginal product is only $14. Consequently, the two pickers retained will become better off; the third will become worse off. Tomato ouput will fall. The value of the average product of labor, however, will rise because $48/2 is greater than $62/3. The correct response is c.

Case 5

THE ECONOMICS OF MINIMUM WAGES

In 1972, the minimum wage for many workers in the United States was $1.60 hour. This means that most firms that engaged in interstate trade legally could not pay any worker less than $1.60 per hour. Currently, pressure is being applied on Congress to raise the minimum wage to $2.00 per hour. The arguments supporting some type of minimum wage legislation in the United States run along the following lines: "No man should be expected to work for a wage less than x cents per hour. The way to help the working poor, those earning very little per hour, is to raise the minimum wage rate to x cents per hour; this will give them a decent living wage." Table 5.a summarizes minimum wage history in the United States.

Unfortunately, the imposition of minimum wage policy, while having laudatory aims, tends to hurt rather than help some of the very people whom it was designed to help—the poor.

Table 5.a

LEGAL MINIMUM WAGE RATE, 1938–1971

Year	Minimum hourly wage rate
1938	$ .25
1939–44	.30
1945–48	.40
1949–55	.75
1956–60	1.00
1961–62	1.15
1963–66	1.25
1967	1.40
1968–71	1.60

You should be in a position to use your knowledge of profit-maximizing behavior of firms to see why this is so. One additional piece of evidence might help you in your analysis. During years of sharp increases in the minimum wage rate, significant decreases in employment occurred in many low-wage-paying industries.

Why should this happen? Would you support an increase in the minimum wage rate today up to $2.00 per hour? Up to $10.00 per hour? Who would benefit from such legislation and who would suffer? Would employment and production increase or decrease? What would happen to firm costs? Try not to confuse the objective of providing a reasonable income for everyone with the means of achieving that end.

SUGGESTIONS FOR ANALYSIS

Competitive firms will hire labor up to the point at which the value of the marginal product of the last laborer hired just equals the wage rate. Given a typical downward sloping marginal product curve, a rise in the wage rate by market or legislative forces would lead firms to hire fewer laborers. Thus, some workers would become unemployed. The workers who remained employed would be better off, but those fired would earn zero income unless they could find employment in firms not covered by minimum wage legislation. But even then, their incomes would fall, or they would have worked for such firms in the first place, had the wage been higher.

Because the price of labor will rise for firms covered by minimum wage legislation, production costs will be higher, and to stay in business, the price of its products must rise. Because it now hires fewer workers, output will be lower and less output means fewer goods and services available to society.

A close look at unemployment in the United States in 1970, for example, indicates that the bulk of unemployment was concentrated among low-skilled, inexperienced workers. For example, although the overall unemployment rate as a percentage of the labor force was 5.9, for teenagers aged sixteen to nineteen in the labor force the rate was 15.3 percent, and for nonwhite teenagers the rate was nearly twice as large as for white teenagers. There is no economic incentive for firms to hire teenagers or any worker whose marginal product value is less than the minimum wage. The less productive workers are, the more likely they are to be harmed by an increase in the minimum wage.

By all reasonable means, let us make sure every United States family has at least a subsistence standard of living if that is our goal. The minimum wage route, however, may not be a reasonable means.

6

Firm Supply

6.1   In Chapter 5, we analyzed how the productivity of factor inputs determined the

_____ of production at different output levels. We assumed all factor inputs but one (labor, in our farming example) to be fixed. In this chapter, the analysis will continue, and we shall show how the profit-maximizing competitive firm behaves—first when some factor inputs are fixed and then when all are variable. Such analysis is necessary to understand not only how the goods and services we consume daily are produced but also the many interdependencies in our economic system.

6.2   You will recall from Chapter 5 that our farmer had certain fixed costs. He rented a ten-acre field for $100 and paid this $100 _(dependent upon/independent of)_ the level of output.

His labor costs were _____ costs, however, because they varied with the level of output.

6.3   In this chapter, we are going to consider a firm in two different time periods; first in the *short-run*, when some costs, like our farmer's field rental, are _____ and independent of the level of output and second in the *long-run* when no costs are fixed.

6.4   You cannot define the *short-run* in terms of days or months because it varies from example to example. We define the *short-run* to be that period within which some costs are fixed; fixed costs do not vary with changes in output. The _____ -run is that time period in which all costs can vary. In our farm example, the long-run would occur after the farmer's lease on the field expired. Thus, at the expiration of the lease, when he was planning how

ANSWERS

1. costs
2. independent of . variable

3. fixed
4. long . land . no . short

much wheat to grow the following year, he could vary the amount of _____ as well as the amount of labor, that is, _(no/some)_ factor was fixed, independent of the planned

output level. Once he rents a field, however, he is back into a _____ -run situation.

6.5   The reason for this short-run–long-run distinction will be clear by the end of this chapter. We shall first consider the competitive firm in the short-run, and we shall assume that the aim of the firm is *profit maximization.* We wish to know what output a competitive firm should

produce in the short-run in which certain costs are _____ , given that the firm's goal

is to maximize _____ .

6.6   The gross income a firm receives from the sale of its product is known as its revenue. Thus, if we use the jargon of economists, we would say that the total income received by a manufac-

turer from sales in some given time period (say one month) is total _____ .

6.7   When total revenue from some specific output exceeds the total cost of producing that output,

the firm will make a _____ at that level of output. If, however, total costs are greater than total revenue for some specific output, the firm will make a loss (that is, will have

a negative _____) at that level of output.

6.8   Let us consider Table 6.1, which shows total cost, total revenue, and profit for a manufacturer of water beds.

Table 6.1

TOTAL COST, REVENUE, AND PROFIT

Output	Total cost	Total revenue	Profit
0	$ 270	$ 0	$–270
1	360	100	–260
2	410	200	–210
3	440	300	–140
4	460	400	– 60
5	470	500	30
6	500	600	100
7	560	700	140
8	660	800	140
9	830	900	70
10	1,110	1,000	–110

ANSWERS

5. fixed . profit

6. revenue

7. profit . profit

8. output . 1,000 . 400 . 0

This manufacturer produces identical water beds and he can sell as many as he can produce for $100 each. We derive the figures in the third column in Table 6.1 by multiplying $100 by the level of _____ . If the manufacturer sells ten water beds per month, the total revenue for that month would be $ _____ . If he sells four beds, his total revenue will be $ _____ , and if he sells zero beds, the total revenue will be $ _____ .

6.9   Let us now consider the manufacturer's cost of production. When the manufacturer produces zero water beds the only cost incurred will be fixed cost. In this example, fixed cost, which is the same at all levels of output, equals $ _____ . From the first and second columns, we see that total cost (variable plus _____ cost) increases as output _____ .

6.10   We obtain the profit figures in the fourth column by subtracting total _____ from total _____ . If, in some given month, the manufacturer produces no water beds (perhaps everyone is having a month's vacation), the only cost that will be incurred will be _____ cost but because total revenue will be $ _____ , profit will be $ _____ .

6.11   We see that if the manufacturer produces one water bed per month, his loss (negative profit) will be $ _____ . In fact, he makes losses if he produces less than _____ water beds per month or more than _____ .

6.12   It is only in the range of output of _____ to _____ water beds per month that the manufacturers will make positive profit. Given that the aim of the manufacturer is to maximize profit, it is obvious from Table 6.1 that he will produce either _____ or _____ water beds, because either of those outputs gives a maximum profit per month of $ _____ .

6.13   In Figure 6.1, we have plotted the data from Table 6.1. Because each water bed sells for $ _____ , total revenue increases by $ _____ for each additional unit of output. As a result, total revenue is represented in Figure 6.1 by a _____ line.

ANSWERS

9. 270 . fixed . increases
10. cost . revenue . fixed . 0 . –270
11. 260 . 5 . 9

12. 5 . 9 . 7 . 8 . 140
13. 100 . 100 . straight

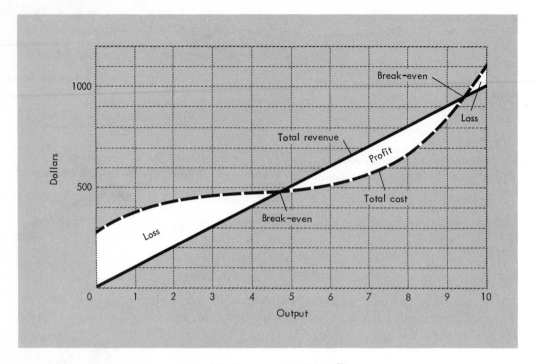

Figure 6.1   Revenue, cost, and profit

6.14   The total cost curve is shaped similarly to the total cost curves we have already analyzed. We

see that at zero output, total cost is $ _____ . At this level of output, total cost

equals _____ cost. As output increases, total cost increases fairly quickly at first,
then more slowly for levels of output between two and seven, and then fairly sharply again
for higher levels of output. We also see that our total cost curve intersects our total revenue

curve at levels of output of between _____ and _____ and also 9

and 10. When this occurs, profit of course is _____ ; the manufacturer is at a
break-even point, making neither profit nor loss.

6.15   For all levels of output less than five, total cost _____ total revenue and, consequently, profit is negative. This situation is similar for levels of output greater than
_____ beds per month where once more total cost exceeds total revenue.

6.16   For levels of output between five and nine water beds, _____ _____

exceeds _____ _____ , and, consequently, _____ is
positive.

ANSWERS

14. 270 . fixed . 4 . 5 . 0   16. total revenue . total cost . profit
15. exceeds . 9

6.17 The level of profit at the monthly output of five water beds could be found by taking the vertical distance between the _____ _____ curve and the _____ _____ curve at a level of output of five beds. This distance would be $30, which would be the _____ for that level of output.

6.18 Because our water bed manufacturer wishes to maximize profit, he will choose that level of output where the distance between _____ _____ curve and the _____ _____ curve is a maximum.

6.19 Thus, our manufacturer will be maximizing _____ if he produces either _____ or _____ water beds per month. In both cases, profit will be $ _____ .

6.20 Just as the distance between total revenue and total cost shows (positive) _____ for outputs of five to nine water beds, so will this distance show a _____ (negative profit) for levels of output less than five and greater than nine. Thus, given the range of outputs in Figure 6.1, maximum loss would be incurred at an output level of _____ water beds per week, and would amount to $ _____ . The level of output that would produce the second highest loss would be _____ water bed(s) per month, at which the extent of the loss would be $ _____ .

6.21 Given our knowledge of costs, there is a more useful way we can calculate the profit-maximizing output for our water bed manufacturer. Look at Table 6.2. In the third column, we have calculated marginal cost, which you will remember is the cost of producing an additional water bed. We see, for instance, that the total cost of producing two water beds is $ _____ , and the total cost of producing one water bed is $ _____ . Thus, the cost of increasing production from one to two water beds is the difference between those two figures, which is $50. Thus, when output is one water bed per month, _____ cost is $50.

Table 6.2

MARGINAL COST AND MARGINAL REVENUE

Output	Total cost	Marginal cost	Total revenue	Marginal revenue
0	$ 270		$ 0	
		$ 90		$100
1	360		100	
		50		100
2	410		200	
		30		100
3	440		300	
		20		100
4	460		400	
		10		100
5	470		500	
		30		100
6	500		600	
		60		100
7	560		700	
		100		100
8	660		800	
		170		100
9	830		900	
		280		100
10	1,110		1,000	

6.22   Similarly, the marginal cost of producing the fifth water bed is $ _____ . This

figure is derived by subtracting the cost of producing _____ water beds, which is

$ _____ , from the cost of producing _____ water beds, which is

$ _____ .

6.23   In a similar fashion, we can calculate marginal revenue. Marginal revenue is the additional

revenue collected by selling one _____ water bed. Because the selling price of
each water bed is the same, the extra revenue from selling an additional water bed is
(less than/equal to) the price. Thus, in this example, marginal revenue is a constant, equal to

$ _____ because price is equal to $ _____ .

6.24   Let us now see how our marginal cost and marginal revenue columns can help us determine
the profit-maximizing output. Suppose, for example, our water bed firm is producing two
units of output and wants to decide whether to produce a third unit. You know from

Table 6.2 that at two units of output, the marginal revenue is $ _____ and the

marginal cost is $ _____ .

6.25   If, by producing an extra bed, revenue is increased by $100 and cost is increased by $30,
would the change be worthwhile? The answer to this question is _(yes/no)_ because such a

change would _(increase/decrease)_ profit (or decrease loss) by $ _____ .

ANSWERS

22. 10 . 4 . 460 . 5 . 470   24. 100 . 30
23. additional . equal to . 100 . 100   25. yes . increase . 70

6.26   Thus, you can see that it will always pay to produce an extra unit of output as long as the marginal revenue (that is, the marginal benefit to the water bed manufacturer) of an extra unit is _(greater/less)_ than the marginal cost.

6.27   At what level of output will there be no gain from producing an extra unit? _____ units. It is here that _____ revenue and _____ cost are equal and _____ is a maximum.

6.28   The extra cost incurred in producing the seventh water bed is _____ than the extra revenue received from its sale. Thus, it is profitable to produce the seventh water bed. The marginal cost of producing an eighth water bed is $ _____ , and the marginal revenue from its sale is $ _____ . Thus, we would say that the manufacturer would be indifferent (he would not care from the viewpoint of maximizing profit) as to whether or not he produced and sold this eighth water bed. He would not, however, produce more than eight water beds because that would take him beyond the point at which _____ _____ equals marginal cost.

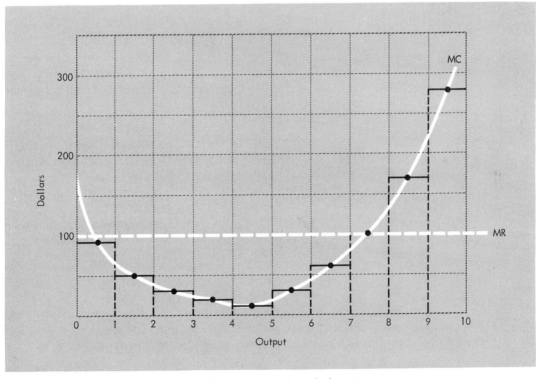

Figure 6.2 Marginal cost and marginal revenue

ANSWERS

26. greater

27. 7 . marginal . marginal . profit

28. less . 100 . 100 . marginal revenue

29. variable

6.29   With the help of one of our earlier diagrams, we can briefly summarize the foregoing analysis.

Adding the ten rectangles in Figure 6.2 would yield the total _____ cost of ten water beds.

6.30   Using the continuous curve (the MC curve) instead, we know that the _____ under the curve also measures the _____ _____ of ten water beds.

6.31   The area under the MR curve between 0 and 10 equals the _____ _____ from selling ten water beds. This area represents $ _____ .

6.32   Thus, ignoring fixed cost for the moment, as long as the area under the MR curve is

_____ than the area under the MC curve, profit will be positive. However, as soon as the MC curve lies above the MR curve, the benefits (revenue) from producing

additional water beds are _____ than the costs of those additional water beds. Consequently, the profit-maximizing entrepreneur will not produce beyond the point where

MR = _____ .

6.33   You should note that it is a necessary condition for profit maximization that _____

_____ equal _____ _____ ; but this is not a sufficient condition. MC must also be rising. For example, the MC curve intersects the MR curve between output levels of 0 and 1, but this is not a profit-maximizing output level because the

_____ curve is falling.

6.34   Thus, we can summarize what we have learned in Figure 6.2 by saying that a profit-seeking entrepreneur will increase output up to that point at which marginal revenue equals marginal cost. It will not pay him to stop before that point is reached because the marginal revenue

collected from each additional water bed exceeds the _____ _____

of producing that water bed. _____ will not be maximized by producing beyond the point at which marginal revenue equals marginal cost, because the marginal revenue col-

lected from sales of additional water beds will be _____ than the marginal cost of producing them.

6.35   Thus, as long as producing and selling additional water beds adds more to total revenue than it does to total cost, it will pay the manufacturer to do so. This statement is the same as saying that a profit-seeking manufacturer should increase his output up to that point at which

marginal revenue equals _____ _____ .

ANSWERS

30. area . variable cost	33. marginal revenue (MR) . marginal cost (MC) .	35. marginal cost
31. total revenue . 1,000	MC	
32. greater . less . MC	34. marginal cost . Profit . less	

6.36   We derived total revenue by multiplying the selling price of each water bed ($100) by the number of units produced. If we wish to calculate average revenue figures from total revenue figures, we reverse the process, that is, we divide total revenue by output. In our water bed

example, we would, of course, obtain a figure of $ _____ as the average revenue for each level of output. Because each additional water bed sold yields $100, the

_____ revenue for each level of output must also be $100.

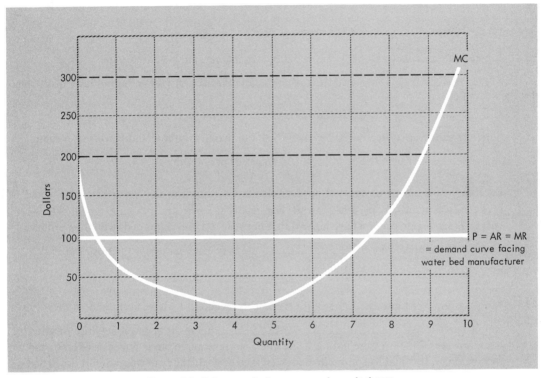

Figure 6.3   Price, marginal revenue, and marginal cost

6.37   In Figure 6.3, we have plotted selling price, average revenue, and marginal revenue against output, with the prices on the vertical axis and output on the horizontal axis. We have one

horizontal line crossing the vertical axis at a price of $ _____ , representing all three. This line is also the demand curve facing the manufacturer. This demand curve shows that the water bed manufacturer can sell as many water beds as he wants at a price of $100 each. It also tells us that the number of water beds our manufacturer can sell at any price

greater than $100 is _____ , because potential water bed customers can buy identical water beds at $100 from a competitor on the next block. Because one manufacturer

ANSWERS

   36. 100 . marginal   37. 100 . 0 . will never

can sell as many water beds as he wishes at $100, but none at a price greater than $100, it _(will/will never)_ be in his interests to charge a lower price.

6.38   If the going price of water beds were $200 each rather than $100, how would our manufacturer react? He would be faced with _(a new/the same)_ demand curve, _(a new/the same)_ P = AR = MR curve, and _(a new/the same)_ MC curve.

6.39   Because his goal is _____ -maximization, he will produce water beds up to the point at which MR = _____ .

6.40   Because the price of water beds is now $200, marginal revenue will now equal

$ _____ . The new MR curve intersects the MC curve at an output level of between

_____ and _____ water beds.

6.41   Similarly, if the price were $300 per water bed, our manufacturer would produce between

_____ and _____ water beds per month.

6.42   Because the marginal cost curve of our manufacturer tells us how many water beds he would produce each month at any price, the MC is in reality the firm's monthly _(demand/supply)_ curve. From Figure 6.3, we have learned that between 7 and 8 water beds would be produced

monthly if the price were $ _____ and between 9 and 10 if the price were

$ _____ .

6.43   In the example just discussed, the firm's revenue exceeded its variable costs, and its short-run

supply curve is its _____ _____ curve. If at the going price of water beds, however, the firm were not receiving sufficient revenue to cover the costs of labor and raw materials, it would lose more than just its fixed cost. If the firm were to shut down and

produce nothing, its losses would equal just its _____ cost. In such a case, it would pay the firm to _(shut down/continue to produce)_ because that would minimize its losses.

6.44   Let us summarize our findings. To have a profitable level of output, _____

_____ must exceed total cost.

ANSWERS

38. a new . a new . the same	42. supply . 100 . 300
39. profit . MC	43. marginal cost . fixed . shutdown
40. 200 . 8 . 9	44. total revenue
41. 9 . 10	

6.45 When total cost equals _____ _____ , we have a break-even level of output, that is, our manufacturer makes neither a _____ nor a _____ at that output level.

6.46 In the short-run, the loss incurred by a manufacturer from closing down will equal his _____ _____ . From a _____ -minimizing viewpoint, this closing down would be rational behavior if there is no level of output that will yield sufficient revenue to at least cover _____ _____ .

6.47 In the short-run, that time period when some costs are fixed, the equilibrium output of the firm will be that output at which _____ _____ equals _____ _____ . This will be an equilibrium position in the sense that the firm will be maximizing _____ . In this short-run, other levels of output may yield a profit, but not a maximum profit.

6.48 In the short-run, therefore, once the firm has reached that _____ position, profit cannot be increased by altering the output level. The short-run supply curve of the firm is its _____ _____ curve for all outputs where variable costs have been met.

6.49 In the real world, consumers' tastes and preferences are constantly changing, new goods and services come into being, research and development discover new uses for natural resources, and technological change is constantly occurring. Because of all this, we would be very surprised if firms ever settled for long, or even reached a long-run equilibrium position, that is, a position from which there would be no incentive to change. However, although firms may never reach a long-run _____ position from which there is no incentive to change, we define *long-run equilibrium* as a position toward which firms move and that would ultimately be reached, in the absence of any other changes. Thus, long-run equilibrium is an abstract concept. It is a position toward which firms would move, were other things to _(remain the same/change)_ .

6.50 In Chapter 1, we recognized that whenever a choice is made we must give up one of the alternatives, that is, we have to accept the _____ cost. Thus, there is a cost to produce a commodity that is over and above the costs that have to be paid out as wages, rent, and so on. This cost is the profit that could be earned by using resources in the best alternative use; it is the entrepreneur's opportunity cost. In our example, the profit that the water bed manufacturer could earn if he produced conventional furniture instead of water beds is his _____ _____ .

ANSWERS

45. total revenue . profit . loss
46. fixed cost . loss . variable cost
47. marginal revenue . marginal cost . profit
48. equilibrium . marginal cost
49. equilibrium . remain the same
50. opportunity . opportunity cost

6.51   In the long-run, in our example, if our water bed manufacturer does not earn enough profit to cover his _____ cost, he will shift his resources to the production of conventional furniture. We can say the same thing a different way. If an entrepreneur cannot earn as much profit in the production of good A as he can in the production of good B, then in the

_____ - _____ he will shift to the production of good B.

6.52   If our water bed manufacturer cannot cover his opportunity cost in the production of water beds, it means that he can earn a _(higher/lower)_ profit in the production of some other commodity, and in the long-run will shift his resources from the production of water beds to the production of that commodity for which the return is highest. Remember, we are assuming he wants the highest return possible.

6.53   In our diagrams, we have included the entrepreneur's opportunity cost as one of the fixed costs of production. Thus, in these diagrams, when a firm is earning a profit, it means that it is earning a profit that is _(greater/less)_ than the profit that could be earned by taking advantage of any alternative opportunity.

6.54   In other words, in our diagrams, when a firm is earning a profit, it means that it is earning enough profit to discourage it from shifting resources to the production of a different commodity. Is this statement true or false? _____

6.55   Thus, if a firm is producing so that total cost equals total revenue, we say that the firm is earning a normal profit. By this we mean that its revenue is just enough to cover all costs

including its _____ cost, but is not earning any profit in excess of what is required to keep the firm in that line of production.

6.56   Consider now the behavior of our water bed manufacturer in the long-run. Because no factors of production are fixed in the long-run, it _(is/is not)_ possible for the manufacturer to increase or decrease the scale of his operations by acquiring a new workshop, larger or smaller store, larger or smaller manufacturing equipment, as well as changing the amount of labor he hires. In the short-run, the firm _(can/cannot)_ change its output, but only by increasing or

decreasing the factors of production that are _____ in the short-run.

6.57   The rule that the water bed manufacturer used for _____ -maximization in the short-run will be used for profit-maximization in the long-run with one important modification. That modification is that marginal revenue must equal *long-run* marginal cost.

ANSWERS

51. opportunity . long-run
52. higher
53. greater
54. true

55. opportunity
56. is . can . variable
57. profit

6.58 The logic is the same as that which we adopted in analyzing short-run profit-maximizing behavior. Consider Figure 6.4.

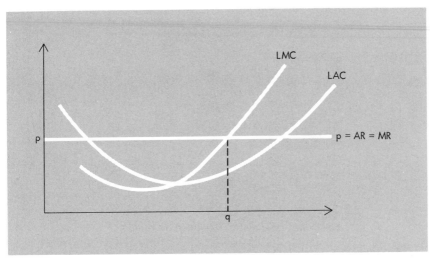

Figure 6.4 Long-run equilibrium of the firm

For outputs less than q, the benefit to our manufacturer from selling one more water bed, that is, that _(MR/LMC)_ , exceeds the cost to him of producing it when all factors are variable, that is, the _____ .

6.59 Similarly, in the long-run for output levels greater than q, MR is less than _____ and, consequently, the production of an additional bed adds more to _____ than it does to revenue, which means that _____ will be reduced.

6.60 The desire to maximize profit, therefore, will indicate to our water bed manufacturer that in the long-run he produces that number of water beds for which marginal revenue equals

_____ - _____ _____ _____ .

6.61 It will also tell him what size of plant or factory or store he should have. He should incur those fixed costs that yield an output for which _____ _____ equals long-run marginal cost.

6.62 For example, if we superimpose this optimally sized plant on our long-run equilibrium diagram, we would have Figure 6.5.

ANSWERS

58. MR . LMC
59. LMC . cost . profit
60. long-run marginal cost (LMC)

61. marginal revenue
62. short-run . long-run (either order)

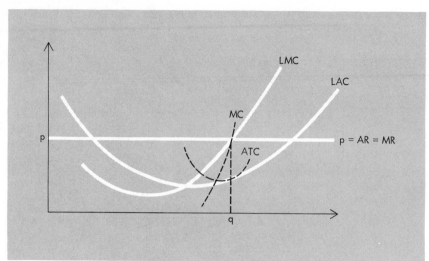

Figure 6.5   Long-run equilibrium of the firm

Here we can see that the firm is in both _____ - _____ and

_____ - _____ equilibrium.

6.63   In other words, for output q in Figure 6.5, any other plant size (incurring any other set of fixed costs) would give a _(higher/lower)_ average total cost than the plant drawn. In other words, our manufacturer would not be on his LAC. Thus, for price p, no other plant size would

allow MR to equal LMC and consequently maximize _____ .

6.64   Of course, once our manufacturer has decided on his optimally sized plant and has incurred

the accompanying _____ costs, he will be back in a short-run situation. If price changes, he will maximize short-run profit by producing that output for which

_____ _____ equals short-run _____ _____ .
Only if price and the state of technology of water bed making and other factors do not change

will he be in both _____ - _____ and _____ - _____

_____ equilibrium. Long-run equilibrium, however, despite all the uncertainties in real life, is the position he will aim for even though he may never actually attain it.

6.65   Because price is equal to marginal revenue for our firm, it will expand output to the level at which price is equal to the long-run marginal cost. Consequently, the long-run supply curve of

the firm will be the long-run _____ _____ curve above the minimum point of the LAC, which is where those curves intersect.

ANSWERS

63. higher . profit   65. marginal cost
64. fixed . marginal revenue . marginal cost .
       short-run . long-run (either order)

6.66 Why, in the long-run, will the firm supply zero output if p is less than LAC? The reason is simple; the firm would not make a _____ ; resources could be used more profitably in some other activity because _____ costs would not be covered.

6.67 So far, we have considered the firm in the short-run, when some costs are fixed, and in the long-run, when all _____ are _____ . We have derived the firm's short-run supply curve, which tells us what output a firm would supply, given its fixed costs, at different prices. We also derived the firm's long-run supply curve, which again tells us what output the firm would supply at different _____ when no fixed costs had been incurred.

6.68 The firm's supply curves, short-run and long-run, are similar to a demand curve in the sense that it involves a "would"–"if" proposition. The firm's supply curves represent hypothetical situations telling us what the firm _____ produce _____ certain prices ruled, other things unchanged. As we shall see in Chapter 8, price is determined by the forces of market demand and market supply. We shall now proceed from firm to market supply in Chapter 7.

REVIEW QUESTIONS

6.1 Suppose that on the day before Christmas, the local florist has a number of cut Christmas trees for sale that he will throw away (at no cost to himself) if they are not sold that day. Each tree cost the florist $3. What price should he set if he wants to maximize profit?

a. A price that gives the greatest profit per tree sold.

b. A price just low enough to make sure that all trees will be sold.

c. A price that maximizes total receipts (that is, price x quantity sold).

d. A price greater than his cost of $3.

Fixed costs are fixed costs and in the short-run should not influence the florist in selling his Christmas trees. The fact that he has paid $3 per tree is irrelevant to the profit maximizing (loss minimizing) decision. Because disposal costs of unsold trees are zero, the florist must attempt to obtain as large a total revenue as possible from the sale of trees, that is, make price times quantity sold a maximum. Thus, the set price need not guarantee either that all trees be sold or that the $3 purchase price be recovered. The correct response is c.

Questions 2, 3, and 4 are based on the following data:

At its present level of output of 400 units, a perfectly competitive firm discovers that its marginal cost is $4. At an output level of 300 units, marginal cost is $3 and is equal to average total cost. The price of the commodity being produced is $5.

6.2   If the firm wishes to maximize profit, which of the following should it do?

a. increase output
b. decrease output

c. raise price
d. lower price

In answering the question, it might help you to draw a diagram. Because the firm is perfectly competitive, the demand curve facing it is represented by a horizontal line. The line also represents price = $5 = average revenue = marginal revenue. Certain points on the marginal cost curve can be plotted. At an output level of 300 units, MC = $3 (and at that point average total cost is at a minimum since MC intersects ATC at its minimum point), and at an output level of 400 units, MC = $4. Let us plot these points and lines.

By projecting the MC curve (given it does not rise vertically at an output level of 400 units), we see that MC intersects MR at an output level greater than 400 units. Thus, to maximize profit, the firm should increase output. It should not change its price, first because it will not be able to sell any output at a price greater than $5 and second because it can sell as much as it can produce at $5—there is no incentive to decrease price. The correct response is a.

6.3   At the present level of output, how much does the four hundredth unit of output add to profit?

a. $5
b. $4

c. $3
d. $1

Using our diagram, in Figure 6.2a, we see that the MC of the four hundredth unit is $4 and MR equals $5. The difference of $1 is what the four hundredth unit adds to profit. The correct response is d.

6.4   The firm will be in equilibrium in the short-run when:

1. it is maximizing profit
2. MC = $5
3. minimum ATC = $5

Which of the above is correct?

a. 1 only
b. 1 and 2 only

c. 1 and 3 only
d. 1, 2, and 3

Again using our diagram, the firm will maximize profit in the short-run when MR = MC = $5. In the long-run, as resources move into the industry in response to the excess profit, the AR = MR curve will fall. The correct response is b.

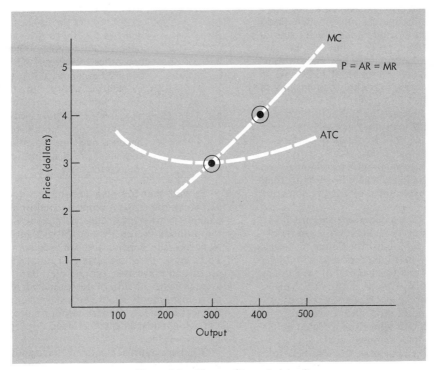

Figure 6.2a   Non-profit maximizing firm

Case 6

AIRLINE TAKES THE MARGINAL ROUTE[1]

Continental Air Lines, Inc., last year filled only half the available seats on its Boeing 707 jet flights, a record some 15 percentage points worse than the national average.

By eliminating just a few runs—less than 5 percent—Continental could have raised its average load considerably. Some of its flights frequently carry as few as 30 passengers on the 120-seat plane. But the improved load factor would have meant reduced profits.

For Continental bolsters its corporate profits by deliberately running extra flights that aren't expected to do more than return their out-of-pocket costs—plus a little profit. Such marginal flights are an integral part of the overall operating philosophy that has brought small, Denver-based Continental—tenth among the 11 trunk carriers—

through the bumpy postwar period with only one loss year.

This philosophy leans heavily on marginal analysis. And the line leans heavily on Chris F. Whelan, vice-president in charge of economic planning, to translate marginalism into hard, dollars-and-cents decisions.

Getting management to accept and apply the marginal concept probably is the chief contribution any economist can make to his company. Put most simply, marginalists maintain that a company should undertake any activity that adds more to revenues than it does to costs—and not limit itself to those activities whose returns equal average or "fully allocated" costs.

The approach, of course, can be applied to virtually any business, not just to air transporta-

[1]From *Business Week,* April 20, 1963. Reprinted with permission of the publisher, ©1963, McGraw-Hill, Inc.

tion. It can be used in consumer finance, for instance, where the question may be whether to make more loans—including more bad loans—if this will increase net profit. Similarly, in advertising, the decision may rest on how much extra business a dollar's worth of additional advertising will bring in, rather than pegging the advertising budget to a percentage of sales—and, in insurance, where setting high interest rates to discourage policy loans may actually damage profits by causing policy-holders to borrow elsewhere.

Whelan finds all such cases wholly analogous to his run of problems, where he seeks to keep his company's eye trained on the big objective: net profit.

Whelan's work is a concrete example of the truth in a crack by Prof. Sidney Alexander of MIT—formerly economist for Columbia Broadcasting System—that the economist who understands marginal analysis has a "full-time job in undoing the work of the accountant." This is so, Alexander holds, because the practices of accountants—and of most businesses—are permeated with cost allocation directed at average, rather than marginal, costs.

In any complex business, there's likely to be a big difference between the costs of each company activity as it's carried on the accounting books and the marginal or "true" costs that can determine whether or not the activity should be undertaken.

The difficulty comes in applying the simple "textbook" marginal concept to specific decisions. If the economist is unwilling to make some bold simplifications, the job of determining "true" marginal costs may be highly complex, time-wasting, and too expensive. But even a rough application of marginal principles may come closer to the right answer for business decision-makers than an analysis based on precise average-cost data.

Marginal analysis in a nutshell

Problem: Shall Continental run an extra daily flight from City X to City City Y?

The facts: Fully-allocated costs of this flight $4,500
Out-of-pocket costs of this flight $2,000
Flight should gross $3,100

Decision: Run the flight. It will add $1,100 to net profit—because it will add $3,100 to revenues and only $2,000 to costs. Overhead and other costs, total $2,500 [$4,500 minus $2,000], would be incurred whether the flight is run or not. Therefore, fully-allocated or "average" costs of $4,500 are not relevant to this business decision. It's the out-of-pocket or "marginal" costs that count.

Proving that this is so demands economists who can break the crust of corporate habits and show concretely why the typical manager's response—that nobody ever made a profit without meeting all costs—is misleading and can reduce profits. To be sure, the whole business cannot make a profit unless average costs are met; but covering average costs should not determine whether any particular activity should be undertaken. For this would unduly restrict corporate decisions and cause managements to forego opportunities for extra gains.

Whelan's approach is this: He considers that the bulk of his scheduled flights have to return at least their fully allocated costs. Overhead, depreciation, insurance are very real expenses and must be covered. The out-of-pocket approach comes into play, says Whelan, only after the line's basic schedule has been set.

"Then you go a step farther," he says, and see if adding more flights will contribute to the corporate net. Similarly, if he's thinking of dropping a flight with a disappointing record, he puts it under the marginal microscope: "If your revenues are going to be more than your out-of-pocket costs, you should keep the flight on."

By "out-of-pocket costs" Whelan means just that: the actual dollars that Continental has to pay out to run a flight. He gets the figure not by applying hypothetical equations but by circulating a proposed schedule to every operating department concerned and finding out just what extra expenses it will entail. If a ground crew already on duty can service the plane, the flight isn't charged a penny of their salary expense. There may even be some costs eliminated in running the flight; they won't need men to roll the plane to a hangar, for instance, if it flies on to another stop.

Most of these extra flights, of course, are run at off-beat hours, mainly late at night. At times, though, Continental discovers that the hours aren't so unpopular after all. A pair of night coach flights on the Houston-San Antonio-El Paso-Phoenix-Los Angeles leg, added on a marginal basis, have turned out to be so successful that they are now more than covering fully allocated costs.

Whelan uses an alternative cost analysis closely allied with the marginal concept in drawing up schedules. For instance, on his 11:11 p.m. flight from Colorado Springs to Denver and a 5:20 a.m. flight the other way, Continental uses Viscounts that, though they carry some cargo, often go without a single passenger. But the net cost of these flights is less than would be the rent for overnight hangar space for the Viscount at Colorado Springs.

And there's more than one absolute-loss flight scheduled solely to bring passengers to a connecting Continental long-haul flight; even when the loss on the feeder service is considered a cost on the long-haul service, the line makes a net profit on the trip.

Continental's data handling system produces weekly reports on each flight, with revenues measured against both out-of-pocket and fully allocated costs. Whelan uses these to give each flight a careful analysis at least once a quarter. But those added on a marginal basis get the fine-tooth-comb treatment monthly.

The business on these flights tends to be useful as a leading indicator, Whelan finds, since the off-peak traffic is more than normally sensitive to economic trends and will fall off sooner than that on the popular-hour flights. When he sees the night coach flights turning in consistently poor showings, it's a clue to lower his projections for the rest of the schedule.

There are times, though, when the decisions dictated by the most expert marginal analysis seem silly at best, and downright costly at worst. For example, Continental will have two planes converging at the same time on Municipal Airport in Kansas City, when the new schedules take effect.

"Continental will have to change its policy or go out of business since any firm which fails to set a price to cover the full average cost of production is headed for bankruptcy. Marginal analysis may be alright for the economics textbook but, for good reason, is not a useful concept to the businessman in determining pricing policies."

Do you agree or disagree? Why or why not?

SUGGESTIONS FOR ANALYSIS

The main lesson of this case is pointed up in the box about halfway through the text. As long as the marginal cost is below marginal revenue, it pays Continental Airlines to increase its output (add more flights), even though the extra income received (marginal revenue) may not cover the full average cost of production. Continental's total profit is larger with the flights in question than without them. Mr. Whelan gets A in Economics I.

But there is a second lesson, too, which Mr. Whelan recognizes in the twelfth paragraph. Although some flights can add to profits, even though they do not cover *full* costs, clearly for all flights together income must cover full costs if the firm is to make a profit and stay in business. Those marginal Continental flights are good business because the company has on hand anyhow the planes, airport docks, reservation clerks, and other facilities needed to operate its business. For purposes of this analysis, these are *fixed* costs; they go on whether or not Continental adds the marginal flights in question. As Whelan says, the out-of-pocket (marginal) approach comes into play only after the line's basic schedule has been set—but income from some flights obviously has to cover all those costs if the company is to make a profit.

Note that this point is related to, but different from, the distinction between long- and short-runs drawn in the text of Chapter 6. In the short-run, some costs are fixed, and the firm should disregard them in deciding how much to produce if it is going to operate at all. As in the Continental case, comparison of marginal revenue with marginal cost gives the right answer on how much to produce. But in the long-run, income must cover *all* costs (that is, price must at least cover average unit cost) or the firm will make losses and drop out of business.

7

Market Supply

7.1   Just as we assumed when discussing the consumer that no single individual was a significant force affecting prices and output in competitive markets, so we shall make the same assumption for firms as suppliers in these markets. In other words, our water bed manufacturer producing 6 or 7 or 8 water beds per month *(does/does not)* significantly affect the price of water beds. His production is an insignificant part of total production. All water bed manufacturers taken together in some market, however, will have a significant impact on price.

7.2   In Figure 7.1, consider three water bed manufacturers, A, B, and C producing identical products. Assume the going price of a water bed is $100.

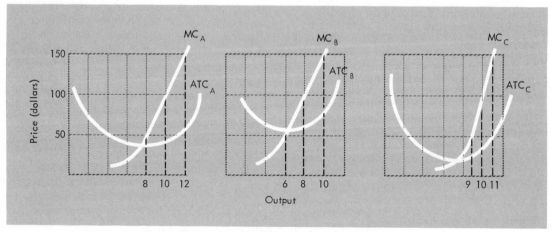

Figure 7.1   **Cost curves for three different firms**

ANSWERS
     1. does not   2. 10   .   marginal revenue

How many beds will A produce? _____ . Quite correct, he will produce 10 beds because at this output the benefit to A of producing the tenth bed, that is, the _____ _____ , just equals the marginal cost.

7.3   Similarly, in order to maximize short-run _____ , B and C will produce _____ and _____ beds per month respectively. If the price per water bed were $150 instead of $100, how many water beds would each produce? A–_____ : B– _____ ; C–_____ . In similar fashion, we could repeat this process for every possible price, asking how much each manufacturer would produce if a certain price were to rule.

7.4   Figure 7.2 is derived from Figure 7.1 and shows the   *(firm/market)*   supply, assuming the only suppliers are A, B, and C. For example, at a price of $150 per water bed, the total supplied by the three firms would be 12 + 10 + 11, which adds up to 33 beds.

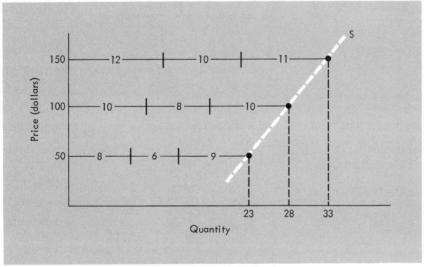

Figure 7.2   Market supply in the short-run

7.5   Just as the short-run supply curve of the individual firm is its _____ _____ curve above the minimum point of its average variable cost curve, so the aggregate supply curve S will be the summation of all the firms' short-run supply curves, that is, a summation of their

_____ _____ curves.

ANSWERS

3. profit . 8 . 10 . 12
   . 10 . 11

4. market
5. marginal cost . marginal cost

7.6   The relationship between the short-run market supply curve and the short-run supply curve for a typical firm is shown in Figure 7.3.

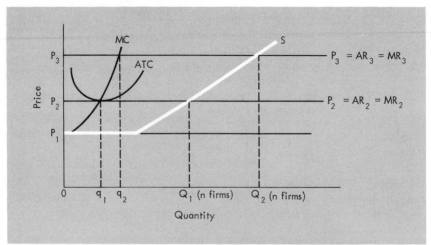

Figure 7.3   Firm and market supply in the short-run

At price P_2, the firm represented by ATC and MC would produce output _____ .
From the market supply curve S, we can see that the n firms taken together would produce

_____ .

7.7   Because market supply for prices below P_1 equals _____ , we can conclude that

no firm has an _____   _____   _____ curve whose minimum
point is less than P_1 .

7.8   At price of P_3, the individual firm in Figure 7.3 would produce _____ . Why?
Because at that output MR = _____ . The n firms taken together would produce

_____ .

7.9   In Figure 7.3, when the price is P_3, the firm will be making _____ ; over and above
the opportunity cost of the resources employed, by producing that level of output at which

P_3 (which is equal to AR and MR) = _____ .

7.10   Now consider what will happen in the long-run. Businessmen will observe _____
being made by firms in the industry depicted in Figure 7.3 and, being profit-motivated, will
divert resources into the industry.

ANSWERS

6. $0q_1$. $0Q_1$
7. zero . average variable cost
8. $0q_2$. MC . $0Q_2$

9. profit . MC
10. profit

7.11   First, consider the case in which the movement of new firms into the industry does not increase the prices of the factors of production employed in this industry. Thus, the

_____ of producing a unit of output will not increase as new firms move in.

7.12   In the long-run, new firms will continue to move into the industry as long as _____ exists. Profit will exist as long as price is greater than the average total cost of production; that

is, as long as the _____ is above the minimum point of the average total cost curve.

7.13   In Figure 7.3, because firms would continue to enter the industry as long as price is greater than

P_2, industry output would _____ for prices greater than P_2. Zero output would be supplied in the long-run for prices below P_2, however, because for prices less than P_2, long-

run average _____ _____ of production will not be covered. There-fore, in this example, the long-run market (or industry) supply curve will be represented by a horizontal line at price P_2.

7.14   Remember we are assuming here that the _____ of production does not increase as more firms move into the industry. The short-run industry supply curve, of course, will be a *(negatively inclined/horizontal/positively inclined)* line, but the long-run industry supply

curve, a _____ line.

7.15   This can be seen in Figure 7.4. If there were 50 identical firms in the industry, total industry

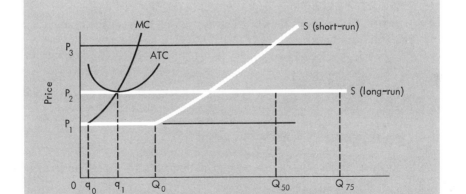

Figure 7.4 Long-run supply (constant cost)

ANSWERS

11. cost

12. profit . price

13. increase . total cost

14. cost . positively inclined . horizontal

15. $0q_1$. $0Q_{75}$

supply at a price of P_2 would be $0Q_{50}$. Each firm would produce _____ . If there were 75 identical firms instead and the price were still P_2, total industry supply would be

_____ . Each firm still would produce $0q_1$.

7.16   For any price below P_2, firms would be unable to cover average total _____ and consequently in the long-run would divert resources to other industries.

7.17   Thus, no long-run _____ curve exists for prices below P_2, and, because resource

costs do not rise as more firms enter the industry, the market long-run _____ curve is a horizontal line at the price P_2.

7.18   Remember the assumption we have made, however, to arrive at such a long-run industry supply curve. We have assumed that an increase in demand for factor inputs resulting from an increase in production would not cause any increase in their prices, and consequently,

there would be no resulting increase in the _____ curves of the firms in the industry.

7.19   How realistic this assumption is may depend on the size of the industry. Most industries compete in the same markets for factor inputs. The automobile industry, the ship-building industry, the consumers' durables industries, and many more all compete, for instance, for steel just as they all compete for labor and many more factor inputs. Now, if an industry is very small relative to all others competing for those factor inputs, a small increase in its demand for, let us say, steel may have a negligible influence on the market price of steel; and

thus, as far as steel is concerned, this industry could expand without causing an _____ in the cost of steel to itself or to the other industries using steel as a factor input.

7.20   Thus, if one industry is small and is only one of many using certain factor inputs, the

(more/less) likely it will be to have an influence on the _____ of any factor input, and, thus, the more *(elastic/inelastic)* will be this industry's long-run supply curve. In the limiting case where the industry can expand without increasing the price of any factor

input, the long-run supply curve will be completely _____ .

7.21   For most industries, however, if we assume that additional factor inputs are forthcoming only

at higher prices, the long-run industry _____ curve will not be a _____ line, but will be upward sloping.

ANSWERS

16. cost
17. supply . supply
18. cost

19. increase
20. less . price . elastic . elastic (horizontal)
21. supply . horizontal

7.22 Consider Figure 7.5. In this instance, as firms move into the industry in their search for

_____ , the increased demand for factor inputs causes their price to rise. (We shall see precisely how prices are determined in the next chapter.)

7.23 As factor prices increase, the cost of producing a unit of output would _____ , and, consequently, the average total cost curve of each firm would shift up.

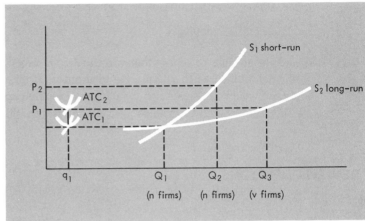

Figure 7.5
Long-run supply (increasing cost)

7.24 Originally at a price of P_1, the firm depicted in Figure 7.5 was producing output _____.
There were n firms in the market, and the total quantity supplied was _____ .

7.25 If the price rose to P_2, marginal revenue would, of course, increase from P_1 to P_2. Each firm would _____ its output to the point at which marginal revenue equalled marginal _____ , that is, each firm would increase output to _____ .

7.26 There would still be only n firms in the short-run, but each would be earning a profit because price or average revenue would be greater than _____ _____

_____ .

7.27 Profit would attract new firms. If such entry caused factor prices to rise, we can depict the rise in costs by shifting _(upwards/downwards)_ the average total cost curve.

7.28 Looking at Figure 7.5, we can see the shift of ATC_1 to ATC_2. With this rise, a price of _____ is required to cover average total costs.

ANSWERS

22. profits
23. increase
24. $0q_1$. $0Q_1$
25. increase . cost . $0q_2$

26. average total cost
27. upwards
28. P_3

7.29   Thus, with only n firms in the market, market supply equaled _____ at a price of P_1. Each firm was covering its average total costs.

7.30   With a larger market supply in the long-run, we now have more firms (v firms), and although

each, if identical, is supplying _____ , average total costs have risen. It therefore

requires a _____ price to cover the higher costs. Thus, in the long-run, because a greater supply is forthcoming, only at a higher price will the long-run supply curve be

_____ sloping.

7.31   It could be possible, of course, to have a situation in which an increase in demand for factors of production would lead to a decrease in their prices. If this did happen, the firm's average total cost curve would *(rise/fall)* and the long-run supply curve of the industry would be *(positively/negatively)* inclined. Because this is the unlikely situation, we can ignore it.

REVIEW QUESTIONS

Questions 1 and 2 are based on the following information.
   In an economy where there is unrestricted competition in all markets, coal is the primary source of heat for most households. Suppose a supply of natural gas that can provide heat at a much lower cost is discovered.

7.1   Assuming the cost per ton of coal changes in the same direction as industry output, what effect will the discovery have on the price of coal and the quantity of coal produced?

   a. price will increase; quantity will decrease   c. price will decrease; quantity will increase
   b. price will decrease; quantity will decrease   d. price will increase; quantity will increase

7.2   Which of the following statements is correct?

   a. The supply curve in the gas industry is posi-   c. The supply curve in the coal industry is
       tively inclined.   positively inclined.
   b. The supply curve in the gas industry is neg-   d. The supply curve in the coal industry is
       atively inclined.   negatively inclined.

As consumers switch from coal heating to gas heating, the demand for coal will decline, that is, at any given price the quantity demanded will be smaller than before. Because costs increase as industry output increases in the coal industry, that is, the supply curve is positively inclined, the gas discovery will lead to a lower price and a smaller output in the coal industry. We are given no information on costs in the gas industry. The correct response to 7.1 is b and to 7.2 is c.

ANSWERS

29. $0Q_1$ 31. fall . negatively
30. $0q_1$. higher . upward

7.3   If a competitive industry were in long-run equilibrium, which of the following would be correct?

1. Price would equal firm short-run marginal cost.
2. Price would equal firm long-run marginal cost.
3. The industry supply curve would be a horizontal line.

    a. 1 only   c. 1 and 2 only

    b. 2 only   d. 1, 2, and 3

In industry, equilibrium in a competitive industry price must equal both a firm's long-run and short-run marginal cost. This says nothing, however, about the shape of the long-run industry supply curve, which could be horizontal, or positively or negatively inclined. The correct response is c.

7.4   If an increase in the demand for aircraft causes the price of aluminum to rise, how will this, other things unchanged, affect the aluminum can industry? (Although it is not true, assume there is only one quality of aluminum.)

    a. Output in the aluminum industry will increase.   c. The long-run supply curve of the aluminum can industry will shift to the left.

    b. The long-run supply curve of the aluminum can industry will shift to the right.   d. The long-run supply curve of the aluminum can industry will be unaffected.

As the price of aluminum rises, the cost curves of the aluminum can industry will shift up, that is, aluminum cans will be more expensive to produce. In the long-run, therefore, to cover costs the price of aluminum cans must rise, that is, the same quantity will be forthcoming only at a higher price. The long-run supply curve will shift upwards or to the left. The correct response is c.

Case 7

THE ECONOMICS OF CHANGING AGRICULTURAL OUTPUT OVER TIME

The main lesson of Chapter 7 is how industries' outputs or supplies are determined in both the short- and long-run. Agriculture in the American economy provides an interesting case study.

Table 7.a presents data on expenditure for and production of food in the U.S. since 1929.

Question: Has the U.S. economy responded effectively to changing consumer demands for food? From what you have learned in earlier chapters and looking at the data in Table 7.a, what changes have taken place over time in the factors that determine the supply of food?

SUGGESTIONS FOR ANALYSIS

Although Table 7.a provides only a small subset of the data for a complete answer, it has the crucial information on most of the important points.

First, what happened to consumer demand for food over the four decades? Line 1 shows that consumers bought about three times as much food in 1970 as 1929. (Total spending on food rose more, but a part of the increase was merely higher prices, and this inflation has been eliminated by converting all years to the same [1967] prices.) Thus, the line shows both growing consumer

Table 7.a

FOOD IN THE UNITED STATES, 1929-1970

	1929	1947	1970
1. Consumer expenditures on food (billions of 1967 dollars)	$38	$72	$115
2. Food as % of total consumption	29	28	21
3. Number of farms (millions)	6.2	5.5	2.9
4. Number of farm workers (millions)	13	10	4
5. Farmers as % of total population	25	16	5
6. Output per farm worker (1967=100)	17	33	112
7. Investment per farm worker (1967=100)	34	71	104
8. Acres devoted to farming (millions)	974	1155	980
9. Farm per capita income as % of nonfarm*	29	37	28

* Farm income excludes government payments and nonfarm earnings.

demand (mainly more people) and farmers' increased production in response to that demand. But line 2 shows an equally important fact about demand. Demand for food grew much less rapidly than demand for other goods and services; food's share of total consumer spending fell from 29 to 21 percent as the American people became more affluent.

How did the economy respond? We know from line 1 that production grew to meet growing demand. Lines 3 through 9 tell us more, that people have persistently moved out of farming to the rest of the economy where consumer demand has grown more rapidly—but that fewer and fewer farms and farmers nonetheless managed to produce the increase in food demanded. Lines 3 through 5 show the big exodus from farming to the rest of the economy, and line 9 suggests why—average farm incomes have persistently been far below those in nonfarm occupations. Millions of farm proprietors and workers have moved out of low-profit and low-income farming to other industries where income prospects are higher, just as economic theory says they will.

Lines 6 through 8 tell how the farm industry managed a big increase in food production nonetheless. Land devoted to farming remained virtually unchanged, while farmers invested large sums in tractors, chemicals, and other modern capital equipment that dramatically raised output per worker and per acre. The average farm tripled in size; indeed, with modern farm technology, increasingly only very large farms can produce at the lowest costs per unit of output. (If the table

showed individual food products, you would also see dramatic shifts within farming as demands changed, notably away from grains toward meats, fruits, and vegetables.)

Over all, Table 7.a suggests that the economy has responded reasonably well to changing food demands. It has produced the increased food demanded, it has done so with increasing efficiency, and it has shifted a large number of no-longer-needed workers into other industries where consumer demand has grown faster, all as the long-run supply curves in Chapter 7 suggest it should.

But this is only an early illustrative case, which has simplified away some of the difficult problems faced in the actual economy. It omits the problems faced by many farm families in moving when consumer demand passes them by, especially in depression periods. The fact that per capita farm incomes are still far below nonfarm incomes suggests that not enough people have shifted occupations yet. The table says nothing of the elaborate government farm aid program, which, incidentally, has probably impeded more than speeded movement of excess resources out of agriculture. It says nothing of excess farm production bought up by the government in some years. And the whole international market for food products is omitted. But these omissions do not change the basic adjustment process summarized by Table 7.a. The purpose of Chapter 7 is only to develop a simple model of industry supply curves and to show how production adjusts to changing demands. The qualifications will come later.

8

Price Determination
and Market Equilibrium

8.1 Let us see how the price and quantity of a commodity are determined in the market by the interaction of the industry demand and supply curves. We can begin with the short-run equilibrium position of the industry. Consider now Table 8.1. The first two columns, if plotted, would give a normally shaped _____ curve for sweat shirts. This _____ curve would slope _____ from left to right. The position of this curve would be determined by a set of _____ , the independent variable being _____ and the dependent variable being _____ .

Table 8.1

DEMAND AND SUPPLY SCHEDULES OF SWEAT SHIRTS

Price per sweat shirt	Quantity that would be demanded	Quantity that would be supplied
$ 1	180	0
2	160	40
3	140	80
4	120	120
5	100	160
6	80	200
7	60	240
8	40	280
9	20	320
10	0	360

ANSWERS
1. demand . demand . downwards   . parameters . price . quantity

8.2   If each sweat shirt were priced at $7, the quantity that would be demanded at this price

would be _____ . If the price of sweat shirts were to change to $6 per unit, the demand curve represented by the first and second columns would shift. *(yes/no)*

8.3   The figures in the first and second columns are for a time period of a given length, say one week. If we were to draw the demand curve for a time period of five weeks, it would be to the *(left/right)* of the demand curve for a time period of one week.

8.4   In a similar fashion, if we were to draw a curve for the first and third columns in Table 8.1,

we would have a _____ curve that would slope upwards from _____

to _____ . This curve would be similar to our demand curve in the sense that its

position would be determined by a set of _____ . The dependent variable would

again be _____ and the independent variable _____ .

8.5   Imagine that all potential buyers of your college's sweat shirts get together with all the potential suppliers of sweat shirts, and they hire an auctioneer. Imagine that the auctioneer starts with a price of $3, saying to the potential buyers, "How many sweat shirts would you buy at a

price of $3?" The potential consumers will answer _____ . Then, the auctioneer asks the suppliers, "How many sweat shirts would you be willing to supply at $3?" The poten-

tial suppliers will answer _____ . The auctioneer will see that at a price of $3 the

quantity that would be demanded is _____ than the quantity that would be supplied.

8.6   Since it is the purpose of the auctioneer to achieve an equilibrium solution, that is, to have no unsatisfied buyers or sellers, $3 cannot be the equilibrium price. As long as the quantity that would be supplied is less than the quantity that would be demanded, some consumers would

not be in _____ , because they would be willing to buy the good at the market price but would be unable to find any of the good left for sale. In order to reach an equilib-

rium, the auctioneer must change the _____ .

8.7   The auctioneer has taken a course in economics and knows about normally shaped demand and supply curves. He knows that if he chooses a higher price, the quantity that would be demand-

ed will be _____ , and the quantity that would be supplied will be _____ than the corresponding quantities at a price of $3.

ANSWERS

2. 60 . no
3. right
4. supply . left . right . parameters
   . quantity . price

5. 140 . 80 . greater
6. equilibrium . price
7. less . greater

8.8   Suppose the next price he chooses is $6 per unit. Again he asks the potential buyers how many sweat shirts they would buy at a price of $6, and they reply _____ . And the potential suppliers tell him they would supply _____ sweat shirts at a price of $6.

8.9   He sees that at a price of $6 the quantity that would be demanded is _____ than the quantity that would be supplied. At a price of $3, we would have excess demand (the quantity that would be demanded is in excess of the quantity that would be supplied), and, as you might expect, at a price of $6, we would have a situation of excess _____ .

8.10   It is only at a price of $ _____ per unit that the quantity that would be demanded is equal to the quantity that would be supplied in that time period. Thus, we would say that in the market under consideration, a price of $ _____ per unit of good X is the equilibrium price, and a quantity of _____ is the equilibrium quantity.

8.11   This price is known as the equilibrium price because once this price has been established in this market, there will, *ceteris paribus*, be no tendency for the price to move from $4 because at this price the quantity that would be demanded just _____ the quantity that would be supplied.

8.12   We saw that at a price of $3 in this market, we had excess _____ and at the price of $6, we had excess _____ . But, at a price of $4, both excess _____ and excess _____ are zero. Thus, at a price of $4, the market is just cleared. The quantity that would be demanded equals the quantity that would be supplied. Excess demand and excess supply are both zero, and consequently, $4 is the _____ price.

8.13   In Figure 8.1, we have drawn the demand curve and supply curve from the data in Table 8.1. As you can observe, those curves intersect at a price of $ _____ and at a quantity of _____ .

8.14   We can observe in Figure 8.1 what we saw in Table 8.1. At a price of $3, the quantity that would be demanded is _____ , and the quantity that would be supplied is _____ . The difference of 60 is a measure of excess _____ at a price of $3 per unit.

ANSWERS

8. 80 . 200
9. less . supply
10. 4 . 4 . 120
11. equals

12. demand . supply . demand . supply
   . equilibrium
13. 4 . 120
14. 140 . 80 . demand

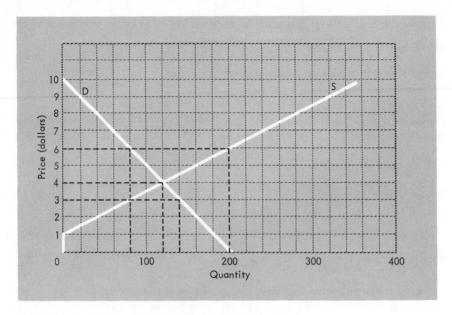

Figure 8.1 Demand and supply curves

8.15 Similarly, at a price of $6 per unit, the quantity that would be demanded is _____ ,
and the quantity that would be supplied is _____ . The difference of 120 is a
measure of excess _____ at this price. At a price of $4 per unit, and only at this
price, is the quantity that would be demanded _____ to the quantity that would
be supplied, and, consequently, excess supply and excess demand both equal _____ .
Given the shape of the demand and supply curves in Figure 8.1, is it possible for any price other
than $4 per unit to be an equilibrium price? _____ Given that the demand and
supply curves remain in the same position as they are in Figure 8.1 for several time periods,
would the equilibrium price change? _____

8.16 Thus, $4 would remain the _____ price, and 120 units would remain the
_____ quantity, because there would be no economic forces at work tending to
change either that price or quantity.

8.17 Before the equilibrium price of $4 was reached, buyers were competing against each other,
tending to drive price upwards, and sellers or suppliers were competing against other suppliers
in an attempt to sell their goods, tending to drive _____ downwards. This is

the competitive higgling of a free market. Only when ＿＿＿＿＿＿ has been reached have opposing forces cancelled each other out; those forces determine equilibrium

＿＿＿＿＿＿ and ＿＿＿＿＿＿ .

8.18 In the real world, there are factors existing in markets that may prevent ideal market situations from occurring. Although an equilibrium price may never be established or, if established, may never remain at equilibrium long, the market mechanism we have just analyzed describes what happens in many markets in the United States. That is, in the free market situation, price tends

toward the ＿＿＿＿＿＿ level.

8.19 We must now investigate what happens when we relax our *ceteris paribus* assumptions, or in other words, what happens when other things do not remain equal in our market. Let us return to our example in Table 8.1 and Figure 8.1. Let us imagine that the number of potential buyers in this market increases, and this causes the quantity that would be demanded in time period to double at every price. Thus, in Table 8.2, at a price of $1 per sweat shirt, the new quantity that would be demanded will be 360 and at the price of $3 per unit, the new quantity

that would be demanded will be ＿＿＿＿＿＿ .

8.20 What has happened in this example is that one of the ＿＿＿＿＿＿ determining the position of the demand curve has changed, and this has caused us to have a new demand curve for sweat shirts. Let us represent the old and the new market situations in Figure 8.2.

Table 8.2

SHIFT IN DEMAND

Price per sweat shirt	Originial quantity that would be demanded	New quantity that would be demanded	Quantity that would be supplied
1	180	360	0
2	160	320	40
3	140	280	80
4	120	240	120
5	100	200	160
6	80	160	200
7	60	120	240
8	40	80	280
9	20	40	320
10	0	0	360

ANSWERS

18. equilibrium
19. 280

20. parameters

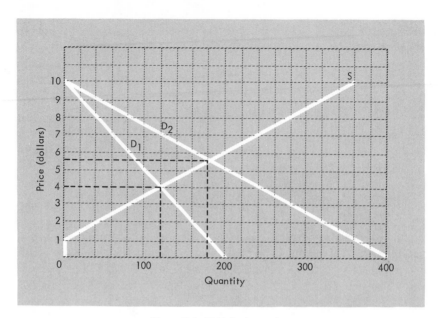

Figure 8.2 Shift in demand

8.21   We can see from Figure 8.2 that the intersection of D_1 and S occurs at a price of $_____ per sweat shirt and at a quantity of _____ sweat shirts.

8.22   Let us now consider the shift of the demand curve. We have a shift of the demand curve because one of the _____ determining the position of the demand curve has changed. (In this case, it is the number of consumers.) If we observe where D_2 intersects S, we shall discover what the new _____ price and quantity are. In this example, the new equilibrium price lies between $_____ and $_____ per sweat shirt, and the new equilibrium quantity is _____ sweat shirts.

8.23   In Figure 8.2, the demand curve shifts upwards and to the right. When this occurs, we say we have an increase in demand. Thus, an increase in demand occurs when a) one of the _____ determining the position of a demand curve changes, and b) this change causes the demand curve to move to the _____ .

8.24   As you might expect, a decrease in demand occurs when one of the _____ determining the position of the demand curve changes in such a way that the demand curve moves to the _____ . (Remember Chapter 4.)

ANSWERS

21. 4 . 120
22. parameters . equilibrium . 5 . 6
    . 180

23. parameters . right
24. parameters . left

8.25 Thus, when we speak of an increase or a decrease in demand, we are talking of a _____ of the demand curve. This has to be carefully distinguished from a movement along a demand curve.

8.26 When we have a movement along a demand curve, none of the parameters determining the position of the demand curve change, but we are considering the hypothetical situation of the different _____ of a good that _____ be demanded at various prices.

8.27 It is important that you distinguish between movements along and movements of a demand or a supply curve. Failure to do so can cause analytical errors in economics. If the market depicted in Figure 8.2 by D₂ and S were in equilibrium, which of the following would cause:

   a. a movement along the demand curve,
   b. an increase in the demand curve,
   c. a decrease in the demand curve?

   1. An increase in the incomes of consumers who normally purchase good X: _____

   2. A decrease in price of a competitive product: _____
   3. An increase in the price of a complementary product caused by a leftward shift of the supply curve for that product: _____
   4. An increase in the price of a complementary product caused by an increase in the demand for that product: _____

   5. A shift of S down and to the right: _____
   6. A decision by the suppliers of good X to offer smaller quantities of good X at each price: _____

   7. The discovery that consumption of good X is detrimental to health: _____
   8. Given that we have very competitive sellers supplying good X, a technological breakthrough that makes the production of good X much cheaper than it was previously: _____

8.28 Let us now consider some rather special cases in demand and supply analysis on which you can bring your knowledge of elasticity to bear. Consider a street in a residential area where there are no vacant plots. Thus, the supply of houses on this street _(is/is not)_ fixed, and, consequently, the supply curve of houses for this street would be represented on a figure by a _____ line, which would have the property of being completely _(elastic/inelastic)_, that is, quantity supplied would not be responsive to price changes.

8.29 If each house on this street were identical, then the _____ price of houses on this street would be determined by where the demand curve for houses on this street intersected the supply curve. Let us imagine the equilibrium price to be $50,000 per house.

ANSWERS

25. shift
26. quantities . would
27. b . c . c . b . a . a . c . a

28. is . vertical . inelastic
29. equilibrium

8.30   If there is now an increase in demand for houses on this street, the demand curve will shift to

the _____ , the equilibrium price will _____ , but the equilibrium

quantity will _____ _____ , because the supply curve is completely

_____ .

8.31   When considering most of the goods and services we consume in our daily lives, we would

expect that suppliers would be willing to supply _____ of a good at higher prices.
But many examples exist in the real world in which an increase in supply will not be forth-
coming no matter what the price offered. We have examples of the number of original Mona
Lisa paintings, the number of Rose Bowl tickets, and many more you can think of in which

the supply is completely _____ . In those cases, an increase in demand in a

competitive market will lead to a _____ equilibrium _____ .

8.32   At the other end of the spectrum, we can consider a completely elastic supply, which would be

represented in a figure by a _____ line. We discussed this case in Chapter 7, when

the entry of new firms did not cause factor prices to rise. The long-run industry _____
curve was a horizontal line. Given that we start off from an equilibrium position once more, an
increase in demand _(will/will not)_ lead to a higher equilibrium price. What we would have

in this situation would be a larger _____ _____ .

8.33   The supply curves, representing most of the goods we consume in our daily lives, lie somewhere
between the extremes of complete elasticity and complete inelasticity. Consequently, an

increase in demand normally results in a _____ equilibrium price and a larger

_____ quantity.

8.34   You should now be able to see rather easily why it is that some goods that are very valuable
cost so little. If you take a good, such as air, that is very valuable because without it life could
not exist, it should become obvious why we do not pay for air. The demand curve for air is

obviously _(elastic/inelastic)_ , but the supply of air is unlimited at _____ cost.

8.35   Thus, although we might be prepared to pay a very high price for air if we had to, if we look at
the demand for and the supply of air in a figure similar to the demand and supply figures we

have already analyzed, we would have an _____ demand curve that would inter-

ANSWERS

30. right . increase . remain unchanged
    . inelastic
31. more . inelastic . higher . price
32. horizontal . supply . will not
    . equilibrium quantity

33. higher . equilibrium
34. inelastic . zero
35. inelastic . zero . horizontal

sect a horizontal supply curve at a price of $ _____ . That is, for all practical intents and purposes, the supply curve for air in the world would be the _(vertical/horizontal)_ axis.

8.36   Goods with this type of supply curve are known as free goods. They are free goods because

the _____ is greater than the amount demanded at a zero price. Traditionally, air has been regarded as a free good. Although air was extremely valuable—without it, we could not survive—it was also extremely cheap. In many cities today, however, there is less clean air than people want and to provide more is proving to be very expensive.

8.37   Let us now use our knowledge of demand and supply analysis to discover what happens when a central body, such as a government, interferes with this free price system. In Figure 8.3, we have the demand and supply schedules of steak in a local community. Under competitive

conditions, the equilibrium price per pound of steak would be $ _____ and the

equilibrium quantity would be _____ pounds, per time period under consideration.

8.38   Let us imagine, however, that for some reason the local government decides to fix a price ceiling on the price of steak. Suppose that this price ceiling is $2 per pound. In other words, the legal maximum price that may be charged for steak is $2 per pound. At a price of $2 per

pound, however, we can see from Figure 8.3 that we have a situation of excess _____

because the quantity that would be demanded at this price is _____ pounds and

the quantity that would be supplied is _____ pounds. Thus, the amount of excess

_____ at $2 per pound is _____ pounds.

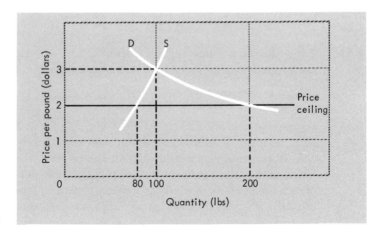

Figure 8.3
Price ceiling in the market for steak

ANSWERS

36. supply
37. 3 . 100

38. demand . 200 . 80 . demand . 120

8.39 Without a price ceiling existing in this market, and if indeed suppliers of steak had started off by selling steak at $2 per pound, they would have discovered that this price was _____ the equilibrium price and consequently, price would have _____ to $_____ per pound.

8.40 At the equilibrium price, the question of who obtains steak is relatively simple. Those people who are prepared to pay $3 per pound for steak will be able to buy as much steak as they want at that price because $3 is the _____ price.

8.41 However, with a price ceiling of $2 per pound, not all demands will be satisfied, because the quantity that would be demanded at that price is _____ than the quantity that would be supplied. Thus, we have a situation of excess supply. *(true/false)*

8.42 With a price ceiling of $2 per pound as we have in Figure 8.3, the price mechanism is obviously inadequate in allocating steak among potential buyers, and some other allocating mechanism will have to be sought because there are only _____ pounds of steak available from suppliers at a price of $2 per pound to be distributed to buyers who actually want _____ pounds of steak at this price.

8.43 One method would be to have a rationing system in which each household would be limited to a certain quantity of steak. Another way to allocate the 80 pounds of steak would be on a first-come-first-served basis. Or, the suppliers of steak may sell steak to regular customers to the exclusion of nonregular customers. But, whichever method is adopted, the _____ _____ will not be the allocating mechanism as it is in a freely competitive market situation.

8.44 Consumers and suppliers might also resort to a black market system, which would be an illegal mechanism for circumventing the price ceiling and which would essentially be resorting to an illegal, but competitive, _____ system.

8.45 The reason that a case such as the one depicted in Figure 8.3 is important is because many countries resort to price ceilings during wars when there are shortages of many basic commodities. Because many of these basic commodities are essential to the survival of families, it is felt unfair that those individuals who cannot pay the high equilibrium prices should be deprived of such commodities. Thus, a price ceiling system is often adopted for many goods, and this, together with a rationing scheme, ensures a distribution of available supplies that seems more

ANSWERS

39. below . risen . 3
40. equilibrium
41. greater . false
42. 80 . 200

43. price mechanism
44. price (market)
45. demand . price mechanism

equitable to many people. Thus, in situations similar to the one we have in Figure 8.3, price ceiling and rationing schemes can be used in situations of excess _____ , and from the point of view of economic analysis, we see that the goods in question will not be allocated completely by a _____ _____ .

8.46 The opposite of a price ceiling is a price floor, and if we look at Figure 8.4, we have a situation of a price floor. If, in the time period under consideration, we were to allow competitive forces to operate in the market depicted in Figure 8.4, the equilibrium price per bushel of wheat would be $ _____ , and the equilibrium quantity would be _____ million bushels.

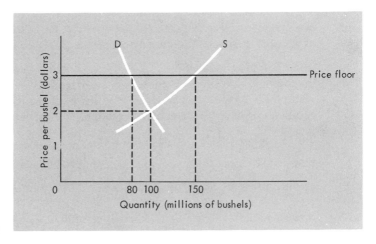

Figure 8.4
Price floor in the market for wheat

8.47 However, let us imagine that the government decides, in order to help raise the incomes of farmers, to enforce a price floor of $3 per bushel of wheat. This means that no one may legally sell wheat for less than $3 per bushel, and that no one may legally buy wheat for less than $3 per bushel. With the price floor enforced, the quantity of wheat that will be demanded at this price per time period will be _____ million bushels, and the quantity that will be supplied will be _____ million bushels.

8.48 Thus, with a price floor of $3 per bushel, we will have a situation in this market of _____ _____ to the extent of _____ million bushels of wheat.

8.49 The question now arises, what will happen to the excess supply of wheat? One solution would be for the government to buy the excess supply of wheat, which in this case amounts to _____ million bushels per time period, and give or sell this to other nations.

ANSWERS

46. 2 . 100
47. 80 . 150

48. excess supply . 70
49. 70

8.50   Another possible solution would be for the farmers to dispose of, let us imagine by burning, this excess supply of wheat. Would this action ever be profitable for the farmers? To answer that question, we must, of course, discover the revenues and costs involved. What will be the farmers' total revenue in this market per time period if there are no price floors (remember total revenue is derived by multiplying price per bushel by number of bushels sold)?

_____ What will be the farmers' total revenue under a price floor situation as

depicted in Figure 8.4? _____

8.51   Thus, we can see total revenue is actually _____ under a situation of a price floor than it is under competitive conditions.

8.52   In a situation such as that depicted in Figure 8.4, the government may also restrict the supply of wheat. We can see from the supply schedule in Figure 8.4 that at a price of $3, farmers

would be willing to supply _____ million bushels of wheat per time period. What the government might do is require farmers to reduce the amount of wheat they would supply at this price so that the amount of wheat that would be produced would just equal the amount of wheat that would be demanded at that price. If this were to occur in Figure 8.4, the govern-

ment would require farmers to produce only _____ million bushels of wheat per

time period instead of _____ million bushels of wheat, which they would normally

produce were the price floor _____ per bushel.

8.53   Now, at a price of $3, we would have farmers producing exactly the amount of wheat that

people would demand at $3 per bushel, that is, _____ million bushels of wheat per time period. Under this type of situation, the farmers are definitely _(better off/worse off)_ than they would be in a freely competitive system because in a freely competitive system

total revenue from the sale of _____ million bushels of wheat would amount to

$ _____ million, whereas under the new system, total revenue from sales of wheat

will amount to $ _____ million per time period at a production level of

_____ million bushels of wheat. Farmers are also definitely _(better off/worse off)_ in this situation because, if we assume that the supply schedule of wheat is normally shaped and reflects cost of production, the total costs of producing 80 million bushels of wheat will be

(less than/greater than) the total cost of producing _____ million bushels of wheat per time period, which the farmers would do in the freely competitive situation.

ANSWERS

50. $200 million . $240 million
51. greater
52. 150 . 80 . 150 . $3

53. 80 . better off . 100 . 200 . 240
. 80 . better off . less than . 100

8.54 Using our knowledge of elasticity, we can see why indeed farmers get a larger total revenue at a price of $3 compared with a price of $2 per bushel. It is because the demand curve for wheat in this price range is _(elastic/inelastic)_ , as a 50 percent increase in price leads to _(less than/ greater than)_ a 50 percent decrease in quantity that would be demanded.

8.55 Let us now turn to Figure 8.5 and another example. D and S are the demand and supply schedules of a hypothetical good Y. We see that the demand for this good in the price range in the figure is completely _____ . The equilibrium price per unit is $ _____ , and the equilibrium quantity is _____ .

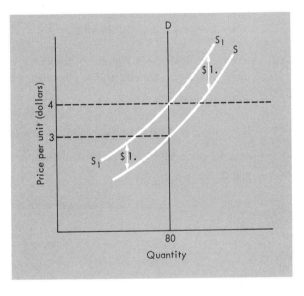

Figure 8.5
Tax effect

8.56 Now let us imagine that the government imposes a $1 tax on each unit of the good that the suppliers sell. Before the imposition of this tax, as is shown by SS, suppliers would be willing to supply _____ units of this good at $3 per unit, but because they now have to pay the government $1 on each unit they sell after the imposition of a tax, they will be willing to supply _____ units of this good only at a price of $4 per unit as is shown by $S_1 S_1$. We see that the imposition of a tax has caused an upwards and leftwards shift of the _____ schedule, that is, less will now be produced at each price.

8.57 Thus, the new effective supply schedule will be $S_1 S_1$. The new equilibrium price will be $ _____ , and the new equilibrium quantity will be _____ .

ANSWERS

54. inelastic . less than
55. inelastic . 3 . 80

56. 80 . 80 . supply
57. 4 . 80

8.58   In the situation before the tax, total revenue, if the market were in equilibrium, would amount

to $ _____ . After the tax has been imposed, total revenue will amount to

$ _____ , of which the supplier will receive $ _____ and the govern-

ment will receive $ _____ .

8.59   Now obviously, the suppliers of this good are no worse off than they were before, as

_____ _____ received by the suppliers has not changed. Thus, the
whole burden of the tax has been borne by the consumers because each individual who now

buys a unit of the good is paying $ _____ instead of $ _____ , as he
would have in the nontax situation.

8.60   In the case depicted in Figure 8.5, therefore, we would say that the incidence of the tax is completely on the consumers, and as you might guess, this is because the demand curve for this

good is completely _____ .

8.61   Now consider the case in Figure 8.6. In this situation, we have a completely _____

demand curve, and in the pretax situation the equilibrium price is $ _____ per unit

and the equilibrium quantity _____ . After the tax has been imposed, the equilib-

rium price is $ _____ per unit, and the equilibrium quantity is _____ .

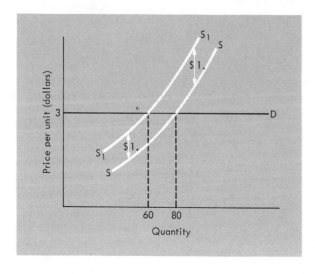

Figure 8.6
Tax effect

8.62 Again, we can see that the imposition of a $1 per unit tax has caused the _____ schedule to shift to the left. Now, had consumers purchased only 60 units of the good in the pretax situation, the total revenue collected by the suppliers would have been $_____. After the tax has been imposed, however, the equilibrium quantity that will be purchased will actually be 60 units. And in this case, the total revenue will again be $ _____ , but out of this sum suppliers will have to give $ _____ to the government. Thus, we see that the total incidence of the tax in this situation is on the _(consumers/suppliers)_ .

8.63 We have chosen extreme examples to show how to determine the incidence of the tax. You should now work through some examples for yourself with normally shaped demand and supply curves, bearing in mind that the more elastic the demand curve is relative to the supply curve, the greater will be the burden of tax borne by the _____ , whereas the more inelastic the demand curve is relative to the supply curve, the greater will be the burden of the tax borne by the _____ .

8.64 If we return to the world of perfectly competitive markets, we are now in a position to analyze the importance of the price mechanism in allocating scarce productive _____ .

8.65 We have assumed throughout that all consumers and firms are competitors. This means that when making consumption and production decisions, consumers and firms act as price takers. That is, they do not consider that their decisions to buy or produce a good will have any noticeable effect on the _____ of that good in the competitive markets.

8.66 Let us pull together the main ideas and basic economic tools that we have learned, and show the role of the price mechanism in allocating resources. In the discussion of demand, we assumed that consumers would spend their _____ according to their preferences. Formally, we say that consumers allocate their limited income in such a way as to maximize total _____ . The condition for such a maximum to be attained is that the _____ utility from the last dollar spent be the same for all goods and services.

8.67 When the price of a particular good falls, the amount of that good that a dollar can buy _(increases/decreases)_ . Consequently, when the price of a good falls, the marginal utility derived from the last dollar spent on a good will _(increase/decrease)_ . This will encourage consumers to buy more of that good to meet the marginal equivalency condition necessary for a maximum.

ANSWERS

62. supply . 180 . 180 . 60 . suppliers   65. price
63. suppliers . consumers   66. income . utility . marginal
64. resources   67. increases . increase

8.68   Another way to say the same thing is that the demand curve, which shows the quantity that will be demanded at different prices, slopes *(upward/downward)* from left to right.

8.69   In the discussion of supply, it was assumed that firms try to maximize _____ . Like a consumer, each perfectly competitive firm is a price taker, not a price maker.

8.70   To the perfectly competitive firm, the going market price for a good, be it a water bed or a sweat shirt, is the price the firm receives for each unit sold or for one additional unit; it equals

average _____ and also _____ _____ .

8.71   In order for a competitive firm to maximize profit, it is necessary to produce that level of out-

put at which the _____ of the product is equal to _____ cost.

8.72   The price of a product tells how much will be added to the *(revenue/cost)* of a competitive firm if an extra unit is produced. The marginal cost tells how much will be added to

_____ if an extra unit of output is produced.

8.73   If price is greater than marginal cost, the production of an extra unit of output will add *(more/ less)* to revenue than to cost; that is, profit will *(increase/decrease)* if an extra unit is pro- duced. If price were less than marginal cost, it would be possible to add to profit by *(increasing/decreasing)* output.

8.74   Only at the level of output where price equals marginal cost will _____ be at a maximum.

8.75   This way of expressing the marginal equivalency condition for profit maximization enables us to derive the supply curve for a firm. The supply curve of a firm, of course, shows the

_____ that a firm will be willing to produce at different _____ .

8.76   A profit-maximizing competitive firm will always expand output to the point where

_____ equals _____ _____ . As a result, for any particular

price, the quantity that will be produced will be given by the marginal _____ curve. In other words, the marginal cost curve shows the quantity that a competitive firm will supply at different prices. That is to say, the marginal cost curve is the competitive firm's

_____ curve.

ANSWERS

68. downward
69. profit
70. revenue . marginal revenue
71. price . marginal
72. revenue . cost

73. more . increase . decreasing
74. profit
75. quantities . prices
76. price . marginal cost . cost . supply

8.77   The foregoing discussions were put to use to show how, in the market for any commodity, the

equilibrium _____ and _____ of that commodity would be determined by the forces of supply and demand.

8.78   In any market, unless the quantity that consumers demand equals the quantity that firms

supply, competition among consumers and among firms will lead to changes in _____
until supply and demand are equal.

8.79   The importance of this result can be easily seen. Suppose, for example, that consumers' preferences change so that they consider books to be more satisfying commodities than was previously the case. This would have the effect of shifting the demand curve for books

_____ and to the _____ .

8.80   At the old price for books, the quantity demanded will now exceed the quantity supplied, and

the price of books will _____ . As the price increases, publishers will be induced to
(move along/shift) their supply curve and produce more books. This process will continue

until supply and demand are _____ .

8.81   To take another example, suppose that publishers discover a new, more efficient way to produce books. This will have the effect of shifting down firms' cost curves with the result that
they will be prepared to produce more books at each price. This change in technology, then,

shifts the supply curve _____ and to the _____ .

8.82   At the old price, the quantity _____ will be greater than the quantity

_____ , and competition among firms will lead to a fall in _____ .

8.83   As the price of books falls, consumers will respond by *(moving along/shifting)*   their demand

curves. This process will continue until _____ and _____ are equal.

8.84   In both of these examples, we have seen how the utility and profit-maximizing behavior of
consumers and competitive firms led to a change in the amount of resources used in the production of a commodity as conditions changed. In the first example, the change in consumers'

preferences was reflected in a shift in the _____ curve. This led to a change in

_____ , which signaled firms to increase production.

ANSWERS

77. price . quantity
78. price
79. upwards . right
80. increase . move along . equal

81. downward . right
82. supplied . demanded . price
83. moving along . demand . supply
84. demand . price

8.85   In the second example, the change in costs was reflected in a shift in the _____

curve. This led to a change in _____ , which induced consumers to increase

expenditures on the commodity in question.

8.86   In each case, the change in price acted as a signal. In the first case, the rise in price signaled to

_____ that consumers would prefer to consume more books and also made it

profitable for firms to produce more books. In the second case, the fall in price signaled to

_____ that books could be produced with fewer resources and enabled them to

purchase books at a lower price.

REVIEW QUESTIONS

8.1   When influenza vaccine first became available in the United States, the government set the price
equal to the cost of production. At that price, output was insufficient to fill orders, and the
government regulated the distribution of the vaccine. Had the vaccine been sold privately without government intervention,

a. the price would have been higher.

b. the price would have been lower.

c. the price would have been the same.

d. whether the price would be higher or
lower cannot be determined from the
information given.

At the price set by the government, excess demand existed. Thus, the price required to clear
the market exceeded the set price. It should be noted that had the vaccine been sold privately
at the "equilibrium" price, the problem of vaccine distribution would have been solved differently, that is, having set a price at which excess demand existed, the government then had to
decide who was going to receive the vaccine and who, while willing to pay the set price, was
going to be excluded. In a competitive market, distribution would have been determined by
competition among buyers, with those able and willing to pay receiving the vaccine. The correct response is a.

8.2   Which, if either, of the following statements would be correct when applied to a private enterprise economy?

1. One of the principal effects of competition is to force prices to the lowest level consistent
with normal profits.
2. One of the principal functions of profits is to indicate to the government where wages are
too low.

a. 1 only

b. 2 only

c. both 1 and 2

d. neither 1 nor 2

ANSWERS

85. supply . price

86. firms . consumers

Although profits indicate where capital can be most efficiently allocated, they yield no information about the wage level, which in a private enterprise economy is determined by the demand for and supply of labor. Thus, for any given firm, no causal relationship need exist between profit and wage level. In addition, concluding that a wage is "too low" involves making a value judgment. In a private enterprise economy, resources will be allocated in accordance with consumers' wants only if firms' production decisions are responsive to consumers' expenditure decisions. An increase in demand for a good will at first be reflected in higher prices of that good and in higher profits from producing it. Firms will try to take advantage of this higher profitability by producing more of that good, but only if there is competition will firms fully accommodate consumers' preferences by expanding output to the point where consumers' valuation just matches the cost (including normal profit) of production. The correct response is a.

8.3   A city has decided to build 5,000 dwelling units and to lease them to low income persons at a rental below cost and the going rate in the private market. Other things, such as population, being the same, what effect would you expect this to have on the market for private housing?

a. A decrease in rent, followed later by a decrease in the quantity supplied.
b. A decrease in tenants followed later by an increase in rents.
c. An increase in rents followed later by an increase in the quantity supplied.

d. No effect, because the poor persons who will be eligible for the 5,000 city built dwelling units cannot afford acceptable private housing.

There is a demand for rental housing and a supply of rental housing. The intersection of those schedules yields the equilibrium market output and price. When the 5,000 city dwelling units are complete, the demand curve for private housing will shift to the left as people move into the city dwelling units. In the short-run, given the supply of private housing is fixed, the rental price must therefore fall. This will cause returns in the market to decrease and in the long-run resources to move out, that is, a decrease in the quantity supplied. The correct response is a.

8.4   "If at the going price there is excess demand, competitive firms will shift their supply curves to the right causing prices to rise and quantity to increase until an equilibrium is reached." Which of the following is correct with regard to competitive markets?

a. The above statement is essentially correct in describing how equilibrium is reached.
b. The above statement is correct regarding how suppliers behave, but ignores buyers' reactions.

c. The above statement is incorrect, because the supply curves will not shift.
d. The above statement is incorrect, because it confuses shifting supply curves with shifting demand curves.

Because excess demand exists, at the going prices the market is not in equilibrium. Consequently, the price will rise until demand equals supply or in other words until the excess demand has been eliminated. Neither the demand nor supply curve will shift. The correct response is c.

Case 8

CONSUMER PROTECTION—USURY LAWS

Throughout the Middle Ages, to charge interest for the use of money was improper under Catholic Church doctrines (most lending was done by Jews) and was prohibited by law in many kingdoms—with violation sometimes punishable by death. Such laws were commonly evaded by borrowers and lenders because of the obvious benefits to both of borrowing-lending, and, with the Protestant Reformation and the commercial and industrial revolutions, official antagonism to lending at interest faded rapidly. Yet today, most states still have laws limiting the interest rates that can legally be charged on loans, presumably to safeguard borrowers against greedy lenders.

State laws have varied widely, but most have had a general ceiling (say 10 percent or so on business loans) with an escape provision permitting higher rates where (as on small loans to consumers) extra costs or risks of lending can be shown. In such cases, upper limits of 30 to 42 percent were not uncommon.

The volume of such lending is large—about $100 billion of consumer credit was outstanding at mid-1971 on department store installment credit, credit cards, bank loans, auto purchase loans, and the like.

In response to the recent wave of "consumerism," the National Uniform Credit Act was passed to limit to 1½ percent per month (18 percent per annum) the interest rate that department stores, credit card companies, automobile dealers, banks, and others can charge borrowers. This was well below the going rate for many borrowers, especially high-risk, low-income individuals and families. Moreover, by mid-1971, four states had gone still further and reduced the legal ceiling rate to 10 (Arkansas) or 12 percent (Minnesota, Washington, and Wisconsin). Consumer protection groups are pushing such legislation in other states.

What do you predict will be the results of these new consumer protection laws? Who will gain and who will lose? Should your state pass such a law? The analytical concepts of Chapter 8 provide the tools for at least partial answers to these questions.

SUGGESTIONS FOR ANALYSIS

Simple supply and demand analysis can help on this problem. The new laws are fixing a price ceiling (interest rate) on loans below the free market price. Suppose the supply and demand curves for consumer credit in your state are as follows:

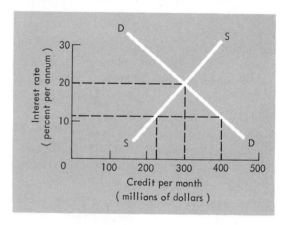

The free market interest rate would be 20 percent per annum, and $300 million would be offered and borrowed per month. The supply curve says that lenders would offer more at higher interest rates, less at lower ones. Why? Because at higher interest rates on consumer loans, it will pay to divert more credit from other potential borrowers, and because at higher rates it will pay to lend to higher-risk borrowers. The demand curve says that more will be borrowed at lower than at higher rates. Obviously, the "finance charge" (of which the interest rate is a big part) helps determine whether or not people can afford a new refrigerator or car. The lower the interest rate, the lower the monthly payments and the effective price of the product to people who buy on credit rather than paying cash.

Suppose, now, the state legislature decrees that no lender shall charge consumers more than 1 percent monthly—12 percent per year. At that rate, lenders will lend only $225 million monthly, but consumers will want to borrow $400 million. Clearly, there is a large excess demand—$175 million of unsatisfied consumer wants for credit. The first effect of the new law is that some consumers get cheaper credit, but some who were previously borrowing at 20 percent now get nothing. Seventy-five million dollars less is lent and an additional $100 million of demand goes unsatisfied. We can be sure there are going to be a lot of angry consumers who get a friendly but firm "no" from auto dealers, banks, finance companies, department stores, and credit card companies. And the lenders are not going to be very happy alienating their present and potential customers.

But the law is the law. Who gets the limited supply of consumer credit? Probably the well-established, good, low-risk customers of the lenders. But pity the consumer who applies for a new credit card, or charge account, or finance company loan in your state, especially if his income is low and he does not look like a top-notch credit risk. If you were a lender, you would stick with your good, established, sure-pay customers for what credit you have to lend—and that is just what lenders did in Arkansas, Minnesota, Washington, and Wisconsin. If the free price system does not decide who gets the available credit, lenders will have to ration it out on some other basis—unhappy customers or not.

What other effects would you expect? Rejected borrowers who live near the state boundary can reasonably be expected to take their business next door where credit is available and of course use scarce resources in traveling to other states. This is not calculated to make your home-state merchants very happy. Some borrowers and lenders may cheat a little—some of those rejected potential borrowers may offer to slip the finance man, auto dealer, or credit card manager a little something on the side to get credit, or a new credit card. "Black markets" can develop in credit just as they did in butter and gasoline, which were price-fixed and rationed back in World War II. For sure, angry consumers turned away will complain bitterly to their legislators that they are being treated unfairly—they were supposed to get cheaper credit, but in fact they are getting none. It is those greedy money-lenders trying to gouge them again, especially the poor, minority groups, and others who need the credit most if they are to buy.

Last, and a bit outside our assumptions, the whole supply curve (SS) is likely to move to the left—because big consumer lenders, like the nation-wide finance companies, may essentially drop out of business in your state. Why suffer the criticisms and take the lower interest rates there if they can make more money with happier customer relationships in other states? Move the SS curve to the left and see what that does to the problem.

Who has gained and who has lost from the new law? Should your state legislature be the next to put a 1 percent monthly ceiling on customer credit rates?

9

Efficiency
of the Market

9.1 What is the economic incentive for people to live under a free enterprise system or under any economic system for that matter? First what does "free" mean? "Free" in the free enterprise system implies the freedom of households to bid for the goods and services they want and freedom of firms to bid for the resources they need to produce those goods and services. People hire out their services, primarily labor services, and with the income they receive they buy the

_____ and _____ they help produce.

9.2 Why are individuals or families not self-sufficient, producing for themselves what they want? In early times, many families were self-sufficient, building their own homes, making their own clothes, and doing their own hunting. It became obvious to such people that they could be _(better off/worse off)_ by doing those things they were best at and exchanging goods with other people who were better at doing other things.

9.3 To fully understand this principle, let us build on what we know. You have already learned that in any given time period the more of any one good you consume, the smaller the

_____ _____ .

9.4 Imagine that living in a primitive society are two individuals who both enjoy nuts and fish. Chips is an excellent fisherman who can, on the average, catch four fish per day, which will spoil if not eaten that day. Coco is an excellent tree climber who can collect six nuts (also perishable) per day. Coco cannot fish; Chips cannot climb trees. Further, suppose that the following figures apply to both Chips and Coco.

ANSWERS

1. goods . services
2. better off

3. marginal utility
4. nut . fish

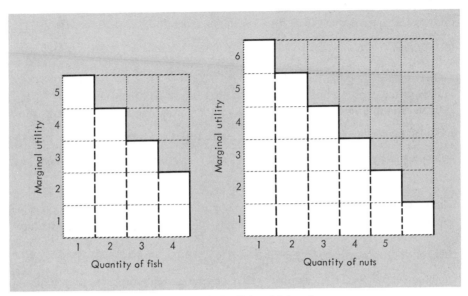

Figure 9.1 Marginal utilities of fish and nuts

Both Chips and Coco would prefer, in any given day, a first _____ rather than a first _____ by a ratio of 6/5.

9.5 For the sake of simplicity, assume we can measure satisfaction or utility in terms of utils. From Figure 9.1, we can calculate how many utils Chip receives from consuming his four fish. From the first fish he receives _____ utils, from the second, _____ utils, and so on. From the four fish, therefore, he receives _____ utils, the area under the "steps."

9.6 How many utils does Coco enjoy in consuming his six nuts? _____ utils.

9.7 Now let Chips and Coco meet. Would Chips be better off giving up one fish for one coconut? _____ . The marginal cost of giving up a fish is _____ utils; the marginal benefit of a coconut to Chips is _____ utils, so, he is _____ utils better off.

9.8 If Chips gains 4 utils, Coco must lose 4 utils. _(true/false)_ Not only is the answer false, but we see that Coco also gains; the _____ _____ of giving up one nut is 1 util, whereas the _____ _____ of obtaining one fish is 5 utils. Thus, Coco gains _____ utils on the exchange.

ANSWERS

5. 5 . 4 . 14
6. 21

7. yes . 2 . 6 . 4
8. false . marginal cost . marginal benefit . 4

9.9   If Chips exchanges a second fish for a second nut from Coco, is he better off? _____.
By how much? _____ utils. By how many utils is Coco better off? _____
utils.

9.10   Trading would continue until neither Chips nor Coco could become better off. Although this
example is a bit farfetched, the principle is very important. By merely exchanging or trading
goods, all individuals involved can _____ their total utility. And note that each
person is trading benefits without an _____ in the quantity of goods available.

9.11   Two important lessons emerge from our example. Not only are people better off after trading
without an increase in total output but the opportunity to trade allows each individual to
specialize in producing what he does best, thus _(increasing/decreasing)_ total utility.

9.12   How much division of labor occurs in a society is limited by the extent of the market. In some
communities, the local doctor provides all the medical attention. As the market _____,
some doctors specialize in children's ailments (pediatricians), others in skin diseases (derma-
tologists), and so on. As specialization increases, quality and quantity of services also increase,
making society _____ off. In Chapter 21, we shall extend the discussion to show
how nations become better off by engaging in international trade.

9.13   The opportunity for individuals to specialize in the production of different goods and exchange
them for other goods in free markets will have a substantial impact on the supply and demand
for each good. In the preceding chapter, we analyzed the way in which supply and demand
interact and determine the equilibrium _____ and _____ in the mar-
ket for any single commodity. In so doing, we analyzed the basic mechanics of a market economy. But the solution, or equilibrium, determined in any single market constitutes only a
partial equilibrium because it does not take into account the interdependence among markets.

9.14   What happens in the market for trucks certainly has an effect on the market for steel because
steel is needed to produce trucks. What happens in the market for steel certainly has an effect
on the market for iron ore because iron ore is needed to produce steel. What happens in the
market for iron ore has an effect on the market for trucks because trucks are needed to carry
iron ore. This is just a simple example of what it means to say that _____ are
interdependent.

9.15   But although it would be difficult, in fact impossible, to describe the millions of such interdependencies that exist in an economy like the United States', competitive markets, in bringing

ANSWERS

9. yes . 2 . 2
10. increase . increase
11. increasing
12. increases . better

13. price . quantity (either order)
14. markets
15. markets

about a *general equilibrium* of prices and quantities, automatically take these interdependencies into account. It is possible for competitive _____ to perform this complex task for two reasons.

9.16 First, no single individual or organization has to make all the decisions. Consumers and firms all pursue their own interests and the general _____ solution is the result of all those individual decisions taken together.

9.17 Second, markets can give out signals that convey to the many individual decision makers the information necessary to plan their expenditure or production. These signals are, of course,

_____ .

9.18 As individual consumers and firms make their decisions they affect the _____ of commodities. In turn, the prices that are signals to consumers and firms will influence their decisions. Changes in prices and in quantities supplied and demanded will occur until equilibrium in all markets is achieved. We call this solution _____ equilibrium.

9.19 Thus, through individuals pursuing their own ends—utility, in the case of the consumer, and profit, in the case of the entrepreneur—in a competitive economy, _____ will be allocated according to those ends.

9.20 The decisions of individual consumers and firms, acting freely and independently, are reflected in prices and outputs in the many competitive _____ that exist in a competitive free enterprise system. Equilibrium is reached in all markets when the combination of commodities demanded is equal to the combination of commodities supplied, just as _____ . is reached in any individual market when the amount of a commodity consumers are willing to buy just equals the amount firms are willing to produce.

9.21 We have not yet seen, however, whether the equilibrium that is reached in a competitive market economy provides an efficient solution to the problem of resource allocation. In the remaining part of this chapter, we will show under what conditions competitive _____ economy will tend toward an efficient equilibrium.

9.22 What is meant by the term *efficiency*? One kind of efficiency can be called technological efficiency. If a firm, in producing a given output, uses up the smallest possible quantity of resources, it would be technologically _____ . That is, it would incur the least possible cost in producing a given output.

ANSWERS

16. equilibrium
17. prices
18. prices . general
19. resources

20. markets . equilibrium
21. market
22. efficient

9.23   For an economy as a whole, if a given combination of commodities is produced with the smallest possible cost (quantity of resources), it will be _____ efficient.

9.24   Will an economy with competitive markets tend to be technologically efficient? Suppose, for example, that some firms in the home construction industry were not efficient in this sense. This would mean that they were using more _____ to build houses than necessary. As a result, these firms would be incurring greater costs and earning smaller _____ than would be the case if they were efficient.

9.25   If these firms are trying to maximize profit, it would clearly be in their own interest to reduce costs by becoming technologically _____ .

9.26   But if, for some reason, these firms did not adopt efficient methods of production, it would be profitable for competing, more efficient firms to produce and sell houses at a lower _____ and bid away the customers of less efficient firms. The more efficient firms would be able to sell houses at a lower price and still earn a profit because their _____ are lower.

9.27   The effect of this competitive behavior would be to force inefficient firms to reduce costs or, eventually, to force them out of business. Thus, if self-interest does not bring about technological efficiency, then the force of _____ will.

9.28   Thus, a competitive market economy will tend to be technologically efficient, because, for any combination of commodities produced, _____ will force firms to adopt the least-cost methods of production.

9.29   But, before an economy can be called economically efficient, it must be more than just technologically efficient. In other words, economic efficiency requires something more than just that the combination of commodities be produced with the fewest possible _____ .

9.30   It would be possible, for example, for an economy to produce nothing but paperweights and still be technologically efficient. Such an economy would not be _____ efficient, however, because it clearly would not be producing the best (from the viewpoint of consumers) combination of commodities.

ANSWERS

23. technologically
24. resources . profits
25. efficient
26. price . costs

27. competition
28. competition
29. resources
30. economically

9.31   If it is consumers' wants that should be satisfied, then economic efficiency requires that resources be allocated among the production of different commodities in accordance with consumers' preferences. The paperweight economy would not be efficient, because it would

be possible to increase the utility of consumers by shifting at least some _____ from the production of paperweights to the production of goods such as food and clothing.

9.32   We have seen that a competitive market economy will tend to be _____ efficient.

Will it also tend toward _____ efficiency? Let us see.

9.33   Earlier, it was shown that a consumer who spent his income in such a way as to maximize

utility would make the _____ utility from the last dollar spent equal for all goods.

9.34   For simplicity, consider only two goods, A and B. For the _____ -maximizing consumer, it must be true that

$$\frac{\text{marginal utility of A}}{\text{price of A}} = \frac{\text{marginal utility of B}}{\text{price of B}}$$

9.35   This says, of course, that if A costs twice as much as B, its marginal utility would have to be _(twice/half)_ that of B to make it worthwhile to buy the last unit of A.

9.36   It has also been shown that a profit-maximizing competitive firm will produce that level of out-

put for which price equals marginal _____ . For goods A and B, it will be true, in

a _____ market economy, that price of A equals marginal cost of A and that price

of B equals marginal cost of B. If we consider together the behavior of _____-max-

imizing consumers and _____-maximizing firms in a competitive economy, we can see that there will be a tendency for resources to be allocated efficiently.

9.37   Using symbols, we know in equilibrium that

(1) $$\frac{MU_A}{P_A} = \frac{MU_B}{P_B}$$

for all consumers.
In words: in equilibrium, the ratio of marginal utility to price for any commodity must be equal to the ratio of marginal utility to price for any other commodity. If, for any consumer, for any two commodities, the ratios were not equal, the consumer would not be in equilibrium; he could increase his satisfaction by reallocating his expenditure.

ANSWERS

31. resources
32. technologically . economic
33. marginal
34. utility

35. twice
36. cost . competitive . utility . profit
37. MC_A . MC_B

Again, using symbols, we also know in equilibrium that

(2) $P_A = MC_A$ and $P_B = MC_B$

for all producers of A and B.

In words: in equilibrium the price of a commodity must equal its marginal cost. Now consider (1) and (2) together.

(1) $$\frac{MU_A}{P_A} = \frac{MU_B}{P_B}$$

(2) $P_A = MC_A$; $P_B = MC_B$

Let us replace the prices (P's) in (1) with marginal costs (MC's) from (2). Thus, in (1) we will replace P_A with _____ and P_B with _____ . This gives the result

(3) $$\frac{MU_A}{MC_A} = \frac{MU_B}{MC_B}$$

What does this mean?

9.38   Because MU_A is the utility gained from consumption of the last unit of A, and MC_A is the dollar amount of resources used to produce the last unit of A, $\frac{MU_A}{MC_A}$ is the _____ gained from the last dollar's worth of _____ in the production of A. Pause here and make sure you understand frame 38.

9.39   Likewise, $\frac{MU_B}{MC_B}$ is the _____ gained from the last dollar's worth of _____ used in the production of B.

9.40   Equation (3), then, says that for each consumer in a competitive economy, the utility gained from the last dollar of resources used in the production of A, that is, $\left(\frac{MU_A}{MC_A}\right)$, and the utility gained from the last dollar of resources used in the production of B, that is, $\left(\frac{MU_B}{MC_B}\right)$, are _____ .

9.41   Suppose that this equality does not hold. Suppose, for example, that

$$\frac{MU_A}{MC_A} = \frac{4}{2} \text{ and } \frac{MU_B}{MC_B} = \frac{3}{2} .$$

ANSWERS

38. utility . resources
39. utility . resources

40. equal
41. 2 . 3

We can show that this is not an equilibrium situation. Suppose that $2 worth of resources were shifted away from the production of B to the production of A. Because the MC_B is

_____ , this will mean one less unit of B. What will be the loss in utility just from this reduction in the amount of B? _____

9.42 Because the MC_A is also $2, the resources obtained from industry B, when put to use in

industry A, will produce _____ unit(s) of A. What will be the gain in utility just from this increase in the amount of A? _____

9.43 Will it be worthwhile in this case for the economy to shift resources from B to A? _(yes/no)_ .

Why? Because there will be a net gain in _____ by doing so.

9.44 It will pay to shift resources from one industry to another until

$$\frac{MU_A}{MC_A} = \frac{MU_B}{MC_B}.$$

In other words, this is a marginal equivalency condition for efficiency for the economy as a whole. And, as we saw before, a competitive economy will move toward an equilibrium where this condition _(is/is not)_ met.

9.45 For this reason, we say that a competitive economy tends to be economically _____.
When a competitive economy attains equilibrium, there can be no increases in efficiency by

reallocating _____ .

9.46 In other words, a _____ market economy will allocate scarce _____

among alternative uses in such a way as to satisfy consumers' _____ as fully as possible.

9.47 In the preceding frames, we said that a competitive market economy will tend to be efficient. By this, we mean two things: first, such an economy will tend to produce the combination of

commodities that is most in accordance with the preferences of _____ ; second, it will tend to produce that combination of goods and services with the smallest possible quan-

tity of _____ .

9.48 In the preceding frame, we used the expressions "tend to be efficient" and "tend to produce..." Why can we not say unequivocally that a competitive market economy will be

ANSWERS

42. 1 . 4
43. yes . utility
44. is
45. efficient . resources

46. competitive . resources . wants
47. consumers . resources
48. might never be

efficient and will produce that combination of commodities most in accordance with consumers' wishes, using the smallest possible quantity of resources? There are several reasons. First, the real world does not stand still. New goods and services are constantly appearing, just as old ones are disappearing. Thus, for some firms, long-run equilibrium _(might never be/is always)_ reached.

9.49 Rapidly changing technology—compare the 747 with the piston aircraft or the containerized vessel with the sailing ship, which incidentally still transported wheat during this century, or zippers in pants instead of buttons—makes the attainment of long-run equilibrium for many

firms well nigh impossible. Firms, however, still attempt to reach _____

_____ equilibrium because their goal is _____ maximization.

9.50 Changes in population, changes in consumers' tastes and preferences, and changes in the relative supplies of different factors of production and accompanying price changes can force firms to adopt different combinations of factor inputs. Not so many years ago, roads were constructed with relatively large amounts of labor and little capital goods. Today, the reverse is true. Heavy capital equipment and relatively few men are used, implying that over time the relative cost of labor to capital in this industry has _(risen/fallen)_ and firms have economized on the _(more/less)_ expensive factor inputs in an attempt to maximize profit.

9.51 The greater the rate of technological advance, of course, the _____ the output of goods and services available for society, but the faster the rate of changes taking place in

society, the less likely firms and consumers are to reach _____ _____ equilibrium. Thus, although change is something we welcome, it also necessitates caution in making claims about what actually occurs in a free enterprise system.

9.52 In this chapter, we have seen why a competitive market will tend to be _____ . This is a very important result that is the ultimate justification for reliance on market forces in an economy. This "wonderful world of perfect competition," however, does not include a large amount of economic activity in our economy (for example, producing national defense and decreasing pollution), and as we shall see in Chapter 10, there is a legitimate role for government or collective action on the part of society to achieve efficiency in allocating resources. We shall also see in Chapter 11 why some goods are not produced by perfectly competitive firms, for example, telephone services and automobiles.

9.53 Despite exceptions, however, a significant portion of economic activity takes place in our economy as though it were a competitive free enterprise economy. Thus, it is important that you understand how such an economy functions and also be aware of exceptions to general rules. Were there no exceptions, of course, a competitive _____ _____

ANSWERS

49. long-run . profit
50. risen . more
51. greater . long-run

52. efficient
53. free enterprise . resources

system would tend to be efficient by providing the goods and services consumers desired, using the least amount of scarce _____ .

9.54 Let us briefly summarize how the competitive free enterprise system functions. Consumers allocate their incomes to the goods and services they want most. In so doing, each consumer attempts to maximize his total _____ .

9.55 Businessmen attempting to maximize _____ produce the goods and services demanded by consumers. Businessmen will produce additional output as long as the revenue from the production of one extra unit is greater than the _____ of producing that unit.

9.56 More technically, as long as marginal _____ exceeds _____ _____ , more will be added to revenue than to cost, and profit will increase.

9.57 Businessmen compete with each other in resource (land, _____ , and capital) markets and attempt to combine resources (factors of production) in the most efficient manner. Thus, the average cost of each unit of output will be least when factors are purchased at the minimum _____ and combined as efficiently as possible.

9.58 The prices that businessmen pay for those resources will be the incomes received by the owners of the resources. Thus, what are costs to the businessmen are _____ to the resources' owners, who in turn attempt to maximize _____ by allocating their income on the goods and services they want most.

9.59 In the markets for goods and services, competition will force down the _____ of each commodity to the minimum average cost of production. Profit will disappear and only a normal return on investment will remain.

9.60 If in any industry prices move higher than average minimum production cost, excess _____ will exist, and resources will move into that industry in search of that excess _____ . This process will continue until excess profit (over and above a normal return) disappears. On the other hand, if price is below average minimum production _____ , resources will move out of that industry in search of _____ elsewhere.

ANSWERS

54. utility
55. profit . cost
56. revenue . marginal cost
57. labor . price

58. incomes . utility
59. price
60. profit . profit . cost . profit

9.61   Thus, in equilibrium in a competitive free enterprise system, businessmen will be producing just as much of each product as consumers are willing to buy at the price that just covers

production cost. The _____ that just covers production cost is the price that is just necessary to command the factors of production needed to produce the amount demanded.

9.62   In equilibrium, therefore, the price that consumers must pay for any good will equal the marginal cost of production. Because in equilibrium this will be true for all commodities, there

would be no way to allocate resources more _____ .

9.63   Also in equilibrium as you will recall from Chapter 5, the price a businessman must pay for a factor of production will equal the value of its marginal product. If the value of the marginal

product is _____ than the price paid for the resource, it will add more to revenue than to cost, if the businessman continues to hire additional units of the factor. This will be

true for any factor input until the value of its marginal product equals its _____ .

9.64   Thus, in equilibrium, each factor will be paid a price equal to the value of its _____

_____ . The income, therefore, that any resource owner will earn will be deter-

mined by the value of the _____ _____ of the resource owned, which

in turn will be determined by the _____ for and _____ of the commodities that require that resource in the production process.

9.65   In equilibrium, therefore, when the _____ of each resource equals the value of

its _____ _____ , no resource could earn a higher return by moving to
any other field of production.

9.66   We can now see how, in a competitive free enterprise system, scarce _____ are
allocated efficiently through innumerable interdependent markets and incomes are paid to
resource owners based on the value of their marginal products. In this remarkable system,
there is no central control or planning. The actions of utility-seeking consumers and profit-

motivated entrepreneurs lead to a general _____ solution, in which resources
will be allocated in the most efficient fashion. Whether or not you like such an economic system may well be influenced by your income, that is, by the value of your marginal product
or by how quickly you feel goods and services are distributed through the price system. This
is the function of income distribution that we shall study in Chapter 12.

ANSWERS

61. price
62. efficiently
63. greater . price
64. marginal product . marginal product
   . demand . supply

65. price . marginal product
66. resources . equilibrium

REVIEW QUESTIONS

9.1 In a perfectly competitive free enterprise economy, which of the following statements would be correct?

1. Technological efficiency implies economic efficiency.
2. Economic efficiency implies technological efficiency.
3. For any consumer, marginal utilities will all be equal.

   a. 1 only   c. 1 and 2 only

   b. 2 only   d. 1, 2, and 3

Economic efficiency means not only that goods are being produced at least cost, that is, technological efficiency, but also that the utility of consumers is being maximized. Technological efficiency implies nothing at all about utility maximization. Utility will be maximized for each consumer when

$$\frac{MU_A}{MC_A} = \frac{MU_B}{MC_B},$$

and so on, not when

$$MU_A = MU_B.$$

The correct response is b.

9.2 In a perfectly competitive economic system in equilibrium, which of the following will be true?

   a. Incomes will be equal if all men are born with equal ability.

   b. Incomes will differ only insofar as people differ in how long or hard they work.

   c. Average income could not be increased by labor moving from one firm to another.

   d. Average income will be sufficiently high so that no working individual will starve.

If a perfectly competitive economy were in equilibrium, by definition each factor market, including the labor market, would be in equilibrium and each laborer would receive the value of his marginal product. Under these circumstances, total income could not be increased by moving labor from one industry or firm to another. The value of someone's marginal product, and consequently his wage, however, may be so low that even subsistence living will not be possible. Different individuals make different work-leisure decisions. Thus, equal abilities do not produce equal incomes. There are, of course, many other reasons for unequal incomes with equal abilities, that is, inherited wealth. The correct response is c.

9.3 Imagine a perfectly competitive economic system in equilibrium. Then, $\frac{MU_A}{MC_A}$ will equal $\frac{MU_B}{MC_B}$ will equal $\frac{MU_C}{MC_C}$, and so on. Technological advance significantly reduces costs in industry B.

After a time, equilibrium is reestablished in the economy. Which of the following will be true?

a. Prices will have risen in industry B.

b. Prices will have fallen in industry B.

c. Marginal utility will have risen for good B.

d. Total utility will have remained the same.

Due to the technological advance in industry B, costs will fall, and excess profits will appear. Resources will move into industry B from other industries until those excess profits are eliminated. Price, however, will be lower in the new situation because of the cost reduction, and at lower prices consumers will buy more B, reducing the marginal utility of B but increasing total utility. The correct response is b.

9.4   If two individuals were to voluntarily trade with each other, each would become better off for which of the following reasons?

1. Total output would be greater.
2. Total utility would be greater.
3. Costs of production would be lower.

    a. 1 only

    b. 2 only

    c. 3 only

    d. 1, 2, and 3

For two individuals to benefit from trade, neither need total output be greater nor costs of production lower. By each swapping a good that has low marginal utility for him but high marginal utility for his neighbor, an increase in total utility will result. The correct response is b.

Case 9

ECONOMIC ANALYSIS OF THE DRAFT

President Nixon, several aspiring presidential candidates, and many senators and congressmen (not forgetting students) have expressed dissatisfaction with the manner in which manpower needs are currently satisfied in the United States Army. The current lottery system, they maintain, is both unfair and economically inefficient. The army should compete for labor like any firm and should pay the going wage rate for the labor it needs. Currently, a lottery system exists for draftees; those who are unfortunate enough to draw the "two of clubs" and by fair means or foul cannot escape, serve up to two years in the army at wage rates significantly below those ruling in the private sector.

Furthermore, those conscripted cannot (at least the majority cannot) buy their way out. For example, if you are drafted, you cannot pay someone else to take your place. This was not always the case. During the Civil War, for example, draftees were allowed to send replacements; such a system must have made both the draftee and the replacement better off, or both parties would not have agreed to the deal. The price (bribe?) was negotiated by the draftee and potential replacements in the open market.

Some countries, such as Britain, have abolished a draft system and currently have volunteer armies in the same sense that United States Steel, General Motors, and the local liquor store have volunteer employees. The employees do not volunteer their services free but they have the freedom to apply for jobs at going wage rates. If, at going wage rates, a firm finds it has an excess demand for labor it raises its offer price; this, many people argue, is what the United States Army should do. Under a market system applied to the army, in equilibrium, the demand for and supply of men would intersect at the equilibrium wage. In 1970, at prevailing military salaries, the quantity of men demanded by the armed services exceeded the voluntary supply, so it was necessary to rely on the draft to meet manpower requirements. *The Report of the President's Commission on an All-Volunteer Armed Force* published in 1970 estimated that 60 percent of the army was composed of true volunteers (making due allowance for those driven to volunteer by the existence of the draft) and 40 percent draftees.

What would happen if the United States decided to have an all-volunteer armed force? How large should it be? Who would benefit and who would lose by switching from the draft to the volunteer system? Would it be more or less economically efficient than the current system? Would a volunteer army ensure enough fighting men during wartime?

SUGGESTIONS FOR ANALYSIS

In deciding how large the draft should be, from the point of view of economic efficiency the output of the armed services should be treated like any other good, that is, the last dollar spent on the army should yield the same level of social benefit as the last dollar spent on any other good or service. The fact that the marginal social benefit of military service is difficult to measure, as the President and the Congress well know, is no reason not to attempt to do so. Once the estimates have been made, output should be planned to equate the marginal benefit divided by the marginal cost for the army with the corresponding ratio for civilian goods and services.

The real cost to society of having an army, of course, is not the monetary payments made for all factors of production but the real civilian output foregone, that is, the opportunity cost. In considering adding one more soldier to the army, therefore, the real cost to society is what he could have produced in civilian employment, which is reflected by his civilian salary. Under the draft system, the cost of a draftee, consequently, is *not* the $2,000 or whatever he receives as army pay, but the salary he would have earned in civilian life.

For example, consider the situation in which Jim Plunkett, the football star, is drafted into the army and is paid $2,000 per annum. Does this

mean that Plunkett's services in the army is costing the United States $2,000 dollars? Again, the answer is no. You have to consider what Plunkett's opportunity cost is. If the value of his marginal product with the New England Patriots is, say, $500,000 per year (it is not clear he is paid anything like the value of his marginal product because of the football draft system—think about that), then the real cost to society of drafting Plunkett is the $500,000 of football services he no longer produces. Unless the benefit of having Plunkett in the army exceeds $500,000, it is a misallocation of resources to draft him.

How would the volunteer system allocate resources? To answer this question, consider Figure 9.a, which shows the demand curve for and supply curve of soldiers.

The demand curve reflects the social benefit of an additional soldier. Its traditional downward slope is due to the fact that the benefit to national defense of adding men decreases with the size of the army. The supply curve reflects the social cost of an additional soldier. Its traditional upward slope is indicative of the fact that at higher pay, more men would find military employment more rewarding than their civilian alternatives. The slopes of these curves reflect diminishing marginal benefit and increasing opportunity cost. At the point where the curves intersect, the marginal social benefit equals the marginal social cost. This shows the optimal army size and the equilibrium wage. It is clear that under the volunteer system at that wage Plunkett would not join, but workers who had civilian alternatives that were less desirable than the army at that wage would join.

The equilibrium under the volunteer system features both higher pay and a smaller army than under the present system. The higher pay comes about because the government is forced by the market to pay soldiers their marginal opportunity cost. The smaller size results because government decision makers and ultimately taxpayers now have to take into account the full cost of labor to be used by the army. As can be seen from Figure 9.a, under the current system the size of the army is Oq_2 and the pay is P_0. At this rate of pay, only Oq_0 volunteer and q_0q_2 are drafted. In this situation, the real cost to society of drafting the

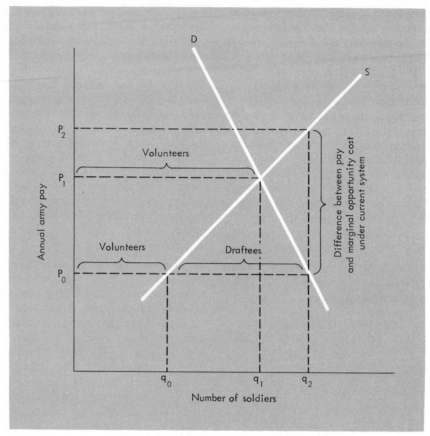

Figure 9.a   Demand for and supply of soldiers

soldier with the highest opportunity cost is P_2, but the benefit is only p_0.

Now, consider who would gain and who would lose under the two systems. The draft system causes draftees to bear a disproportionate share of the costs of national defense. If Plunkett, with potential civilian annual earnings of $500,000, were drafted and paid only $2,000, he would be paying an implicit tax rate of over 99 percent. At the same time, a worker unwilling to serve for $2,000 but willing to serve if he were paid the marginal social benefit of military service (that is, the pay depicted in Figure 9. a) is also worse off under the draft system. Clearly, both Plunkett and the worker could benefit if they were allowed to negotiate a deal, for example, if Plunkett were allowed to pay the worker even $50,000 to take his place in the army, or if there were a voluntary system.

The people who *do* benefit under the present system are those individuals who are not drafted and who would not join under the volunteer system, and those who pay lower taxes to meet the $2,000 draftee wage than they would have to pay under the volunteer system with its higher wages.

With respect to the comparative efficiency of the two systems, freedom of choice in a market situation makes the volunteer system more efficient. Why? Because under the volunteer system, the U.S. government will hire those people who implicitly can contribute more to society in the army than in civilian life. For example, assuming Plunkett and our typical worker would make equally good soldiers, total output would be higher under the volunteer system. Plunkett could produce more in civilian life than in the army, and our worker more in the army than in civilian life. In other words, the draft system, even though it costs less in military pay, is more expensive in terms of output foregone.

One potential drawback of the volunteer system could arise in time of war. In terms of Figure 9.a, we could expect society's demand curve to shift far to the right and at the same time the supply curve of volunteers to shift to the left. The possibility could occur that these curves would not intersect at a practical price. That is, an insufficient number of men would volunteer at a price that society could pay because of the enormous danger to soldiers. In such a situation, a draft system may be in society's interests, but not necessarily in the interests of those who are drafted.

10

Externalities and Public Goods

10.1 Although a considerable amount of economic activity takes place in our economy as though it were a competitive _____ _____ economy, there are areas of economic activity where efficiency would not be achieved if we were to rely upon market forces.

10.2 Besides studying those areas in this and the next chapter, we shall also analyze areas in which the government chooses to "interfere" with the working of the competitive economy. The two principal reasons that, as a society, we choose not to let market forces completely determine the allocation of scarce _____ are first to help achieve economic efficiency and second to alter the distribution of goods and services.

10.3 The forces determining the distribution of incomes will be pursued in Chapter 12. You should be aware at this point, however, that when we were analyzing the economic efficiency of a competitive free enterprise system, we took as given the initial distribution of ownership of human and nonhuman resources. That is, the initial distribution _(was/was not)_ questioned. No value judgment was made as to whether such a distribution was fair or just.

10.4 For instance, it is possible to have an _____ allocation of resources in a competitive market system with a very uneven distribution of resources, output, and income. The existence of a population made up of 10 percent millionares and 90 percent paupers _(must/does not)_ necessarily imply that resources are being inefficiently allocated.

ANSWERS

1. free enterprise
2. resources

3. was not
4. efficient . does not

10.5 Conversely, we would imagine an economy in which everyone had the same amount of resources and income. Although some people might think that this is an ideal distribution—all men equal in certain respects—would it imply that resources were being efficiently allocated? _(yes/no)_

10.6 For the present, let us return to efficiency, specifically to those areas of economic activity in which competitive market forces would not lead to economic efficiency. Given that such areas exist, we _(must modify/leave alone)_ market forces so that efficiency might be achieved.

10.7 In the preceding chapter, we saw that a competitive market economy will tend to be efficient. By this, we mean two things: first, such an economy will tend to produce the combination of commodities that is most in accord with the preferences of _____ ; second, it will tend to produce that combination of goods and services with the smallest possible quantity of

_____ .

10.8 Underlying this discussion was an important assumption, which was never stated explicitly. It was assumed that whenever a firm produced a commodity, it would have to pay all the costs of production, and in turn would be paid by all consumers who benefited from its product. Knowing the going market price of any good, a profit-maximizing firm, when making its decision about what to produce, will consider the _____ it has to pay and will disregard whatever _____ it does not have to pay. It will also base its decision not on how many consumers could be benefited by its product but on how much consumers will _(enjoy/pay for)_ its product.

10.9 As we shall see, when the costs that firms must pay differ from total costs, or when not all consumers have to pay to enjoy the benefits of firms' products, a competitive economy will not tend to allocate _____ efficiently.

10.10 In order to understand why this is true, let us consider two examples, one in which firms do not have to pay for all the _____ of production of a commodity, and one in which consumers can enjoy the benefit of a commodity without having to _____ for it.

10.11 Imagine a large power plant that supplies electricity to a city. Suppose that this power plant burns coal to obtain energy to drive its turbines, and that it is located in the middle of the city. What are the costs of producing electricity? There are the costs of the scarce _____

ANSWERS
5. no
6. must modify
7. consumers . resources
8. costs . costs . pay for
9. resources
10. costs . pay
11. resources . scarce

needed to produce electricity. The firm must pay for the land, labor, and capital it uses because these resources are _____ .

10.12 There is another cost, however, that this firm does not have to pay. In burning coal, the power plant gives off large quantities of smoke that pollutes the air. As a result, for persons living in this city, health suffers, residences are more difficult to keep clean, and the general tenor of life is less pleasant. Air pollution, then, is a real _____ of producing electricity that the firm _(does/does not)_ have to pay.

10.13 In a competitive market economy, nothing exists to force the firm to take the costs of air pollution into account. As a result, in a competitive market economy, resources will be allocated as if such costs _(do not exist/are too great)_ . Let us see why, when some costs are not taken into account, the allocation of resources in a competitive market economy will not be efficient.

10.14 You will remember that a competitive firm will maximize _____ if it produces the level of output for which price equals marginal cost. If the firm pays only some of the costs of production, it will maximize profit, producing the level of output at which _____ equals the _____ _____ paid by the firm.

10.15 If, for example, an air-polluting firm took into account all the costs of producing its output, price would be _(higher/lower)_ and output would be _____ .

10.16 If consumers spend their income to maximize utility, then, in general equilibrium for a competitive economy, it will be true that the extra utility obtained from the last dollar paid of production cost of a commodity will be _(the same/different)_ for all commodities.

10.17 Returning to our example, if we consider for simplicity just two commodities, electricity (E) and gas (G), it would be true in equilibrium for a competitive economy that

$$\frac{MU_E}{\text{paid } MC_E} = \frac{MU_G}{\text{paid } MC_G} \quad .$$

But we know that, in this example, the costs of producing electricity are _____ than the costs paid by firms producing electricity. As a result, in terms of all costs (whether paid by firms or not), it will be true in equilibrium that

$$\frac{MU_E}{MC_E} \text{ is } \underline{(less/greater)} \text{ than } \frac{MU_G}{MC_G}$$

ANSWERS

12. cost . does not
13. do not exist
14. profit . price . marginal cost

15. higher . lower
16. the same
17. greater . less

10.18 Because it is a necessary condition for efficiency that the utility gained from the last dollar of cost be the same for all commodities, we can see from the preceding frame that a competitive economy _(will/will not)_ be efficient when some costs are not paid by producers.

10.19 Historically, communities have recognized this problem and have tried to solve it by modifying the competitive economy in different ways. In terms of our smoke example, zoning has sometimes been used to require that plants which make surrounding areas unpleasant to live in be located in areas distant from residential areas. This approach forces firms to take into account the costs of air pollution by locating in an area where these costs are _(high/low)_ .

10.20 An alternative approach that has been used is to require power plants to use filters and other devices to prevent smoke from pouring out into the air. In this case, firms are forced to take into account the possible costs of air pollution by the requirement that they do whatever is necessary to _(eliminate/create)_ harmful quantities of smoke.

10.21 Consider another example, the one of industrial firms that dump their wastes into lakes and rivers. Although those firms _(are/are not)_ paying the costs of labor and other resources used, they _(are/are not)_ paying the full costs of the output they are producing.

10.22 The fish that will die and never be consumed, the water that can neither be drunk nor bathed in, the polluted beaches children cannot play upon, and the general ugliness forced upon society are all _____ that society must pay in addition to the price of the products produced by such firms.

10.23 Again, as in the smoke example, market forces _(do/do not)_ force firms to consider all the costs of production. Again, therefore, _____ will not be achieved by reliance on market forces.

10.24 Such pollution, or cost, appears in communist and socialist as well as capitalist economies. All economies are becoming increasingly aware of pollution problems and to differing degrees solutions are being sought. In our economy, policies to fight pollution constitute a kind of interference in the workings of a competitive market economy, but it is an interference directed at situations that a competitive economy _(can/cannot)_ handle efficiently.

10.25 Why does any society tolerate pollution? Why does any society tolerate poverty? Why does every family not have all the goods and services it wants? The answer, of course, to each question is that any society's productive _____ are limited and more of any one good, by definition, means _____ of some other good. If the electricity-producing firms polluting the atmosphere or the industrial firms polluting rivers and lakes, in our earlier

ANSWERS

18. will not
19. low
20. eliminate
21. are . are not

22. costs
23. do not . efficiency
24. cannot
25. resources . less . higher . more . less

examples, were to pay all the costs in producing their goods through other means of waste disposal, production costs of these goods would be _____ because *(more/fewer)* resources would be required. Society would have cleaner air and less water polution but _____ of all other goods and services.

10.26   More pure air and nonpolluted rivers and lakes means _____ resources for other goods and services people want. Just think of the resources that would be required to make every beach litter-free, including, incidentally, seaweed, rocks, and driftwood that many people consider to be litter.

10.27   Do we really want litter-free beaches if we have to give up schools, hospitals, horror comics, and switchblade knives to obtain them? The answer, of course, is that society should allocate its _____ so that the last dollar spent on each good or service yields the same _____ .

10.28   To summarize briefly, when there are costs of producing a certain commodity that firms do not have to pay, a competitive market economy will tend to allocate resources _____ . By having society impose restrictions that force such firms to take into account all costs of production, it may be possible to restore the tendency of a market economy toward economic _____ .

10.29   Let us consider now an example of a *public good*. Here, consumers are able to enjoy the benefits of a commodity without having to pay for it. Suppose there is a mosquito swamp that makes life miserable for everyone in the neighboring town. It would appear that such a situation would make it profitable, in a competitive market economy, for a firm to produce and sell swamp-clearing services. Because a large number of persons would like to enjoy the benefits of such services, presumably they _(would/would not)_ be willing to pay for them.

10.30   Now, suppose some swamp-clearing firm could perform such services. Would it be able to sell this service? There is no economic reason why any consumer in this town would be willing to pay for this service after the swamp had been cleared, because now it _(would/would not)_ be necessary to pay in order to enjoy a mosquito-free evening. That is, a resident could enjoy (consume) a mosquito-free evening at zero cost.

10.31   Thus, after the service is rendered (after the swamp is cleared), consumers are able to enjoy the benefits of this service without having to _____ for it.

ANSWERS

26. fewer   29. would
27. resources . benefit   30. would not
28. inefficiently . efficiency   31. pay

10.32 Suppose the firm recognizes this problem and decides to have consumers agree to pay before the swamp is cleared. Because in a competitive economy consumers make their expenditures individually, not as a group, our firm would have to deal with consumers _(as a group/ individually)_ .

10.33 It is unlikely, even though he might be bothered by mosquitos a great deal, that any one consumer would be willing on his own to hire a firm to clear the swamp. He might say to himself: "It really isn't worth it to me to have the swamp cleared if I have to pay the entire cost. Besides, if any one else decides to have the swamp cleared, I will benefit just as much as if I paid for it myself. What's more, if I were to have the swamp cleared, everyone else would benefit without paying any of the cost." As a result, _(no one/some one)_ is likely to buy the services of the swamp-clearing firm.

10.34 An enterprising firm might then hit upon the idea of selling shares so that no single individual would have to pay the entire cost. Unfortunately, however, if consumers really were to behave independently and in their own interest, they would reason to themselves: "Why should I buy a share? The small amount of my contribution is not going to make any significant difference. If everyone else buys a share, the swamp will be cleared, and I will benefit, whether I buy a share or not. If no one else buys a share, the swamp will not be cleared, even if I were to buy a share." As a result, once again, our firm _(will/will not)_ find swamp clearing a profitable activity.

10.35 Because there is no way of preventing people who do not pay for the service from consuming it, it is very difficult in a competitive market economy to get anyone to pay for a service like swamp clearing. This is unlike most commodities. If you want to wear a coat, you must

_____ for your own coat. If you want to drive a car, you must _____ for your own car. But if you want to be free of mosquitos, you can be so just as well if someone else clears the swamp as if you clear the swamp.

10.36 Thus, even though everyone would benefit by having the swamp cleared, it _(will/will not)_ be cleared in a competitive market economy if no one is willing to pay for it.

10.37 There is a way, however, in which the swamp can be cleared to most people's satisfaction. This solution requires that consumers do not behave independently or competitively. If all consumers got together as a group and agreed that each citizen would be taxed to pay part of the cost of clearing the swamp, it would be possible to pay for the project. But collective or group consumption of this kind is different from the behavior assumed when we talk about a

_____ _____ economy.

ANSWERS

32. individually
33. no one
34. will not

35. pay . pay
36. will not
37. competitive market

10.38   Society has long recognized the need for collective consumption. In fact, one of the principal activities of governments is to make expenditures, on behalf of consumers as a group, for goods that most people want but that will not be produced in a competitive economy. These goods are frequently called "public goods." Examples of _____ goods are national defense, police and fire protection, scientific research, education, public highways, parks, and recreational areas. For each of these, it is at least partially true that consumers will be free to enjoy them whether or not they pay for them.

10.39   When governments make expenditures, they "interfere" with the workings of a competitive market economy. But when these expenditures are for _____ goods, they make it possible for goods to be produced that consumers want produced, but that would not be produced in adequate quantities in a _____ _____ economy.

10.40   In a society such as ours, we elect representatives to form a government. This government, as we have just seen, makes economic decisions designed to _____ economic welfare. Most of the expenditures made by the government are financed out of taxes paid by individuals and firms.

10.41   In earlier chapters, we studied how individuals spent their incomes on those goods that yielded the highest _____ . It was an individual or family decision. With government expenditure, however, the decision of who pays for a public good, for example, is sometimes based upon who can afford to pay rather than upon who benefits.

10.42   Consider national defense for example. Suppose we assume that every individual living in the United States benefits equally from national defense. One might argue, then, that such individuals should pay an equal share of the cost. Families with lower incomes in this case would pay _(a larger/an equal/a smaller)_ proportion of their incomes for national defense.

10.43   If families were taxed an equal proportion of their incomes to pay for national defense, the poorer families in dollar terms would pay _(less than/the same as/more than)_ families with larger incomes.

10.44   Thus, once the decision has been made to deploy a certain amount of resources for national defense, the question of who pays for this defense will affect the income distribution within the country. The more any one individual is taxed to pay for any public good, the _____ income he will have available for all other goods and services and the _(worse/better)_ off he will be.

ANSWERS

38. public	42. a larger
39. public . competitive market	43. less than
40. increase	44. less . worse
41. utility	

10.45 How much national defense should there be? Society should allocate its resources so that the last dollar spent on national defense yields the same _____ as the last dollar spent on any other good or service. This rule determines, in principle, how much should be spent on national defense, but because this good is a _____ good, there is no rule for telling which members of society should pay for it. This decision must be made on grounds such as equity or ability to pay; there is no economic rule to yield an answer.

10.46 Now consider the case of a detergent-producing firm polluting a river. Suppose the community decides that the pollution must stop and that the most technologically efficient way to stop the pollution requires expenditures of $1 million dollars annually, that is, $1 million dollars worth of _____ are required to avoid pollution.

10.47 Who should pay? Before you decide that the detergent-producing firm should pay, consider the following. Why not have the people who want a nonpolluted river pay the $1 million per year? After all, if you want an automobile or a can of beer, it is _(you/your neighbors)_ who should pay because it is _____ who receive the benefit from the car or the beer.

10.48 In the river pollution case, no matter who pays, the same amount of _____ is going to be required, namely $1 million dollars worth. Thus, the question of who pays is a question of income distribution. Those who pay will have _____ income to spend on other goods.

10.49 If the detergent-producing firm pays the $1 million dollars to clean up the river, the cost of producing detergent to the firm will _____ . Because, in the long-run, the price of any product must reflect costs borne by the firm, the _____ of detergent must rise, and households using detergent, if they pay the higher price, will have _____ income to spend on other goods. Consequently, the detergent users will be paying for cleaning up the river.

10.50 On the other hand, if the local community pays the $1 million out of taxes, the price of detergents _(will/will not)_ rise, and, to the extent that the local community is composed of detergent and nondetergent users, _(the same/a different)_ distribution of income will result.

10.51 To reinforce the point, consider two people in a room—a smoker and a nonsmoker. A widget, costing $1, placed on the end of a cigarette gets rid of the smoke pollution. Who should pay the $1—the smoker causing the pollution or the nonsmoker who wants clean air? No matter

ANSWERS

45. utility . public
46. resources
47. you . you
48. resources . less

49. rise . price . less
50. will not . a different
51. 1 . resources

who pays, the cost is going to be $ _____ ; who actually does pay (or partially pays, for example, 50 cents each) affects the income distribution between the two people, not the amount of _____ required for clean air.

10.52   No one likes pollution as pollution, but getting rid of pollution requires _____ .

The more resources society devotes to lessening pollution, the _____ resources available for other goods and services.

10.53   If someone else is prepared to pay to get rid of pollution in your community, you would welcome this because you would become _____ off at no cost to you. But if you or your community must pay the bill, you may decide that the cost is too high.

REVIEW QUESTIONS

Questions 1 and 2 are based on the following information:

Factories in a city with a population of 500,000 cause a serious smog problem. Imagine that the smog could be completely eliminated if 100 new air purification vacuum plants were built. The annual cost of operating the 100 plants would be $400,000.

10.1   Assuming that no single household can afford to pay for the project, but the project's annual benefits to the community as a whole are $600,000, which of the following conditions would be sufficient to prevent a private firm from making a profit by carrying out the project and selling its services to residents?

1. Each household acts independently of other households in spending its income.
2. When it is to their advantage, households cooperate with one another and act as a single buyer.
3. It is impossible to prevent households that do not pay from enjoying smog-free air.

    a. 1 only   c. 1 and 3 taken together
    b. 2 only   d. 2 and 3 taken together

The nature of the good in question is such that if any household purchases smog-free air, it will automatically purchase smog-free air for all, and those households that refuse to pay cannot be excluded from enjoying the smog-free air. It is impossible for each household to buy its own little piece of clean atmosphere in the same way it can buy bread. Given this all-or-nothing situation, because no single household can afford to pay the $400,000 annual cost of the project, as long as households act independently, it will be unprofitable for a private firm to carry out the project. Note that condition 3 by itself is not sufficient to make the project unprofitable for a private firm, for as long as households are free to cooperate they might find it to their advantage to make a collective decision to contract with a private firm on profitable terms. The corrrect response is c.

ANSWERS

52. resources . fewer   53. better

10.2 Suppose that, instead of a private firm, the city government were to build and operate puri-fication plants. The amount of smog left in the atmosphere will depend on the number of plants in operation. Assuming the government can calculate the benefit and cost of each plant, how many plants should be built to achieve the most efficient use of the city's resources?

a. That number at which average benefit minus average cost is maximum.

b. That number at which the benefit minus the cost of the last plant built is maximum.

c. That number at which the benefit from an extra plant is zero.

d. That number at which the benefit minus the cost of an extra plant is zero.

As long as the gain to society, or to an individual, from producing one extra unit of a commodity exceeds the cost of that unit, society will be better off if the unit is produced. Welfare will be at a maximum when production for each good is continued until the benefit from the last unit produced just equals the cost or, as in this example, until the benefit minus the cost of an extra plant is zero. The correct response is d.

Questions 3 and 4 are based on the following information:

A conflict over the use of the Yat River has arisen between commercial fishermen, who have traditionally caught large quantities of salmon in the river, and a large producer of chemicals, who has discovered that it is possible to dispose of wastes by depositing them in the river. The fishermen claim that the high quantity of wastes being dumped into the river is killing a large number of fish and the chemical producers should be prohibited from using the river as a sewer. No other benefits (for example scenic) are derived from the river.

10.3 This use of the river does not constitute an economical use of resources because:

a. the river is better used as a source of fish than as a sewer.

b. although the chemical producer con-siders the benefits, he does not take into account all the costs of using the river as a sewer.

c. killing the fish is a waste of natural resources.

d. although chemical wastes can be disposed of elsewhere, fish require their natural habitat.

The river is a source of only two benefits—waste disposal and commercial fish. The greater the amount of waste deposited in the river, the greater the number of fish killed and consequently the smaller the commercial fishing catch. Because the benefits and costs to society from both activities—dumping waste and commercial fishing—are not enumerated, we do not know the best mix of these two uses of the river. What we do know is that the chemical producer, in deciding to dump wastes into the river, is considering the private cost of waste disposal, that is, the cost to himself, not the social cost. He ignores the cost his actions impose on the com-mercial fishermen, and as a result the marginal social benefit from this waste disposal is less than the marginal social cost. This implies that efficiency would be increased if less waste were dumped in the river and more fish were caught, even though it would mean higher-priced chemicals. The correct response is b.

10.4 If the government wants to promote efficient resource use, which of the following policies should it adopt? It should:

a. refuse to intervene.
b. prohibit the chemical producer from dumping wastes into the river.

c. encourage fishermen to fish elsewhere and compensate them for any loss in income.
d. allow the chemical producer to dump wastes into the river but charge him the decrease in value of the river as a fishery.

Because private and social costs differ, as discussed in tne answer to 10.3, efficient resource allocation will not result when each individual pursues his own interests. Because the private cost understates the total cost of producing chemicals, the output of the chemical industry will be too large and the output of all other industries too small for efficient resource allocation. The government can promote efficiency by eliminating any difference between private and social costs. It can do this by charging the chemical producer the difference between his private marginal cost and social marginal cost, that is, by charging him the decrease in the value of the river as a fishery. The correct response is d.

Case 10

POLLUTION AND THE METAL CASTING INDUSTRY IN ST. LOUIS

THE INDUSTRY

The metal-casting industry is the sixth largest among manufacturing industries in the United States (after motor vehicles, steel, aircraft, chemicals, and communications equipment). A metal casting is the result of pouring molten metal into a mold that has been patterned to give the metal the desired shape. In its most elementary form, casting thus involves the melting of some metal, its being poured into a previously made mold, and the solidification of the metal, after which the mold is removed. Such casting, done in foundries, is by far the cheapest way to produce blocks of metal in desired shapes, much cheaper than machining metal into the shapes needed. Castings are made with a wide variety of metals, but iron castings are by far the largest in terms of total output.

In 1967, there were about 5,400 foundries in the United States, employing 350,000 men, a high proportion of whom were unskilled. Most foundries are small. In 1967, about 60 percent of all independent foundries had sales of less than $1 million, on which, in a typical

foundry, profits *before taxes* would be about $60,000 in a good year.[1]

Nearly all iron foundries are similar in operation. They use a tall cupola with a high, outside smokestack. Coke is burned in these cupolas, and air is forced up through the cupola at very high velocity to increase the heat of the coke when it burns. The pig iron and scrap iron are melted in this heat and poured into the mold. Under the intense heat, the air expands and rushes out the top of the cupola into the atmosphere. This discharge over an hour from a typical small cupola will contain as much as 128 pounds of fly-ash particulate, about 16 pounds of dirt per ton of metal melted per hour.

Cast iron foundries are one of the oldest of man's inventions for handling metals, and until recently no one paid much attention to the pollution problem surrounding such foundries. According to government tests, of the dust that

[1] The factual information in this case is largely drawn from "Pollution Control and the Metal Casting Industry" (Boston: Intercollegiate Case Clearing House, 1969).

is blown up through the stacks, about 80 percent in a gray-iron foundry (the common type) is large particles that are too heavy to travel far and that usually fall very near the cupola. The additional 20 percent is smaller particles. These are light enough to be carried further away by the wind and provide a serious nuisance in the form of soot and dirt for the surrounding area. Some of the particles (perhaps 5 percent of the total) are very small and are taken into the atmosphere or dispersed, and some of them are eventually inhaled.

Pollution control. Most gray-iron foundries operate either 8- or 16-ton-melt-per-hour-capacity cupolas. The larger foundries differ from the smaller ones more in the number of hours per day that the cupolas operate than in the number of cupolas used. Thus, the problem of putting emission control equipment in the cupolas is about equally expensive on the installation side for small and for larger foundries. Following the federal Clean Air Act of 1967, industry and government experts agreed that a "wet-cap" emission control system with 60 to 75 percent collection efficiency (insufficient to meet pollution controls in most areas) could be installed at between $1,000 and $9,000 per ton-hour cupola melt capacity—that is, $8,000 to $72,000 per cupola for an 8-ton cupola. High efficiency systems cost substantially more. "Bag-house" systems, with 99 percent efficiency, cost from about $6,000 to $38,000 per ton for installed systems. In addition to those installation costs, there are substantial operating maintenance expenses, generally proportionate to the cupola size. These extra operating costs range from about $500 to $2,800 per ton of hourly melt capacity per cupola for the simplest systems, up to $2,300 to $12,000 per hour for maximum effectiveness "bag-house" systems. Moreover, the industry pointed out, installation of such equipment raised the stated value of the plants, and thereby raised property taxes proportionately because most local governments tax industrial properties on their values.

THE ST. LOUIS PROBLEM

Iron foundries are scattered all over the United States, but are generally concentrated in industrial cities, especially in the eastern half of the United States. St. Louis is one such city. Moreover, St. Louis was chosen as an early pilot study area by federal authorities when the original antipollution bill was enacted in 1963 (the 1967 bill was a revision). St. Louis had thirteen iron foundries in 1967.

When St. Louis authorities examined their air pollution problem, they soon found that automobile emissions were the largest single cause. But they also found little enthusiasm on the part of the citizens for doing anything to control automobile emissions. Thus, to reduce air pollution, they decided to concentrate on nonautomobile causes. In accordance with the federal act, the city commission decided in 1967 on a region-wide air pollution reduction goal of 39 percent. Because this was all to be achieved through industry, the city's foundries were first told to reduce their emissions by at least 71 percent to meet their share of the goal. In fact, this standard was a good deal looser than those in some other cities, for example Los Angeles, and some city officials thought that emission standards should be tightened up still more. The foundry owners, on the other hand, were most alarmed at the costs involved. Nonetheless, as discussions continued, by 1968 the city commission had established a reduction quota of 86.3 percent for the foundries, far in excess of the industry's earlier expectation of a 71 percent reduction figure. Again, the industry protested vigorously that it could not meet these standards and stay in business; industry leaders suggested a compromise by which they would undertake to reduce their emissions by 83.2 percent instead of the 86.3 percent demanded.

From the industry's point of view, the difference between the two figures meant much more than 3.1 percent. For all St. Louis iron foundries, emission reductions of 83.2 percent would require an investment of about $1 million. To meet the higher 86.3 percent figure would cost the industry over $3 million. The $2 million marginal cost yielding a marginal benefit of 3.1 percent pollution reduction would, they argued, mean the difference between death and survival for most of the foundries in St. Louis, but it would change the overall cleanliness of St. Louis's atmosphere by only a tiny fraction of 1 percent. City officials were said to have conceded that, because of the roughness of measurement techniques for measuring pollution emission, the 3.1 percent difference was "hardly measurable." For a typical foundry, with a $500,000 sales and $30,000 profit *before taxes* each year, installation of the lower efficiency system would cost about $60,000, and maintenance charges per year would be about $17,000. Adherence to the higher standards would require installation of a higher efficiency "scrubber" system costing about $180,000 plus annual operating costs of $50,000.

Last, foundry operators pointed out that if they went out of business, the burden of the closedown would fall largely on unskilled workers in the area, most of whom were blacks. St. Louis has had a serious racial and unemployment problem in recent years, with a large "hard core" group of unemployed workers. "What you're going to do," bitterly protested one foundry owner, "is to throw a lot of poor blacks out of work, drive us out of business, and make it impossible for many businesses to find any place to buy iron castings. What happens if a business wants to get an iron part made and there are no longer small jobbing foundries around? Do you think they are going to get the job done by Ford or General Electric at their big captive foundries in the East?"

Many of the issues in the cases are both complex and difficult. You might try to answer the following questions.

Should concerned students picket the St. Louis foundries because they are polluting the atmosphere?

What, if any, pollution standards should St. Louis establish for iron foundries?

What, if any, air pollution standards should the Federal Government establish for iron foundries?

Would a tax per pound of particles emitted into the atmosphere be more or less efficient than an absolute standard of the sort described in the case?

Who should pay the cost of eliminating air pollution from iron foundries?

SUGGESTIONS FOR ANALYSIS

In the iron foundry case, the dirt poured out on the surrounding neighborhood is a real cost to the people who live there, but it is not a cost borne by the iron foundry itself. Thus, in the absence of government, or some other collective action, the price of iron castings will only reflect private cost, that is, will only cover the cost of producing iron castings and will not include the cost of cleaning up the windowsills, clothes, and lungs of the people who live near the foundry, or of preventing this pollution.

This, like other externalities, is a case that requires collective action if society is to have the full cost of producing iron castings reflected in the price charged to the purchase of them. Without some collective action to incorporate the pollution costs into the price of the finished castings, buyers of castings are getting them too cheap, and too many castings are being produced.

To maximize profit, each firm will produce up to the point at which marginal cost equals price. Iron casting consumers will purchase until the ratio of $\frac{MU}{P}$ for castings is equal to the corresponding ratio for any other good. However, because price now equals private, not total social, marginal cost, price does not cover the full social marginal cost of production. To achieve allocative efficiency, the cost of producing castings should include the full social cost rather than merely the economic, or accounting, cost as seen by the individual firm. The marginal equivalency conditions should be met with marginal social costs included.

Here, as in most other cases, the principle of marginalism applies. If we were to eliminate all pollution from iron foundries (zero dirt emission from the cupolas), we would probably end up raising the price of castings so high that few, if any, would be bought. As a practical matter, this standard might well force the production of metal blocks by other devices, such as machining or new electric processes for molding metals. These costs could be very high, and the shift would not necessarily be desirable socially. Just how far we should force the iron foundries to go in eliminating emissions from their cupolas should be determined by balancing off the marginal costs of installing and operating the emission against the marginal benefits derived (the cleaner air). There is no general way of saying just when this equation of marginal costs with marginal benefits will be reached in any given case—it depends on the particular circumstances involved. In the St. Louis case, for example, you may or may not feel that going from the 83 percent emission control level to the 86 percent level is worth the added cost. In the end, consumers of iron products are going to end up paying the higher costs.

The principle of marginalism also throws light on the question of whether a flat rule is more efficient than a tax (charge) per unit of pollution emitted into the air. The absolute limit (say 83 percent emission control) falls very unevenly on different-sized firms. The cost of installation is about the same for a very small firm (one that uses its furnace only an hour or two a day) as for a very large firm (which may run its furnace many hours per day and hence emit far more pollution into the air). The principle of marginalism says efficiency would be achieved by charging a tax, or charge, of so much per pound of particles emitted into the air. This would mean that the larger firm would have to pay a much larger tax than would the smaller firm because it emits so much more dirt into the air per day. This seems fairer, for one thing. But more importantly, the larger tax burden on the larger producer would put a much heavier pressure on him to reduce his emissions than it would on the small producer, whose tax

would be much lighter as a result of his lesser emissions of dirt. Thus, the tax would put financial pressure where it would do the most to clean up pollution.

If St. Louis imposes rigorous emission control standards on its iron foundries, clearly this will raise their costs and they will have to raise their prices or go out of business. If they do raise their prices, and if iron foundries elsewhere do not have to meet the same emission standards, it is pretty clear that St. Louis foundries will go out of business at the higher prices; customers will simply take their orders where they can buy iron castings cheaper. Another alternative would be for St. Louis citizens to pay for the cleaner air they want by using tax money to subsidize foundries to end pollution. Thus, the people of St. Louis must decide whether the benefits of additional clean air through foundry legislation are worth the extra cost. Remember that St. Louis residents showed no enthusiasm for doing anything about auto emissions—the major air pollutant. If St. Louis decided to live with its air pollution, and if all such pollution were local, federal legislation that imposed air pollution standards more severe than St. Louis citizens wanted would be inefficient. Why? Because St. Louis citizens would be forced to use scarce resources to produce a good—clean air—that they did not believe was worth the cost.

11

Imperfect Competition

11.1   In Chapters 1 through 9 we analyzed markets in which competition prevails, that is, markets in which many consumers compete with each other on the demand side and in which many suppliers compete with each other on the supply side. The price of a commodity is determined

by the forces of _____ and _____ . In those competitive markets, no

single buyer or seller has a significant influence on the _____ of the commodity being sold in the market, although each can buy or sell as much of the commodity as he wishes

at that _____ .

11.2   Obviously, in the U.S. economy not all markets are characterized by perfect competition. In the automobile industry, for instance, four companies account for almost all domestic sales, with General Motors producing over 50 percent. Each company can have a substantial effect on the price of automobiles. Thus, the automobile industry in the United States is not a

_____ _____ industry. We shall begin our study of such types of firms with the complete opposite of perfect competition: monopoly.

11.3   *Monopoly* means one seller. Between the extremes of _____ and perfect competition, we have duopoly (two sellers), oligopoly (a few sellers), and monopolistic competition (a substantial number of sellers but fewer than the number required for perfect competition). We shall return later to the question of whether monopoly is a "good thing" or a "bad thing." For now, we shall merely analyze how price and output are determined in monopolistic situations.

ANSWERS

1. demand . supply . price . price   3. monopoly
2. perfectly competitive

11.4 Suppose the demand schedule for good X is represented by the following data and further suppose that the supplier in the market is a monopolist. If a consumer wishes to purchase some of good X, he must purchase it from that monopolist. Should the _____ decide not to produce any of good X, there will be none available in this market, as he is the only producer. (We assume that X is a good, such as insulin, for which there is no close substitute.)

Table 11.1

DEMAND SCHEDULE

Price per unit	Quantity that would be demanded
$10	0
9	20
8	40
7	60
6	80
5	100
4	120
3	140
2	160
1	180
0	200

11.5 From Table 11.1, we can draw a normally shaped _____ curve. Suppose the profit-maximizing monopolist has access to these data. He will wish to know how many units of good X he should produce per time period or how much he should charge for each unit of good X. Now, it is important to note that, given the market demand schedule, he cannot decide how much to produce (sell) and also what price to charge. For instance, if he decides to produce and sell 140 units per time period, the only price that will clear the market of excess demand or excess supply will be $ _____ per unit. Thus, once he makes either an output or a selling-price decision, the market, if it is to be cleared, will automatically determine the other for him.

11.6 Because the monopolist is a profit-maximizing entrepreneur, we must discover which output and price will yield maximum _____ . For any given level of output, this will be

ANSWERS

4. monopolist
5. demand . 3

6. profit . revenue

170 Imperfect Competition

found by subtracting the total costs of producing from the total _____ received
from selling that level of output.

Table 11.2

DEMAND AND REVENUE SCHEDULE

(1) Price per unit	(2) Quantity that would be demanded	(3) Total revenue	(4) Average revenue	(5) Marginal revenue
10	0	0	—	
9	20	180	9	9
8	40	320	8	7
7	60	420	7	5
6	80	480	6	3
5	100	500	5	1
4	120	480	4	-1
3	140	420	3	-3
2	160	320	2	-5
1	180	180	1	-7
0	200	0	0	-9

11.7 In Table 11.2, we have calculated total, average, and marginal revenue from the data in
Table 11.1. Total revenue is found by multiplying each _____ by the quantity
that would be demanded at that price. Thus, TR = P X Q.

11.8 Average revenue is _____ _____ divided by quantity. In symbols,

$$AR = \frac{TR}{Q}.$$

_____ revenue is the extra revenue from the sale of one additional unit of output.

Thus, _____ revenue is the increase in revenue divided by the increase in output.
That is,

$$MR = \frac{\Delta TR}{\Delta Q}.$$

ANSWERS

7. price   8. total revenue . marginal . marginal

11.9 The data from Table 11.2 have been plotted in Figure 11.1. The average revenue curve is, of course, the same as the demand curve. We saw in perfect competition that the _____ curve facing the firm was also the firm's average revenue curve. In the monopoly case, however, the industry demand curve will be the demand curve faced by the monopolist because the monopolist has the only firm in the industry. Thus, the demand curve facing a monopolistic firm _(will/will not)_ be a horizontal line as was the case in the demand curve facing a competitive firm.

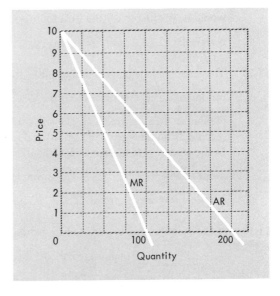

Figure 11.1
Average and marginal revenue

11.10 We can also see from Figure 11.1 that marginal revenue no longer equals _____ revenue as it did in the case of perfectly competitive firms. Thus, for any positive level of output, the monopolist price _(will/will not)_ equal marginal revenue.

11.11 Imagine that the demand (equals _____ _____) curve in Figure 11.1 is for some magic elixir, which comes from only one spring owned by a monopolist. Let us further imagine that the elixir rises from the ground and thus costs nothing to produce. If the monopolist's aim is to maximize profit, how many gallons of elixir should he put up for sale each month? Alternatively, what price per unit should he charge if his aim is profit maximization? $ _____ .

11.12 Profit, of course, equals total _____ minus total _____ . Because, in this example, production cost is zero, the monopolist's profit will be the same as _____ _____ . Thus, profit will be a maximum when _____ _____ is a maximum.

ANSWERS

9. demand . will not
10. average . will not

11. average revenue . 5
12. revenue . cost . total revenue . total revenue

11.13 From Table 11.2, we see that total revenue will be a maximum when the monopolist charges a price of $ _____ per unit and sells _____ units. Total profit will equal total _____ will equal $ _____ .

11.14 In studying competitive firms, we saw that the profit-maximizing level of output was that output at which marginal revenue equaled _____ _____ . As long as a firm could add more to its revenue than to its cost by producing an extra unit of output, it would be profitable for the firm to do so. Thus, firms would produce up to the point at which marginal _____ equaled _____ cost.

11.15 The same holds true for a monopolist. In our example, however, the marginal cost of producing an extra unit of elixir is _____ . If the monopolist wishes to maximize _____ , he will produce elixir up to the point at which the extra revenue from the sale of one additional unit of elixir equals the cost of producing that unit. In the case of zero marginal cost, therefore, the monopolist will produce elixir up to the point at which _____ revenue equals zero. From Figure 11.1, we see that marginal revenue is zero at _____ units of output.

11.16 If the monopolist were to produce beyond this point, marginal revenue would be _____ than marginal cost, because marginal revenue would be negative and marginal cost would be _____ .

11.17 Thus, by producing beyond this point, although the monopolist adds nothing to _____ , he actually detracts from total revenue, and _____ would therefore fall, were he to produce more than 100 units.

11.18 Most monopolists do not have the fortune of owning a magic elixir spring but have to pay positive prices for factors of production. Imagine, therefore, that our monopolist is the sole supplier of an exotic liquor, but that his cost curves are similar in shape to those of the competitive firms we studied earlier. Assume, however, that the demand curve for this liquor is the demand curve in Figure 11.1. This then will be the _____ _____ facing our monopolist.

ANSWERS

13. 5 . 100 . revenue . 500
14. marginal cost . revenue . marginal
15. zero . profit . marginal . 100

16. less . zero
17. cost . profit
18. demand curve

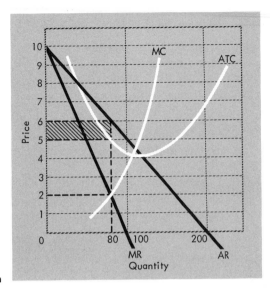

Figure 11.2
Monopolistic equilibrium

11.19 In Figure 11.2, we show the revenue and cost curves. If the monopolist wishes to maximize _____ , he will produce up to that point at which marginal revenue equals marginal _____ . As long as producing an extra unit of output adds more to _____ than it does to _____ , it will be profitable to produce that unit.

11.20 If the production of an additional unit adds more to _____ than it does to _____ , however, it will not be profitable to produce that unit. Thus, in Figure 11.2 the profit-maximizing level of output will be _____ units.

11.21 Once the monopolist has decided what his _____ -maximizing level of output is, the maximum price he can charge will be determined by the demand or _____ _____ curve. In Figure 11.2, we see that this price is $ _____ .

11.22 From the ATC, we see that the average cost of producing one unit of output at this output level is $ _____ , and thus average _____ per unit is $1. Total profit will, therefore, be average profit X the number of units of output, or $1 X _____ . Total profit is represented by the shaded area in Figure 11.2.

ANSWERS

19. profit . cost . revenue . cost
20. cost . revenue . 80

21. profit . average revenue . 6
22. 5 . profit . 80

11.23   Thus, our monopolist will be in equilibrium, producing an output for which marginal revenue _____ marginal cost, and he will be making a _____ over and above a normal return.

11.24   If our monopolist will not allow others to see his secret recipe for his liquor, or if the government has granted him the sole rights of production, other firms will not be able to enter this industry seeking the excess _____ that exists. Does the presence of the monopolist therefore lead to an inefficient allocation of resources in the economy?

11.25   To answer this question, let us see whether the marginal equivalency condition for efficient allocation of resources will be satisfied when there is monopoly. We showed in Chapter 9 that resources would be efficiently allocated only if

$$\frac{MU_A}{MC_A} = \frac{MU_B}{MC_B} = \cdots = \frac{MU_N}{MC_N}$$

If this did not hold true, it _(would/would not)_ be possible to make consumers better off by reallocating resources.

11.26   We derived the condition by showing first how consumers would maximize _____ when

$$\frac{MU_A}{P_A} = \frac{MU_B}{P_B},$$

and so on, and second, how, when goods were being produced as efficiently as possible by competitive firms, the _____ of each good would equal its marginal cost, that is, $P_A = MC_A$, $P_B = MC_B$, and so on. By substituting MC's for price, we arrived at

$$\frac{MU_A}{MC_A} = \frac{MU_B}{MC_B},$$

and so on.

11.27   In the monopoly example we have been discussing, from Figure 11.2 we can see that at the profit-maximizing level of output, marginal cost is $ _____ , and the price is

_____ .

11.28   Thus, price exceeds marginal cost, and the marginal equivalency condition for efficient resources allocation _(does not hold/holds)_ because we cannot substitute MC for price in the equivalency equation.

ANSWERS

23. equals . profit
24. profit
25. would

26. utility . price
27. 2 . 6
28. does not hold

11.29 Imagine that the government, on seeing that the marginal equivalency condition was not met when monopoly existed and consequently that _____ were not being allocated optimally, decided to force each monopoly to produce on the level at which MC equalled demand or average revenue.

11.30 Now consider our monopolist in Figure 11.2. The government order would mean that his output would _____ and the price that would clear the market, that is, where MC = AR, would be _____ than before.

11.31 In fact, output would exceed 100 units and the price would fall below $5. But now price would equal _____ _____ , and economic efficiency would be established because $\dfrac{MU}{MC}$ for the monopolistically produced good would equal $\dfrac{MU}{MC}$ for competitively produced goods.

11.32 More resources would now be employed in the monopolist sectors because output would be larger and consequently _____ _____ would be employed in the competitive sectors. Society would become _(better off/worse off)_ .

11.33 Why, then, does any economy tolerate firms that are not perfectly competitive? Would welfare and efficiency not be increased if a government forced all firms to become perfect competitors? Economics would be a very simple subject if the answers in the previous sentence were always yes. Let us see why the answers are not necessarily yes. If, as a firm expands, the average cost of producing a unit of output decreases, the average total cost curve of that firm will _(rise/fall)_ as output increases. This must mean that the marginal cost of production is _(decreasing/less than average cost)_ .

11.34 There are many reasons why such a situation is possible. Each employee can become highly specialized and very efficient in doing only one job. Assembly line production and the installation of very expensive equipment, such as computers, may be profitable if the output level is sufficiently high. Bulk buying of raw materials may result in a lower per unit cost. For those and for many other reasons, therefore, it is quite conceivable that average _____ of production can be lower, the higher level of output.

11.35 Imagine that Figure 11.3 represents the average total cost curves for a firm for different possible scales of operation. It is quite clear that the minimum average total _____ of production occurs with ATC_4, at an output level of _____ .

ANSWERS

29. resources
30. increase . lower
31. marginal cost
32. fewer resources . better off

33. fall . less than average cost
34. cost
35. cost . q_4

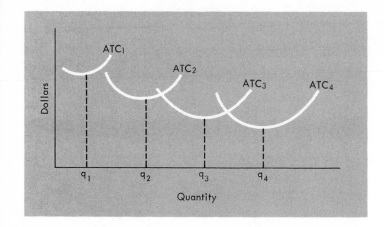

Figure 11.3
Economies of scale

11.36   Let us now superimpose on Figure 11.4 the aggregate demand curve for the commodity whose cost curves appear in the figure. If we insist on this being a competitive industry, we require a large number of firms. In order to have a large number of competitive firms, we cannot allow any firm to produce more than q_1. Thus, all firms would produce q_1 at minimum cost for that output level, which means that all firms would operate the scale of output given by ATC_1. In "equilibrium," aggregate demand would equal aggregate supply.

The equilibrium price would be _____ , and the equilibrium quantity for the

industry would be _____ .

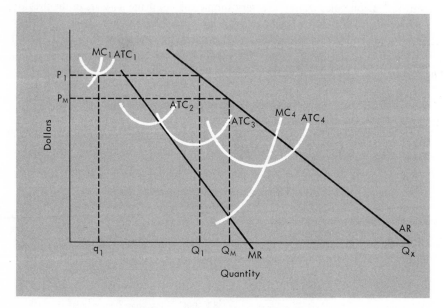

Figure 11.4   Monopoly vs. competition

ANSWERS

36. P_1 . Q_1

11.37 Each firm would be producing at the minimum point of ATC_1, and, important for our efficiency considerations, marginal cost would equal _____ .

11.38 Consider now the monopoly solution if we have only one firm with ATC_4. The monopolist will maximize _____ by producing up to that output at which marginal revenue equals marginal cost. The equilibrium price will be _____ . and the equilibrium output will be _____ .

11.39 Now, the monopolist is certainly not producing that level of output at which MC = P but is producing where MC = _____ . Consequently, P is *(greater/less)* than MC We have just seen, however, that under the marginal equivalency condition of a competitive price system, resources are inefficiently allocated when price does not equal _____ _____ .

11.40 Consider, now, the situation in Figure 11.4, when we insisted on many competitive firms rather than a monopoly. It was certainly true that we had _____ equal to marginal cost, but, in this situation, the "equilibrium" price was _____ , and the equilibrium quantity Q_1. In the monopoly situation, the equilibrium price is _____ , and the equilibrium quantity is _____ . That is, in this example under monopoly, price is lower and quantity greater than in the competitive case.

11.41 Consider this case from the viewpoint of consumers. Under monopoly, compared with competition, consumers can enjoy a _____ quantity at a _____ price. Thus, obviously, in the case where we have decreasing-cost industries, competition will not lead to optimum resource allocation, nor will perfect competition prevail.

11.42 If we begin with many competitive firms, each one will realize that average total _____ can be reduced by expanding the scale of operation. In Figure 11.4 however, we can see that if each firm expanded to a size represented by ATC_4, (and if each produced only Q_M *(less/more)* than output at the minimum point of ATC_4), the aggregate quantity supplied would be in excess of the aggregate quantity demanded, which is _____ at a price of zero.

ANSWERS

37. price
38. profit . P_M . Q_M
39. MR . greater . marginal cost

40. price . P_1 . P_M . Q_M
41. larger . lower
42. cost . less . Q_X

11.43   In this example, only one firm would find it profitable to remain in this industry in the long-run—that firm that would be allowed to be a _____ .

11.44   If you consider the real world, there are many examples of firms that, although not pure monopolists, are certainly far removed from being perfect competitors. The local gas and electricity companies and the telephone company are a few examples. You do not need to be an economist to imagine the inconvenience, inefficiency, and waste of resources that would result if there were thousands of telephone poles and cables side by side on the highways belonging to thousands of competitive telephone companies. The saving of scarce

_____ is obviously large by having only one telephone company.

11.45   It is in society's interest to have large firms in decreasing cost industries. Because such firms, however, will not equate _____ with _____ _____ , there may be a legitimate reason for government to regulate prices in those industries. And the government often does so in industries such as public utilities. The telephone company, for instance, must apply to the Federal Communications Commission (FCC)—an agency of the federal government—for permission to change telephone rates. Also, if the FCC considers the telephone company's profits too high, it can force the telephone company, in the public interest, to charge _(lower/higher)_ prices. Thus, if the government can force such firms to

produce where price equals marginal cost, economic _____ can be achieved and the advantages of economies of scale enjoyed.

11.46   So far, we have considered the extremes in types of firms—the perfectly _____ firm and the _____ firm. In between those extremes lie the majority of the firms we observe daily. They are known as imperfect competitors and to those firms we now turn.

11.47   One of the assumptions of perfect competition is that suppliers in a given industry produce an identical product. Consequently, consumers _(are/are not)_ indifferent as to whose output they consume. Most consumers, for instance, are _____ as to which particular farmer's wheat was used to make today's loaf of bread.

11.48   Another assumption is that the number of suppliers is sufficiently _____ so that no single supplier has an appreciable effect on _____ through changing his rate of output.

ANSWERS

43. monopolist
44. resources
45. price . marginal cost . lower .
    efficiency

46. competitive . monopolistic
47. are . indifferent
48. large . price

11.49 If you stop for a moment and consider the commodities you consume daily, you will realize that relatively few meet these "perfect competition" tests. Do you randomly shop for beer or hamburgers or books, or are you like most people and frequent your favorite or most convenient store? If the answer is yes, you obviously __*(are/are not)*__ indifferent about suppliers, and perfect _____ is not ruling in those markets.

11.50 If you were an automobile producer you might be indifferent about which company's steel you purchased, that is, the steel could be identical. But when you realize that relatively few companies produce the bulk of steel in the United States, you know that the steel industry is not perfectly _____ and that each large company can have a significant effect on the _____ of steel.

11.51 In what way does the presence of imperfectly competitive firms affect efficient resource allocation in our economy? The answer, you might guess, is that similar to monopoly, equilibrium price does not equal _____ _____ in imperfectly competitive industries, and thus our marginal _____ condition for efficient resource allocation is violated.

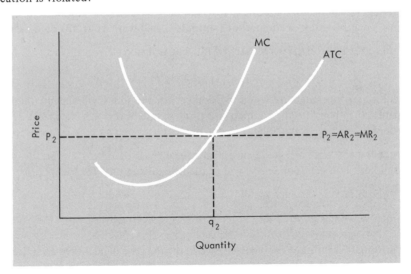

Figure 11.5 Perfectly competitive firm in equilibrium

11.52 Figure 11.5 shows a perfectly competitive firm in equilibrium producing output _____ at a price of P_2. We know the firm has no incentive to change output

ANSWERS

49. are not . competition
50. competitive . price

51. marginal cost . equivalency
52. q_2 . marginal cost . loss

because q_2 is the equilibrium output—marginal revenue equals _____

_____ ; any other output would cause a _(profit/loss)_ .

11.53 The demand curve D facing this firm is a _____ line (at a height equal to

_____ = _____ = _____), and consequently is

completely price _(elastic/inelastic)_ . This means that if the supplier attempted to charge a

price greater than P_2, he would not sell any of his commodity. All his buyers would switch to

a competitor's indistinguishable product at a price of _____ .

11.54 In imperfect competition, the demand for the product of a firm is not completely price

elastic. The more elastic is the demand curve facing a firm, the _(greater/smaller)_ the

response of buyers to a price change. Although the demand curve facing many imperfect

competitors is highly price elastic, that is, a small _____ increase will cause a

relatively large decrease in quantity demanded, it is not completely elastic as is the case under

perfect competition, where a small _____ increase causes the firm's sales to fall to

zero.

11.55 In imperfect competition, therefore, a firm can raise its _____ and although some

consumers may switch to a competitor's output, not all will. Thus, the demand curve facing

this firm _(will/will not)_ be a horizontal line but will slope _____ from left to

right.

11.56 The decision of consumers to switch to a competitor's product will depend upon how close

a substitute they consider the competitor's product and how much cheaper it is. Most

cigarette smokers have some loyalty to one brand, but, given an increase in the price of only

their brand, many smokers would switch to a close _____ . To the extent that

some smokers, however, remained loyal to their brand and paid the higher price, the demand

curve for that brand, although highly _____ , would not be completely so and,

consequently, would slope _____ from left to right.

11.57 If the information in frame 56 is correct, we know that the demand for cigarettes irrespective

of brand is elastic. _(true/false)_ How do you know? _____

_____

_____

ANSWERS

53. horizontal . P_2 . AR_2 . MR_2 .
    elastic . P_2
54. greater . price . price
55. price . will not . downward

56. substitute . elastic . downward
57. false . we were given information on the elasticity
    of demand for one brand, not for all cigarettes

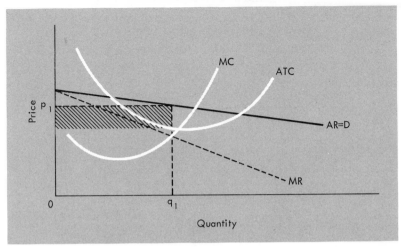

Figure 11.6   Imperfectly competitive firm

11.58   Figure 11.6 represents a typical imperfectly competitive firm. This profit-maximizing firm will produce output _____ at a price P_1 and will make an excess profit (over and above a normal return), represented by the shaded area, that is, average revenue minus average cost at q_1 $\times$ number of units of output 0_{q_1}.

11.59   We know this is an imperfectly competitive firm because _____
_____

11.60   If a situation such as that depicted in Figure 11.6 existed in the short-run, what would happen in the long-run? Other resources' owners would see excess _____ being made in this industry and would divert _____ into it.

11.61   To the extent that some buyers switch to the newcomers' products, the demand curve facing the firm in Figure 11.6 will shift to the _(right/left)_ , that is, one of the _____ determining the position of D will have changed.

11.62   Firms will continue to enter this industry until all excess _____ disappears. Figure 11.7 depicts the long-run equilibrium position.

11.63   How do you know that only normal returns are being earned by resources in Figure 11.7?
_____

ANSWERS

58. 0_{q_1}
59. the demand curve it faces is not horizontal (perfectly elastic)
60. profit . resources

61. left . parameters
62. profit
63. at output q_E, ATC = AR, that is, neither profit nor loss is being made

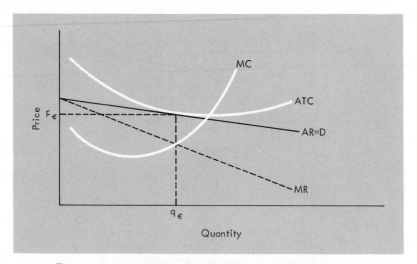

Figure 11.7   Imperfectly competitive firm in long-run equilibrium

11.64   How do you know q_E is the equilibrium output of the firm in Figure 11.7? _____

_____

11.65   Now consider Figure 11.8, in which we have placed a perfectly competitive firm, B, in long-run equilibrium alongside our imperfectly competitive firm A of Figure 11.7:

When firm A is in equilibrium,_____ exceeds MC. In addition, the firm _(is/is not)_ producing at minimum average cost; unused capacity exists in the firm.

11.66   Thus, in comparing A with B, we see that in imperfect competition price is _____

and output is _____ .

11.67   Because price exceeds MC for firm A, the $\dfrac{MU_A}{MC_A}$ _(will/will not)_ equal $\dfrac{MU_B}{MC_B}$, and utility could

therefore be increased by diverting resources towards industry A.

11.68   If, of course, consumers believed that one brand of cigarettes, soup, gasoline, or aspirin were a perfect substitute for another and acted accordingly, and if entry to each industry were free, we could imagine the D curve for firm A tilting until it was a horizontal line, that is, until we

had a _____ _____ firm. Then, MR would equal MC and our

_____ _____ condition would be established.

ANSWERS

64. at output q_E, MR = MC . any price other   66. higher . lower
    than P_E would involve a loss to the firm   67. will not
65. price . is not   68. perfectly competitive . marginal equivalency

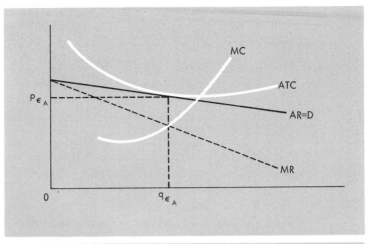

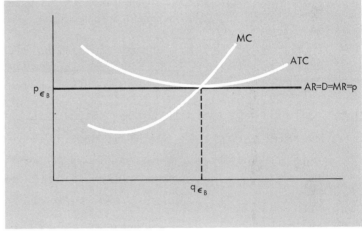

Figure 11.8
Long-run equilibria compared

11.69 When no real product differentiation exists, that is, brand X aspirin at 89 cents per fifty tablets is no different from ordinary aspirin at 15 cents per fifty, advertising might convince consumers that the two products are different. This will cause the average price of aspirin to rise not only because the demand curves for individual brands would become downward

sloping but also because advertising would add to the _____ of production. As a consequence, advertising that serves only to create imaginary product differentiation will

result in _____ being misallocated and welfare being lower than it otherwise could be.

11.70 To the extent that product differentiation is real, that is, soup K is better than soup L, the

manufacturers of soup K have some discretionary power—they can _____ the price and sales will not fall to zero.

ANSWERS

69. cost . resources   70. increase

11.71   Real or imagined product differentiation gives a downward sloping _____ curve, an intersection of MR with _____ at an output less than minimum ATC, an equilibrium price greater than _____ , and a ratio of MU to MC _(greater/less)_ than the corresponding ratio for a perfectly competitive industry.

11.72   As we have shown in the case of monopoly, as long as P ≠ MC, it is always possible to reallocate _____ so that society is better off, that is, so that at least one person is better off and no one is worse off. This means that as long as such a reallocation can take place, society _(is/is not)_ using its resources as efficiently as possible.

11.73   As we move from the perfectly competitive firm to the imperfectly competitive firm and towards the monopolist, we encounter the oligopolistic firm that is relatively large in its industry and that has an appreciable effect on _____ —not as much as the monopolist, but more than the imperfect competitor.

11.74   We could categorize much of our heavy industry in the United States as being oligopolistic (for example, automobiles, steel, aluminum) because a _(small/large)_ number of _(small/large)_ firms produces the bulk of each industry's output.

11.75   Again, the demand curve facing an oligopolist is _____ sloping. Again, a firm will maximize _____ by producing that output at which marginal revenue equals marginal cost. And once again, because price will exceed _____ _____ , the marginal equivalency condition will not hold, though significant economics of scale may exist.

11.76   Matters would become ever worse if oligopolists formally established a cartel or tacitly cooperated in setting prices. In these cases, the oligopolists would achieve the market power of a _(monopolist/competitive firm)_ and the difference between price and marginal cost would _____ .

11.77   In oligopolistic industries, compared with imperfectly competitive industries, entry by other firms is often extremely expensive, and the existence of excess or above-normal _____ may not attract resources into this industry. Or other barriers to entry, such as patents, may exclude potential competitors. In an attempt to lessen the power of oligopolists and monopolists, antitrust laws have been passed, beginning with the Sherman Act in 1890. Those laws are not only aimed at limiting the power of oligopolists but also constitute an attempt to achieve more efficient resource allocation.

ANSWERS

71. demand . MC . MC . greater
72. resources . is not
73. price
74. small . large

75. downward . profit . marginal cost
76. monopolist . increase
77. profit

REVIEW QUESTIONS

11.1   Yoyos are produced by many competing firms. At present levels of production, costs per yoyo would increase if output increased. If a profit maximizing monopolist were to buy out all the present producers, how would the quantity produced compare with output under competitive conditions?

a. The quantity produced by the monopolist would be lower.
b. The quantity produced by the monopolist would be the same.
c. The quantity produced by the monopolist would be higher.

d. The relative quantity that would be produced by the monopolist cannot be determined from the available information.

By buying out all competitive firms, the monopolist would be able to set the price that would yield him maximum profit without fear of any competitor setting a lower price to attract customers and eventually forcing him to decrease his price or lose all his customers. If the monopolist were to continue to produce at the competitively determined quantity of output, he would find that the revenue obtained from the last unit sold would be less than its cost of production. Consequently, in order to maximize profit, the monopolist would reduce output and set a higher price. The correct response is a.

11.2   In an industry in which there are economies of large-scale production, a monopolist is the only firm. The government legislates that the monopoly be broken up and that a number of equal-sized firms replace it. In the new situation:

a. price will be higher, industry output will be higher.
b. price will be lower, industry output will be higher.

c. price will be lower, industry output will be lower.
d. insufficient information exists to determine whether price or quantity will be higher or lower.

Because economies of scale exist, the larger the firm, the lower per unit cost of output. Thus, at the limit when only one firm is operating, that is, the monopoly situation, per unit costs will be lower than they would be if several firms were operating. Such cost information, however, does not indicate whether the selling price of output will be higher or lower. The profit maximizing monopolist would produce that output where marginal revenue equaled marginal cost, and although the resulting equilibrium price would yield monopoly profit, the price might still be lower, because of scale economies, than the competitive price. Thus, because two factors, economies of scale and monopoly power, set up forces that pull in opposing directions, insufficient information exists to determine the net changes in price and quantity when the monopoly is broken up. The correct response is d.

11.3   If, for a manufactured commodity, a monopolist were allowed to charge that price that maximized profit, which of the following statements would be correct?

1. The revenue received from the last unit produced would equal the cost of producing that unit.
2. The total revenue (price X quantity) for the monopolist would be maximum.

a. 1 only   c. both 1 and 2
b. 2 only   d. neither 1 nor 2

The monopolist will produce up to the point at which MR = MC. This will be the profit-maximizing level of output. However, at the level of output, price will exceed both marginal revenue and marginal cost. The correct response is b.

11.4 The government has decided to allow two major automobile companies to merge into one. It rejected the advice of a panel of economists who argued that the government should prohibit the merger and apply antitrust laws to restore rigorous competition.

Which of the following arguments would suggest that the government's decision would lead to greater economic efficiency than would the economists' proposal?

a. Larger firms can produce automobiles   c. Prices in competitive markets are determined
   at lower cost.   by the forces of supply and demand.
b. Competitive firms would attempt to   d. If there were many firms, too many different
   maximize profits.   models of automobiles would be produced.

If economies of scale existed in the automobile industry, it would mean that marginal cost was falling as output increased within the firm. To take advantage, therefore, of such scale economies, the merger would be a good thing. Of course, you might want government regulation over price as in the regulated industries to stop the new automobile company taking advantage of its nonmonopolistic position. The correct response is a.

Case 11

U.S. vs. VON'S GROCERIES

Over the years, Congress has passed several anti-trust laws to preserve competition and outlaw at least certain monopolistic practices. The Celler-Kefauver Antimerger Act of 1950 has been the basis for most of the federal government's anti-trust suits in recent years.

The Von's Groceries case, excerpts from which follow, illustrates some of the problems faced by courts in applying antitrust legislation. The excerpts first summarize the majority decision against the Von's merger, and then the minority dissent. In your judgment, which argument is correct? What are the main issues in this case?

THE MAJORITY DECISION

On March 25, 1960, the United States brought this action charging that the acquisition by Von's

Grocery Company of its direct competitor Shopping Bag Food Stores, both large retail grocery companies in Los Angeles, California, violated #7 of the Clayton Act which, as amended in 1950 by the Celler-Kefauver Anti-Merger Bill, provides . . .

"No corporation engaged in commerce . . . shall acquire the whole or any part of the assets of another corporation engaged also in commerce, where in any line of commerce in any section of the country the effect of such acquisition may be substantially to lessen competition, or to tend to create a monopoly."

The market involved here is the retail grocery market in the Los Angeles area. In 1958 Von's retail sales ranked third in the area and Shopping Bag's ranked sixth. In 1960 their sales together were 7.5 percent of the total two and one half billion dollars of retail groceries sold in the Los

Angeles market each year. For many years before the merger both companies had enjoyed great success as rapidly growing companies. From 1948 to 1958 the number of Von's stores in the Los Angeles area practically doubled from 14 to 27, while at the same time the number of Shopping Bag's stores jumped from 15 to 34. During that same decade, Von's sales increased fourfold and its share of the market almost doubled while Shopping Bag's sales multiplied seven times and its share of the market tripled. The merger of these two highly successful, expanding and aggressive competitors created the second largest grocery chain in Los Angeles with sales of almost $172,488,000 annually.

In addition the findings of the District Court show that the number of owners operating a single store in the Los Angeles retail grocery market decreased from 5,365 in 1950 to 3,818 in 1961. By 1963, three years after the merger, the number of single-store owners had dropped still further to 3,590. During roughly the same period from 1953 to 1962 the number of chains with two or more grocery stores increased from 96 to 150. While the grocery business was being concentrated into the hands of fewer and fewer owners, the small companies were continually being absorbed by the larger firms through mergers. According to an exhibit prepared by one of the Government's expert witnesses, in the period from 1949 to 1958 nine of the top 20 chains acquired 126 stores from their smaller competitors . . . . These facts alone are enough to cause us to conclude contrary to the District Court that the Von's Shopping Bag merger did violate #7 . . . . .

From this country's beginning there has been an abiding and widespread fear of the evils which flow from monopoly—that is the concentration of economic power in the hands of the few. On the basis of this fear, in 1890, when many of the Nation's industries were already concentrated into what Congress deemed too few hands, it passed the Sherman Act in an attempt to prevent further concentration and to preserve competition among a large number of sellers. Several years later in 1897 this Court emphasized this policy of the Sherman Act by calling attention to the tendency of powerful business combinations to restrain competition "by driving out of business the small dealers and worthy men whose lives have been spent therein, and who might be unable to readjust themselves in their altered surroundings." United States v. Trans-Missouri Freight Assn., 166 U.S. 290, 323.

Like the Sherman Act in 1890 and the Clayton Act in 1914, the basic purpose of the 1950 Celler-Kefauver Bill was to prevent economic concentration in the American economy by keeping a large number of small competitors in business. In stating the purpose of the bill, both of its sponsors, Representative Celler and Senator Kefauver, emphasized their fear, widely shared by other members of Congress, that this concentration was rapidly driving the small businessman out of the market. The period from 1940 to 1947, which was at the center of attention throughout the hearings and debates on the Celler-Kefauver bill, had been characterized by a series of mergers between large corporations and their smaller competitors resulting in the steady erosion of the small independent business in our economy. As we said in Brown Shoe Co. v. United States, 370 U.S. 294, 315, "The dominant theme pervading congressional consideration of the 1950 amendments was a fear of what was considered to be a rising tide of economic concentration in the American economy." By using terms in #7 which look not merely to the actual present effect of a merger but instead to its effect upon future competition, Congress sought to preserve competition among many small businesses by arresting a trend toward concentration in its incipiency before that trend developed to the point that a market was left in the grip of a few big companies. Thus, where concentration is gaining momentum in a market, we must be alert to carry out Congress' intent to protect competition against ever-increasing concentration through mergers.

The facts of this case present exactly the threatening trend toward concentration which Congress wanted to halt. The number of small grocery companies in the Los Angeles retail grocery market had been declining rapidly before the merger and continued to decline rapidly afterwards. This rapid decline in the number of grocery store owners moved hand in hand with a large number of significant absorptions of the small companies by the larger ones. In the midst of this steadfast trend toward concentration, Von's and Shopping Bag, two of the most successful and largest companies in the area, jointly owning 66 grocery stores merged to become the second largest chain in Los Angeles.

Appellee's primary argument is that the merger between Von's and Shopping Bag is not prohibited by #7 because the Los Angeles grocery market was competitive before the merger, has been since, and may continue to be in the future. Even so, #7 "requires not merely an appraisal of the immediate impact of the merger upon competition, but a prediction of its impact upon competitive conditions in the future; this is what is meant when it is said that the amended #7 was intended to arrest anti-competitive tendencies in their 'incipiency.' " (United States v. Philadelphia Nat. Bank, 374 U.S., p. 362.) It is enough for us that Congress feared that a market marked at the same time by both a continuous decline in the number of small businesses and a large number of mergers would, slowly but inevitably gravitate from a market of many small competitors to one dominated by one or a few giants, and competition would thereby be destroyed . . .

THE MINORITY DISSENT

First, the standards of #7 require that every corporate acquisition be judged in the light of the contemporary economic context of its industry. Second, the purpose of #7 is to protect competition, not to protect competitors, and every #7 case must be decided in the light of that clear statutory purpose. Today the Court turns its back on these two basic principles and on all the decisions that have followed them.

The court makes no effort to appraise the competitive effects of this acquisition in terms of the contemporary economy of the retail food industry in the Los Angeles area. Instead, through a simple exercise in sums, it finds that the number of individual competitors in the market has decreased over the years, and, apparently on the theory that the degree of competition is invariably proportional to the number of competitors, it holds that this historic reduction in the number of competing units is enough under #7 to invalidate a merger within the market, with no need to examine the economic concentration of the market, the level of competition in the market, or the potential adverse effect of the merger on that competition. This startling per se rule is contrary not only to our previous decisions, but contrary to the language of #7, contrary to the legislative history of the 1950 amendment, and contrary to economic reality.

The concept of arresting restraints of trade in their "incipiency" was not an innovation of the 1950 amendment. The notion of incipiency was part of the report on the original Clayton Act by the Senate Committee on the Judiciary in 1914, and it was reiterated in the Senate report in 1950. That notion was not left undefined. The legislative history leaves no doubt that the applicable standard for measuring the substantiality of the effect of a merger on competition was that of a "reasonable probability" of lessening competition." The standard was thus more stringent than that of a "mere possibility" on the one hand and more lenient than that of a "certainty" on the other." I cannot agree that the retail grocery business in Los Angeles is in an incipient or any other stage of a trend toward a lessening of competition, or that the effective level of concentration in the industry has increased. Moreover, there is no indication that the present merger, or the trend in this industry as a whole, augurs any danger whatsoever for the small businessman. The Court has substituted bare conjecture for the statutory standard of a reasonable probability that competition may be lessened.

I believe that even the most superficial analysis of the record makes plain the fallacy of the Court's syllogism that competition is necessarily reduced when the bare number of competitors has declined. In any meaningful sense, the structure of the Los Angeles grocery market remains unthreatened by concentration. Local competition is vigorous to a fault, not only among chain stores themselves but also between chain stores and single-store operators. The continuing population explosion of the Los Angeles area, which has outrun the expansion plans of even the largest chains, offers a surfeit of business opportunity for stores of all sizes. Affiliated with cooperatives that give the smallest store the buying strength of its largest competitor, new stores have taken full advantage of the remarkable ease of entry into the market. And, most important of all, the record simply cries out that the numerical decline in the number of single-store owners is the result of transcending social and technological changes that positively preclude the inference that competition has suffered because of the attrition of competitors.

Section 7 was never intended by Congress for use by the Court as a charter to roll back the supermarket revolution. Yet the Court's opinion is hardly more than a requiem for the so-called "Mom and Pop" grocery stores—the bakery and butcher shops, the vegetable and fish markets—that are now economically and technologically obsolete in many parts of the country. No action by this Court can resurrect the old single-line Los Angeles food stores that have been run over by the automobile or obliterated by the freeway. The transformation of American society since the Second World War has not completely shelved these specialty stores, but it has relegated them to a much less central role in our food economy. Today's dominant enterprise in food retailing is the supermarket. Accessible to the housewife's automobile from a wide radius, it houses under a single roof the entire food requirements of the family. Only through the sort of reactionary philosophy that this Court long ago rejected in the Due Process Clause area can the Court read into the legislative history of #7 its attempt to make the automobile stand still, to mold the food economy of today into the market pattern of another era.

The District Court found that the Von's stores were located in the southern and western portions of the Los Angeles metropolitan area, and that the Shopping Bag stores were located in the northern and eastern portions. In each of the areas in which Von's and Shopping Bag stores competed directly, there were also at least six other chain stores and several smaller stores competing for the patronage of customers. On the basis of a "housewife's 10-minute driving time" test conducted for the Justice Department by a government witness, it was shown that slightly more than half of the Von's and Shopping Bag stores were not in a position to compete at all with one another in the market. Even among those stores which competed at least partially with one another, the overlap in sales represented only approximately 25% of the combined sales of the two chains in the overall Los Angeles area. The present merger was thus three parts market-extension and only one part horizontal, but the Court nowhere recognizes this market-extension aspect that exists within the local market itself. The actual market share foreclosed by the elimination of Shopping Bag as an independent competitor was thus slightly less than 1% of the total grocery store sales in the area . . .

Moreover, it is clear that there are no substantial barriers to market entry. The record contains references to numerous highly successful instances of entry with modest initial investments. Many of the stores opened by new entrants were obtained through the disposition of unwanted outlets by chains; frequently the new competitors were themselves chain-store executives who had resigned to enter the

market on their own. Enhancing free access to the market is the absence of any such restrictive factors as patented technology, trade secrets, or substantial product differentiation.

Numerous other factors attest to the pugnacious level of grocery competition in Los Angeles, all of them silently ignored by the Court in its emphasis solely on the declining number of single-store competitors in the market. 3,500 single-store firms is a lot of grocery stores. The large number of separate competitors and the frequent price battles between them belie any suggestion that price competition in the area is even remotely threatened by a descent to the sort of consciously interdependent pricing that is characteristic of a market turning the corner toward oligopoly. The birth of dynamic new competitive forces—discount food houses and food departments in department stores, bantams and superettes, deli-liquor stores and drive-in dairies—promises unremitting competition in the future. In the more than four years following the merger, the District Court found not a shred of evidence that competition had been in any way impaired by the merger. Industry witnesses testified overwhelmingly to the same effect. By any realistic criterion, retail food competition in Los Angeles is today more intense than ever.

The emotional impact of a merger between the third and sixth largest competitors in a given market, however fragmented, is understandable, but that impact cannot substitute for the analysis of the effect of the merger on competition that Congress required by the 1950 amendment. Nothing in the present record indicates that there is more than an ephemeral possibility that the effect of this merger may be substantially to lessen competition. Section 7 clearly takes "reasonable probability" as its standard. That standard has not been met here . . .

SUGGESTIONS FOR ANALYSIS

The preceding chapters establish a strong presumption that market competition leads to an efficient allocation of society's scarce economic resources. In the absence of competition, businesses may keep prices above marginal cost and restrict output to maximize their profits. But just how many firms are needed to assure the main benefits of competition is often a complex practical problem. And what shall we do if larger firms (say, supermarkets) are more efficient than small ones? Shall we permit a smaller number of larger firms and hope that competition will still be enough to keep prices down and stimulate progress? Or shall we insist on many small firms even though we know that lower average unit costs are available with larger firms using modern technology and large-scale buying? And Von's raises still another issue: do we want smallness in business for its own sake, efficiency notwithstanding?

Von's illustrates that there is no simple answer to these questions. Ask yourself and answer these questions to focus up your thinking:

1. What do we want competition to accomplish for us? (Chapter 10 provides a direct foundation for this answer.)

2. How many firms does it take (for example, in the Los Angeles grocery market) to assure these benefits? (Suppose you are a housewife—what is your answer? Obviously, there is no one "right" answer to this question, but you should be able to see the central issues. For example, with only two or three grocers in an isolated shopping area, how actively would you expect them to compete on price and quality? What if other shopping centers were located only a few minutes drive away?)

3. If modern technology (for example, supermarket buying and selling methods) provide substantial cost savings, how shall we balance these off against the potentially greater competition of more small but higher-cost stores? (Remember question 1 above. Clearly, little stores can be so small as to be unable to sell at as low a price as the supermarkets, but many little stores assure that no one can dominate the business. In steel production, for example, it is clear that insisting on hundreds of basic steel producers would make each so small that costs per ton of steel produced would be very high, and consumers would be worse off in spite of assured active competition. The minority decision suggests that the same may be true of the grocery business in Los Angeles. The majority says, maintain lots of competitors no matter if the costs of small firms are higher.)

4. Beyond economics, should we prefer smallness for its own sake, regardless of the economic efficiency issues? (The majority opinion says, yes; the minority says that can drive us to silly results—insisting on protecting small competitors rather than assuring the low costs and prices that are the main objectives of competition. How would you have ruled in the Von's case?)

12

Income Distribution

12.1 In earlier chapters, we learned the meaning of economic efficiency and the conditions under which economic efficiency would be achieved in an economy. The more efficiently a society's resources are used, the _____ total output and total income.

12.2 In determining how well off individuals or families are in a society, however, we must consider not only how large total _____ and total _____ are but also how they are distributed. In this chapter, we shall analyze the forces determining income distribution and the means adopted by governments for changing the market-determined income distribution to a more desirable one.

12.3 A nation's total annual income divided by its population yields that nation's annual *per capita income.* As will be discussed in Chapter 13, per capita income is a rough measure of how well off, on the average, an individual is. This is only an *average* measure, however, and _(takes/does not take)_ into account how total income is distributed within a nation.

12.4 By looking at per capita income figures by country, despite lack of detail on distribution, you would see that some individuals have a relatively high income and others a very low income. Average per capita income in the United States, for example, is almost $5,000, whereas in India it is approximately $100. That is, accepting those figures, the average American has _____ times more income than the average Indian. Such figures do not say that every American citizen has an annual income of $5,000 and every Indian an annual income of $100. _(true/false)_

ANSWERS

1. larger
2. output . income (either order)
3. does not take
4. 50 . true

12.5   Some United States citizens, admittedly only a few, have annual incomes in excess of $1 million, while others have annual incomes of less than $200. Thus, the economic system of the United States _(does/does not)_ produce equal incomes for all; in fact, without some redistribution of income on the part of the government, some people would not have sufficient income to subsist.

12.6   Table 12.1 contains income distributions for white, nonwhite, and all families for different years. The income levels are given in 1969 prices to adjust for changes in the price level and to reflect changes in real income; such adjustments are discussed in Chapter 13.

Table 12.1

INCOME DISTRIBUTION IN THE UNITED STATES (PERCENTAGE OF FAMILIES)

Income Level (1969 Prices)	1950			1960			1969		
	White	Nonwhite	All	White	Nonwhite	All	White	Nonwhite	All
Under $3,000	21.6	52.4	28.9	14.3	38.4	19.5	8.1	24.0	9.3
$3,000 - $4,999	24.4	29.2	29.1	14.3	22.3	18.0	9.6	19.3	10.8
$5,000 - $6,999	24.1	11.6	20.6	18.8	15.7	21.6	11.8	17.0	12.3
$7,000 - $9,999	17.7	4.0	13.6	25.6	14.4	22.5	21.9	19.5	12.7
$10,000 - $14,999	12.1	2.6	7.9	18.3	6.9	13.3	28.0	15.5	26.7
$15,000 and over				8.5	2.2	5.3	20.6	8.3	19.2

What can be seen from Table 12.1 is that for both whites and nonwhites the percentage of families in the lower income brackets has _____ over time and the percentages of familes and individuals in the upper income brackets has _____ over time. In other words, a larger proportion of U.S. families enjoyed higher incomes in 1969 compared to 1950 or 1960, and a _____ proportion had lower incomes.

12.7   The proportion of nonwhites in lower income brackets, however, has remained substantially higher than the proportion of whites. The _(reverse/same)_ holds true for the upper income brackets.

12.8   Today, there are about 10 million families in the United States who are below what is often called a poverty level income—around $4,000 per annum for family of four people. Does this imply that economic efficiency is not being achieved in the United States? _(yes/no)_

ANSWERS

5. does not

6. decreased . increased . smaller

7. reverse

8. no

12.9 Although an economic system may yield an uneven distribution of income and also be economically efficient, one could imagine the reverse—an economy in which all incomes were equal but in which resources are not _____ allocated.

12.10 What determines an individual's income and consequently his claim on the economy's output? As you will recall from Chapter 9, just as the equilibrium price of a good is determined by the forces of _____ and _____ , so is the equilibrium price of a factor of production.

12.11 The supplies of Jim Plunketts, Mohammed Alis, and Elizabeth Taylors and the demands for their services intersect at relatively _____ prices compared to the intersection of the demands for and supplies of babysitters, street cleaners, and hospital attendants.

12.12 Why does the glamorous movie star earn more than your hard working college professor? It is all a matter of _____ and _____ determining price.

12.13 The demands for goods and services will determine the demands for the scarce factors or resources required to produce them. These demands, taken with the supplies of the various resources, will determine their _____ .

12.14 Thus, the more of any scarce resources you own, the _____ your income. If you own one of football's few good throwing arms or possess a deadly knockout punch or a unique singing voice, you will, other things equal, command a higher price for your particular resources than your less gifted neighbor.

12.15 You might, of course, also acquire a scarce, highly-priced resource through training and/or education. Most doctors, dentists, and lawyers earn high incomes because the _____ for their services will equal the supply only at a high price.

12.16 Just as nature bequeathed Willie Mays with fine baseball skills that put him into a very _____ income bracket, so some families bequeath their children with property or part ownership of businesses, both of which are _____ resources that earn income for their owners.

12.17 In Chapter 5, when we discussed productivity and costs, we analyzed how many units of a factor input a firm would hire. Figure 12.1 summarizes the analysis using engineers as an example.

ANSWERS

9. efficiently	14. higher
10. demand . supply (either order)	15. demands
11. high	16. high . scarce
12. demand . supply (either order)	17. W . demanded . supplied
13. prices	

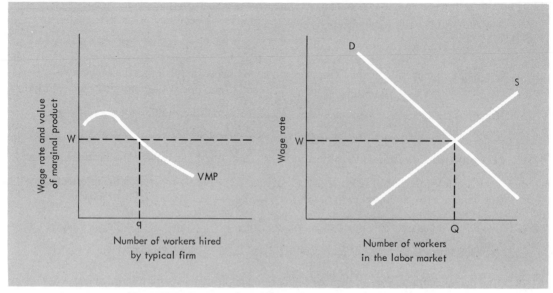

Figure 12.1   Market and firm demand for and supply of engineers

In the factor market for engineers, the equilibrium wage rate is $ _____ , and at that price for labor the quantity _____ equals the quantity _____ .

12.18   For the firm, we have held constant all other factor inputs and drawn the marginal value product curve for engineers. This curve tells by how much the value of _____ will increase if one additional engineer is hired.

12.19   The firm is a price taker and sees that the going price for an engineer is $ _____ . How many engineers will the firm hire? _____

12.20   The firm will not hire more than oq because doing so would add more to cost than it would to _____ ; that is, for each engineer hired beyond oq, the cost, $ _____ , exceeds the _____ _____ .

12.21   If, in the market for engineers, the supply curve shifts to the right and the demand curve remains at D, the equilibrium _____ will fall and the equilibrium output will _____ .

ANSWERS

18. output
19. W . oq

20. revenue . W . marginal product
21. price . increase

12.22 At the lower price, the firm will hire _(more/less)_ than oq, but the return to each engineer (that is, the wage rate) will be _____ than W.

12.23 Thus, in the free enterprise system, the forces of _____ and _____ will determine the returns to resource owners and consequently will determine the distribution of _____ .

12.24 What will happen in such a system if an individual possesses no talents or skills that are marketable? His income will be _____ .

12.25 Most individuals who earn zero or very low incomes do so because their potential contribution to a firm, that is, the value of their _____ _____ , is extremely low.

12.26 If an individual's marginal product for a week to some firm is $20, that is, he increases the value of _____ by $20 if hired, the profit-maximizing firm will not pay him more than $ _____ .

12.27 At the other extreme, if Jim Plunkett, by joining any football team, could raise its revenues by $500,000 in a season, and if competition were allowed to prevail in the National Football League, it would be worthwhile for a club to pay him up to $500,000, the value of his

_____ _____ .

12.28 Thus, although it is stated that all men are born equal, they are _(certainly/certainly not)_ born equal with regard to income potential.

12.29 Those born with superior intellects, unique sporting or entertaining abilities, wealthy parents, or a great capacity for hard work are, other things equal, likely to finish up at the upper end of the _____ distribution. Those born with low intelligence, in ghettos, denied good schooling, or with no parental encouragement and no inherited wealth are, with some exceptions, likely to end up at the _____ end of the income distribution.

12.30 The competitive free enterprise system rewards individuals according to their _(needs/ability to produce)_ , not according to their _(needs/ability to produce)_ .

ANSWERS

22. more . less
23. demand . supply . income
24. zero
25. marginal products
26. output . 20

27. marginal product
28. certainly not
29. income . lower
30. ability to produce . needs

12.31 Should we have such an economic system? The answer to such a question requires value judgments and involves ethics and morals. It *(can/cannot)* be answered by economic analysis. What economic analysis can do, however, is explain what distributions of income are likely to prevail under different economic systems, without saying which distributions are desirable or undesirable.

12.32 Typically, people in the upper end of the income distribution favor the system, while many at the lower end do not. Part of the reason that this is so is that with a given amount of material income or output, redistributing income in favor of the poorer people must mean

_____ income for those at the upper end of the distribution.

12.33 Although few of the high-income recipients would vote for an equal distribution of income, many favor some type of redistribution so that no family need live below a poverty line. Any

such redistribution, of course, means taking from the "rich" and giving to the _____ . That is, with fixed national income, to make some group better off, some other group is going

to be made _____ _____ .

12.34 Society has long recognized the problem of poverty or unequal income distribution, and

many welfare programs that are designed to make the distribution of _____ more equitable exist here and in other countries.

12.35 Food stamp programs, aid to dependent children, welfare payments, and medicare are programs under which people essentially receive income or payments in excess of their

economic contribution to society, that is, in excess of the value of their _____

_____ .

12.36 The Federal and local governments supply many public goods, such as national defense, police and fire protection, education, and so on. Although all families enjoy to a greater or

lesser degree those _____ goods, not all families contribute an equal share of the cost. Of course, the more resources are used by the public sector (government), the

_____ are available for use in the private sector. The more such goods are paid for by the higher income families, however, the *(less/more)* unevenly incomes will be distributed.

12.37 The federal income tax structure in the United States is progressive. This means that higher

income families, other things equal, pay a higher proportion of their _____ in taxes

ANSWERS

31. cannot
32. less
33. poor . worse off
34. income

35. marginal products
36. public . fewer . less
37. incomes . more

than do lower income families. Were all incomes taxed by the same proportion, for example 20 percent, the resulting distribution of after-tax income would be __*(more/less)*__ unequal than the progressive system's yield.

12.38   A system under which each family paid the same dollar amount of tax (not the same percentage) would lead to an even __*(more/less)*__ unequal distribution of after-tax income.

12.39   Unfortunately, for the lower income groups in our society, not all taxes are _____ , as is the federal income tax; some are the opposite: regressive.

12.40   Consider, for example, a 5 percent sales tax on a commodity. Independent of your income, you must pay a 5 percent tax for buying the item. If both a high-income and low-income individual spends $1 on the commodity, each is paying only _____ cents in tax, but this is a _____ proportion of the poor man's income than the rich man's.

12.41   In fact, if all taxes in the U.S. were taken into account, it would be found that some of the lower income groups actually pay a higher proportion of their income in taxes than do middle and some upper income groups. That is, in some ranges, we have a _____ tax system.

12.42   Many proposals for achieving a more equitable income distribution have been suggested. They range from a complete reform of the tax structure to the negative income tax discussed in the case later in this chapter. What is clear in all redistribution schemes of a fixed amount of national income is that to make any one income group better off, some other income group(s) must become _____ _____ .

12.43   Up to now, we have assumed that equilibrium is attained in all markets, including the labor market. But, as you know from reading the newspapers, unemployment is a frequent problem in the United States. This means that __*(all/not all)*__ workers can always find jobs.

12.44   The type of labor that often bears the brunt of unemployment is the least-skilled and lowest-income earning group. Thus, one way to promote a more even distribution of _____ is to pursue policies designed to keep the economy employing all its scarce productive _____ , that is, at full employment.

12.45   By also pursuing policies that retrain unemployed workers for better jobs and by providing better education and training for deprived children, we are implicitly raising skill levels in the

ANSWERS

38. more
39. progressive
40. 5 . higher
41. regressive

42. worse off
43. not all
44. income . resources
45. products . higher . less

labor force. Higher skills, that is, higher marginal _____ , are associated with
(higher/lower) wages. To the extent that the poor benefit disproportionately from such
programs, the distribution of income will become _(more/less)_ unequal.

12.46 Not all income is payment for labor services. Just as labor earns a return in its market, so do

the owners of nonlabor input earn returns according to the value of the _____

_____ of those inputs. For example, the individual who owns and leases
property earns a rent that reflects the marginal contribution of that real estate to production.

12.47 In 1971, total income payments to factors of production was $794 billion, of which three-
quarters was labor income. The remaining one-quarter took the form of rents, interest,
dividends, and proprietor's income. Most of this nonlabor income is distributed to families
who are in upper income brackets. Consequently, the distribution of income is made
(more/less) uneven when we add nonlabor income to labor income.

12.48 One reason the poor are poor is that the value of the _____ _____
of their labor is _(high/low)_ . Another reason is that they own few nonhuman resources.

12.49 Throughout modern industrial history, disagreement over what is a fair division of income
between wages and profits payments has been the source of much debate and has had a
profound influence on the development of economic institutions. As you might expect,

workers have typically felt that _(wage/profit)_ income should be higher and _____
income lower. Have you ever heard of workers striking for lower wages?

12.50 In an attempt to redress what workers have felt was _(a fair/an unfair)_ division of returns to
factors of production, unions have been formed to strengthen the power of labor in the
market place. By representing all workers in a market, a union may effectively eliminate
competition among workers for jobs and force employers to deal with union leaders
(representing workers collectively) rather than with workers individually. Thus, one goal of
the union may be to provide workers with _(monopoly/competitive)_ power in the market
for labor.

12.51 If we imagine successful unionization in what previously had been a competitive labor
market (with competition among employers as well as among workers), and if we further
suppose that the union negotiates a wage rate above the competitive equilibrium wage rate,

then profit-maximizing employers will respond by equating the value of the _____

_____ of labor with the new wage rate. Because for the typical firm there are
diminishing returns to any given factor input (that is, there is a downward-sloping marginal
product curve for labor), employers will hire _(more/fewer)_ workers than before.

ANSWERS

46. marginal products
47. more
48. marginal product . low

49. wage . profit
50. an unfair . monopoly
51. marginal product . fewer

12.52 Note that the establishment by unions of a higher-than-equilibrium wage rate will have an effect that is similar to that of an imposition by government of a higher-than-equilibrium minimum wage rate, as was discussed in Case 5. Those workers who remain employed will become _(better/worse)_ off, while those who are laid off will become _____ off.

12.53 In certain situations, however, it is possible for unionization to lead to a higher wage rate and no decrease in unemployment. Those situations occur where there is no effective competition for labor among employers. Lack of competition among buyers is called *monopsony*. This is the counterpart of a lack of competition among sellers, which is called _____ . In these situations, by establishing _____ power for workers, unions can offset the _____ power of employers.

12.54 An example of monopsony power occurs in the "company town" where one firm provides the bulk of employment opportunities. If such a firm were to try to hire more labor, it would normally have to increase the wage rate to attract workers from other towns, out of retirement, off the farm, and so on. In other words, it does not face the completely _(elastic/inelastic)_ supply curve of labor facing the competitive firm. The supply curve slopes _____ from left to right.

12.55 The cost to the firm of hiring an additional worker, that is, the _____ cost of hiring labor, would equal the higher wage necessary to attract the new worker plus the increase in wages the firm would have to pay all workers currently employed. (The increase for existing workers would result because the employer would be unable to pay two different wage rates for equal work.) Thus, the marginal cost of hiring labor to the firm is _(greater/less)_ than the wage rate.

12.56 The profit-maximizing monopsonistic firm will hire labor up to the point at which the benefit to the firm of hiring one more worker (that is, the value of the _____ _____ of labor) is equal to the cost to the firm of hiring that worker (that is, the _____ _____ of hiring labor). Consequently, the monopsonistic firm will not hire labor up to the point at which the value of the marginal product is equal to the wage rate. (Remember, the marginal cost of hiring labor for the monopsonist is greater than the wage rate.) The wage rate will be _(less/greater)_ than the value of the marginal product of labor. This is what economists mean by *exploitation* of labor. As we shall see in Chapter 23, this definition of *exploitation* differs from the Marxian definition.

ANSWERS

52. better . worse
53. monopoly . monopoly . monopsony
54. elastic . upward

55. marginal . greater
56. marginal product . marginal cost . less

12.57   When dealing with monopsonist employers, by successfully negotiating a fixed wage rate that is higher than the initial wage rate, a union can actually reduce the marginal cost of hiring labor. At the new fixed wage, the firm can hire an additional worker at the negotiated rate and _(will/will not)_ have to pay existing workers higher wages whenever an additional worker is hired. Thus, even though the wage rate is higher, the employer will hire _(more/fewer)_ , because the marginal cost of hiring labor is lower.

12.58   In monopsony situations, unionization and collective bargaining shift the supply curve of labor facing the firm so that it becomes a horizontal line instead of an upward sloping line. In other words, the cost to the firm of hiring an additional worker _(rises above/remains constant at)_ the negotiated wage up to the point where there are no more people willing to work at that wage.

12.59   Much of the debate over the effectiveness and desirability of unionization centers on the extent to which they decrease employment opportunities by artificially restricting the supply of labor to firms, or alternatively make all workers better off by eliminating exploitation of labor. Put another way, the issue is whether unions create _____ power for workers or offset _____ power of employers.

REVIEW QUESTIONS

12.1   Is the following statement correct or incorrect and why?

"Economic analysis has shown that to increase economic welfare any policy that would increase economic efficiency should always be undertaken."

a. Correct, because an improved allocation of resources *will* increase every person's real income.

b. Correct, because an improved allocation of resources *can* increase every person's real income.

c. Incorrect, because an improved allocation of resources *can* increase every person's real income, but *may* reduce some person's income.

d. Incorrect, because an improved allocation of resources *cannot* increase every person's real income.

An increase in economic efficiency, for example, producing more goods than before from the same resources, means it is possible to make some people better off without making anyone worse off. However, an increase in economic efficiency does not guarantee that some people will not suffer. Thus, while improved resource allocation can increase every person's real income, the actual reallocation of resources, for example, introducing cheaper production methods in agriculture and reducing labor requirements, may make some people worse off. To conclude that any increase in efficiency should *always* be undertaken requires a value

ANSWERS

57. will not . more
58. remains constant at

59. monopoly . monopsony

judgment regarding the distribution of income. Consequently, it is incorrect to say that economic analysis has shown that all changes that increase economic efficiency should be made because economic analysis can only draw positive, not normative, conclusions. The correct response is c.

12.2   Questions 2 and 3 are based on the following information.

For a particular income tax system, the first $900 of income is exempt and the remainder is taxed at a 90 percent rate.

How is the ratio of a high income (say $10,000 before tax) to a low income (say $1,000 before tax) affected by the tax system?

a. The after-tax ratio is higher, that is, the system is regressive.

b. The after-tax ratio is lower, that is, the system is progressive.

c. The after-tax ratio is the same, that is, the system is proportional.

d. The after-tax ratio could be higher or lower, depending upon the income level.

For incomes greater than $900, even though the marginal tax rate (the tax rate on the last dollar of income) is constant, it exceeds the average tax rate (total tax divided by total income). Consequently, the average tax rate increases as income increases and the system is progressive. For example, an income of $1,000 will be taxed $90, which gives an average tax rate of 9 percent. An income of $10,000 will be taxed $8,190, which gives an average tax rate of 81.9 percent. In this example, the ratio of the two incomes before tax was 10:1 and the ratio after tax was approximately 2:1. A rising average tax rate is consistent with a constant marginal tax rate because the first $900 is exempt from tax. This relationship is similar to that between average cost and marginal cost for a firm with positive fixed cost. The correct response is b.

12.3   Under this tax system, Ritchie, who is paid 50 cents per hour, chooses to work 2,000 hours per year. If the exemption were decreased to $100 and the tax rate on income over $100 were decreased to 10 percent, he would:

a. be no worse off and work no fewer than 2,000 hours.

b. be no worse off and work no more than 2,000 hours.

c. be no better off and work no fewer than 2,000 hours.

d. be no better off and work no more than 2,000 hours.

Under both sets of exemptions and rates ($900 and 90 percent, $100 and 10 percent), Ritchie could earn $1,000 per annum pretax and $910 posttax. Because under the new exemption and rate ($100 and 10 percent) Ritchie can earn as much posttax income as previously by working the same number of hours, he can be no worse off than before, but he may be better off. He will be better off if the after-tax hourly income of 45 cents for an additional hour's work is worth more to him than an extra hour of leisure. By choosing to work only 2,000 hours, initially we know that an extra hour of leisure was worth more than 5 cents—the after tax return for one extra hour worked. If the 45 cents posttax rate is worth more than an extra hour of leisure, not only will Ritchie be better off, he will work more than 2,000 hours. The correct response is a.

12.4   On which of the following can an economist offer only a personal opinion, not professional analysis?

a. whether farmers' incomes would increase if all price supports were removed
b. whether taxes should be changed to distribute income more evenly
c. whether a decrease in telephone rates would lead to an increased use of telephone facilities
d. whether increased economic efficiency would result if the computer industry were broken up into a large number of small firms

An economist can offer professional analysis on "what would happen if" propositions, but only a personal opinion on what "should" happen. The fact that an economist might be wrong, for instance, in predicting whether economic efficiency would result if the computer industry were broken up is irrelevant. The economist might have insufficient information or an inadequate model for making the correct prediction but neither prohibits professional analysis. What is the "right" distribution of income requires a value judgment and is, therefore, a matter of personal opinion. The correct response is b.

Case 12

THE NIXON FAMILY-ASSISTANCE PLAN

Although there is general agreement that public assistance to the poor is a legitimate activity for government, there is wide disagreement as to how this should be achieved. There is strong criticism of existing welfare programs from two main points of view: First, they are considered by many to be inadequate; and, second, it is argued that they provide strong incentives for recipients not to work or save.

The present welfare program is really a collection of separate programs that deal with different aspects of poverty and many of which involve nonpoor persons as well. Although there were some 438 Federal aid programs in 1970, out of the 25 million persons living in poverty, only about 14 million persons were on the welfare rolls.

The largest single program to help the poor is Aid to Families with Dependent Children. During the 1960s, the number of persons receiving AFDC assistance increased from 3 to 9 million, largely because many poor people have become increasingly aware of their rights and many have moved from the South, where very restrictive welfare policies prevail, to Northern cities, where liberal regulations have been adopted.

Perhaps the most distressing aspect of the AFDC program is the effect it has on incentives

to work and save. Before a person can qualify for aid, he must pass a means test. He must show that he has no substantial savings, and if he earns any income, much of this income is deducted from the standard of need in determining his potential welfare payment.

Aware of these problems, the Nixon Administration submitted to Congress in 1969* the following welfare program:

The government would assure an income foundation throughout every section of America for all parents who cannot adequately support themselves and their children. For a family of four with less than $1,000 income, this payment would be $1,600 a year; for a family of four with $2,000 income, this payment would supplement that income by $960 a year.

Under the present welfare system, each State provides "Aid to Families with Dependent Children," a program we propose to replace. The Federal government shares the cost, but each State establishes key eligibility rules and determines how much income support will be provided to poor families. The result has been an uneven and unequal system. The 1969 benefits average for a family of four is $171 a month across the Nation, but individual State averages range from $263 down to $39 a month.

*Congressional Record, 1969.

A new Federal minimum of $1600 a year cannot claim to provide comfort to a family of four, but the present low of $468 a year cannot claim to provide even the basic necessities.

The new system would do away with the inequity of very low benefit levels in some States, and of State-by-State variations in eligibility tests, by establishing a Federally-financed income floor with a national definition of basic eligibility . . .

For the typical "welfare family"—a mother with dependent children and no outside income—the new system would provide a basic national minimum payment. A mother with three small children would be assured an annual income of at least $1600.

For the family headed by an employed father or working mother, the same basic benefits would be received, but $60 per month of earnings would be "disregarded" in order to make up the costs of working and provide a strong advantage in holding a job. The wage earner could also keep 50% of his benefits as his earnings rise above that $60 per month. A family of four, in which the father earns $2,000 in a year, would receive payments of $960, for a total income of $2,960.

For a 4-person family with a basic payment standard of $1600 and earned income disregard of $720 the schedule of benefits would be:

Earned income	New benefit	Total income
0	$1,600	$1,600
$500	1,600	2,100
$1,000	1,460	2,460
$1,500	1,210	2,710
$2,000	960	2,960
$2,500	710	3,210
$3,000	460	3,460
$3,500	210	3,710
$4,000	0	4,000

How effectively does this proposal overcome the inadequacies of the present program with regard to coverage and incentives? Does it provide a superior alternative to the present program.

SUGGESTIONS FOR ANALYSIS

One of the major problems of economic policy for a free enterprise economy is how to redistri-

bute income in accordance with politically-determined standards of equity while distorting the signals of the price system as little as possible. It is clear that under the existing welfare system, at least as far as AFDC is concerned, the price system is severely distorted. Suppose, for example, the subsistence standard for a family is $3000. Under AFDC, prior to Nixon's welfare proposal, an eligible family received the difference between its earnings and the standard of payment. Under this system, what was the effect of doing more work? If a working mother increased her income from employment from say $500 to $1000 per year, what would happen to her total income? If AFDC guaranteed her $3000, no more, no less, then it would simply reduce the family welfare payment from $2500 to $2000, in which case the net gain from doing more work would be zero. What this means is that under that AFDC program recipients would have nothing to gain from doing more work, they would face what amounted to an effective marginal tax rate of 100 percent. Since 1969, the AFDC program has been modified to reduce the implicit marginal tax rate. At present, only two-thirds of earned income is subtracted from the standard of payment in determining what welfare transfer will be made. This, of course, reduces the marginal tax rate to 67 percent.

How does this compare with Nixon's Family Assistance plan? The table below calculates, from the information provided in Nixon's message to Congress, the effective marginal tax rate, that is, the proportion of extra earned

Earned income	Total income	Marginal tax rate
$ 0	$1,600	0%
500	2,100	28
1000	2,460	50
1500	2,710	50
2000	2,960	50
2500	3,210	50
3000	3,460	50
3500	3,710	50
4000	4,000	42

income that will not be taxed away in the form of reduced benefits. (It should be noted that these and other figures in this case exclude any benefits to the poor from the food-stamp program. See Case 3.)

Although the marginal tax rate for a family earning income in the range of $1000 to $4000 is high, it is nowhere near as high as that implied by the AFDC program. Furthermore, it does not penalize persons who have saved income in the past. Thus, from the point of view of economic efficiency, the proposed Nixon Family Assistance Plan represents a substantial step forward. Not only does it move toward encouraging the poor to help themselves by working and saving more but it also provides an incentive to put more of the economy's productive resources back to work.

With respect to the issue of coverage, the proposed Family Assistance Plan includes many of the poor who are not now covered by existing programs. It would reduce regional welfare benefit differentials, and it would not exclude poor families with working fathers, as the preceding system did.

Despite its many desirable features, Congress has yet to adopt the Nixon welfare program. Since it was originally proposed, the program has been amended in various ways (for example, the basic payment standard has been raised from $1600 to $2400), and it is sure to be revised further before Congress takes final action on it. However Congress decides, it must come to grips with the issue that the Nixon proposal has raised: how can we as a nation provide all people with a guarantee of a minimally acceptable standard of living without destroying the incentive to engage in productive work?

National Output, Expenditure, and Income

13.1 We have seen that an economic problem exists whenever resources are _____ . Scarcity means that it is impossible to satisfy all wants with the available supply of

_____ . Thus, to obtain the maximum possible satisfaction, available resources

must be used _____ .

13.2 Economic activity, then, is the attempt to convert a limited supply of resources into a bundle of commodities (goods and services) that gives _(more/less)_ satisfaction than any other bundle that can be obtained with those resources. When this goal is achieved, resources are being

allocated _____ .

13.3 When considering any nation, it is clear that the level of economic welfare attained depends on two factors:

(1) the quantity of _____ available, and

(2) how _____ these resources are used.

13.4 The more resources an economy has and the more efficiently those resources are used, the _(larger/smaller)_ the *output* of goods and services (commodities) that can be produced in a year. The larger the output that an economy can produce in a year, the _(more/less)_ fully consumers' wants can be satisfied.

13.5 Unfortunately, it is impossible to measure directly the level of satisfaction or *economic welfare* attained by the consumers of an economy. As a result, the amount of output produced in a

ANSWERS

1. scarce . resources . efficiently
2. more . efficiently
3. resources . efficiently
4. larger . more
5. economic . output

year is often used as an indicator of _____ welfare. For example, it is impossible to say how much more satisfied consumers are this year than last, but it is possible to say how

much more _____ is available to consumers this year compared with last year.

13.6 Total output can be calculated in several ways. For example, two possibilities are to count the number of things produced or to measure the weight of those things produced. Whatever calculation is made, however, it is desirable that it provide a guide for measuring the economic

_____ of consumers.

13.7 If there were only one commodity produced, there would be little difficulty in measuring the annual output of an economy. If that commodity were hot dogs, for instance, the annual

_____ could be measured simply by either the number or weight of hot dogs

produced in one _____ . Either measure would enable one to determine whether economic welfare was increasing or decreasing from year to year.

13.8 But because there are many commodities produced in an economy, calculating total

_____ by simply adding up the number or weight of items produced will not

provide a good measure of economic _____ .

13.9 Even if there were only two commodities produced, the simple counting procedure would not work well. Suppose the two commodities were hot dogs and hot rods. Assume production for the past two years was as follows:

	This year	*Last year*
Hot dogs	1,000	2,000
Hot rods	500	5

In which year was output greater? The simple counting procedure would indicate that output

was greater _____ year. But if people considered a hot rod to represent consider-

ably more output than a hot dog, they would say that output was greater _____ year. This example makes clear that when there is more than one kind of commodity produced, the number of units produced _(is/is not)_ generally a useful measure of output.

13.10 What is a good measure? Consider the possibility of using weight as a measure. Suppose that the only two commodities are bread and bricks and that weight is used as a measure of output. Because a brick is much heavier than a loaf of bread, an economy that produced very few

ANSWERS

6. welfare
7. output . year
8. output . welfare

9. last . this . is not
10. more . poor . economic

loaves of bread but many bricks would appear to have a lot _(more/less)_ output than an economy that produced many loaves of bread but few bricks. If the economy with more bread and fewer bricks satisfied consumers' wants more fully, using weight of goods produced as a measure of output would be a _(good/poor)_ guide to _____ welfare.

13.11 The difficulty with using either number of items or weight as a measure of output is that neither is a good guide to the amount of satisfaction different commodities give to customers. For example, a beautiful painting may give more satisfaction than many hot rods or a ton of hot dogs. To measure _____ by either the number or the weight of goods produced _(does/does not)_ provide a good indicator of economic welfare.

13.12 In constructing a measure of output that is a meaningful guide to the level of economic welfare, it is desirable that the importance attached to each item produced be in proportion to its *value* to consumers. If consumers consider a loaf of bread to be more valuable to them than a brick, a loaf of bread should be treated as a _(larger/smaller)_ amount of output than a brick.

13.13 Suppose that consumers consider a loaf of bread to be ten times as valuable as a brick. Further suppose that the production of bricks and bread for the last two years was as follows:

	This year	*Last year*
Bread	200 million	100 million
Bricks	500 million	900 million

If output should be measured to reflect its value to consumers, in which year was output greater? Because consumers consider a loaf of bread to be ten times as valuable as a brick, _____ year's output was greater. This is true even though the weight and number of the items produced were greater _____ year.

13.14 To be useful as a guide to the level of economic welfare, an output measure should count each item produced in proportion to the _____ attached to it by consumers.

13.15 For an economy like the United States, with millions of commodities and millions of consumers, this seems an impossible task. Nevertheless, information on the way consumers value different commodities is readily available and this information is required to construct a measure of _____ that counts each commodity in proportion to the value given it by _____ .

ANSWERS

11. output . does not

12. larger

13. this . last

14. value

15. output . consumers

13.16 You will recall from Chapter 3 on consumer choice that if consumers spend their income to maximize their utility, they will adjust their expenditure patterns to make the last dollar spent on each commodity yield the same satisfaction. In other words, utility-maximizing consumers will try to make the marginal _____ of a commodity divided by the

_____ of that commodity the same for all commodities.

13.17 If consumers spend their income so that the MU/p is the same for all commodities, then additional units of commodities that have a high price will be commodities that provide consumers with a *(high/low)* level of satisfaction. For this reason, it can be expected that

the _____ paid for different commodities will reflect their values to consumers.

13.18 In constructing a measure of output that would serve as a useful guide to the level of economic

welfare, it is necessary to have information on the _____ of different commodities to consumers. Information on the values of different commodities to consumers can be found

in the _____ of these commodities.

13.19 How can prices be used to construct a measure of total output produced in a year? If prices of different commodities reflect their relative importance to consumers, then a unit of any

commodity can be measured by its _____ . The total output of any commodity

would then be the number of units times the _____ per unit.

13.20 The total output of all commodities would be the sum of the total outputs of the individual commodities. For the brick-bread economy, output would be calculated as follows (fill in the missing numbers):

THIS YEAR

	Quantity	Price	Output
Bread	200 million	$.25	$ 50 million
Bricks	500 million	.05	25 million
Total output			_____ million

ANSWERS

16. utility . price
17. high . prices
18. value . prices

19. price . price
20. 75 . 25 . 45 . 70

LAST YEAR

	Quantity	Price	Output
Bread	100 million	$.25	$ _____ million
Bricks	900 million	.05	_____ million
Total output			_____ million

13.21 Counting each commodity in proportion to its value in the market, output was greater _____ year.

13.22 The reason market values of the production of different commodities are used as measures of their output is that the _____ of these commodities reflect their values to consumers.

13.23 By "weighing" each unit of a commodity by its price, instead of in pounds and ounces, a measure of output is obtained that counts each commodity in proportion to the value placed on it by _____ .

13.24 Thus, by counting each commodity as it is valued in the market—that is, by multiplying the quantity of the commodity by its _____ —a measure of total output is obtained that serves as a guide to the level of economic welfare in the economy. The procedure of measuring total _____ by the market value of the goods and services produced underlies the official national output statistics for the United States.

13.25 Several problems arise in actually trying to measure the market value of output. One problem arises because many goods that are produced are used up in the production of other goods. In the case of steel and automobiles, for example, some of the _____ that is produced is used up in the production of _____ .

13.26 Because steel is used up in the production of automobiles, part of the market value of automobiles comes from the value of the steel used. For this reason, if the total output of these two commodities is obtained by adding up their separate market values, part of the output of _____ will be counted twice, once in its own market value and again as part of the _____ _____ of automobiles.

ANSWERS

21. this
22. prices
23. consumers

24. price . output
25. steel . automobiles
26. steel . market value

13.27   If we add together the market value of the steel used in the automobile and the market value of the automobiles, we will be including the value of the steel twice. This is known as *double counting* since we are including the value of steel _____ . In the above example, simply adding up the market values for all commodities would give a calculated output that would overstate total production because of _____ counting.

13.28   Commodities used to produce other commodities during the same period in which they themselves are produced are called *intermediate goods*. Steel is an example of an _____ good because during the period in which it is produced it is used up in the production of automobiles. All other commodities are called *final* goods. Automobiles are _____ goods because they _(are/are not)_ used up in the production of other goods in the period in which they are produced.

13.29   It is possible for part of the production of a commodity to be counted as an intermediate good and part as a final good. In this example, if part of the year's production of steel was used up in the production of automobiles and part was accumulated as *inventories* and stored for future use, the part used up would be counted as an _____ good and the part accumulated as _____ would be counted as a _____ good.

13.30   Because the market value of final goods includes the market value of the intermediate goods, one way to avoid _____ counting would be to exclude from the calculation of total output all _____ goods. The justification for such an exclusion is that those goods are already counted in the output of the _____ goods that they helped to produce. Thus, the definition of *total output* should be modified to be the market value of all _____ goods produced during the time period under consideration.

13.31   A second problem in measuring output arises because the *capital goods* (for example, machinery and buildings) that are used to help produce output decrease in value due to aging and wear and tear. The production of automobiles, for example, will result in some _(increase/decrease)_ in the value of the _____ goods used to help produce automobiles.

13.32   The decline in the value of capital goods due to aging and wear and tear is called *depreciation*. The reduction in the value of capital goods, which is called _____ , reflects the fact that the older capital goods are, and the more they have been used, the _(more/less)_ output they are capable of producing.

ANSWERS

27. twice . double
28. intermediate . final . are not
29. intermediate . inventories . final
30. double . intermediate . final . final
31. decrease . capital
32. depreciation . less

13.33   In calculating the total amount of output produced in the economy, it is important to take into account the _____ that accrues on the capital goods needed to produce the output.

13.34   Thus, to have a complete account of the gain from productive activity during any period, the depreciation on the capital goods that has occurred during that period should be _(added to/subtracted from)_ the market value of the final goods produced.

13.35   Failure to deduct depreciation in the calculation of total output is similar to the mistake of double counting. Depreciation can be thought of as the amount of _____ goods used up in the production of current output. In this way, capital goods are like intermediate goods, except that _____ goods are produced in the same period in which they are used up, whereas _____ goods are produced in earlier periods.

13.36   Because the value of any capital good was counted as part of total output for the year it was produced, failure to deduct the part of that capital good used up in current production would be to count that part of the _____ good a second time. In other words, when _____ is not deducted from current output, some output, produced in an earlier period, is counted again as part of current output.

13.37   Because depreciation cannot be observed directly, it is difficult to measure accurately, and comparisons of output for different years may be distorted by changes in the way depreciation is measured. As a result, many economists consider the value of output produced without a deduction for depreciation to be a better basis for comparisons over time. For this reason, the official statistics report total output both ways: with and without a deduction for

_____ .

13.38   The value of total output for an economy in a year *without* a deduction for depreciation is termed the *gross national product*, frequently abbreviated GNP. The value of that output *with* a deduction for depreciation is *net national product*, or NNP. Of course, NNP +

_____ = GNP. For the reasons cited above, the most commonly used measure of output is GNP, even though _____ is conceptually preferable for many purposes.

13.39   Both GNP and NNP measure the market _____ of all the final goods and services produced in a given period of time. The only difference is that _____ does not include a deduction for depreciation, whereas _____ does.

ANSWERS

33. depreciation	37. depreciation
34. subtracted from	38. depreciation . NNP
35. capital . intermediate . capital	39. value . GNP . NNP
36. capital . depreciation	

13.40   Much of our analysis will be in terms of GNP, but you should be aware that, although for most

purposes it makes little difference which measure of total output is used, _____ is

preferred by reason of statistical accuracy and _____ is preferred by reason of
conceptual correctness. Thus, the second problem of how to account for the capital goods
used up in production cannot be completely solved because of data limitations.

13.41   The production of output is carried out in order to satisfy consumers' wants. Not all current

production, however, is used to satisfy _____ _____ in the present.
Some of current output may enlarge the possibilities for satisfying consumers' wants in the

_____ .

13.42   Output that is used to satisfy consumers' wants in the present is called *consumption.* The
production of musical entertainment by a rock group at a concert is an example of

_____ .

13.43   Output that provides for higher satisfaction of wants in the future is called *investment.* In
the automobile and steel production example, the accumulation of inventories of steel was a

form of _____ . Similarly, the production of new capital goods, for example,

new machinery, makes possible higher consumption in _____ periods.

13.44   Any output that is not used for consumption during the period in which it is produced is

called _____ because it makes possible higher levels of _____ in
future periods.

13.45   In deciding whether output is consumption or investment, the criterion is whether it is used

to satisfy wants in the present. If it is, the output is _____ ; otherwise it is

_____ . Whether certain goods are classified as consumption or investment
depends on the length of the time period for which output is being measured.

13.46   Many goods, such as a loaf of bread, are not consumed the instant they are produced and
might show up as investment in the form of inventories if the time period were very
(long/short) . Typically, however, output is measured for a year or a quarter of a year,

and bread would be regarded as _____ because almost all bread produced would
be consumed within a time period of such length.

ANSWERS

40. GNP . NNP
41. consumers' wants . future
42. consumption
43. investment . future

44. investment . consumption
45. consumption . investment
46. short . consumption

13.47   It is difficult to decide how to classify many goods bought by consumers. Most durable goods bought by consumers, such as furniture and automobiles, are consumed in part in the present but also contribute to future consumption. The production of such goods, therefore, is part

_____ and part _____ . Because of the difficulty involved in measuring which part is which, the official national output statistics count all output of consumers' durable goods as current consumption and none as _____ .

13.48   A similar problem is encountered in the case of the production of houses. But here, the overwhelming portion of such production provides for future use and, consequently, is classified

as _____ . The production of inventories, machinery, buildings, and houses is all regarded as _____ .

13.49   Total output, as measured by GNP, whether it be used for consumption or investment, is the

_____ _____ of all final goods and services produced in a year. Most output is sold by its producers to consumers, other businesses, or governments. To this extent, output is matched by *expenditure* for _____ goods and services.

13.50   Because most output is sold in the marketplace, that part of output is equal in value to the

_____ made for it. But what about output, produced by businesses, that does not get sold in the period for which output is measured?

13.51   Goods that are produced by a business but not sold to consumers, other businesses, or governments are classified as *inventories*. When producers accumulate inventories of their own product, they are considered to purchase the goods from themselves. As a result, it is assumed that

even output that takes the form of _____ is matched by an expenditure of an equal amount.

13.52   As a result, total output—that is, the market value of all _____ goods and services—is matched by an equal amount of _____ for those goods and services.

13.53   As will be seen in subsequent chapters, it is useful when trying to explain how GNP is determined to classify final product according to the type of purchaser. Thus, GNP is fre-

quently referred to as the sum of all _____ for final goods and services made by consumers, businesses, and governments. For 1971, GNP was broken down as follows:

ANSWERS

47. consumption . investment (either order)
    investment
48. investment . investment
49. market value . final

50. expenditure
51. inventories
52. final . expenditure
53. expenditure

Type of purchaser	Type of expenditure	Amount
Consumers	Consumption	$662 billion
Businesses	Investment	152 billion
Governments	Government	233 billion

13.54 Consumption expenditure in 1971 was $ _____ billion. This includes all new

consumption goods purchased by _____ . It also includes consumers' purchases
of some goods that are part consumption and part investment but that are treated as only

_____ in the national income accounts.

13.55 Investment expenditure in 1971 was $ _____ billion. This includes all newly

produced inventories, machinery, buildings, and other _____ goods purchased by
businesses. It also includes the new houses purchased by consumers, who are treated as

_____ when they purchase new houses.

13.56 The third category of expenditure is _____ expenditure. This type of expenditure
includes any purchase of a good or service by a government (federal, state, or local). Expenditure for highway construction or public school education _(would/would not)_ fall into this
category. It includes any purchase of newly produced output by government, regardless of
whether it is for consumption or investment.

13.57 All three types of expenditure include only purchases of final _____ and

_____ . That is, consumption, investment, and government expenditures are
defined as outlays for output produced in the current period.

13.58 The purchase of a used automobile by a consumer _(would/would not)_ be included in
consumption expenditure because it is not an outlay for currently produced output. Such
a transaction does not reflect the creation of a good or service to satisfy wants but merely the
transfer of _(a new/an existing)_ commodity from one person to another.

13.59 Similarly, the purchase of common stock or corporate bonds cannot be considered investment

expenditure because it is *not* the purchase of newly produced _____ that provides
for greater future consumption. Again, this transaction simply represents the _(transfer/_
production) of an already existing item from the seller to the buyer.

ANSWERS

54. 662 . consumers . consumption   57. goods . services (either order)
55. 152 . capital (investment) . businesses   58. would not . an existing
56. government . would   59. output (goods) . transfer

13.60 As with consumers and businesses, not all outlays by the government are expenditure for newly produced final goods and services. Many items in government budgets are *transfer payments* from the government to private persons or groups, such as welfare payments to poor persons. The purchase of a missile would be included in _____ _____ , whereas social security benefits are _____ _____ .

13.61 In any year, total output, which is measured by the market value of all _____ goods and services produced, equals the total _____ for final goods and services by consumers, businesses, and governments and implicitly incorporates the value of all _____ goods and services that are used up in their production.

13.62 The same measure of total output can be derived in a different manner by answering this question: What is the *value added* to total output by each industry during the year? In our previous automobile-steel example, the _____ added by the steel industry is the value of the steel produced, and the _____ _____ by the automobile industry is the value of the automobiles produced _(minus/plus)_ the value of the steel used up in the production of automobiles.

13.63 In this example, the value of the steel used up in automobile production could be included either as the _(final goods produced/value added)_ by the automobile industry or the _(final goods produced/value added)_ by the steel industry.

13.64 Whether total output is measured by summing up the market value of _____ _____ produced by each industry or the _____ _____ by each industry, the result will be the same.

13.65 As was indicated above, the value added by an industry is equal to the total output produced by the industry minus the value of the _____ goods purchased by that industry. In other words, part of the total receipts of an industry from selling its output goes for the purchase of _____ _____ . But what happens to the rest of total receipts?

13.66 Obviously, part of these receipts are used for payment of income to factors of production hired by the industry. For example, part of the total receipts of an industry is paid out in wages in return for the _____ hired to help produce the industry's output.

ANSWERS

60. government expenditure . transfer payments
61. final . expenditure . intermediate
62. value . value added . minus
63. final goods produced . value added
64. final goods . value added
65. intermediate . intermediate goods
66. labor . income

Another example would be payment of rent in return for use of land and buildings that are used but not owned by the industry. Both wages and rent represent payments of

_____ in return for use of resources hired to help produce the industry's output.

13.67   What about the portion of total receipts not used to purchase intermediate goods and not used to hire factors of production? The amount left is what the owners of the firms in the

industry can pay themselves; this is called *profit*. The payment of _____ to owners of businesses is in return for the contribution made to total output by the factors of production provided by the owners. Like wages and rent, profit is a type of

_____ payment.

13.68   As a result, the amount paid out as income payments (including profit) to factors of production and the value added _(must be/cannot be)_ equal. That is, it is possible to measure the value added of an industry either by calculating total receipts minus purchases

of intermediate goods or by adding together all payments of _____ to factors of production.

13.69   Thus, for each business it is true that the _____ added equals total

_____ payments. Adding together the value added by all producers gives total output. At the same time, adding together the incomes paid by all producers gives total income. As a result, for the economy as a whole total output must be equal to total

_____ .

13.70   For the economy as a whole, total output and total income _(must/can)_ be equal because

all the value added by each producer is paid out as different types of _____ ,

including the _____ received by the owners of the business in return for the resources that they provide.

13.71   In this chapter, two fundamental equalities have been identified. One is the equality between total output and total expenditure. The other is the equality of total output and total income.

The importance of the fact that total output is equal to both total _____ and total

_____ is that it makes it possible to consider the rate of economic activity from two different points of view.

ANSWERS

67. profit . income
68. must be . income
69. value . income . income

70. must . income . profit
71. expenditure . income (either order)

13.72 In any given year, the total output of an economy (GNP) can be measured in two ways that yield __*(the same/a different)*__ result. Just as it is possible to identify a penny by either its head or tail side, so it is possible to measure GNP by either total _____ or total

_____ .

13.73 Consider the illustration below.

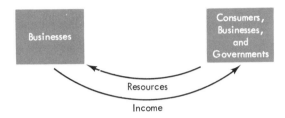

Resource owners provide businesses with resources in return for payments called

_____ . The most common transaction of this type in our economy is the payment

of _____ to consumers for labor services. Another example is the payment of rent to another business for the use of its building.

13.74 Thus, in the simplified diagram above, there is a flow of resources from their owners to

_____ , and a flow of _____ in the opposite direction from businesses to resource owners.

13.75 Now look at the following illustration.

This illustration shows a flow of _____ goods and services in return for the

_____ made for them.

13.76 Combining both illustrations, the circular flow of income and expenditure becomes apparent.

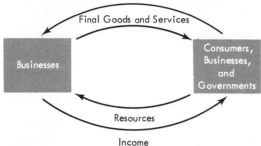

Income is earned in the production of output and in turn is used to make _____ for that output. At the same time, expenditure for output provides the funds with which businesses make _____ payments.

13.77   Because *GNP* is defined as the market value of final goods and services, it is equal both to total _____ for final goods and services by consumers, businesses, and governments and to total _____ earned by the owners of resources used in production.

13.78   The following table shows for 1970 both the expenditure and income flows that took place as a consequence of producing the _____ for that year.

U.S. NATIONAL EXPENDITURE AND INCOME, 1971
(Billions of Dollars)

Expenditure		Income	
Consumption	662	Wages and salaries	642
Investment	152	Rents	24
Government	233	Interest	36
		Depreciation	95
		Profits and other business income	153
		Indirect business taxes	102
		Statistical discrepancy	−5
Total expenditure (GNP)	1047	Total income (GNP)	1047

ANSWERS

77. expenditure . income   78. GNP (output)

13.79 Both total expenditure and total income are equivalent measures of an economy's

_____ . As a result, by considering either the expenditure or income side of this table, it is possible to determine that the market value of final goods and services

produced in the United States in 1971 was $ _____ billion. Note that a part of total income (indirect business taxes) does not take the form of a payment to any factor of production. Because these taxes—for example, excise taxes—are levied before the income

can be distributed to the productive factors, they are _____ taxes on income.

13.80 Because of the many receipts and payments that must be tabulated to produce the results shown in the above table, it should not come as a surprise that there will be some error in measuring expenditure and income. Because of this error, measured total expenditure and total income are not exactly equal, even though the true values of these two flows must be

_____ . This error of measurement, which is usually quite small, is shown on the income side of the table as the statistical discrepancy. In 1971, the statistical discrepancy was

$ _____ billion or less than 1 percent of total GNP.

13.81 The other items shown on the income side represent the earnings of the different factors of production used to produce output in 1971. For example, in return for providing labor

services, employees were paid _____ and _____ in the amount of $642

billion. Also, landlords were paid rents of $ _____ billion in return for the use of their property.

13.82 Not all earned income, however, is available to the owners of resources to spend as they like.

For example, as was discussed earlier in this chapter, indirect business _____ represent income that was earned by resources but that was never paid to their owners. This

income is taken by the _____ in the form of sales, property, and certain other taxes before resource owners receive it.

13.83 In addition to indirect business taxes, the government also takes income away from individuals

by taxing their income directly. Direct personal taxes are another example of _____

that individuals earn but do not have to _____ as they choose.

13.84 The government affects the amount of income that individuals have to spend in a way other than collecting taxes. One of the uses of government tax revenue is to supplement the income of certain people through *transfer payments*. Taxes are payments from individuals to

the _____ , and transfer payments are made by the government to _____ .

ANSWERS

79. GNP (output) . 1047 . indirect
80. equal . −5
81. wages . salaries (either order) . 24

82. taxes . government
83. income . spend
84. government . individuals

13.85   To calculate how much income consumers have to make consumption expenditure, it is necessary to subtract the amount households pay in ＿＿＿＿＿＿＿ and add the amount they receive in ＿＿＿＿＿＿ ＿＿＿＿＿＿ .

13.86   As in the case with consumers, not all the income received by businesses is retained by businesses. Some of it is paid to the government in the form of direct business ＿＿＿＿＿＿＿ . The higher business taxes are, the lower the amount of income that ＿＿＿＿＿＿＿ have to spend as they like.

13.87   In addition to taxes, businesses usually pay part of the income they earn to their owners, in the form of *dividends*. When a business pays ＿＿＿＿＿＿＿ to its owners (who, of course, are individual consumers), the spendable income of businesses goes _(up/down)_ while that of consumers goes _(up/down)_ .

13.88   To determine how much income businesses have available to make investment expenditure, it is necessary to take into account the amounts they pay to the government in the form of ＿＿＿＿＿＿＿ and to consumers in the form of ＿＿＿＿＿＿ .

13.89   Even though governments do not receive income in return for providing resources for use in production, they do have income to spend because of the various ＿＿＿＿＿＿＿ they collect. Not all tax receipts, however, are available for purchases of goods and services because some are used to supplement the income of consumers in the form of ＿＿＿＿＿＿＿ payments.

13.90   The income that governments can use for government expenditure is equal to ＿＿＿＿＿＿＿ receipts minus ＿＿＿＿＿＿＿ payments.

13.91   In the preceding table showing expenditure and income flows, total income was divided into different types of income, such as wages and salaries, rents, and so on. For some purposes, it is useful to divide total income into the amounts available to consumers to make ＿＿＿＿＿＿＿ expenditure, to businesses to make ＿＿＿＿＿＿＿ expenditure, and to the government to make ＿＿＿＿＿＿＿ expenditure.

13.92   The income that consumers have available to spend is called *disposable income*. Previously, it was noted that ＿＿＿＿＿＿＿ income is equal to the income earned by individuals plus

ANSWERS

85. taxes . transfer payments
86. taxes . businesses
87. dividends . down . up
88. taxes . dividends

89. taxes . transfer
90. tax . transfer
91. consumption . investment . government
92. disposable . taxes . transfer payments

the income paid to consumers by businesses in the form of dividends less the income paid by consumers to governments in the form of _____ plus the income paid to consumers by governments in the form of _____ _____ .

13.93 The income that businesses can spend is called *retained earnings.* Retained _____ , of course, are equal to depreciation, profits, and other business income minus _____ paid to the government minus _____ paid to consumers.

13.94 The income available to governments is called *net taxes,* which is equal to total _____ paid to the government minus government _____ _____ to consumers.

13.95 These definitions of the *spendable income* of consumers, businesses, and governments are shown in the following table.

wages, salaries, interest, rents
+ dividends
- direct personal taxes
+ transfer payments   = _____ _____

profit, other business income
+ depreciation
- direct business taxes
- dividends   = _____ _____

indirect business taxes
+ direct personal taxes
+ direct business taxes
- transfer payments   = _____ _____

13.96 Because all total income must show up as the spendable income for one or another sector of the economy, the sum of disposable income, retained earnings, and net taxes must add up to total _____ , or GNP.

13.97 The following table shows expenditure and income for 1971 with the new breakdown of income into spendable income by sector.

ANSWERS

93. earnings . taxes . dividends
94. taxes . transfer payments
95. disposable income . retained earnings . net taxes

96. output
97. expenditure . income . GNP

U.S. EXPENDITURE AND INCOME, 1971

(Billions of Dollars)

Expenditure		*Income*	
Consumption	662	Disposable income	723
Investment	152	Retained earnings	116
Government	233	Net taxes	213
		Statistical discrepancy	-5
Total expenditure (GNP)	1047	Total income (GNP)	1047

As this table shows, after allowing for the statistical discrepancy, both the total

_____ made by consumers, businesses, and governments and the total

_____ that these groups have available to spend are equal to _____ .

REVIEW QUESTIONS

13.1   For any particular receipt to be counted as part of an economy's total income, which of the following must be true?

a. It must be in return for a good or service.

b. It must be in return for the use of resources in the production of current output.

c. It must represent repayment for a loan.

d. It must represent an increase in the welfare of the recipient.

GNP is the total money expenditures for final goods and services produced. Total income, which by definition must equal GNP, is the total income flow to resource owners whose resources produced all the final goods and services. For any particular receipt, therefore, to be included in total income, it must be a return for the use of resources in the production of current output. The correct response is b.

13.2   For the economy as a whole, which of the following is correct with respect to investment expenditure?

a. It does not benefit consumers.

b. It makes possible higher levels of consumption in the future.

c. It is primarily the purchase of stocks and bonds.

d. It is part of GNP but not NNP.

Investment expenditure, by increasing the stock of capital in the economy, increases potential GNP and consequently makes possible higher levels of consumption in the future. Thus, it benefits consumers. The difference between GNP and NNP is capital depreciation—both include new investment as well as C + G. However, *investment*, as you now use the word, that is, creation of new capital, does not mean swapping money for existing claims on the capital stock, which is what we mean by the expression "investing in stocks and bonds." The correct response is b.

13.3   If you were to add up all the sales in the economy for a given year, which of the following would be true with respect to the grand total for that year?

a. It would equal GNP.

b. It would exceed GNP.

c. It would be less than GNP.

d. It would ignore consumers' valuation of the goods and services produced.

Adding together all sales in the economy would be double counting. For instance, the sale of wheat would be added to the sale of flour, which would be added to the sale of the final loaf of bread—the wheat would be included three times in the example. Thus, the sum would exceed GNP. The rational buyer's purchases, however, whether he be a miller or baker or bread buyer would reflect his valuations of the commodity. The correct response is b.

13.4   Last year, a small island economy produced only the following commodities:

$150,000 worth of fish
$ 35,000 worth of bait
$ 20,000 worth of nets

During the year, $10,000 worth of nets became damaged and had to be discarded. For this economy, which of the following is true?

a. GNP and NNP were $205,000 and $215,000 respectively.

b. GNP and NNP were $170,000 and $160,000 respectively.

c. GNP and NNP were $205,000 and $195,000 respectively.

d. GNP and NNP cannot be derived from the above information.

The final consumption good in the island economy is fish, and thus the $150,000 worth of fish enters both GNP and NNP. The bait is an intermediate good assisting in the "production" of fish, and the value of output of fish includes the output of bait. Nets are investment goods. Of the $20,000 worth of nets produced, $10,000 worth wear out or are used up in the production process. Thus, during the year, the output of final goods was $150,000 worth of fish and the $20,000 worth of nets. GNP, therefore, was $170,000. Depreciation was $10,000; thus, NNP was $160,000. The correct response is b.

Case 13

IS GNP A GOOD MEASURE OF ECONOMIC WELL-BEING?

As you know from Chapter 13, GNP attempts to measure the market value of final goods and services produced in a year. The justification for focusing on the market value of output is that this counts goods and services according to what people are willing to pay for them, which presumably reflects the relative marginal utilities of different goods. But you have already seen that

GNP is not a perfect measure of welfare because it fails to take into account the depreciation of capital goods that occurs during the year. And there are many other ways, not discussed in Chapter 13, in which GNP is defective as an indicator of economic well-being.

Many economists have advocated that the national income accounts be revised to come up with a new concept of GNP that takes into account the many deficiencies of the present concept. In the following discussion,[1] a distinguished economist argues for the retention of current GNP accounting practices because an all-encompassing measure of economic welfare is impossible. In reading his argument, make sure you understand the deficiencies of our GNP measure and what difficulties would be involved in trying to devise a more comprehensive measure of welfare.

The national accounts system is a great accomplishment of modern quantitative economics; it supplies an intelligible, integrated, and invaluable body of information about the functioning of the nation's economy. Its big summary number—the gross national product—has become a household word and has even been enshrined in a clock in the lobby of the Department of Commerce.

Yet, even as your numbers are receiving greater use and attention than ever before, they also are receiving more criticism. Put simply (perhaps caricatured), the fundamental criticism is that, even after correction for price and population change, the gross national product does not yield an unambiguous measure of national welfare; a rise in real GNP per capita does not necessarily mean that the nation has become better off. This diagnosis may be followed by either of two prescriptions: (1) ignore GNP, or (2) fix GNP so that it does measure social welfare.

I know you will not ignore the GNP. I urge you to bear the criticism with pride as a symbol of your success. I urge that you not try to "fix" it—to convert GNP into a purported measure of social welfare. You are doing your job so well that people are asking you to take on a different and bigger job. Resist at all costs, for you can't do that job; indeed, nobody can. Producing a

[1]Arthur M. Okun, "Should GNP Measure Social Welfare," *The Brookings Institution Bulletin*, Summer 1971.

summary measure of social welfare is a job for a philosopher-king, and there is no room for a philosopher-king in the federal government.

. . . Obviously, any number of things would make the nation better off without raising its real GNP as measured today. We might start the list with peace, equality of opportunity, the elimination of injustice and violence, greater brotherhood among Americans of different racial and ethnic backgrounds, better understanding between parents and children and between husbands and wives, and we could go on endlessly. To suggest that GNP could become *the* indicator of social welfare is to imply that an appropriate price tag could be put on changes in all of these social factors from one year to the next. This would hardly be a minor modification of the national accounts. As I have suggested, it would be asking the national income statistician to play the role of philosopher-king, quantifying and evaluating all changes in the human condition. And it is absurd to suggest that if the national income statistician can't do that job, the figure he writes for GNP is not interesting.

. . .

What you can and do measure as national income statisticians is the output resulting from market-oriented activity. The key to market oriented activity is the presence of price tags—the essential ingredient in an objective standard of measurement. Price tags enable you to sum up physicians' prescriptions and phonograph records and pounds of steak and packages of beans, or all the things that money can buy. But if you were to be seduced by your critics into inventing price tags that neither exist nor can be reasonably approximated for things that money can't buy, you would have sacrificed the objective yardstick.

. . .

As we have known for decades, the guiding principles still leave some fuzzy boundary areas. Some of the questions about where to draw lines are terribly perplexing. But the current system is a workable arrangement, and when I don't like its answers I can roll my own, relying on the detailed information you provide. You should continue to think about the difficult boundary-line issues. But you should not. I would insist, introduce major changes in the concept of productive activity, the boundary lines between final and intermediate product, and the evaluation of externalities. Let me run through some examples of changes you should *not* make.

*Imputation of The Value of Housewives'
Services and of Leisure*

For good reasons, you violate the normal
institutional boundary between business and
consumers when you include in GNP the imputed
rental value of owner-occupied housing. You do
this because the owner-occupant is short-circuiting
the market that tenants go through. You do the
same for the food farmers produce and consume
within their own households rather than sending
to market. Why, so the argument goes, should
you not similarly treat the housewife as short-
circuiting the market by providing services that
other families obtain by hiring domestic workers?
I find it a compelling argument that a housewife
is not a maid—and that this difference is of a
higher order than the difference between the title
to a house and a lease. The valuation of the
housewife's hourly services by the wage rate of
maids, or any multiple thereof, would not really
translate her activity into dollars and cents.

I have never been disturbed by the well-known
paradox that when the bachelor marries his cook,
the national product goes down. The GNP
measures the output of market-oriented activity,
and the market-oriented activity is reduced by
the cook's marriage. Why is this any more
paradoxical than the fact that the national
product will go down if I take a month's unpaid
vacation in order to travel around the world? In
both cases, the nation's marketable output is
reduced, but that doesn't mean that welfare is
reduced.

The vacation example brings us to the largest
element of what might conceivably be viewed as
potentially marketable services that do not show
up in the national accounts—that is, time allocated
to everything but work. I suspect that if we
lived in a world in which everyone had the
choice of working precisely as many hours as he
wanted every week at a fixed and known wage
schedule, a plausible—though still not compelling—
argument could be made for evaluating leisure as
a consumption good. In such a world, one
might argue that the individual must explicitly
decide to withhold some portion of his potentially marketable services, and thus to sell that
time to himself for consumption purposes. But
since the real world has more or less standard
work weeks and imperfect opportunities for
moonlighting, the current practice of ignoring
leisure in the GNP is the only sound and sensible
treatment. Leisure is a good thing, but it is
one of many good things that do not bear a

reasonably determinate price tag. It is an
important subject for analysis and research, but
it does not belong in GNP.

. . .

"Regrettable Necessities."

It is obvious that many of the things consumers
buy are not intended for pure enjoyment, but
are rather a means of avoiding discomfort or
preventing deterioration of physical and human
capital. Yet you count them all as final product.
You have been urged to try to eliminate
"regrettable necessities" from final product and
thus to classify them as a cost of living rather
than a source of satisfaction. Don't start down
that path. If you should do so (regrettably and
unnecessarily), you would find that it winds along
forever. Costs of physicians' services and other
medical care are obviously regrettable necessities.
So are the services of lawyers, policemen, firemen,
sanitation workers, and economists (including
national income statisticians). So are heating and
air-conditioning outlays. Except for the few
people who live to eat rather than eating to live,
food is a regrettable necessity. Indeed, it is hard
to imagine any output that clearly serves the
purpose of pure, unmitigated enjoyment. But
even if you could invent some arbitrary definition
that kept final-product consumption from falling
to zero, the exclusion of regrettable necessities
would make no sense. It would deny the distinction between meeting one's needs and failing to
meet them. If air-conditioning is a regrettable
necessity in 1971 to those who enjoy it, then it
must be a regrettable necessity to someone who
doesn't have it. Thus, excluding the services of
items that might be deemed regrettable necessities
is palpably unsatisfactory.

Imputations for Externalities.

It is obvious that the producer does not incur all
the costs of producing certain types of output,
nor does the consumer get all the benefits.
The producer whose factory belches smoke or
sends effluents into the river is imposing a cost
on society that is not reflected in private costs
of production. On the other hand, draining a
swamp or building a park may create benefits
that are equally absent in your measure of the
gross national product. Why, then, should you
not try to estimate the net deterioration (or
improvement) of the environment as a cost of
productive activity, netting it out of GNP?

Again, I must ask how such a valuation could

be made, if the market and the democratic process didn't provide price tags. Following your present rules, you will report the costs and benefits that society recognizes and responds to. If a ban is placed on activity that is inherently dangerous, or fees and taxes are imposed, you will follow the signals and properly reflect them in your valuation of output. If society changes its mind, you will make some rather puzzling changes in your definition and coverage of outputs. But any puzzles that arise concern the volatility of the nation's collective judgment, not of your practices. Your principle of excluding the output of illegal activity from the national product abides by the social judgment that some activities have such important negative externalities that they subtract from society's output even though somebody is willing to pay for them as an ultimate consumer. However sensible or foolish it was for the nation to decide that the sale of alcoholic beverages was illegal and then that it was legal again, it was completely sensible for the national income accountant to follow those verdicts. Regulations and tax incentives or subsidies are less extreme ways of outlawing an activity, and they are subject to the same accounting principles.

. . .

In short, the GNP is not the whole story of our society or even of our economy, and no conceivable redefinition can turn it into the whole story. You can help in many ways to put together some of the other pieces required to develop the whole story about social performance. But you would not assist by compromising on the proposition that GNP is *not* a measure of total social welfare. The beauty of your present practice is that no sensible person could mistake it for such.

If Okun is right in asserting that GNP should not be redefined, what good is the present concept with all of the inadequacies as a measure of welfare? Would you want to take into account the increasing levels of pollution for calculating how much better off each generation becomes as GNP per capita rises?

SUGGESTIONS FOR ANALYSIS

Even though GNP does not measure all output from economic activity, if it consistently measures a constant proportion of this output, then changes in GNP will reflect what is happening to economic welfare.

The Department of Commerce attempts to measure accurately that part of output that results from market activities. Many users of GNP statistics are interested primarily in just this measure because it can be thought of as the end result of normal business undertakings. For example, as you will see in later chapters, government officials concerned with the problems of inflation and unemployment must know with a high degree of accuracy what is being produced and sold in markets throughout the economy in order to enact appropriate policies to deal with these problems. They are often concerned with just those activities that provide jobs.

Just as we want to know the extent to which our capital stock is depreciated in the production process, so, too, do we want to know the extent to which our natural resources are depleted as a consequence of productive activity. Clearly, if the rate of increase in depletion of our natural resources exceeds the rate of growth of GNP, then a properly adjusted NNP would show a slower increase in per capita output than is shown by present statistics. Because the real costs of pollution are not reflected in any market—we do not have markets for rivers, oceans, and air—it is practically impossible to obtain an accurate measure of the depletion of natural resources.

14

Money,
Real and Potential GNP

14.1 In Chapter 1, the concept of national output was defined and analyzed. The main conclusions were that GNP (total output) in any period is the market value of final goods and services produced in that period, and that GNP can be measured by either the _____ for final goods and services or the _____ earned by the resources used to produce these final goods and services.

14.2 One principal reason for trying to measure output is that, because output can serve as a guide to the economic _____ of a nation, it is useful for policy makers to know whether output is high or low, or rising or falling.

14.3 Measures of the total output of an economy for any particular year have no meaning unless there is something with which they can be compared. For example, suppose you were told that in 1961 Japan's GNP was 17 trillion yen. By itself, this _(would/would not)_ give you any information about the level of economic welfare in the Japanese economy.

14.4 If you also knew that in 1960 Japan's GNP was 14 trillion yen, then the figure for 1961 would acquire meaning, for you would then know that Japan's GNP _(increased/decreased)_ from 1960 to 1961. Similarly, if you knew that in 1961 GNP in the United States was 187 trillion yen, the figure for Japan's GNP would tell you that Japan's annual output was substantially _(larger/smaller)_ than that of the United States.

ANSWERS

1. expenditure . income
2. welfare
3. would not
4. increased . smaller

14.5   Thus, aggregate measures of economic activity __*(do/do not)*__ indicate the *absolute* level of economic welfare, but __*(do/do not)*__ provide information about *relative* levels of economic welfare.

14.6   In other words, measures of total output of an economy for a particular year are __*(useful/only useful)*__ for making comparisons. As in the example of Japan's GNP, a measure of total output for a given country in a given year may be compared with the same kind of measure for a different _____ or a different _____ . Taken by itself, Japan's GNP in 1961 __*(is/is not)*__ a meaningful figure.

14.7   Because changes in a nation's output are of great importance to the well-being of its people, GNP is frequently used to make comparisons over time. And, because it is so important, the next six chapters are concerned with the analysis of those factors that lead to changes in GNP over _____ . That is, most of the following chapters will be devoted to the consideration of changes in _____ for the United States.

14.8   The use of GNP (or similar measures of output) to make comparisons over time involves a number of ambiguities that result from the fact that GNP is a measure of the market _____ of final goods and services produced. This market value is obtained by using the _____ of each commodity to measure the relative importance of a unit of each commodity to consumers.

14.9   The price of a commodity is the amount of *money* that must be given up to obtain one unit of the commodity. If stones were used as money, the price of an automobile would be the number of _____ that must be paid to obtain the automobile.

14.10   In some economies, stones have been used as money. In others, like prisoner of war camps, cigarettes have been used as money. In the United States, currency issued by the government and other items (such as checks) that can be quickly and cheaply converted into currency are used as _____ .

14.11   The basic monetary unit in the United States is the dollar. Thus, the price of an automobile is the number of _____ that must be given up to obtain an automobile.

ANSWERS

5. do not . do
6. only useful . year .
   country (either order) . is not
7. time . GNP (output)

8. value . price
9. stones
10. money
11. dollars

14.12 As you learned in Chapter 8, the price of a commodity in a market economy like that of the United States is determined by the _____ of and _____ for that good. For example, when the quantity demanded exceeds the quantity supplied, the price will tend to _(rise/fall)_ .

14.13 If the markets function properly, the prices of different commodities will move to the point at which the quantities _____ and _____ are equal.

14.14 Consumers help determine the prices of different commodities by the way they spend their _____ . The preferences of consumers will be reflected in the _(supply/demand)_ schedules for different commodities. And the prices that are determined in free markets will reflect the relative values placed on those commodities by _(consumers/producers)_ .

14.15 It is because prices reflect the relative values placed on different commodities by consumers that the market value of all commodities produced, which is _____ , is used as a measure of total output. That is, in using _____ as a measure of total output, the importance or weight given to a unit of any commodity is determined by its _____ .

14.16 Because the prices of different commodities are determined in part by the demand schedule of consumers, and because the quantities supplied by producers depend on prices, it is clear that consumers _(have/do not have)_ an important influence on amounts of different commodities produced. If firms produced commodities that no one would buy, they _(would/would not)_ be able to sell them and _(would/would not)_ be able to earn a profit.

14.17 Because businesses are motivated by the desire for profit, in a competitive market economy they will tend to produce commodities in accordance with the preferences of _____ as reflected in the way _____ spend their _____ .

14.18 As preferences and incomes change over time, the _____ schedules for different commodities will change. Think, for example, of the demand schedule for mini-skirts in 1970 compared with 1960. When demand schedules change, _____ can be expected to change.

ANSWERS

12. supply . demand . rise
13. supplied . demanded
14. income . demand . consumers
15. GNP . GNP . price

16. have . would not . would not
17. consumers . consumers . income
18. demand . prices

14.19   Similarly, as the costs of producing different goods change, their _____
schedules will change. Think, for example, of the supply schedule of radios before and after
the invention of the transistor. When supply schedules change, _____ can be
expected to change.

14.20   Because the supply and demand schedules for different commodities can be expected to shift
in different ways, it can also be expected that _____ of different commodities
will not all change in the same way.

14.21   Because all prices _(do/do not)_ change by the same amount, or even in the same direction,
in order to determine the general movement in prices, it is necessary to find for each period
the *average price level.*

14.22   For example, suppose there were just two commodities—air travel and bicycles—and that
last year the price of a student ticket to Hawaii was $100 and the price of a bicycle was $100.
Suppose that this year the price of a ticket is $110 and the price of a bicycle is $90. What
can be said about the general movement of prices? You know that last year the average of
the two prices, or the average _____ _____ , was $ _____ .

14.23   It is not so clear, however, what this year's average price level is. At first, you might think
that it would be a simple average of the two prices, which would be $\frac{\$110 + \$90}{2}$,
or $ _____ . But what if many tickets and only a few bicycles are sold each year?
Then the increase in the price of tickets is _(more/less)_ important than the decrease in the
price of bicycles.

14.24   That is, if more tickets than bicycles are sold each year, you would have to say that in this
example the average price level _(rose/fell)_ from last year to this year.

14.25   To calculate the average price level by using a simple average of individual prices assumes that
each commodity _(is/is not)_ equally important. Because this is not true, it is necessary to
count the price of each commodity _(more/less)_ heavily, the more important that commodity
is in the economy.

14.26   Measures of the average price level are called *price indexes.* There are several different price
indexes that are widely used in the United States that measure the _____
_____ levels for different groups of commodities. For example, the consumer

ANSWERS

19. supply . prices	23. $100 . more
20. prices	24. rose
21. do not	25. is . more
22. price level . $100	26. average price . index . price index

price _____ measures the average price level for the goods and services consumers buy. The wholesale _____ _____ measures the average price level of goods sold in wholesale trade.

14.27 The price index for any group of commodities is an average of the _____ of the individual commodities in that group. The more important any commodity is, the _(more/less)_ influence its price will have on the index. A small price increase of a very important commodity _(can/cannot)_ result in as large an increase in the price index as can a large price increase of an unimportant one.

14.28 Changes in the average price level become important when you want to compare total output for different years. Suppose you want to compare total output in the United States for the two years 1960 and 1970. To do this, you would want to find out what the GNP was in each of these years. GNP, of course, is the market value of total _____ , and it can be measured either by total _____ for final goods and services or total _____ paid, including depreciation, plus indirect business taxes.

14.29 By looking in the statistical tables in the *Economic Report of the President, 1971,* for example, you would find that GNP increased from $504 billion in 1960 to $977 billion in 1971—an increase of 7 percent per year. If the average price level remained unchanged over this period, it would be clear that the 7 percent per year increase in GNP was all due to an increase in the _(prices/production)_ of final goods and services.

14.30 But suppose that between 1960 and 1971 the average price level rose by 7 percent per year while production remained unchanged. With this price increase, the market value of output, or GNP, would have _(increased/remained the same)_ even though there was no increase in production.

14.31 This example shows that if one knew that GNP rose from 1960 to 1970 by 7 percent per year, one _(could/could not)_ be sure that there was an increase in output. All that one would know is that the _____ value of output increased by 7 percent per year. In other words, prices could have risen with output constant, output could have risen with prices constant, or (as actually happened) both output and prices could have risen, each by less than _____ percent.

14.32 One way to determine how much of the increase in GNP was due to an increase in real output would be to find out by how much the average _____ _____

ANSWERS

27. prices . more . can
28. output . expenditure . income
29. production
30. increased
31. could not . market . 7
32. price level . all . 2

increased. If the average price level did not increase at all, then it would be true that
(all/none) of the 7 percent per year increase in GNP was due to an increase in production.
If the average price level increased by 5 percent per year, then the increase in GNP due to
increased production would be only _(2/5/7)_ percent per year.

14.33 In this example, what would it mean if all the increase in GNP was due to an increase in
prices? Would it mean that consumers obtained greater satisfaction from output produced
in 1970 than in 1960? Although it is possible that consumers *might* derive more satisfaction
from the same quantity of goods and services in one year than in another, the fact that the
prices of these commodities rose would not *imply* that this was true. That is, the increase in
GNP due merely to an increase in prices _(does/does not)_ indicate an increase in economic
welfare.

14.34 An increase in GNP due to an increase in prices indicates only that output produced is sold
for more dollars now than before. It does not indicate an increase in _____

_____ . If it is assumed that consumers' tastes and preferences remain unchanged,
it means only that the value of money has _(increased/decreased)_ because it now takes
more dollars to obtain the same quantity of goods and services as before.

14.35 The reason for considering price increases as a decrease in the value of _____
rather than as an increase in the real value of output is that goods and services, not money,
satisfy consumers' wants. Because consumer satisfaction cannot be measured directly, it
is necessary to be content with a measure of output as a guide to economic welfare. As a
result, increases in economic welfare are assumed to result from increases in real _____

_____ , but not from increases in _____ .

14.36 If you were to look up the official GNP figures for the United States, you would find that
GNP is shown in two ways. One way, which is GNP in *current prices,* is simply GNP as it
has been described so far. The other, which is GNP in *constant prices*, is adjusted to eliminate

the effects of _____ changes and to provide a basis for finding the changes in

real _____ .

14.37 GNP in constant prices is output valued in terms of prices in some particular year (the *base*
year). For example, GNP for 1960 in 1958 prices is simply the market value of the output

produced in 1960 valued in terms of the _____ that existed in 1958. GNP for

1960 valued in terms of 1960 prices is GNP in _____ prices.

ANSWERS

33. does not
34. economic welfare . decreased
35. money . output (production) . prices

36. price . output
37. prices . current

14.38 Similarly, GNP for 1970 in 1958 prices is the market value of the output produced in _____ valued in terms of _____ prices. GNP for 1970 in 1970 prices is GNP in _____ prices.

14.39 Any price changes that occurred between 1960 and 1970 will not influence the change in output as measured by GNP in _____ _____ because each year's output is valued in terms of *(the same/different)* prices.

14.40 Earlier, it was noted that GNP in current prices increased by 7 percent per year from 1960 to 1970. Over the same period, GNP in 1958 prices increased by 4 percent per year. In other words, over this eight-year period, the annual real output increased by _____ percent per year, and the price level increased by _____ percent per year.

14.41 To emphasize the difference between these two GNP concepts, GNP in current prices is frequently called *money GNP*, and GNP in constant prices is frequently called *real GNP*. The term *money GNP* emphasizes that GNP in _____ prices measures the annual money expenditure. The term *real GNP* emphasizes that GNP in _____ prices measures increases in the annual production of goods and services.

14.42 The reason money GNP and real GNP can change in different ways is that, even when there are no changes in the production of output, changes in money expenditure for output can reflect changes in _____ .

14.43 It should be emphasized that prices play an important role in the construction of both money and real GNP. Both GNP measures use the prices of different commodities to determine the relative importance of units of these commodities. If commodity A has a low price and commodity B a high price, a unit of A makes up a relatively *(small/large)* part of total output and a unit of B makes up a relatively *(small/large)* part of total output.

14.44 The only difference between money GNP and real GNP is that each uses a different set of _____ to value output for any year. For the output of 1970, for example, money GNP uses the prices for _____ , whereas real GNP uses the prices for some _____ year.

ANSWERS

38. 1970 . 1958 . current
39. constant prices (1958 prices) . the same
40. 4 . 3
41. current . constant

42. prices
43. small . large
44. prices . 1970 . base

14.45   The reason money GNP should not be used for making comparisons of output over time is that it is affected by both _____ and _____ changes. By using real GNP, a change in GNP will reflect only changes in _____ .

14.46   Figure 14.1 indicates the quantitative importance of the distinction between money and real GNP. Because 1958 was chosen as the base year in Figure 14.1, money and real GNP are _____ in that year.

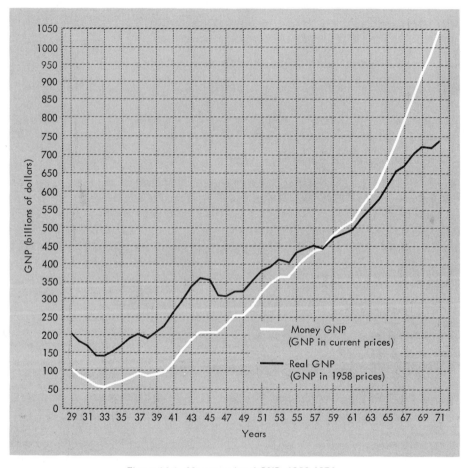

Figure 14.1   Money and real GNP, 1929-1971

14.47   The fact that money GNP lies _(above/below)_ real GNP before 1958, and _(above/below)_ after 1958, indicates that there has been a general _(upward/downward)_ trend in the average price level.

14.48   In practice, real GNP is obtained by dividing money GNP by a price index for all final goods and services. This index, which is called the GNP *deflator*, measures the average

_____ _____ of all final goods and services. The GNP deflator is

shown in Figure 14.2. Because 1958 is the base year, the GNP _____ for 1958 has a value of 1.00. The annual percentage increase in the GNP deflator is shown in Figure 14.3.

14.49   In other years, the GNP deflator in Figure 14.2 will be different from 1.00. This difference

is due to the fact that the average _____ level was different in those years from the 1958 level. For example, as shown in Figure 14.2, the value for 1971 was about

_____ . This means that the average price level in 1971 was about _____ percent higher than the 1958 level.

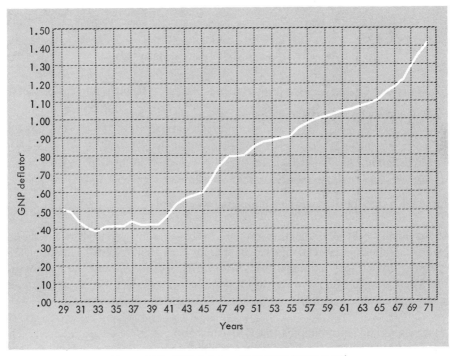

Figure 14.2   GNP deflator, 1929-1971 (1958=1.00)

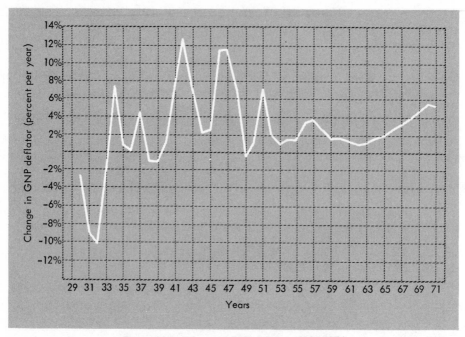

Figure 14.3   Change in GNP deflator, 1930-1971

14.50   The GNP _____ is a price _____ . It shows how the price level in any year compares with the price level in the _____ year.

14.51   An increase in the price level is called *inflation*. Similarly, a decrease in the price level is termed *deflation*. As Figures 14.2 and 14.3 show, since 1933 the GNP deflator has _(increased/decreased)_ in most years. As a result, one would conclude from this information that for the most part this period was one of _____ .

14.52   Although practically all economists would agree that over this period there have been many years of inflation, many economists argue that the changes in the GNP deflator are *biased* upwards. By this, they mean that the GNP deflator tends to overstate the amount of inflation in the economy. That is, they believe that when in fact there is average price stability, the GNP deflator is likely to _(increase/decrease)_ somewhat.

14.53   What reason is there to think that the GNP deflator shows more _____ than there really is? Consider the case of one commodity: film.

ANSWERS

50. deflator . index . base   52. increase
51. increased . inflation   53. inflation

14.54 Suppose that the price of film had remained constant from 1929 to 1971. Would the buyer of film in 1929 or in 1971 have obtained more for his money? Because the quality of film has increased substantially over this period—for example, film is now available in color and is both faster and more light sensitive—you would have to say that the _(1929/1971)_ film would be a better buy.

14.55 In fact, the price of film has risen since 1929. But because the _____ of film has also increased over this period, it is not clear that, even though the price has increased, you would not get more for your money buying film in 1971 than you could have in 1929.

14.56 If the quality increase just matched the price increase, then it would be possible to conclude that if film were the only commodity, there _(was/was no)_ inflation.

14.57 The actual increase in the price of a commodity would provide an accurate measure of the real price increase only if the nature of the commodity _(remained the same/changed)_ . If the quality of a commodity increases, the actual price increase will be _greater/smaller)_ than the real price increase.

14.58 When one considers the range of commodities for which substantial increases in quality have occurred, the importance of this problem becomes apparent. Despite the familiar saying that "they don't make things the way they used to," it is clear that the improvements in the

_____ of such different commodities as automobiles and medical services, typewriters and clothing, records and the packaging and processing of food make it difficult

to identify the true rate of _____ from the GNP deflator.

14.59 Although an attempt is made to take quality changes into account, it is practically impossible to measure the improvements in quality of some commodities. Consequently, in the construction of price indexes some portion of quality change may be ignored, and for this reason

many economists consider changes in the GNP deflator to be biased _____ .

14.60 Because it is important always to use _____ GNP when making comparisons over time, whenever the term *GNP* is used in that context in this book it should be understood to mean real GNP. For example, if the statement is made that GNP in 1968 was 5 percent

greater than in 1967, it means that _____ GNP, not _____ GNP, was 5 percent greater. In reading newspaper reports of changes in GNP, however, it is important to find out which of these concepts is being discussed.

ANSWERS

54. 1971
55. quality
56. was no
57. remained the same . greater

58. quality . inflation
59. upward
60. real . real . money

14.61   Real GNP gives a measure of the output actually produced. What real GNP is in any year depends on the quantity of _____ used in production and how efficiently those _____ are used.

14.62   Unfortunately, there have been periods when the quantity of resources used has been less than the quantity available. As a result, in those periods real GNP has _(been equal to/ fallen below)_ the level that could have been obtained if all available resources had been utilized. The level of output that *can* be obtained when resources are fully utilized is called *potential GNP.*

14.63   When actual GNP is equal to potential GNP, the economy's _____ are fully utilized. When the available resources are fully utilized, actual GNP is equal to _____ GNP.

14.64   Figure 14.4 shows, for the period 1929-1971, the percentage of those persons working or seeking work who were unemployed. This number is called the unemployment rate. The year in which the _____ rate was highest was _____ . In 1953, the unemployment rate was considerably lower—only about _____ percent as compared to _____ percent in 1933.

14.65   For an economy like that of the United States, in which there is a great deal of resource mobility, there will always be workers and other factors shifting from one use or location to another. Such reallocation takes time and results in temporary unemployment. If there are always some resources in the process of shifting, the _____ rate will never be zero. If you look at Figure 14.4, you will see that for the years shown the unemployment rate _(has/has never)_ fallen to zero.

14.66   Because unemployment due to the realloaction of resources is considered normal in a free market economy, *full employment* is often defined to exist when the number of workers unemployed is 4 percent of the labor force or less. Thus, it is clear that in 1953, for example, by this definition there was _____ employment, and in 1937 there _(also was/was not)_ full employment.

14.67   Full employment is defined in terms of labor resources because reliable information on the unemployment of other resources is not generally available. As a result, full employment often is said to exist when the percentage of labor force that is unemployed falls as low as _____ percent.

ANSWERS

61. resources . resources
62. fallen below
63. resources . potential
64. unemployment . 1933 . 3 . 25

65. unemployment . has never
66. full . was not
67. 4

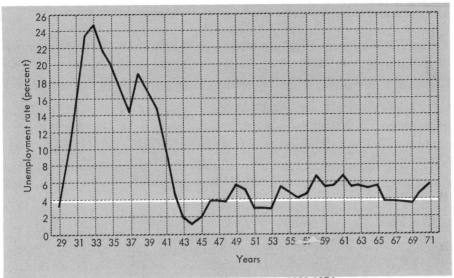

Figure 14.4 Unemployment rate, 1929-1971

14.68 The concepts of potential GNP and full employment are tied together. That is,

_____ GNP is defined to mean the output obtainable if there were full employment. Thus, in order for GNP to be equal to potential GNP, it is not necessary for the

_____ rate to be zero. Potential GNP is the output that would be produced if

the unemployment rate were _____ percent or less.

14.69 If you look at Figure 14.4 again, you will see that, for the years 1943–1945, the unemployment

rate fell well below 4 percent. That is, even though full _____ is assumed to
prevail if the unemployment rate is 4 percent, it _(is/is not)_ impossible to get it even lower.

14.70 It should be made clear, however, that the years in which the unemployment rate fell far
below 4 percent were war years, when the normal functioning of markets was disrupted.
Aside from this period, there _(were/were no)_ years in which the unemployment rate fell
below 3 percent.

ANSWERS

68. potential . unemployment . 4   70. were no
69. employment . is not

14.71   Full employment is often said to exist when the unemployment rate is _____ percent or less. But, to simplify the discussion, henceforth a period of full employment will be referred to as a period during which there is no unemployment. You should remember, however, that the more clumsy phrase "no unemployment above 4 percent of the labor force" would be *(more/less)* accurate.

14.72   From Figure 14.4, it is clear that there were many years between 1929 and 1971 when the unemployment rate rose above 4 percent. In those years, actual GNP fell below

_____ GNP.

14.73   Studies have been made to calculate what GNP would have been in those years if there had

been full employment. The result of those calculations, which is _____ GNP, is shown in Figure 14.5, along with actual GNP, in 1958 prices.

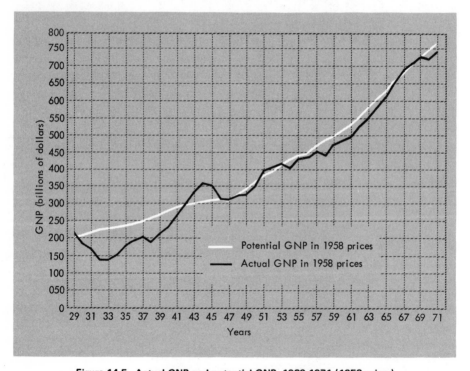

Figure 14.5   Actual GNP and potential GNP, 1929-1971 (1958 prices)

14.74   The difference between actual and potential GNP is the _____ lost when resources are wasted in unemployment.

ANSWERS

71. 4 .   more   73. potential
72. potential   74. output

14.75 To understand how substantial this can be, consider the following information taken from Figures 14.4 and 14.5 for the year 1961:

	GNP in 1958 prices	Unemployment rate
Actual situation	$497 billion	6.7 percent
Full employment situation	$530 billion	4.0 percent

In 1961, the unemployment rate was _____ percent and real GNP was

$ _____ billion. If the unemployment rate had been 4.0 percent, real GNP would

have been $ _____ billion.

14.76 Thus, in 1961, $ _____ billion of output was lost because resources were

wasted in _____ . When you know that this loss was greater than the entire GNP of either Australia or Canada in 1961, you realize how great the costs of unemployment can be.

14.77 In 1968, unlike 1961, the economy was at full employment. This means, of course, that

in 1968 actual GNP was equal to _____ _____ .

14.78 In comparing 1961 and 1968, it is helpful to look at the following table:

	1961	1968
Unemployment rate	6.7 percent	3.6 percent
Potential GNP (1958 prices)	$530 billion	$707 billion
Actual GNP (1958 prices)	$497 billion	$707 billion
Output gap	$ 33 billion	$ 0 billion

Between 1961 and 1968, unemployment fell from _____ to _____
percent of the labor force. As a result, the gap between actual and potential GNP was

reduced from $ _____ billion to $ _____ billion.

14.79 This means that part of the increase in output between 1961 and 1968 resulted from the

fact that some of the resources that were _____ in 1961 were used to produce

output in _____ .

ANSWERS

75. 6.7 . 497 . 530
76. 33 . unemployment
77. potential GNP

78. 6.7 . 3.6 . 33 . 0
79. unemployed . 1968

14.80   Whenever there is above normal unemployment, resources that could be used to satisfy consumers' _____ are being wasted in idleness. In 1961, then, it would have been possible to make many consumers better off if the _____ resources could have been put to use.

14.81   Unemployment, of course, arises when _____ GNP is less than _____ GNP. For this reason, when potential GNP increases, actual GNP must also increase to avoid _____ .

14.82   Frequently, increases in unemployment are blamed on factors that cause potential GNP to rise. According to this view, the way to prevent _____ is to keep _____ GNP from rising. GNP can be thought of as the average GNP per worker times the number of employed workers. If either average _____ per worker or the number of workers in the labor force goes up, potential GNP will go up also.

14.83   Average GNP per worker is usually called *labor productivity*. When the output that the average worker can produce goes up, it is said that there has been an increase in labor _____ .Those who worry about the effect of growth in potential GNP on unemployment are concerned that existing workers will no longer be needed when labor _____ increases or that new workers will not find jobs when the labor _____ increases.

14.84   For this worry to be justified, there must be a reason that actual GNP cannot keep pace with potential GNP. As long as it is possible to increase actual GNP, the best way to prevent unemployment is not to keep _____ GNP from increasing but to make sure that _____ GNP expands along with _____ GNP. In this way, it will be possible to avoid _____ and still have an increasing _____ .

14.85   Over past decades in the United States, there has been substantial growth in both labor productivity and the labor force. That is, growth in potential GNP has resulted from an increase in both average _____ per _____ and the number of _____ .

ANSWERS

80. wants . unemployed
81. actual . potential . unemployment
82. unemployment . potential . GNP
83. productivity . productivity . force

84. potential . actual . potential . unemployment . GNP
85. GNP . worker . workers

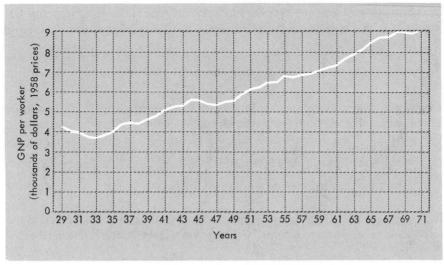

Figure 14.6 GNP per worker, 1929-1971 (1958 prices)

14.86 Figure 14.6 shows the growth in labor productivity since 1929. Throughout most of this period, average GNP per worker has *(increased/decreased)* , so that in 1971 labor

_____ was about *(2/3/4)* times higher than in 1929. This amounts to an average increase of nearly 2 percent per year.

14.87 Given the approximate doubling of labor _____ between 1929 and 1971, it would be possible to produce in 1971 the same GNP as in 1929 with only about

_____ as many workers. At the same time, the number of available workers increased by 80 percent.

14.88 As a result, if output had not increased between 1929 and 1971, there would have been a

very high rate of _____ in 1971—on the order of 70 percent. From Figure 14.4, which showed unemployment rates for this time period, it is clear that the unemployment rate in 1971 *(was/was not)* higher than in 1929, *(nearly/but not nearly)* as high as 70 percent.

14.89 This means that increases in productivity between 1929 and 1971 have not forced the

economy to accept a substantially higher rate of _____ but have made possible

a higher level of _____ .

ANSWERS

86. increased . productivity . 2
87. productivity . half

88. unemployment . was . but not nearly
89. unemployment . GNP

14.90   Even though there have been periods of high unemployment, the fact that actual GNP has repeatedly caught up with potential GNP (see Figure 14.5) indicates that productivity increases need not be wasted in high _____ but can result in higher _____ , as well as potential, GNP.

14.91   The labor force also grew throughout the 1929–1971 period. In 1971, there were over 87 million workers compared to fewer than 50 million in 1929. This represents an average annual increase of 1¼ percent. Even if labor productivity had remained unchanged, actual GNP would have had to increase at annual rate of _____ percent to prevent _____ from rising over the period.

14.92   Because potential GNP equals labor productivity times the number of workers in the labor force, the rate of growth in potential GNP is equal to the rate of increase in labor _____ *plus* the rate of increase in the labor _____ .

14.93   Since 1929, growth in labor productivity has averaged 2 percent per year, while growth in the labor force has averaged 1¼ percent per year. Consequently, potential GNP has grown at an average rate of _____ percent per year. Also, because actual and potential were equal both in 1929 and 1968, the average rate of growth of actual GNP between 1929 and 1968 must have been _____ percent per year. Since 1968, however, actual GNP has grown _(faster/slower)_ than potential GNP, and the unemployment rate has _(risen above/fallen below)_ 4 percent.

14.94   It is clear that labor force growth is the result of population growth. But what is it that causes growth in labor productivity? One factor is the education and skill of the labor force. The better educated and more highly trained workers are, the higher their _____ .

14.95   Education and skill are sometimes referred to as *human capital*. Just like capital goods (machinery, and so on), human _____ can be increased by investment. By devoting output to education and training, it is possible to give workers more _____ and thereby increase their _____ .

14.96   A second factor that has led to higher labor productivity has been the growth in the amount of capital goods. The more capital goods the average worker has to use, the more

ANSWERS

90. unemployment . actual
91. 1¼ . unemployment
92. productivity . force
93. 3¼ . 3¼ . slower . risen above

94. productivity
95. capital . human capital . productivity
96. output . productivity . investment

_____ he can produce, and the greater his _____ will be. The quantity of capital goods has increased over time as a result of _____ expenditure by businesses.

14.97   A third factor that has raised labor productivity has been *technical progress,* which is an improvement in the technological and organizational know-how relating to production. The invention of the transistor and the adoption of mass production are examples of

_____ progress that increased labor _____ .

14.98   For any particular period of time, an economy's potential GNP will have been determined by past events. For this year, to take an example, the labor force in the United States has been determined by _(present/past)_ population growth. This year's births can add to the labor force only in the _(present/future)_ .

14.99   Similarly, the level of labor productivity will have been influenced by past _____ for education and training, plant and equipment, and research and development. But expenditure for these items in the present will only have an effect on future labor

_____ .

14.100   It is possible for events that take place in the current period to affect the potential GNP of future periods. But for the current period, potential GNP can be regarded as having been already determined. That is, in the *long*-run, when allowance is made for the passage of time and the accompanying technological progress and growth in the quantity of resources, potential GNP can be considered to be _(fixed/variable)_ . But, in the *short*-run, when the sole consideration is what occurs in the present period of time, potential GNP can be taken to be _(fixed/variable)_ .

14.101   In the short-run, there is a limit to the level of GNP. For any normal period, _____ GNP cannot exceed _____ GNP. Because in the short-run potential GNP is

_____ , the main policy issue concerns the gap between actual and potential.

14.102   In the long-run, there is no ceiling on GNP. By investing in education, capital goods, and research, it is possible to increase labor _____ and, thereby, _____ GNP. As a result, in the long-run the main interest of policy shifts to the question of whether the economy is investing enough to increase _____ GNP at a fast enough rate.

ANSWERS

97. technical . productivity
98. past . future
99. expenditure . productivity

100. variable . fixed
101. actual . potential . fixed
102. productivity . potential . potential

14.103   In the following chapters, the main topic for discussion will be short-run policy. Two

questions to be answered are: Why does _____ GNP sometimes fall short of

_____ GNP? And, what happens when there is an attempt to raise actual

_____ above potential _____ ?

REVIEW QUESTIONS

14.1   Which, if any, of the following would be a possible consequence of adopting technological innovations that resulted in higher output per worker?

1. lower employment
2. higher national output

a. 1 only	c. both 1 and 2
b. 2 only	d. neither 1 nor 2

If higher national output did not result, an increase in output per worker would be accompanied by a reduction in the number of workers employed and/or a reduction in average hours worked per week. If lower employment did not result, higher output per worker would lend to higher national output. Consequently, both 1 and 2 are possible. Of course, it is also possible with a productivity increase to have simultaneously lower employment and higher national output. The correct response is c.

14.2   If money GNP fell more rapidly than real GNP during some period, which of the following must be true?

a. The average price level must have fallen.	c. The average price level must have risen.
b. The average price level must have fallen more rapidly than production.	d. The average price level must have risen more rapidly than production.

Suppose that money GNP fell by 6 percent and real GNP fell by 4 percent; the average price level must have fallen by 2 percent. Because the price level is the ratio of money GNP to real GNP, the only way for money GNP to fall more than real GNP is for the price level to fall. The correct response is a.

14.3   If the labor force and labor productivity both increase, then:

a. real GNP will increase.	c. either a or b, or both
b. unemployment will increase.	d. None of the above is correct.

An increase in both the labor force and labor productivity will increase potential GNP. Thus, it is possible for real GNP to increase. But because it is possible for actual GNP to fall below potential GNP, real GNP will not necessarily increase. If real GNP failed to increase, unemployment would increase. It is possible, however, that real GNP would increase but not by as much as potential GNP, in which case unemployment would also increase. Either real GNP or unemployment or both must increase. The correct response is c.

14.4 An economy producing just cards and curds had a record of prices and production as follows:

	First year	Second year
Cards		
Output	150	100
Price	$1.00	$2.00
Curds		
Output	700	1000
Price	$ .50	$ .40

Fill in the following table:

	First year	Second year
Money GNP	————	————
Real GNP in first year prices	————	————
GNP deflator	————	————

Money GNP is the market value (price times quantity) of all final goods and services produced using current year prices in each year. Money GNP was $500 for the base year and $600 for this year. Real GNP in first year prices is the market value of output produced using first year prices to value the output in each year. Because the first year is the base year, real GNP in the first year must be the same as for money GNP, $500. For the second year, real GNP in first year prices would be 100 X $1.00 plus 1000 X $.50 or $600. The GNP deflator is the ratio of money GNP to real GNP in each year. In the first year this must be 1.00. For the second year, the ratio is also 1.00, which means there was no inflation between the first year and the second year.

Case 14
THE COSTS OF INFLATION

We live, it seems, in an age of inflation. What are the effects of inflation? What are its costs? Who is hurt by inflation, and who, if anyone, benefits from it? You do not yet have all the analytical tools and the understanding of the macroeconomy needed to answer these questions satisfactorily. But the analytical concepts from Chapters 13 and 14, plus those from the earlier chapters of this text, can help you get the issues well into focus.

First, what do we mean by "inflation" and how do we measure it? The most common meaning of "inflation" is a rise in "the price level." Usually, the government-produced "GNP deflator" or its "consumer price index" (an index of prices paid by consumers in cities) is used to measure changes in the price level. The indices move roughly together. If "the price level" measures included all prices, the purchasing power of $1 over all goods and services would rise or fall just inversely to the changes in the price level. But our standard price indexes measure changes in the prices of only currently produced goods and services that enter the GNP. They thus exclude prices of existing assets, such as houses, securities traded on the stock market, and the like.

Figure 14.2 in the chapter shows clearly the persistent rise in the price level since 1930s. Figure 14.1 shows an important parallel fact. During these years when the price level was rising persistently, both money GNP and real GNP were also rising rapidly. And money GNP rose far more rapidly than the price level; this is shown by the strong rise in real GNP in Figure 14.1. Although there was persistent inflation, it is clear that the American people as a whole were also becoming persistently better off economically (as measured by total annual real GNP) during those years. Their money incomes were rising much faster than the price level, so their real incomes were rising, too. Although $1 today will buy only about one-third of what it would in 1929, total output is almost $800 billion today compared with about $100 billion in 1929 (in 1958 prices). Although $1 will buy a lot less, we have a vastly larger number of dollars of income with which to buy things.

Usually, as Figure 14.1 shows, prices and real output have gone up together. But sometimes they move in opposite directions. Consider 1968 and 1970 as examples.
It is clear that the American public became better off during 1968 (in the sense of having more real goods and services for consumption, investment, and government spending) in spite of the fact that there was a 4 percent inflation. Although $1 would buy 4 percent less, the number of dollars in income received rose nearly 9 percent. How

Table 14.a

CHANGES IN MONEY AND REAL GNP 1968, 1970

	% change in money GNP	*% change in real GNP*	*% change in price level*
1968	+8.9	+4.8	+4.1
1970	+4.8	-0.4	+5.2

about 1970? Then money income rose nearly 5 percent, but prices rose a little more than 5 percent. The result was that the public's real GNP fell slightly. Clearly, the public became worse off economically (in the sense that it had less real GNP for consumption, investment, and government services).

Can we say that the public was worse off in 1970 as a result of inflation? The answer is no. If there had been a 4.8 percent rise in money GNP and no increase in the price level, clearly the public would have been 4.8 percent better off. But we do not know whether inflation caused any or all of the slight decrease in real output. If we were to say that the change in real output was due to inflation in 1970, quite possibly we ought to say the same thing in 1968 and give inflation the credit for raising real GNP by 4.7 percent. The table merely shows what occurred during two years of inflation. Until we have done the analysis in the following chapters, we are unable to say whether inflation in any meaningful sense *causes* real output to rise faster or slower, or to fall. Do not fall into the common fallacy of assuming that just because two things come together, one necessarily causes the other.

But inflation has another effect—typically it changes the distribution of who receives the money and real GNP in the economy. Consider Table 14.b, which shows changes in the percentage shares of the national income going to major groups in the economy during three recent inflation periods.

Clearly, wage and salary receivers were the big gainers during these recent American inflations.

Table 14.b

CHANGES IN PERCENTAGE SHARES OF NATIONAL INCOME 1946-70

	1946-70	*1955-57*	*1965-70*
Wages and salaries	+11	+2	+5
Unincorporated businesses			
farm	-6	0	-1
nonfarm	-5	0	-1
Rents	-1	0	-1
Interest	+3	+1	+1
Corporate profits before tax	-1	-2	-4
Transfer payments to persons	+3	0	+3

This was true for the postwar period as a whole and for the individual inflations in 1955-57 and 1965-70. Conversely, the income shares of both farm and nonfarm unincorporated businesses and of corporations fell during the recent inflations. As with Table 14.a, we do not know that inflation *caused* the changes in income shares shown; but the data do suggest something about the kinds of shifts that may occur in other inflations. If we included in Table 14.b other American inflations, we would find that the figures shift somewhat from case to case. In earlier inflations, wages and salaries sometimes lagged behind corporate profits, but this has clearly not been true since World War II. The substantial shift through transfer payments to individuals is also a recent phenomenon.

Inflation also has a differential effect on debtors and creditors. It is commonly said that inflation hurts creditors and helps debtors, because a rise in prices means that debtors can pay off their debts in dollars with less real purchasing power. For example, if I borrow $100 from you today for a year and the price level rises 10 percent during the year, when I repay the $100 I am really only repaying about $90 of real purchasing power. Unless you expected this effect and charged me an appropriately higher interest rate for the money, you have clearly lost about 10 percent on the trans-

action (leaving interest payments aside), whereas I have gained about 10 percent.

Who are the big debtors and big creditors in our economy who will gain or lose from inflation on that account? Because almost everyone is both a debtor and a creditor to some extent, we need to *net* debts off against credits and examine who are the *net* debtors and *net* creditors. Table 14.c summarizes the facts as of 1970.

Table 14.c

NET DEBTOR AND CREDITOR STATUS OF MAJOR ECONOMIC SECTORS, 1970*

(In billions of dollars)

	1970
Households	+658
Unincorporated business	- 90
Nonfinancial corporations	-187
Financial corporations	- 63
Governments	-326

*A plus sign means net creditors and a minus sign means net debtor.

Table 14.c shows clearly that households are the big net creditors in our economy, while governments (especially the federal government) and nonfinancial businesses are the big net debtors. Thus on debtor-creditor account, inflation will tend to transfer wealth from households to governments and businesses. That is, with inflation, households will have less real purchasing power for their savings (creditor positions), while the weight of debt on governments and businesses will be correspondingly lessened in terms of real purchasing power. But of course governments are all of us, so in a sense inflation would transfer real purchasing power from us as households to us as potential taxpayers. And, of course, individuals own all businesses, so the inflation-transfer effect must be analyzed in more detail as to just who in the economy benefits and who loses. Remember that, given any total amount of real wealth in the economy (which is substantially fixed at a given time) and any level of real GNP (which is also whatever it is in any given year), inflation only *redistributes* income and wealth; it does not change the total. Thus, whatever anyone loses, someone else must gain.

We can look in more detail at household groups to see who is especially heavily in debt and who, therefore, is likely to gain most from inflation on that account. Table 14.d shows how heavily each group is in debt in relation to its total assets.

The top section of Table 14.d shows that middle income groups are most heavily in debt relative to their total assets. This may be surprising, but if you stop to think about it, very poor people are not very good credit risks and find it hard to borrow very much. The heavy debt position of middle income groups reflects primarily large mortgages to help buy houses and consumer debts at stores and elsewhere. Thus, the middle income groups have substantial protection against inflation through their heavy dept position. This protection is relatively less for both very low and very high income levels.

The bottom part of the table is even more striking. Young people go heavily into debt as they set up households, both to buy houses and to acquire all kinds of consumer durables. As they grow older, they gradually pay off these debts, and by the time they reach retirement at

Table 14.d

DEBTS OF HOUSEHOLD GROUPS, EARLY 1969

	Percent of all households	*Debts as percentage of total assets*
All households	100	24
By 1968 money income before taxes:		
Under 3,000	16	9
3,000–4,999	13	16
5,000–9,999	34	27
10,000–14,999	24	31
15,000–24,999	9	23
25,000–49,999	2	20
50,000 and over	0.4	15
By age of head of household:		
18–24	11	49
25–34	23	48
35–44	19	37
45–54	18	23
55–64	14	10
65 and over	14	3

age 65 or so they have very little debt left, on the average. Thus, older people are heavily exposed to inflation on this account. Remember, of course, that this table shows only part of the asset-liability structure of households, so it gives only a partial picture of relative inflation exposures. Now you have more ammunition to tackle the questions posed at the beginning of this case.

SUGGESTIONS FOR ANALYSIS

We can analyze inflation completely only after we have more analytical concepts and better understanding of the macroeconomy. However, you can understand a good deal about the effects (costs and benefits) of inflation with the concepts you already have at hand.

Chapter 14 provides the most important concept in understanding the effects of inflation—the difference between real and money income or GNP. Table 14.a illuminates the point. It is only by looking at the real GNP column that we see the net performance of the economy in real terms. Do not be tricked into thinking that inflation "losses" should be subtracted from changes in real GNP figures. Inflation figures should be subtracted only from the increases in *money* GNP, not from *real* GNP, if you want to get at the increase in real goods and services available for consumption, investment, and government services in any given year.

As was indicated above, you have no basis yet for stating that inflation either increases or decreases real output, other things being equal. As Figure 14.1 shows, usually money GNP and real GNP have risen together, but not always (note the 1970 figures above). Keep an open mind until you have done the following chapters.

If we *assume* that the level of *real* GNP is not affected by moderate inflation of the sort we have recently had in America, then clearly the effects of inflation must be entirely redistributional. Inflation may change the shares of money and real national income going to different groups and the amount of wealth held by different groups through the debtor-creditor effect, but it does not change the total amount of real output or wealth to be divided up.

Analytically, the central principle about how inflation affects the distribution of current income for any given real GNP is: those whose incomes rise faster than the average get bigger pieces of the real GNP pie, and those whose incomes rise slower or not at all get smaller pieces. In a full employment economy, inflation usually means that prices rise at about the same rate as money GNP. Thus, roughly, the man whose income just keeps pace with rising prices will keep about the same size piece of pie.

Remember, however, that this assumes that the amount of current real GNP is given. If there is unemployment in the economy, that is, if some scarce resources are idle, the real GNP may expand at the same time as inflation, and then *everybody's* real income may rise. But the principle controlling the *distribution* remains the same: those whose incomes rise fastest increase their relative shares of the national output; and those whose incomes rise slower get smaller relative shares. Clearly, those on fixed incomes are hit hardest. If real output grows, nobody has to lose if inflation occurs; the fact that someone gains does not necessarily mean someone else loses—this is not a football game. Table 14.b shows the shifts during recent U.S. inflations.

On debtor-creditor effects, the analytical point was stated above. Those who are heaviest net debtors will gain from inflation and those who are heaviest net creditors will lose from inflation, unless they have correctly anticipated inflation and made adjustments for it in the bargains they struck with each other.

This raises one last analytical point about inflation—the importance of expectations. If everyone correctly anticipates inflation, we could reasonably expect that they would take this into account in their planning. Wage earners would demand higher wages, businessmen raise their markups in setting prices, lenders demand higher interest rates, and the like. Similarly, borrowers would be willing to pay higher interest rates, businessmen might be willing to pay higher wages, and the like, because they would see that this would just offset the expected inflation. Thus, in the extreme case in which everybody correctly anticipates inflation, the inflation could be expected to have no redistributional effects at all.

In fact, sometimes inflations are widely anticipated, and something like this effect occurs. Examples are the persistent, rapid inflations in some South American countries (for example, Brazil) where inflation has become a widely recognized way of life. But even in these countries, not everyone is equally *au courant* with the possibilities of future inflation, and some (especially the poor and uneducated) are not able to protect themselves effectively even if they know inflation is coming.

15

Aggregate Demand and Supply

15.1 The annual output of the United States economy has grown substantially in past years. This has been made possible by increases in _____ output.

15.2 But at times, this growth has been accompanied by large increases in the price level. That is, there have been periods of time when the economy faced the problem of _____ .

15.3 At other times, annual output actually decreased, or failed to increase as rapidly as possible. In those periods, output fell below _____ output as resources became

_____ .

15.4 What are the causes of inflation and unemployment? Why is it that in some periods

_____ tend to rise and in others _____ become unemployed? To answer these important questions it is useful to introduce a simple *model* of the economy. A model states relationships among a number of economic variables, such as GNP, the average price level, and so on. In order to be useful, the relationships stated in a

_____ must be a reasonably close approximation to the aspect of the actual economy under study.

15.5 At the same time, however, the model must be simple enough to facilitate the understanding of the actual economy. That is, a _____ of the economy must *(retain/exclude)*

ANSWERS

1. potential
2. inflation
3. potential . unemployed

4. prices . resources . model
5. model . retain . exclude

the essential features of the economy in order to be realistic and must _(retain/exclude)_ the unnecessary details of the real world in order to be simple enough to understand easily.

15.6   Models are important to economists because they enable the economist to isolate and concentrate on the _(more/less)_ important variables and relationships in the economy.

15.7   As a model is developed, the simplifying assumptions will be made explicit so that it is clear how it differs from the real world. But even though the model _(will/will not)_ be an exact replica of the real world, it can help answer the questions that have been asked about inflation

and _____ .

15.8   Because the United States has a market economy, the quantity of output that firms are willing

to produce and the price at which they can sell their output depend on the total _____ for output that consumers, businesses, and governments are willing to make at different price levels.

15.9   As you learned in Chapter 13, total expenditure must be equal to money GNP. A change in

total expenditure must be accompanied by a change in _____ GNP. But, as you learned in Chapter 14, a change in total expenditure _(must/need not)_ be accompanied by a change in real GNP.

15.10 For example, if total expenditure increases by 5 percent, then _____ GNP must

increase by 5 percent. If the price level remains the same, then _____ GNP must also increase by 5 percent. But if the price level increases by 5 percent, real GNP will increase by _(0/5)_ percent.

15.11 Thus, an increase in total expenditure will always result in an increase in _____

GNP, but may or may not result in an increase in _____ GNP.

15.12 In order to understand when an increase in total expenditure will be accompanied by an increase in real GNP, and when by an increase in the price level, it is useful to think in terms of the total expenditure that would be made *if prices were to remain unchanged.* This is called *aggregate demand.* Although very simple, this concept is very important, so be sure you

know its definition. The total expenditure that would be made if _____ were to

remain _____ is called aggregate _____ .

ANSWERS

6. more
7. will not . unemployment
8. expenditure
9. money . need not

10. money . real . 0
11. money . real
12. prices . unchanged . demand

15.13 Sometimes economists use the term *aggregate demand* to mean an increase in spending regardless of what is happening to prices. But here, because it makes the analysis clearer, what we mean by aggregate demand is the total _____ that would result with a _(given/changing)_ price level.

15.14 What will be the effect of a change in aggregate demand on the price level and on real GNP? Suppose the economy were initially at full employment. Then, of course, actual GNP would initially be equal to _____ GNP. Now suppose there were an increase in aggregate demand. This means that, if the price level were to remain unchanged, consumers, businesses, and governments would be willing to purchase _(more/less)_ output than before.

15.15 Because the economy was initially at full employment, it _(would/would not)_ be possible for producers to increase production because there _(would/would not)_ be unemployed resources available.

15.16 Thus, the increase in aggregate demand means that, at initial prices, buyers would be trying to buy _(more/less)_ output than could be produced. In such a situation, competition among buyers would tend to drive the price level _(up/down)_ .

15.17 What this example makes clear is that when aggregate demand exceeds potential GNP valued in initial prices, the price level will _(increase/decrease)_ . Thus, according to our model, inflation will result whenever the level of _____ _____ is greater than _____ _____ in initial prices.

15.18 Suppose that aggregate demand instead of increasing were to decrease. This would mean that at initial prices buyers would be willing to buy _(more/less)_ output than before. Because the economy was initially at full employment, it also means that at initial prices buyers would be willing to purchase _(more/less)_ output than could be produced.

15.19 In this situation, if markets were to function perfectly, competition among producers would tend to drive prices _(up/down)_ . In many markets, however, prices do not respond immediately to a decline in expenditure. Although industries generally respond to an increase in expenditure when there is full employment by raising _____ , many appear to be unwilling to cut prices when there is a decline in _____ .

15.20 If you look at Figures 15.1 and 15.2, you will see, for example, that during the period 1958–1965 actual GNP was _(less than/equal to)_ potential GNP and the price level _(did/did not)_ fall.

ANSWERS

13. expenditure . given
14. potential . more
15. would not . would not
16. more . up

17. increase . aggregate demand . potential GNP
18. less . less
19. down . prices . expenditure
20. less than . did not

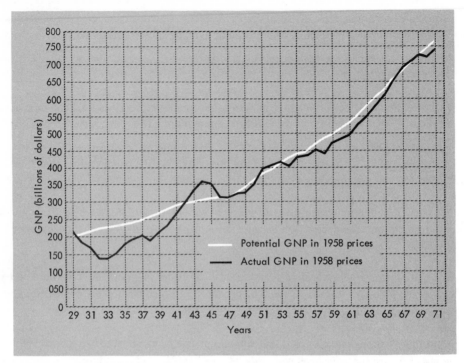

Figure 15.1   Real GNP and potential GNP, 1929-1971 (1958 prices)

15.21   Does this imply that no prices fell during this period? *(yes/no)* . It only implies that when aggregate demand was less than potential GNP in initial prices, the average _____ _____ did not fall.

15.22   In most other periods, when actual GNP fell below potential GNP the price level did not fall. As a result, it is possible to conclude that when aggregate demand falls below potential GNP in initial prices, the price level tends to be *(flexible/rigid)* .

15.23   A careful look at Figures 15.1 and 15.2 will reveal that for most years when actual GNP was less than potential GNP not only did the official price index not fall but it actually rose. It should be recalled, however, that because the GNP deflator fails to fully take account of changes in the _____ of output, it *(under/over)* states the rate of inflation by about 1 or 2 percent. It is for this reason that a small rate of increase in the GNP deflator, as occurred in the 1958-1965 period, *(is/is not)* considered by many to be true inflation.

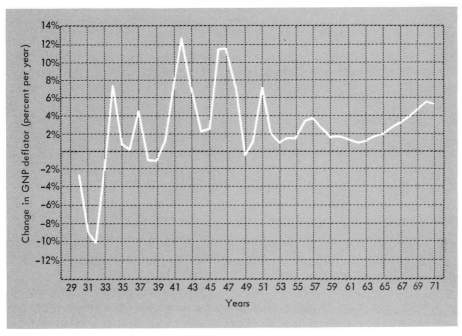

Figure 15.2 Change in GNP deflator, 1930-1971

15.24 The price level is not perfectly rigid when there is unemployment. It is possible for the price level to fall in such periods. If you look at Figure 15.1, you will see that in the 1930-1933 period actual GNP *(remained equal to/fell far below)* potential GNP. This was a period, then, in which aggregate demand fell very sharply and in which there was *(great/little)* downward pressure on prices.

15.25 If you look at Figure 15.2, you will see that in 1930-1933 the price level *(rose/fell)* quite sharply. From this evidence, it can be concluded that even though the price level tends not to fall when there is as much as 6 or 7 percent unemployment, if there is enough downward pressure on prices, the price level *(will/will not)* decline.

15.26 It is also possible when there is unemployment for the price level to rise faster than the 1 or 2 percent considered to be consistent with price stability. Three such periods were 1934, 1937, and 1970-1971. In those years, there was *(high/low)* unemployment, yet the price level *(rose/fell)* sharply. The reasons for price level increases when actual GNP is less than potential will be discussed in Chapter 20.

ANSWERS

24. fell far below . great   26. high . rose
25. fell . will

15.27   Although there have been exceptions, particularly in the 1930s, and more recently in 1970-1971, the general pattern of price changes has been that when actual GNP falls below potential GNP the _____ level stays relatively stable. In the model to be analyzed in this and following chapters, we will assume for the sake of simplicity that it is always true that when actual GNP is less than potential GNP, the price level _(will/will not)_ change.

15.28   Previously, it was concluded that when aggregate demand exceeds potential GNP in initial prices, the price level will _(rise/fall)_ . In the model to be analyzed here, the same result will hold. Thus, in both the real world and in the model analyzed here, the price level will rise when _____ _____ exceeds _____ _____ .

15.29   In the real world, the price level sometimes increases when aggregate demand is below potential GNP. In the model used here, however, it will be assumed that this will not occur. Thus, in the real world the price level has _(sometimes/never)_ risen when aggregate demand is less than potential GNP in initial prices, but in the model it will be assumed that in this situation the price level _(will/will not)_ rise.

15.30   In summary, the model discussed below assumes that whenever aggregate demand is greater than potential GNP, the price level is _(flexible/rigid)_ and prices will _(rise/stay the same)_ . It further assumes that the price level _(will/will not)_ rise under other circumstances.

15.31   If the economy were initially at full employment, a decline in aggregate demand would mean that at initial prices buyers would want to buy _(more/less)_ output than could be produced.

15.32   If prices were to remain at their initial level when aggregate demand falls, producers _(would/would not)_ be able to sell as much output as before. As a result, it would no longer be profitable for them to use as large a quantity of _____ and produce as much _____ as before.

15.33   What this example shows is that when aggregate demand falls below potential GNP valued in initial prices, if there is downward price rigidity, some resources become _____ and actual GNP falls below its _____ .

15.34   Thus, according to our model, unemployment results when _____ _____ falls below _____ in initial prices.

ANSWERS

27. price . will not
28. rise . aggregate demand . potential GNP
29. sometimes . will not
30. flexible . rise . will not
31. less
32. would not . resources . output
33. unemployed . potential
34. aggregate demand . potential GNP

15.35 In summary, our model suggests that whether there will be inflation, unemployment or full

employment with no inflation depends on the level of _____ _____

relative to _____ _____ valued in initial prices.

     a. If there is excess aggregate demand, the result will be _____ .

     b. If there is insufficient aggregate demand, the result will be _____ .

     c. If aggregate demand is just equal to potential output in initial prices, the result will be

         _____ _____ without _____ .

15.36 Thus, the condition of the economy depends critically on the level of _____

_____ . The level of GNP that will result from different levels of aggregate demand

can be summarized in terms of Figure 15.3.

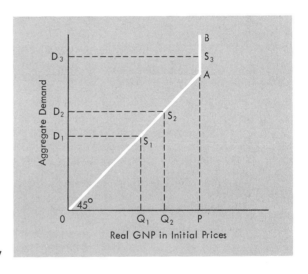

Figure 15.3
Aggregate supply

15.37 In Figure 15.3, the horizontal axis measures _____ _____ in initial
prices. Each point along the axis indicates an amount of real GNP equal to its distance from
the origin.

15.38 For example, the point Q_1 indicates an amount of real GNP equal to the distance from 0 to
Q_1. This amount can be written simply $0Q_1$. Clearly, Q_2 indicates a _(larger/smaller)_ GNP
than Q_1 because $0Q_2$ is a _(greater/smaller)_ distance than $0Q_1$.

15.39   Point P along the horizontal axis indicates the level of potential GNP. Thus, for the economy represented in Figure 15.3, the largest possible real GNP that can be attained is the distance

_____ .

15.40   The vertical axis in Figure 15.3 measures _____ _____ , which is the

total _____ that would be made at initial prices. Point D_3, for example, indicates

a level of aggregate demand equal to _____ . The distance $D_2 D_3$ shows how much greater $0D_3$ is than _(D₂D₃/0D₂)_ .

15.41   In Figure 15.3, there is a kinked line that starts at 0, goes to A, and then rises vertically to B. This line 0AB shows the level of real GNP in initial prices (which is shown along the

_____ axis) that will result for each possible level of aggregate demand (which is

shown along the _____ axis).

15.42   Line 0AB is called the *aggregate supply* curve. It shows the level of real GNP in initial prices

that will be supplied for each possible level of _____ _____ .

15.43   If you know the level of aggregate demand, you can find what the level of real GNP will be

from the _____ _____ curve.

15.44   For example, in Figure 15.3, suppose the level of aggregate demand is $0D_1$. The point on the

aggregate supply curve that corresponds to that level of aggregate demand is _____ .

This point lies directly above point _____ on the horizontal axis. This indicates

that the level of real GNP that will be supplied is _____ .

15.45   As is indicated in Figure 15.3, the segment 0A of the aggregate supply curve makes a

_____ degree angle with each axis. Because of this, any level of aggregate demand that corresponds to a point on 0A will result in a real GNP of an equal amount. For example,

$0D_1$ is the same amount as _____ .

15.46   If aggregate demand were to increase from $0D_1$ to $0D_2$, real GNP would increase from

_____ to _____ . Because line 0A is a 45 degree line, the increase in

aggregate demand, $D_1 D_2$, results in an equal increase in real GNP, _____ .

ANSWERS

39. 0P

40. aggregate demand . expenditure .
    $0D_3$. $0D_2$

41. horizontal . vertical

42. aggregate demand

43. aggregate supply

44. S_1 . Q_1 . $0Q_1$

45. 45 . $0Q_1$

46. $0Q_1$. $0Q_2$. $Q_1 Q_2$

15.47   As you will recall, in this model when aggregate demand falls below potential GNP in initial prices, the price level is _(flexible/inflexible)_ . As a result, a decline in aggregate demand will cause an equal decline in _(output/prices)_ . This is represented in Figure 15.3 by the 45 degree line, along which a change in aggregate demand is accompanied by an _____ change in real GNP.

15.48   A fall in aggregate demand below real GNP in initial prices will reduce _(output/prices)_ instead of _(output/prices)_ . An increase in aggregate demand from a level below potential GNP in initial prices will increase output instead of prices.

15.49   That is, when there is unemployment, an increase in aggregate demand _(will/will not)_ lead producers to increase prices. Instead, producers will hire more _____ and produce more _____ to match the increase in aggregate demand. Again, this is represented by the 45 degree line, along which an increase in aggregate demand is accompanied by an _____ increase in real GNP.

15.50   Thus, when there is unemployment, prices are _(rigid/flexible)_ and the aggregate supply curve is a _(45 degree/vertical)_ line.

15.51   After point A, the aggregate supply curve becomes a _____ line. This indicates that no matter how great the level of aggregate demand, real GNP cannot increase beyond the level indicated by point _____ , which is directly below point A.

15.52   For example, in Figure 15.3, if aggregate demand were equal to OD_3, the corresponding point on the aggregate supply curve would be _____ . This lies directly above point _____ on the horizontal axis, which indicates that real GNP would be _____ .

15.53   The reason that the aggregate supply curve becomes a vertical line above point P is that OP is the level of potential GNP. No matter how great the level of aggregate demand, real GNP cannot exceed _____ GNP. Even if aggregate demand were greater than OD_3, the level of real GNP indicated by the aggregate supply curve would still be _____ , which is equal to potential GNP.

ANSWERS

47. inflexible . output . equal
48. output . prices
49. will not . resources . output . equal
50. rigid . 45 degree

51. vertical . P
52. S_3 . P . OP
53. potential . OP

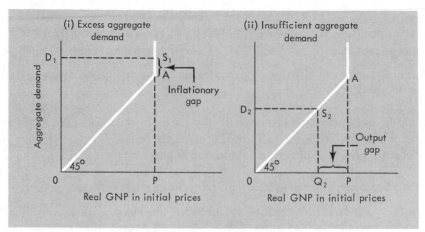

Figure 15.4   Aggregate supply

15.54   The difference between having too much and too little aggregate demand can be seen in Figure 15.4, which shows two typical cases. Here, as in Figure 15.3, the vertical axis measures

_____ _____ , and the horizontal axis measures _____

_____ in initial prices. Again, the aggregate supply curve has two segments: one

makes a _____ degree angle with each axis at the origin, and the other is a vertical

line above point P on the horizontal axis that indicates the level of _____ GNP.

15.55   In case (i) the level of aggregate demand is OD_1. This corresponds to point _____ on the aggregate supply curve. This indicates that when aggregate demand is OD_1, real GNP

will be _____ , which is also the level of _____ GNP. Because real GNP

is OP, in this case, there _(will/will not)_ be full employment.

15.56   Because S_1 is on the vertical segment of the aggregate supply curve, you know that OD_1 is _(greater/smaller)_ than OP. This means that aggregate demand is _(greater/smaller)_ than potential GNP.

15.57   The amount by which aggregate demand exceeds potential GNP is _____ . Because

excess aggregate demand leads to _____ , this amount is called, as noted in Figure

15.4, the _____ gap.

15.58 Whenever there is an _____ gap, it means that the amount of output that consumers, businesses, and governments would be willing to buy at initial prices is _(greater/
smaller)_ than the output that can be produced with available resources. The result, in such a

situation, will be _(unemployment/full employment)_ with _____ .

15.59 Now consider (ii). Here, the level of aggregate demand is $0D_2$. The aggregate supply curve

indicates that when aggregate demand is $0D_2$, real GNP will be _____ . Because
this is _(greater/smaller)_ than $0P$, real GNP will be _(greater/smaller)_ than potential GNP.

15.60 In this case, the difference between real GNP and potential GNP is _____ . This
amount is called, as noted Figure 15.4, the output gap.

15.61 The _____ gap measures the loss in GNP that results when there is

_____ due to insufficient _____ _____ .

15.62 As these two cases show, given the level of potential GNP, whether there will be inflation or

unemployment depends on the level of _____ _____ . Only if

aggregate demand is just equal to potential GNP in initial prices can there be _____

_____ with no _____ . Later, the assumptions of the model will be
relaxed, and you will see why there have been periods of a rising price level at less than full
employment. For the present, however, our simple model will be retained.

REVIEW QUESTIONS

15.1 Whether there will be unemployment or inflation is determined by:

   a. the level of aggregate demand
   b. the level of potential GNP

   c. the size of the output gap relative to the
      inflationary gap
   d. the level of aggregate demand relative to
      potential GNP

Aggregate demand is the expenditure that would be made at initial prices, and potential GNP
is the output that could be produced if all resources were utilized. If aggregate demand
exceeds potential GNP, the result will be inflation; if it falls short of potential GNP, the result
will be unemployment. To know only the level of aggregate demand or only the level of
potential GNP would not be sufficient to know whether inflation or unemployment would

result. It is impossible for there to be both inflationary and output gaps at the same time because aggregate demand cannot both exceed and fall short of potential GNP at the same time. The correct response is d.

15.2   Which of the following explains why an increase in aggregate demand does not always lead to an equal increase in real GNP?

1. Potential GNP is an upper limit to real GNP.
2. There is not a sufficient quantity of resources to produce all levels of real GNP.
3. Resource owners and firms may respond by raising resource and product prices instead of producing more output.

    a. 1 and 2 only   c. 2 and 3 only
    b. 1 and 3 only   d. 1, 2, and 3

By definition, *potential GNP* is the amount of output that would be produced if all resources were utilized. This means that real GNP cannot exceed potential GNP because there are not enough resources to produce at a higher level. Thus, statements 1 and 2 must be correct explanations. Whenever aggregate demand exceeds potential GNP, there will be an excess demand in the market for at least some resources and products. Consequently, prices in these markets will rise, and statement 3 is a correct explanation. The correct response is d.

15.3   Which of the following explains why considerable unemployment can exist in a market economy?

    a. At full employment, national income is not always sufficient to purchase all output produced.

    b. Many product and factor prices respond very slowly when supply exceeds demand.

    c. The rate of productivity increase is not always great enough to permit sufficient growth of actual output.

    d. The growth of productive capacity outstrips the growth of consumers' private wants.

Other things equal, the lower the price of a good or resource, the larger the quantity demanded. Thus, if prices were completely flexible and responded quickly to situations of excess demand and excess supply, all markets including the labor market, would clear. That is, full employment, apart from frictional elements, would always exist. Of the other options, none makes sense. By definition, national income equals national output. If the rate of productivity increase limited the growth of actual output, it would mean the economy was at full employment, and to date no nation has sufficient resources to satisfy all of its citizens' private wants. The correct response is b.

15.4   Which of the following features must a good economics model have in order to help us understand the economy?

1. It must be completely realistic.
2. It must be simple enough to understand.
3. It must capture some essential feature of the economy.

    a. 1 and 2 only   c. 2 and 3 only
    b. 1 and 3 only   d. 1, 2, and 3

The use of simple economic models to explain economic events in the real world is made necessary by the fact that the real world economy is very complex. There are so many interrelationships that it would be impossible to consider and understand all of them at one time. Good models in economics are designed to explain only a limited number of phenomena at one time. Consequently, a good model need capture only that part of reality pertinent to the issue under consideration. It is not necessary, for example, for a model that is designed to explain the causes of inflation and unemployment to also explain the distribution of income and the allocation of resources. The correct response is c.

Case 15

THE COST OF UNEMPLOYMENT

The Great Depression of the 1930s was a cataclysmic event that brought misery to millions of Americans and radically changed the way we view the functioning of our economy and the responsibility of government to promote full employment. In 1929, the economy was at full employment, but by 1933 one out of every four workers was without work and many others had only part-time jobs. In 1933, real GNP per person was only half of what it had been in 1929. By 1939, the unemployment rate was still above 17 percent, or about 2½ times higher than it has been in any year since World War II.

Frightening though these figures may be, they fail to capture the extent of suffering and the depth of despair brought on by the depression. A more personal impression of the plight of many can be obtained from the following excerpts from Arthur M. Schlesinger, Jr.'s account of the period 1929-33.[1]

... Across the country the dismal process was beginning, ushering in a new life for millions of Americans. In the twenties wage earners in general had found ample employment, satisfaction in life, hope for the future. Now came the slowdown—only three days of work a week, then perhaps two, then the layoff. And then the search for a new job—at first vigorous and hopeful; then sober; then desperate; the long lines before the

employment offices, the eyes straining for words of hope on the chalked boards, the unending walk from one plant to the next, the all-night wait to be first for possible work in the morning. And the inexorable news, brusque impersonality concealing fear: "No help wanted here" . . . "We don't need nobody" . . . "Move along, Mac, move along" . . .

As savings end, borrowing begins. If there is life insurance, borrowing on that, until it lapses; then loans from relatives and from friends; then the life of credit, from the landlord, from the corner grocer, until the lines of friendship and compassion are snapped. Meat vanishes from the table; lard replaces butter; father goes out less often, is terribly quiet; the children begin to lack shoes, their clothes are ragged, their mothers are ashamed to send them to school. Wedding rings are pawned, furniture is sold, the family moves into ever cheaper, damper, dirtier rooms. In a Philadelphia settlement house a little boy of three cried constantly in the spring of 1930; the doctor found that he was slowly starving. One woman complained that when she had food her children could barely eat; they had become accustomed to so little, she said, that their stomachs had shrunk. The apple peddlers began to appear on cold street corners, their threadbare clothes brushed and neat . . . .

At the breadlines and soup kitchens, hours of waiting would produce a bowl of mush, often without milk or sugar, and a tin cup of coffee. The vapors from the huge steam cookers mingled with the stench of wet clothes and sweating bodies made the air foul. But waiting in the soup kitchen was better than the scavenging in

[1] Arthur M. Schlesinger, Jr., *The Crisis of the Old Order, 1919-1933* (Boston; Houghton-Mifflin Company, 1957). Reproduced by permission of the publisher.

the dump. Citizens of Chicago, in this second winter, could be seen digging into heaps of refuse with sticks and hands as soon as the garbage trucks pulled out. On June 30, 1931, the Pennsylvania Department of Labor and Industry reported that nearly one-quarter of the labor force of the state was out of work. Clarence Pickett of the Friends found schools where 85, 90, even 99 percent of the children were underweight, and, in consequence, drowsy and lethargic. "Have you ever heard a hungry child cry?" asked Lillian Wald of Henry Street. "Have you seen the uncontrollable trembling of parents who have gone half starved for weeks so that the children may have food?" . . . .

And so, through the winter of 1931–32, the third winter of the depression, relief resources, public and private, dwindled toward the vanishing point. In few cities was there any longer pretense of meeting minimum budgetary standards. Little money was available for shoes or clothing, for medical or dental care, for gas or electricity. In New York City entire families were getting an average of $2.39 a week for relief. In Toledo the municipal commissary could allow only 2.14 cents per meal per person per day. In vast rural areas there was no relief coverage at all. "I don't want to steal," a Pennsylvania man wrote Governor Pinchot, "but I won't let my wife and boy cry for something to eat . . . How long is this going to keep up? I cannot stand it any longer . . . . O, if God would only open a way." . . . .

The Philadelphia Community Council described its situation in July 1932 as one of "slow starvation and progressive disintegration of family life." In the Pennsylvania coal fields, miners kept up a subdued battle against starvation, freezing in rickety one-room houses, subsisting on wild weed-roots and dandelions, struggling for life in black and blasted valleys. In Kentucky they ate violet tops, wild onions, and the weeds which cows would eat (one wrote, "as cows won't eat a poison weeds"). while wan children attended school without coats, shoes, or underclothes. In Logan and Mingo Counties of West Virginia, according to Clarence Pickett's testimony before a House committee, people were breaking into storehouses and stealing supplies. "I would steal before I would starve," interjected Congressman Kent Keller of Illinois. "I think all of us would probably," replied the Quaker official, adding hastily: "I don't know whether you want that in the record."

In Oakland, California, four-year-old Narcisson Sandoval, who had been living on refuse, died of starvation, while her brothers and sisters were rushed to a hospital on the verge of death. In Northampton, Massachusetts, Anthony Prasol, the father of eight children, killed himself because he had no hope of work or assistance. Faith in life itself seemed to be ebbing away; the national birthrate for 1931 was 17 percent below 1921 and 10 percent below 1926 . . .

Although there may never be another major depression, since World War II we have had frequent smaller depressions or recessions. In the late fifties and early sixties, the unemployment rate reached 7 percent and in the early seventies it was as high as 6 percent. Although this is a far cry from the 25 percent of the early thirties, it is still a lot higher than it need be and the loss in output is enormous. As was noted in Chapter 14, in 1961 alone the loss of output that resulted from the unemployment rate being 6.7 percent instead of 4 percent was $33 billion. In 1971, the loss due to unemployment in excess of 4 percent was $40 billion. Taking into account not only those who are unemployed but also those who are forced to accept part-time work, those who are discouraged from looking for a job, and those who are kept on full-time but do less than full time work, the difference between a 4 percent and a 6 percent unemployment rate could be thought of as forcing the average worker to accept a lay-off of about 3 weeks during the year and an income loss of 6 percent.

Tables 15.a and 15.b provide some information on recent unemployment figures in the United States for different groups in the labor force. How bad is this post-World-War II unemployment?

SUGGESTIONS FOR ANALYSIS

As was indicated in the foregoing discussion and in Chapters 14 and 15, a certain amount of unemployment—often assumed to be around 4 percent of the labor force—is a normal aspect of a market economy because people are continually shifting jobs. If this shifting, with its temporary "frictional" unemployment, were prohibited, the loss

Table 15.a

SELECTED UNEMPLOYMENT RATES FOR VARIOUS YEARS

Year	All workers	Both sexes 16–19 years	Men over 19	Women over 19	Married men	Blue- collar workers	All white workers	Negro and other races
1960	5.5	14.7	4.7	5.1	3.7	7.8	4.9	10.2
1969	3.5	12.2	2.1	3.7	1.5	3.9	3.1	6.4
1970	4.9	15.2	3.5	4.8	2.6	6.2	4.5	8.2
1971	5.9	16.9	4.4	5.7	3.2	7.4	5.4	9.9

Table 15.b

AVERAGE UNEMPLOYMENT BY DURATION FOR VARIOUS YEARS

(Thousands of Persons 16 Years of Age and Over)

Year	Total unemployment	Duration of unemployment			
		Less than 5 weeks	5–14 weeks	15–26 weeks	27 weeks and over
1960	3,852	1,719	1,176	503	454
1969	2,831	1,629	827	242	133
1970	4,088	2,137	1,289	427	235
1971	4,993	2,234	1,578	665	517

in economic efficiency would outweigh the gain due to keeping all resources 100 percent employed. And of course, millions of people, especially housewives, students, and elderly persons do not take paid jobs because they do not want them. These people are not involuntarily unemployed; they are not considered to be in the labor force and are not counted as unemployed. Table 15.b emphasizes the existence of widespread frictional unemployment in our market system. In all the years shown, about half of all those unemployed were out of work for less than 5 weeks, primarily shifting from one job to another. About another quarter were unemployed for 5-14 weeks, leaving only about one-quarter victims of what might be termed *long-term unemployment.* But remember that 1960 and 1970-71 were mild recessions, while 1969 was generally a boom year. In a major re-

cession, the long-term unemployment totals rise much faster that does the "frictional" total.

But beyond normal frictional unemployment, further involuntary unemployment has large human and economic costs with few offsetting gains. Consider several separate points.

First, as Table 15.a shows, the burden of unemployment falls most heavily on those who are often least able to afford it—on minorities and lower-income blue-collar workers. It also falls most heavily on teenagers, expecially minority-group teenagers, whose family responsibilities are usually limited, but whose alienation has played an important role in the social disruption of recent years. Understandably, when sales slump, businessmen first lay off the least efficient, least experienced, least skilled workers, generally the groups just listed above. And, understandably, in such periods businessmen are unlikely to hire inexperienced teenagers and other less-skilled groups, so unemployment piles up for them. Conversely, it takes a serious recession to run the unemployment rate for experienced married men up over 3 or 4 percent.

Second, an increase in unemployment is typically associated with a more than proportional drop in total output. Thus, the unemployment figures provide an understatement of the loss to society. The post-war period suggests that a 1 percent decrease in unemployment is usually associated with a 3 percent increase in total output. Why? There are four main reasons.

(1) When recession comes and reported unemployment rises, many who stay employed are cut to shorter work weeks. (2) Some workers move to part-time jobs in which they produce less, although they are considered still employed. (3) Managers at least temporarily often keep more workers than they need in recessions because they do not want to lose skilled, valuable employees, so that the average output per worker falls. (4) Last, during periods of rising unemployment, some workers become discouraged and simply drop out of the labor force (stop looking for jobs), which keeps the unemployment rate correspondingly lower, Conversely, when times improve and reported unemployment drops, total output rises more than proportionately because all these factors work in reverse.

"Moderate" levels of unemployment like those of recent years do not have the devastating impact on society that the great depression did. The numbers unemployed are much fewer, and unemployment insurance, welfare payments, food stamps, and the like help to ease the blow for many unemployed and their families. But the costs are still large, for society, in the form of potential output wasted and for the unemployed themselves, in misery and lost income. Involuntary unemployment is a far cry from the "leisure" that some people say the unemployed enjoy. How to avoid widespread unemployment above "frictional" levels is one of the big problems of modern economic policy, and much of the next few chapters is devoted to precisely this question.

16

Aggregate Demand and the Multiplier

16.1 In the preceding chapter, it was concluded that whether there is inflation or unemployment depends on the relationship between _____ _____ and _____ _____ in initial prices.

16.2 If aggregate demand exceeds potential GNP in initial prices, there will be _____ . If aggregate demand falls short of potential GNP in initial prices, there will be _____ . Only if there is neither excess nor insufficient _____ _____ can there be full employment without inflation.

16.3 What determines the level of aggregate demand? You will recall that aggregate demand is the total _____ that consumers, businesses, and governments would make if prices were to remain unchanged. In other words, it is the sum of consumption, investment, and government expenditures at initial prices.

16.4 Consider consumption expenditure first. Clearly, many factors influence how much any family will spend on goods and services: family size, the ages of its members, preferences, and so on. But one factor that explains most of the differences in expenditure among different families is *income*. The more income a family has, the _(more/less)_ it is likely to spend.

ANSWERS

1. aggregate demand . potential GNP
2. inflation . unemployment .
   aggregate demand

3. expenditure
4. more

16.5   When considering the total expenditure of all consumers, the same factor explains most of the changes that have occurred over time. The principal reason that consumption expenditure has

increased over time is that consumers' total _____ has increased.

16.6   As we have seen, the total income that consumers have available to spend is called *disposable*

income. The greater _____ income is, the greater total _____
expenditure is likely to be.

16.7   Although the level of consumption expenditure in any year depends on the level of

_____ income, it is not necessarily and not usually equal to it. Because on the
average people save part of their income, consumption expenditure is usually *(more/less)*
than disposable income.

16.8   Because consumption expenditure depends on disposable income, it can be said that
consumption expenditure is a *function* of disposable income. For this reason, the relationship
between consumption expenditure and disposable income is called the *consumption function.*

The consumption _____ indicates, for any level of disposable income, what the

level of _____ _____ will be. The consumption function can be shown
diagrammatically, as in Figure 16.1. In this diagram, the horizontal axis measures

_____ _____ , and the vertical axis measures _____

_____ .

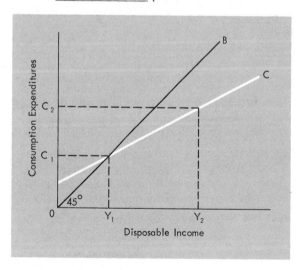

Figure 16.1
The consumption function

16.9   Because the line 0B is a 45 degree line from the origin, any point along that line shows amounts of consumption expenditure and disposable income that are _____ .

16.10   Line C is the consumption function. It shows for any level of disposable income what the level of _____ _____ will be. For example, if disposable income is $0Y_2$, consumption expenditure will be _____ .

16.11   For each level of disposable income, line 0B shows the consumption expenditure that would result if all income were spent. If disposable income is $0Y_2$, consumption expenditure is *(more/less)* than income, and part of income $0Y_2$ will be saved. The amount saved out of $0Y_2$ will be the vertical distance between line 0B and the _____ function.

16.12   If disposable income is $0Y_1$, *(all/not all)* income will be spent because at this income level the consumption function and the 45 degree line intersect. For any level of disposable income less than $0Y_1$, consumption expenditure will be *(less/more)* than disposable income, and some consumers will spend part of their previous savings in addition to their disposable income.

16.13   As is shown by the _____ _____ in Figure 16.1, consumption expenditure depends on _____ _____ .

16.14   Disposable income is closely related to the total income earned in the economy. As you will recall, in Chapter 3 it was emphasized that total income and the market value of total output must be _____ because of the circular flow of income and expenditure. Therefore, disposable income must be related to the market value of total output, which is _____ .

16.15   Disposable income is the income that _____ have available to spend for goods and services. Therefore, if you subtract from GNP (or total income) the income retained by businesses and governments, you will be left with the income retained by consumers, which is _____ _____ .

16.16   The relationship between GNP and disposable income can be summarized as follows:

GNP
less: income retained by businesses $= \begin{cases} \text{depreciation} \\ + \text{ profit} \\ - \text{ direct business taxes} \\ - \text{ dividends} \end{cases}$

ANSWERS

9. equal
10. consumption expenditure . $0C_2$
11. less . consumption
12. all . more

13. consumption function . disposable income
14. equal . GNP
15. consumers . disposable income
16. disposable income

$$\text{less: income retained by governments} \quad = \begin{cases} \text{taxes} \\ -\text{ transfer payments} \end{cases}$$

$$\text{equals: } \underline{\hspace{3cm}} \; \underline{\hspace{3cm}} \quad = \begin{cases} \text{wages, salaries, interest, rent} \\ +\text{ dividends} \\ -\text{ personal taxes} \\ +\text{ transfer payments} \end{cases}$$

16.17   From the above tabulation, you can see that the income earned by each of the three groups in the economy _(is/is not)_ the same as the income retained by each group.

16.18   The business sector, for example, keeps only part of the depreciation and profit that it earns on its investment in capital goods and land. Part is paid out to the government in the form of direct business _____ , and part is paid out to the owners, who are also consumers, in the form of _____ .

16.19   The government sector, although it earns no income, obtains income that it can use for purchases of goods and services by collecting _____ . In addition to indirect business taxes, it collects corporate taxes and personal taxes. The personal taxes include income and social security taxes.

16.20   Not all the income that the government receives in taxes is available to purchase goods and services because part is paid out to consumers in the form of _____ _____ . Thus, the income retained by governments is equal to _____ minus _____ _____ .

16.21   Disposable income, which is the remaining part of GNP, is equal to the income earned by consumers plus the income transfers *from* businesses and governments minus the income transfer *to* the government. The income earned takes the form of wages and salaries, interest, and rents. The income transfers from businesses are _____ , and the income transfers from governments are _____ _____ .

16.22   Put simply, disposable income equals _____ minus the retained income of business, minus taxes, plus transfer payments. Everything else being the same, the greater GNP is, the _(greater/smaller)_ disposable income will be.

ANSWERS

17. is not
18. taxes . dividends
19. taxes

20. transfer payments . taxes . transfer payments
21. dividends . transfer payments
22. GNP . greater

16.23 Because the level of disposable income is closely related to the level of GNP, the consumption function can be constructed in terms of GNP as well as in terms of disposable income. Previously, the consumption function showed the consumption expenditure that would result

for any level of _____ _____ . Taking into account the relationship

between disposable income and GNP, it is possible to show the level of _____

_____ that would result for any level of GNP.

16.24 The consumption function in terms of GNP is shown in Figure 16.2. This time the horizontal

axis measures both _____ _____ and disposable income. The consumption function in terms of real GNP is shown by line C. If GNP were $0Q_1$, the consumption

function indicates that consumption expenditure would be _____ .

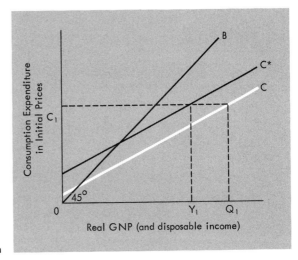

Figure 16.2
The consumption function

16.25 The line C* shows consumption expenditure when the horizontal axis is used to measure disposable income instead of GNP. Because disposable income is _(larger/smaller)_ than GNP, any given amount of GNP, such as $0Q_1$, will be accompanied by a smaller amount of disposable income, such as $0Y_1$. The consumption expenditure indicated by C for a GNP of $0Q_1$ is

_____ . The consumption expenditure indicated by C* for disposable income $0Y_1$

_____ be the same amount.

16.26   For this reason C lies parallel to and to the __*(left/right)*__ of C*. Suppose a disposable income of $500 billion results in consumption expenditure of $400 billion. Because GNP will be greater than disposable income, it will take a GNP that is __*(more/less)*__ than $500 billion to generate $400 billion in consumption expenditure.

16.27   The consumption function C shows how one component of aggregate demand depends on the level of GNP. The higher real GNP, the __*(higher/lower)*__ the expenditure that consumers would be willing to make at initial prices.

16.28   Suppose, for the sake of simplicity, that both investment expenditure and government expenditure were independent of the level of GNP. This means that whatever the level of GNP,

_____ and _____ expenditures would be the same.

16.29   The independence of GNP for these two types of expenditures is shown in Figure 16.3. Diagram (i) shows the investment function I as a __*(horizontal/vertical)*__ line. This indicates, for example, that whether GNP is $0Q_1$ or $0Q_2$ investment expenditure will be _____ .

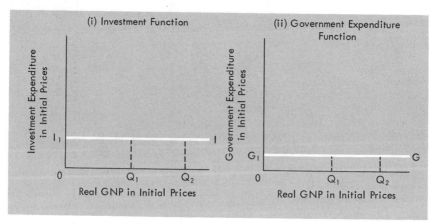

Figure 16.3   Investment and government expenditure

16.30   Diagram (ii) shows the government expenditure function G as a _____ line. In this case, whether GNP is $0Q_1$, $0Q_2$, or any other amount, government expenditure will be

_____ .

16.31   Because aggregate demand is the total _____ that would be made at initial prices, it will be equal to the sum of _____ , _____ , and _____ expenditures.

ANSWERS

26. right . more
27. higher
28. investment . government
29 horizontal . $0I_1$

30. horizontal . $0G_1$
31. expenditure . consumption . investment .
    government

16.32 By adding together the consumption, investment, and government expenditures functions from Figures 16.2 and 16.3, it is possible to obtain an _____ _____ curve. This is shown as the AD curve in Figure 16.4

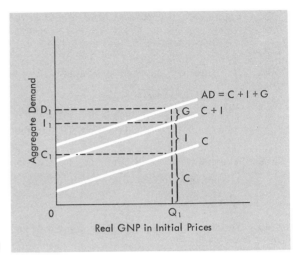

Figure 16.4
Aggregate demand

16.33 In Figure 16.4, the C curve is, of course, the _____ _____ from Figure 16.2. It shows for different levels of real GNP the consumption _____ that would be made by households.

16.34 The C + I curve is obtained by adding to the consumption expenditure, given by the C curve for each level of real GNP, the _____ expenditure given by the investment function shown in Figure 16.3 (i). The C + I curve shows the sum of consumption and investment expenditures that would be made by households and businesses for each level of _____ _____ in initial prices.

16.35 Finally, the AD curve is obtained by adding to the _(C/C + I)_ curve the government expenditure given by the G curve in Figure 16.3 (ii). The AD curve shows the level of _____ _____ that would result for each level of _____ _____ in initial prices.

16.36 Suppose real GNP were $0Q_1$. At this level of real GNP, consumption expenditure would be _____ , investment expenditure would be _____ , and government

ANSWERS

32. aggregate demand

33. consumption function . expenditure

34. investment . real GNP

35. C + I . aggregate demand . real GNP

36. $0C_1$. $C_1 I_1$. $I_1 D_1$. $0D_1$

expenditure would be _____ . Aggregate demand, which would be the sum of these three, would be _____ .

16.37   By putting the aggregate demand curve together with the aggregate supply curve from Figure 15.3, it is possible to see what level of real GNP will result, and whether there will be _____ or _____ . This is done in Figure 16.5.

16.38   In Figure 16.5, suppose that initally GNP were $0Q_0$—what would happen? At that level of real GNP, aggregate demand would be _____ , which would be _(greater/less)_ than real GNP. This means that the amount of output that buyers would want to buy at that level of real GNP is _(greater/less)_ than the amount produced.

16.39   At a real GNP of $0Q_0$, there will be _____ resources. Because aggregate demand exceeds real GNP, producers _(will/will not)_ hire more resources and will increase _(prices/output)_ .

16.40   Thus, real GNP would not be maintained at $0Q_0$ because at that level aggregate demand would be _(greater/less)_ than aggregate supply. The behavior of producers in such a situation would cause _(an increase/a decrease)_ in real GNP.

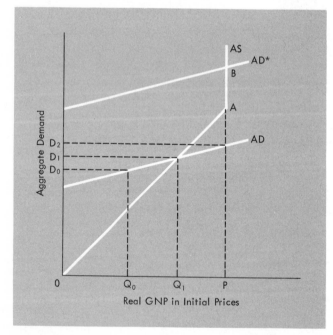

Figure 16.5
Aggregate demand and aggregate supply

ANSWERS

37. inflation . unemployment (either order)   39. unemployed . will . output
38. $0D_0$. greater . greater   40. greater . an increase

16.41 As long as real GNP is less than $0Q_1$, aggregate demand will be _(greater/less)_ than aggregate supply, and real GNP will _(increase/decrease)_ .

16.42 Suppose real GNP were initially equal to 0P. Here, aggregate demand would be equal to _____ , which is _(greater/less)_ than real GNP. Producers would find that they are producing more output than they can sell and will act to _(increase/decrease)_ real GNP by reducing their employment of resources and producing less output.

16.43 As long as real GNP is greater than $0Q_1$, producers will act to _(increase/decrease)_ GNP.

16.44 Because real GNP will increase if it is below $0Q_1$ and decrease if it is above $0Q_1$, it can be expected that real GNP will adjust to the level _____ . This is the level where aggregate demand and aggregate supply are _____ . This is the *equilibrium* level of real GNP.

16.45 The level of real GNP where aggregate demand and aggregate supply are equal is called the _____ level of GNP. The economy is in equilibrium when there is no tendency to change. In Figure 16.5, it is clear that $0Q_1$ is the only _____ level of real GNP.

16.46 Suppose, in Figure 16.5, that the AD curve were AD* and intersected the aggregate supply curve in the vertical segment AB. If this occurred, firms would find that at initial prices buyers would be willing to purchase _(more/less)_ output than they could produce. Because firms could not expand production enough to match aggregate demand, the result would be _(unemployment/inflation)_ .

16.47 In short, whether there is inflation, unemployment, or neither depends on the relative positions of the aggregate _____ and _____ curves.

16.48 Looking back to Figure 16.5, if the aggregate demand curve is AD*, there will be an _____ gap of _____ , whereas if the aggregate demand curve is AD, there will be an _____ gap of _____ .

16.49 In terms of the simple model of the economy shown in Figure 16.6, the equilibrium level of real GNP depends on where the aggregate demand curve intersects the aggregate supply curve.

ANSWERS

41. greater . increase
42. $0D_2$. less . decrease
43. decrease
44. $0Q_1$. equal
45. equilibrium . equilibrium

46. more . inflation
47. demand . supply (either order)
48. inflationary . AB . output . Q_1P
49. 0Q

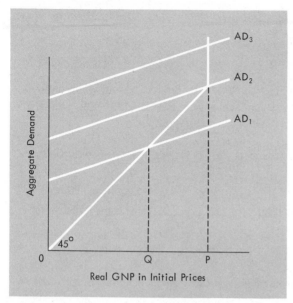

Figure 16.6
Aggregate demand and aggregate supply

For example, for aggregate demand curve AD_1, the equilibrium real GNP is _____ .

16.50   If real GNP deviates from its equilibrium level, the amount of output that consumers, businesses, and governments would be willing to buy and the amount of output produced _(would/would not)_ be equal. In such an event, producers would adjust production to match aggregate demand and real GNP would adjust to its _____ level.

16.51   Thus, in Figure 16.6, real GNP cannot permanently diverge from 0Q as long as the aggregate demand curve is _____ . Thus, ignoring temporary deviations from equilibrium, in order for real GNP to change it is necessary for the _____ _____ curve to shift.

16.52   If the aggregate demand curve were to shift up from AD_1 to AD_2, real GNP would increase from _____ to _____ .

16.53   Similarly, if aggregate demand were initially AD_3, to eliminate the inflationary gap it would be necessary for the aggregate demand curve to shift to AD_1, inflation would be avoided, but _____ would result.

16.54   Aggregate demand is the total expenditure in initial prices made by consumers, businesses, and governments. The higher the level of real GNP in initial prices, the _(higher/lower)_ the level

ANSWERS

50. would not . equilibrium
51. AD_1 . aggregate demand
52. 0Q . 0P

53. unemployment
54. higher . disposable . consumption

of aggregate demand. One reason for this is that when there is an increase in real GNP, there

is also an increase in _____ income and, as a result, an increase in _____
expenditure.

16.55 An increase in real GNP will result in an increase in _____ _____ .
Such a change in aggregate demand is called an *induced* change in expenditure because it is

induced, or caused, by the change in _____ _____ .

16.56 An increase in aggregate demand that is caused by factors other than an increase in real GNP
is called an *autonomous* change in expenditure. The difference between an induced and an

autonomous change in aggregate demand is that an _____ change is caused by a

change in real GNP, whereas an _____ change is caused by some other factor.

16.57 If consumption expenditure and, therefore, aggregate demand increase because of an increase

in real GNP, this would be an _____ increase in aggregate demand. If investment
expenditure increases because a survey of consumers' spending intentions make businesses

more optimistic about future demand for their output, this would be an _____
increase in aggregate demand.

16.58 In terms of the aggregate demand curve, a movement along the curve as real GNP changes is

an _____ change in aggregate demand.

16.59 How would an autonomous change in aggregate demand be represented diagramatically?
Suppose that all of a sudden consumers decided to consume more of their income. This means
that at any level of real GNP, total consumption expenditure would be _(higher/lower)_ than
it was before. Or, in other words, the consumption function would shift _(upward/downward)_ .

16.60 Such a change in consumers' behavior is represented in Figure 16.7 (i), in which the

_____ _____ shifts from C_1 to C_2. Because aggregate demand is the
sum of consumption, investment, and government expenditures, a shift in the consumption

function from C_1 to C_2 will cause the _____ _____ curve to
_____ from AD_1 to AD_2. This assumes, of course, _(an/no)_ autonomous change
in investment and government expenditures.

ANSWERS

55. aggregate demand . real GNP
56. induced . autonomous
57. induced . autonomous
58. induced

59. higher . upward
60. consumption function . aggregate demand .
    shift . no

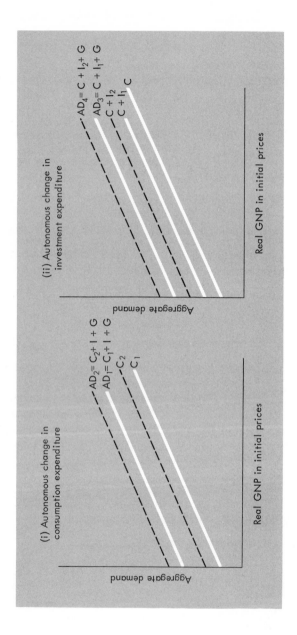

Figure 16.7 Autonomous changes in aggregate demand

16.61   In this example, a change in aggregate demand due to a change in consumers' preferences resulted in a _(shift in/movement along)_ the aggregate demand curve. In fact, any

_____ change in consumption expenditure will result in a shift in the aggregate demand curve.

16.62   Suppose consumers became worried about a possible depression, and they decided to save more and consume less of their present income in order to provide for that "rainy day." This would be an _____ change in expenditure and would result in a _(shift in/movement along)_ both the consumption function and the aggregate demand curve.

16.63   Suppose that the depression did come, and the decline in GNP and disposable income caused consumption expenditure to decline. This would be an _____ change in expenditure and would result in a _(shift in/movement along)_ both the consumption function and the aggregate demand curve.

16.64   Changes in investment expenditure can be analyzed in the same way. You will recall that for the sake of simplicity we assumed investment expenditure was _(dependent on/independent of)_ the level of real GNP. In terms of induced and autonomous changes in expenditure, we assumed that there were no _____ changes in expenditure. Consequently, in our simplified analysis we will consider only _____ changes in investment expenditure.

16.65   Suppose that a series of new inventions makes investment in capital goods more profitable to undertake. This increase in the profitability on investment means that, for any level of GNP, businesses will want to make _(greater/less)_ investment expenditure than before. As a result, the investment _____ will shift up.

16.66   In terms of Figure 16.7 (ii), even though the _____ function remains unchanged, the shift in the _____ function raises the $C + I_1$ curve to $C + I_2$ and the aggregate demand curve from _____ to _____ .

16.67   What is the effect of an autonomous change in aggregate demand? In Figure 16.8, an autonomous increase is represented by an upward shift in the aggregate demand curve from AD_1 to AD_2. The amount of this shift, as is shown on the vertical axis is _____ .

ANSWERS

61. shift in . autonomous
62. autonomous . shift in
63. induced . movement along
64. independent of . induced . autonomous

65. greater . function
66. consumption . investment . AD_3 . AD_4
67. D_1D_2

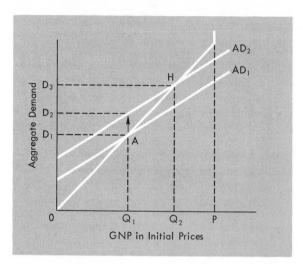

Figure 16.8
Autonomous and induced changes
in aggregate demand

16.68   The effect of this upward shift in the aggregate demand curve will be to shift its point of

intersection with the aggregate supply curve from _____ to _____ .
This indicates that, as a result of the shift from AD_1 to AD_2, aggregate demand will increase

from _____ to _____ .

16.69   Thus, the autonomous increase in aggregate demand of _____ will lead to a total

increase in aggregate demand of _____ . As you can clearly see, the total increase
is _(greater than/equal to)_ the autonomous increase. And, because there is unemployment,
the increase in real GNP will be _(greater than/equal to)_ the autonomous increase in aggregate
demand.

16.70   How is it that an autonomous increase in aggregate demand can lead to a greater total increase
in aggregate demand and real GNP? Because there is unemployment, the autonomous increase

in aggregate demand will lead, at first, to an equal increase in _____

_____ . But that increase in real GNP will induce a further increase in aggregate
demand. That is, an autonomous increase in aggregate demand will lead to an increase in real

GNP that, in turn, will lead to an _____ increase in aggregate demand.

16.71   Now, the induced increase in aggregate demand will lead to a further increase in real GNP,

which will in turn lead to another _____ increase in aggregate demand

16.72   This process can be seen in Figure 16.9. Here, the autonomous increase in aggregate demand

ANSWERS

68. A . H . OD_1 . OD_3 70. real GNP . induced
69. D_1D_2 . D_1D_3 . greater than .   71. induced
     greater than   72. BC . CD . DE . H

of AB will lead, at first, to an equal increase in real GNP of _____ . This in turn will lead to an induced increase in aggregate demand of _____ , which will lead to a further increase in real GNP of _____ . This will continue until point _____ is reached.

16.73 The total increase in aggregate demand will be AB, which is the _____ increase, plus CD, EF, and so on, which are the _____ changes in aggregate demand.

16.74 Similarly, the increase in real GNP will be the sum of _____ , _____ , _____ , and so on.

16.75 As Figure 16.9 makes clear, an autonomous change in aggregate demand will have a multiplied effect on real GNP. This multiplied effect is called the *multiplier*.

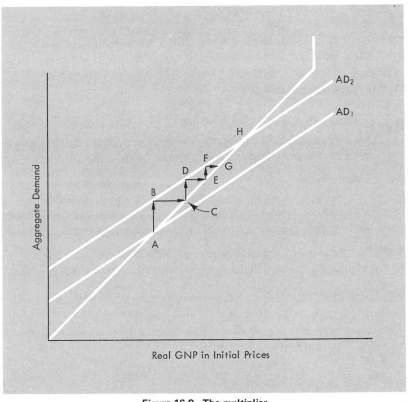

Figure 16.9 The multiplier

ANSWERS

73. autonomous . induced   75. autonomous
74. BC . DE . FG

The multiplier shows how many times greater the total increase in real GNP will be than an _____ increase in aggregate demand.

16.76   If an autonomous increase in aggregate demand of $10 billion will cause a total increase in real GNP of $30 billion, the _____ is 3. If an autonomous decrease in aggregate demand of $5 billion will cause a total decrease in real GNP of $10 billion, the _____ is _____ .

16.77   The reason there is a multiplier is that an autonomous increase in aggregate demand leads to an increase in real GNP, which leads to an _____ increase in aggregate demand, which leads to an increase in _____ _____ , which leads to . . . and so on.

16.78   At first, you might think that this process would continue to increase real GNP indefinitely. However, as Figure 16.9 makes clear, each round of increase in real GNP will be _(larger/smaller)_ than the preceding one.

16.79   The reason for this is that an increase in real GNP will not lead to an equal increase in consumption, investment, and government expenditures. Rather, it will induce an increase in aggregate demand that is _(greater/less)_ than itself. That is, _(all/not all)_ of an increase in real GNP (or total income) will be spent.

16.80   In general, consumers will spend _(part/all)_ of an increase in disposable income and save _(part/none)_ . The increase in consumption expenditure divided by the increase in disposable income is called the *marginal propensity to consume*, or *MPC*. Because part of an increase in disposable income will be saved, the _____ must be less than 1.

16.81   For simplicity, it will be assumed here that all of any increase in real GNP will take the form of an increase in disposable income. Under this assumption, the induced increase in consumption expenditure divided by the increase in real GNP will be the _____ . For example, if an increase in real GNP of $3 billion will induce an increase in consumption expenditure of $2 billion, the MPC is _____ . In general,

$$\frac{\text{the change in consumption expenditure}}{\text{the change in real GNP}} = \underline{\hspace{3cm}},$$

or, using the symbol Δ for "change in,"

$$\frac{\Delta C}{\Delta GNP} = \underline{\hspace{3cm}}.$$

16.82   The MPC tells you how much __*(autonomous/induced)*__ consumption expenditure will result from a change in real GNP. If the MPC is 1/2, a decrease in real GNP of $100 billion will cause a decrease in consumption expenditure of $ _____ billion.

16.83   Under the simplified assumption that investment expenditure was independent of real GNP, an increase in real GNP would not result in any _____ investment expenditure. Similarly, government expenditure is not considered to change systematically with changes in real GNP. Following this assumption, an increase in real GNP __*(will/will not)*__ induce an increase in government expenditure.

16.84   Thus, the amount of induced aggregate demand that results from an increase in real GNP depends on the _____ . For example, if the MPC is 0.7, an increase in real GNP of $10 billion will induce an increase in consumption expenditure of $ _____ billion and in aggregate demand, $ _____ billion.

16.85   Because the induced change in consumption is less than the change in the real GNP that caused it, the MPC is __*(less than/equal to/greater than)*__ 1. It is because MPC is less than _____ that, in the multiplier process, the successive increases in real GNP become __*(larger/smaller)*__ . This can be seen in Table 16.1, which shows the multiplier effect of an _____ increase in investment expenditure of 10 when the MPC is 0.5. In this example, it will be assumed that there is a sufficient quantity of unemployed resources so that an increase in aggregate demand will result in an equal increase in _____ _____ .

16.86   In the first round, ΔI is _____ , which is the _____ change in investment expenditure that starts the multiplier process. Because there is no autonomous change in consumption, in the first round ΔC is _____ , ΔAD is _____ , and ΔGNP is _____ .

ANSWERS

82. induced . 50
83. induced . will not
84. MPC . 7 . 7

85. less than . 1 . smaller . autonomous . real GNP
86. 10.0 . autonomous . 0.0 . 10.0 . 10.0

Table 16.1

THE MULTIPLIER EFFECT OF AN AUTONOMOUS INCREASE IN EXPENDITURE

	Assume: *Autonomous change in investment expenditure = 10 and MPC = 0.5*			
Round	ΔC	ΔI	ΔAD	ΔGNP
1	0	10.0	10.0	10.0
2	5.0	0	5.0	5.0
3	2.5	0	2.5	2.5
4	—	—	—	—
5	0.625	0	0.625	0.625
6	0.3125	0	0.3125	0.3125
·	·	·	·	·
·	·	·	·	·
·	·	·	·	·
·	·	·	·	·
—				
Total Change	10.0	10.0	20.0	20.0

16.87 The increase in real GNP that results from the autonomous increase in investment expenditure in the first round generates an _____ increase in aggregate demand in the second round. In the second round, then, because the MPC 0.5 ΔC is _____ , and because we are assuming no induced changes in investment, ΔI is _____ . As a result, ΔAD is _____ , which causes an increase in real GNP of _____ .

16.88 In the third round, ΔC is _____ , ΔI is _____ , and ΔAD is _____ . All these changes are _____ by the change in real GNP that resulted in the second round. In turn, they cause another increase in real GNP, of

_____ .

16.89 You can calculate for yourself and fill in the table the fourth round effects that result from the third round increase in real GNP. The figures in the ΔAD and ΔGNP columns are, of course, equal because for levels of GNP below potential GNP a change in aggregate demand results in an equal change in _____ _____ .

ANSWERS

87. induced . 5 . 0 . 5 . 5   89. real GNP
88. 2.5 . 0 . 2.5 . induced . 2.5

16.90 Because MPC is less than 1, each successive round has _(larger/smaller)_ changes than the one before. As the number of rounds increases, these successive changes become closer and closer to _(0/1/10)_ and become negligible.

16.91 As can be seen from the table, the sum of all the autonomous and induced changes in aggregate demand is _____ . As a result, the total increase in real GNP is also _____ . Because the autonomous change in aggregate demand was 10 and the total increase in real GNP was 20, the multiplier in this case is equal to _____ .

16.92 It is no accident that the value of the multiplier in this example was 2. It resulted directly from the fact that the MPC out of real GNP was 5/10, 1/2. Suppose, for example, the MPC had been 2/3. In the second round, the increase in aggregate demand and real GNP would have been _(larger/smaller)_ . As a result, if the MPC had been 2/3 instead of 1/2, the multiplier would have been _(larger/smaller)_ .

16.93 If the MPC had been 2/3, you would have found that an autonomous increase in expenditure of 10 would have led to a total increase in real GNP of 30. The larger the MPC, the _(larger/smaller)_ will be the _____ . An MPC of 2/3 yields a multiplier of 3, and, as we have seen, an MPC of 5/10, or 1/2, yields a multiplier of _____ . The formula for calculating the multiplier is:

$$\text{Multiplier} = \frac{1}{1-\text{MPC}} \cdot$$

16.94 The exact relationship between the multiplier and the marginal propensity to consume can easily be derived from what has already been discussed. You know that the final change in GNP will be equal to the _____ change and the _____ change in aggregate demand. You also know that the induced change is equal to the _____ times the final change in GNP. In symbols, then, these facts can be summarized as follows:

$$\Delta\text{GNP} = \text{autonomous } \Delta\text{AD} + \text{MPC} \times \Delta\text{GNP}$$

16.95 Subtracting "MPC X ΔGNP" from both sides of this equation results in the following equation:

$$\Delta\text{GNP} - \text{_____} \times \text{_____} = \text{autonomous } \Delta\text{AD}.$$

ANSWERS

90. smaller . 0
91. 20 . 20 . 2
92. larger . larger

93. larger . multiplier . 2
94. autonomous . induced (either order) . MPC
95. MPC . ΔGNP

16.96   Factoring out "ΔGNP" on the left hand side of this equation enables you to rewrite it in the following form:

$$\text{\underline{\hspace{4cm}}} \times (1\text{-MPC}) = \text{autonomous } \Delta\text{AD.}$$

Multiplying both sides of the equation by $\dfrac{1}{1\text{-MPC}}$ gives the final result:

$$\Delta\text{GNP} = \text{\underline{\hspace{4cm}}} \times \text{autonomous } \Delta\text{AD}.$$

16.97   In words, this equation says that the final change in GNP is equal to the _____ change in aggregate demand times $\dfrac{1}{1\text{-MPC}}$. In other words, the multiplier is equal to

_____ .

16.98   In the example analyzed in Table 16.1, the MPC was 1/2. In this case, $\dfrac{1}{1\text{-MPC}}$, which is the

_____ , equals $\dfrac{1}{1\text{-}1/2} = \dfrac{1}{1/2} = $ _____ . This, you recall, _(was was not)_ the value of the multiplier calculated from the total change in GNP and the autonomous change in aggregate demand.

16.99   If MPC were 2/3, what would the multiplier be? In this case,

$$\frac{1}{1\text{-MPC}} = \frac{1}{1\text{-}2/3} = \frac{1}{1/3} = \text{\underline{\hspace{3cm}}}.$$

If the MPC were 3/4, what would the multiplier be? _____ Suppose the MPC were 5/8, what would the multiplier be? _____ .

16.100   This relationship between the multiplier and the MPC was derived under the assumption that there was no induced change in _____ or government expenditure and that any change in GNP showed up as a change in _____ income. If any change in GNP induced a change in I, for example, we would also have a marginal propensity to invest (MPI) and, consequently, a _(larger/smaller)_ multiplier because any autonomous change in expenditure would bring about greater induced changes in expenditure. In this case the formula for the multiplier would be:

$$\text{Multiplier} = \frac{1}{1\text{-}(\text{MPC+MPI})}.$$

In terms of out diagrams, for example Figure 16.9, the slope of the aggregate demand curve would be steeper, and the multiplier would be _(larger/smaller)_ .

ANSWERS

96. ΔGNP . $\dfrac{1}{1\text{-MPC}}$

97. autonomous . $\dfrac{1}{1\text{-MPC}}$

98. multiplier . 2 . was
99. 3 . 4 . 2-2/3
100. investment . disposable . larger . larger

16.101 In summary, when there are unemployed resources, an _____ increase in aggregate demand will have the effect of increasing real GNP by a *(larger/smaller)* amount.

16.102 The increase in real GNP will be equal to the _____ times the autonomous increase in aggregate demand. The size of the multiplier will depend on the _____ , which indicates how much an increase in aggregate demand will be induced by an increase in real GNP. More precisely, the multiplier will be equal to _____ .

16.103 It should be emphasized that there will be a full multiplier effect only when it is possible for real GNP to change in response to a change in aggregate demand. When there are no unemployed resources, an autonomous increase in aggregate demand *(will/will not)* lead to a multiplied increase in real GNP. Instead, the increase in aggregate demand will lead to

_____ .

16.104 In terms of the aggregate demand and supply diagram, there will be a full multiplier effect on real GNP from an autonomous increase in aggregate demand only if the new aggregate demand curve does not intersect the vertical portion of the aggregate supply curve. If it were to do so, part of the multiplier effect would take the form of an increase in the _____ level instead of an increase in _____ _____ .

16.105 This can be seen in Figure 16.10, which shows an _____ increase in aggregate demand represented by a shift in the aggregate demand curve from AD_1 to AD_2. In order for the full multiplier effect to be realized, it must be possible for the economy to reach point B. This is impossible because real GNP cannot exceed _____ _____ , which is equal to 0P.

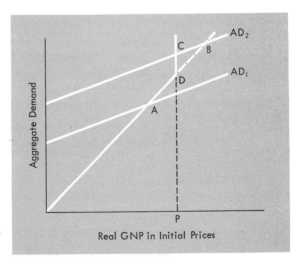

Figure 16.10
The absence of a full multiplier effect

ANSWERS

101. autonomous . larger

102. multiplier . MPC . $\frac{1}{1-MPC}$

103. will not . inflation

104. price . real GNP

105. autonomous . potential GNP

16.106   As a result, instead of increasing real GNP beyond 0P, this shift in the aggregate demand curve will cause an increase in the price level. This is indicated by the _____ gap CD.

REVIEW QUESTIONS

For all the review questions in this chapter, assume that investment expenditure remains unchanged and that consumption expenditure depends only on the level of disposable income.

16.1   Last year in a certain economy, a $400 million increase in investment expenditure was accompanied by a $1 billion increase in consumer spending. Which of the following is the most likely explanation of why the consumer spending increase exceeded the investment expenditure increase?

a. In most economies, consumer expenditures in any year exceed investment expenditures.

b. Increased investment expenditures are usually accompanied by increased government expenditures.

c. Increased spending by those with higher take-home pay, caused by the increased investment expenditure, led to increased income and spending by others.

d. The increased $1 billion of consumer spending equaled the $400 million increase of investment expenditure plus the $600 million increase in government expenditure.

The multiplier process is that process by which, given unemployed resources, an exogenous increase in expenditure will generate or induce a second round of new expenditure, which in turn will induce a third round, and so on. Thus, other things remaining unchanged, an investment expenditure increase will lead to an even greater total spending increase. Although it is true that in most economies consumer expenditures in any year exceed investment expenditures, this is not the reason that increases in investment expenditure lead to increases in total spending. The correct response is c.

16.2   An autonomous increase in government expenditure must always lead to which of the following?

1. an induced increase in expenditure
2. an increase in the price level

a. 1 only

b. 2 only

c. either 1 or 2 or both

d. both 1 and 2

If sufficient unemployed resources exist, an increase in government expenditure will lead to an induced increase in expenditure. If there are not sufficient unemployed resources to make possible an increase in output to match the increase in government expenditure times the multi-

ANSWERS

106. inflationary

plier, an increase in government expenditure will lead to an increase in the price level, since it will cause excess aggregate demand. Thus, either 1 or 2 or both must result. Both 1 and 2 need not occur simultaneously, however. The correct response is c.

16.3   If the value of the marginal propensity to consume were to increase, which of the following would result?

1. The value of the multiplier would increase.
2. Potential GNP would increase.
3. The level of investment expenditure would increase.

    a. 1 only   c. 1 and 2 only
    b. 3 only   d. 1 and 3 only

The value of the multiplier is $\frac{1}{1-MPC}$. Therefore, the higher the value of MPC, the higher the value of the multiplier. For example, an MPC of .5 yields a multiplier of 2, whereas an MPC of .8 yields a multiplier of 5. Neither potential GNP nor the level of expenditure depend upon the value of the MPC. The correct response is a.

16.4   The following data refer to a hypothetical economy for 1972.

$$C = \$500 \text{ million}$$
$$I = \$100 \text{ million}$$
$$G = \$100 \text{ million}$$
$$\text{Potential GNP} = \$1 \text{ billion}$$
$$\text{Value of the MPC} = \frac{2}{3}$$

Had investment expenditures been increased by $50 million and government expenditures increased by $40 million, which of the following would have occurred?

    a. an increase in GNP of $90 million   c. an increase in GNP of $540 million
    b. an increase in GNP of $270 million   d. a rise in the price level

With an MPC of $\frac{2}{3}$, the value of the multiplier is 3. The increase in autonomous expenditure of $90 million ($40 million + $50 million) would lead to an increase of GNP of $90 million ✕ 3 = $270 million. Because actual GNP equals $700, the increase of $270 is still less than potential GNP of $1 billion. Thus, there is no increase in the price level. The correct response is b.

Case 16

MUST WARS CAUSE INFLATION?

A large part of the blame for the recent inflationary experience in the United States is commonly assigned to the Vietnam War. One reason for this is that anyone familiar with

Table 16.a

THE RATE OF INFLATION, DEFENSE EXPENDITURE, AND UNEMPLOYMENT, 1929–1971

	Average annual rate of increase in GNP deflator	*Average annual defense expenditure as as a percent of GNP*	*Average unemployment rate*
1929–1940	–1	1	16.8
1941–1945 (World War II)	7	34	3.9
1946–1950	6	4	4.6
1951–1953 (Korean War)	5	12	3.1
1954–1965	2	9	5.3
1966–1970 (Vietnam War)	4	9	3.9

American history knows that whenever the U.S. has been involved in a major war, prices have risen at a rapid rate. And, by historical standards, the inflation we have had during this war—about 4 percent per year—has been modest indeed. During the Civil War, for example, the rate of inflation was about 25 percent per year, and during World War I the rate was 12 percent per year. Table 16.a records the rate of increase in the GNP deflator for different subperiods since 1929, together with defense expenditure and the unemployment rate.

What is obvious from this data is that there has definitely been a higher rate of inflation during war time (about 5 percent per year overall) than during peace time (about 1 percent per year overall). But what is more disturbing, perhaps, is the apparent inevitability of the association of inflation with war time. Is there something special about defense expenditure that causes prices to rise? Does the economy function differently during war time? Must wars cause inflation? Does the theory spelled out in this and the preceding chapter help to understand this phenomenon?

SUGGESTIONS FOR ANALYSIS

Before trying to answer these questions, let us briefly review what we know from the theory of aggregate supply and demand about inflation. This theory says that as long as there are idle resources in the economy, an expansion in spending will result primarily in an increase in output without much of an increase in the price level. But, when output expands to the level of potential GNP, any further increase in aggregate demand will result primarily in an increase in the price level. Thus, inflation results whenever there is excess aggregate demand.

How well does this theory fit the facts about inflation during war-time years? As Table 16.a shows, involvement in a major war requires very large increases in defense expenditure. And, as was discussed in detail in this chapter, autonomous increases in any kind of expenditure will tend to generate a multiplied increase in aggregate demand. If the resulting increase in aggregate demand were to exceed potential GNP, inflation would result. Thus, if the increases in defense expenditure that occurred during these major wars were large enough to create excess aggregate demand, the war-time inflation phenomenon would be entirely consistent with the theory. How can we determine whether the increase in defense spending created excess aggregate demand? One way would be to look at the unemployment rate. If there were excess aggregate demand we could expect to see the unemployment rate below 4 percent. As can be seen in Table 16-a, in every one of these war-time periods the unemployment rate was below 4 percent. Actually, these average unemployment figures understate the extent of the excess aggregate demand. During World War II, the unemployment rate fell as low as 1.2 percent, and during the Korean and Vietnam Wars the unemployment rate hit lows of 2.5 and 3.3. What these figures suggest is that there is nothing unexpected or inexplicable about war-time inflation. It is exactly what our theory would predict.

Although it is somewhat reassuring to know that our theory fits real world experience, it is not so comforting to realize that our policy makers were unable to prevent the inflation from occurring. Does our theory not provide some guidance as to how the inflation could be avoided? The answer is a resounding "yes." If an increase in defense expenditure, in the absence of any other autonomous changes in expendi-ture, would create excess aggregate demand, what obviously is required is a sufficient auton-omous decrease in other components of aggregate demand to eliminate the inflationary gap. Looking ahead to the next 3 chapters, the government does have policy tools that can bring about such a decrease. The government has often not had the political courage to use these tools. If other components of aggregate demand are to be reduced, consumers and business will have to be induced to cut their consumption and investment expenditure. Because consumers and business will not enjoy the prospect of being pressured through higher taxes and higher interest rates into cutting their expenditures, the implementation of anti-inflationary policies cannot be expected to over-joy the electorate. Thus, economic theory tells us what needs to be done to avoid inflation—even during wars. The question is whether we have the will to do what must be done.

17

Fiscal Policy

17.1 In Chapters 15 and 16, it was shown that it is possible for aggregate demand to exceed or fall short of potential GNP in initial prices. If, in the simple model, there is excess aggregate demand, the result will be _____ . If there is insufficient aggregate demand, the result will be _____ .

17.2 Only if aggregate demand is just equal to potential GNP in initial prices can there be

_____ _____ without _____ .

17.3 In Chapter 16, it was shown that in order to shift the aggregate demand curve to eliminate either excess or insufficient aggregate demand there must be an _____ change in some component of aggregate demand.

17.4 Many factors can cause an autonomous change in aggregate demand. Unfortunately, the factors that would generate the autonomous change necessary to avoid unemployment or inflation do not always exist in a market economy. This is made evident by the data presented in Chapter 14, which show that in the United States there _(have/have not)_ been frequent periods of unemployment and of inflation.

17.5 Fortunately, however, it is possible for the government to take policy measures that will cause autonomous changes in aggregate demand. That is, by taking the right policy measures the government can help to avoid _____ and _____ .

ANSWERS

1. inflation . unemployment
2. full employment . inflation
3. autonomous
4. have
5. inflation . unemployment (either order)

17.6 It is possible for the government to change the level of aggregate demand through *fiscal policy*, which is the general name for government expenditure and tax policies. Because the government will always be making expenditures and collecting taxes, it will always have a

_____ policy even though it may not consciously take into account its effect on

the level of aggregate demand. The question here is how can _____ policy be used to help achieve full employment without inflation?

17.7 There are several ways in which fiscal policy can be used to change the level of aggregate demand. The most obvious way is by changing government expenditure. You will recall that

government expenditure includes only government purchases of _____ and

_____ . A change in government purchases of goods and services is an example of

_____ _____ .

17.8 You will also recall that aggregate demand is the sum of consumption, investment, and

_____ expenditures. Therefore, a change in government expenditures, as long as it does not directly cause offsetting changes in private spending, is an example of how fiscal

policy can be used to change the level of _____ _____ .

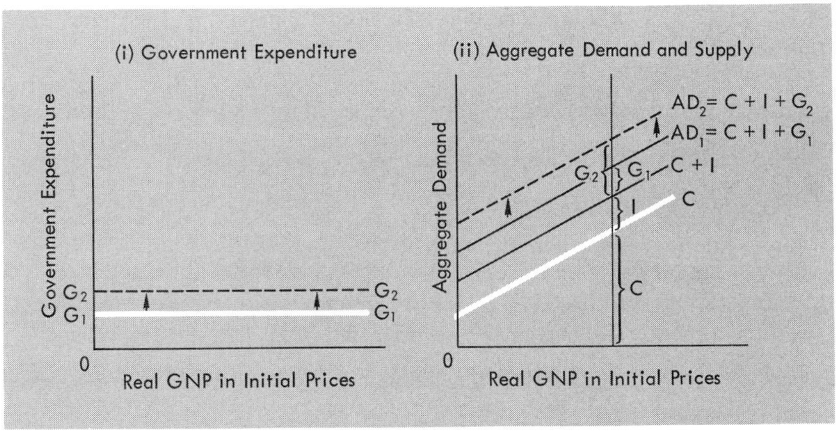

Figure 17.1 Government expenditure and aggregate demand

17.9 That is, given the consumption and investment functions, an increase in government expenditure will cause the _____ _____ curve to shift *(upward/downward)* by an equal amount. This can be seen in Figure 17.1, which shows in (i) the change in government expenditure and in (ii) the effect of that change on the aggregate demand curve.

ANSWERS

6. fiscal . fiscal
7. goods . services . fiscal policy
8. government . aggregate demand
9. aggregate demand . upward

17.10 An increase in government expenditure from $0G_1$ to $0G_2$, as shown in Figure 17.1 (i), will result in an upward shift in the aggregate demand curve from _____ to _____ , as shown in Figure 17.1 (ii).

17.11 This will be the result as long as the increase in government expenditure does not cause an offsetting shift in the _____ and _____ functions. Is there any reason to believe that an increase in government expenditure would cause such an offsetting shift?

17.12 You might make this argument: "In order to increase government expenditure, it is necessary to raise taxes. The tax increase will reduce disposable income and, therefore, reduce consumption expenditure." This argument, however, is incorrect because it is not necessary to raise _____ in order to increase _____ _____ .

17.13 It would be possible, obviously, to increase government expenditure if tax receipts were initially *(greater/less)* than government expenditure. Even if this were not true, however, by borrowing the money the government *(could/could not)* increase its expenditure without increasing taxes.

17.14 Although it is true, as will be seen later, that a change in taxes will affect consumption expenditure, it *(is/is not)* true that a change in taxes need accompany a change in government expenditure.

17.15 Thus, a fiscal policy that increases government expenditure while keeping taxes unchanged *(is/is not)* feasible. And such a policy can be expected to increase _____ _____ as shown in Figure 17.1.

17.16 Look now at Figure 17.2, which shows how changes in government expenditure (without a change in tax receipts) can be used to eliminate an output gap or an inflationary gap. In Figure 17.2 (i), if the aggregate demand curve were AD_1, in equilibrium the level of aggregate demand would be _____ , real GNP would be _____ , and there would be an _____ gap of QP.

17.17 In order to eliminate the output gap, real GNP must increase from _____ to _____ . In order to obtain this increase without causing inflation, it is necessary

ANSWERS

10. AD_1 . AD_2
11. consumption . investment (either order)
12. taxes . government expenditure
13. greater . could
14. is not
15. is . aggregate demand
16. $0D_1$. $0Q$. output
17. $0Q$. $0P$. $0D_1$. $0D_2$. D_1D_2

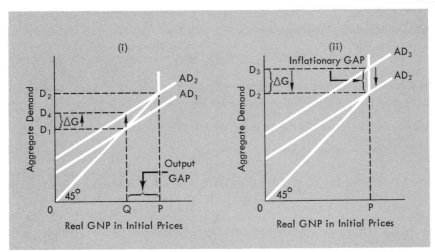

Figure 17.2   Government expenditure policy for full employment without inflation

to raise the equilibrium level of aggregate demand (measuring along the vertical axis) from

_____ to _____ , that is, by an amount _____ .

17.18   In order to have a total increase in aggregate demand of $D_1 D_2$, it is necessary to shift the

aggregate demand curve from AD_1 to _____ . To have a total increase of $D_1 D_2$

requires an autonomous increase in aggregate demand of only _____ because of

the _____ effect.

17.19   In this example, then, an increase in government expenditure of the amount $D_1 D_4$ (with tax

receipts unchanged) will result in a total increase in aggregate demand of _____

and the elimination of the _____ gap without _____ .

17.20   Suppose that initially the aggregate demand curve had been AD_3, as shown in Figure 17.2 (ii),

instead of AD_1. In this case, the economy would be at full employment but would also be con-

fronted with an _____ gap. It would be possible for the government to eliminate

this gap by   _(increasing/decreasing)_   its expenditure.

17.21   If government expenditure were reduced by the amount _____ , the aggregate de-

mand curve would shift to _____ , and the economy could have full employment

(with/without)   inflation.

ANSWERS

18. AD_2 . $D_1 D_4$. multiplier   20. inflationary . decreasing
19. $D_1 D_2$. output . inflation   21. $D_2 D_3$. AD_2 . without

17.22   If government expenditure were reduced by an amount greater than $D_2 D_3$, the inflationary gap __(would/would not)__ be eliminated. At the same time, however, such a policy would cause

_____ .

17.23   What these examples indicate is that in our simple model of the economy changes in government expenditure __(can/cannot)__ be used to move the economy toward full employment without inflation, because a change in government expenditure will shift the _____ _____ curve.

17.24   As was indicated earlier, to change government expenditure is not the only way in which fiscal policy can be used to eliminate either excess or insufficient _____ _____ . An alternative to a change in government expenditure is a change in taxes.

17.25   The exact effect of a change in taxes on the economy depends in part on the type of tax that is changed. For example, a change in corporate profits taxes will affect the rate of return that businesses earn on capital goods and can, therefore, be expected to affect _____ expenditure. A change in personal income taxes, however, will affect disposable income directly and can, therefore, be expected to affect _____ expenditure.

17.26   Changes in taxes of different types, although they vary in many ways, will have similar effects on aggregate demand. For this reason, only one type of tax change will be analyzed in detail. Consider the effects of a change in the personal income tax on aggregate demand. You will recall that the income consumers have available to spend is called _____ income. It is equal to GNP minus retained business income __(plus/minus)__ transfer payments __(plus/minus)__ taxes.

17.27   Given the level of GNP, then, an increase in income taxes will __(increase/decrease)__ disposable income and a decrease in income taxes will __(increase/decrease)__ disposable income.

17.28   You will also recall that disposable income appears to be the basic determinant of _____ expenditure. When disposable income increases, _____ expenditure _____ .

17.29   Thus, given the level of real GNP, because an increase in taxes will __(increase/decrease)__ disposable income, it will also cause __(an increase/a decrease)__ in consumption expenditure.

ANSWERS

22. would . unemployment
23. can . aggregate demand
24. aggregate demand
25. investment . consumption

26. disposable . plus . minus
27. decrease . increase
28. consumption . consumption . increases
29. decrease . a decrease

17.30 Similarly, a decrease in taxes will cause __*(an increase/a decrease)*__ in consumption expenditure.

17.31 The immediate result of a change in taxes, then, is an __*(induced/autonomous)*__ change in consumption expenditure, and therefore in aggregate demand as well. It is an _____ change because it is brought about by a factor *other* than a change in real GNP.

17.32 Like any other autonomous change in aggregate demand, an autonomous change brought about by tax policy will lead to _____ changes in aggregate demand as well. That is, tax changes will cause autonomous changes in aggregate demand that will have a _____ effect.

17.33 These results can be seen in Figures 17.3 and 17.4, which show the effects of tax reduction on disposable income, consumption expenditure, aggregate demand, and real GNP. Look at Figure 17.3 (i). This diagram shows consumption expenditure as a function of _____ _____ .

17.34 Suppose that real GNP is 0Q, as shown in Figure 17.3 (ii), and that with initial taxes, disposable income is $0Y_1$. Then, consumption expenditure will be _____ .

17.35 Now suppose there is a tax cut in the amount of $Y_1 Y_2$. Then, at the same level of GNP 0Q, disposable income will increase to _____ , and consumption will increase to _____ .

17.36 You will recall that the proportion of any increase in disposable income that will be spent by consumers is called the marginal propensity to consume, or MPC. Thus, the increase in consumption expenditure, $C_1 C_2$, will be equal to the _____ times the change in disposable income, $Y_1 Y_2$.

17.37 For a given level of real GNP, then, a decrease in taxes of $Y_1 Y_2$ will increase _____ _____ by the same amount, as is shown in Figure 17.3 (i). This will result in a __*(shift in/movement along)*__ the consumption function in terms of disposable income and an increase in consumption expenditure equal to the _____ times the tax cut.

ANSWERS

30. an increase
31. autonomous . autonomous
32. induced . multiplier
33. disposable income

34. $0C_1$
35. $0Y_2$. $0C_2$
36. MPC
37. disposable income . movement along . MPC

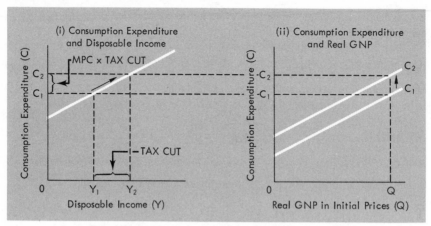

Figure 17.3 The consumption function and tax reduction

17.38 Look now at Figure 17.3 (ii). This diagram shows consumption expenditure as a function of

_____ _____ . As you know from the analysis of Figure 17.3 (i), with

taxes at their initial level, when real GNP is $0Q$, disposable income will be $0Y_1$, and con-

sumption expenditure will be _____ . In Figure 17.3 (ii), this is indicated by the

consumption function _____ .

17.39 After the tax cut, however, when real GNP is $0Q$, disposable income will be _____ ,

and consumption expenditure will be _____ . That is, for the same real GNP, con-

sumption expenditure will now be *(higher/lower)* than before the tax cut.

17.40 At any level of real GNP, consumption expenditure would be higher after the tax cut than

before. As a result, the effect of the tax cut will be an *(induced/autonomous)* increase

in consumption expenditure and, in Figure 17.3 (ii), an upward *(shift in/movement along)*

the consumption function.

17.41 The amount of this autonomous increase in consumption expenditure will, of course, be equal

to the _____ times the decrease in taxes. For this reason, the amount of the shift

in the consumption function (in terms of real GNP) is also equal to the _____

times the decrease in _____ .

ANSWERS

38. real GNP . $0C_1$. C_1
39. $0Y_2$. $0C_2$. higher

40. autonomous . shift in
41. MPC . MPC . taxes

17.42   The effect of tax reduction on aggregate demand and real GNP can be seen in Figure 17.4. This diagram shows how a change in taxes can be used to eliminate unemployment without causing inflation. With a consumption function of C_1 and the corresponding aggregate demand curve of AD_1, the equilibrium level of real GNP will be _____. Without policy action by the government, the result will be *(unemployment/inflation)* and an

_____ gap of QP.

17.43   In this situation, a policy of *(increasing/decreasing)* taxes would be appropriate. *(An increase/A decrease)* in taxes would shift the consumption function up by an amount

equal to the _____ times the tax *(increase/decrease)* .

17.44   Such a policy action is depicted in Figure 17.4. Both the consumption function and the aggregate demand curve shift up by the MPC times the tax decrease. This will lead to further

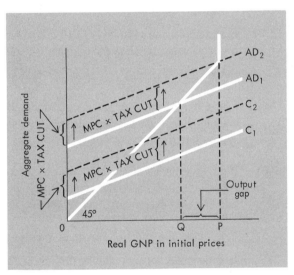

Figure 17.4
Tax reduction to achieve full employment

_____ increases in aggregate demand and a total increase in real GNP equal to the

_____ times the initial autonomous increase in aggregate demand.

17.45   A smaller tax cut would have reduced, but would not have completely eliminated, the output gap. A larger tax cut *(would/would not)* have eliminated unemployment but at the same

time would have caused _____ .

ANSWERS

42. 0Q . unemployment . output
43. decreasing . A decrease . MPC . decrease

44. induced . multiplier
45. would . inflation

17.46   Thus, you have seen that tax policy as well as expenditure policy, if used properly, is a power-ful tool for maintaining the economy at _____ _____ without

_____ .

17.47   In addition to changes in government expenditure and taxes, fiscal policy to influence aggregate demand can take the form of changes in transfer payments. You will remember that most trans-fer payments are transfers of income from the _____ to _____ .
An increase in transfer payments, therefore, will *(increase/decrease)* disposable income.

17.48   Furthermore, an increase in transfer payments will have the same effect on disposable income as *(an increase/a decrease)* in taxes of an equal amount. For this reason, policy action that takes the form of an increase in transfer payments *(will/will not)* have the same effect on aggregate demand as a decrease in taxes of the same amount. The same applies, of course, for a decrease in transfer payments and *(an increase/a decrease)* in taxes.

17.49   For example, a tax increase of $10 billion or a decrease in transfer payments of $10 billion would each result in an autonomous *(increase/decrease)* in consumption expenditure equal

to the _____ times $10 billion.

17.50   In summary, then, given our simple model, if it appears that there will be either inflation or unemployment, the government *(could/could not)* prevent it from occurring by using appropriate fiscal policy.

17.51   If inflation threatens, it would be appropriate for the government to *(increase/decrease)* taxes, *(increase/decrease)* transfer payments, or *(increase/decrease)* government expendi-ture. Or the government could undertake any combination of these three actions.

17.52   In this case, the effect of any or all of these policies would be to *(increase/decrease)* aggre-gate demand, thereby reducing the _____ gap.

17.53   The government would have to use caution in taking any of these policy actions, for too great a decrease in aggregate demand would create an _____ gap and cause _____ .

17.54   If unemployment is the problem, the government would reduce it by doing any or all of the following: *(increase/decrease)* taxes; *(increase/decrease)* transfer payments; *(increase/ decrease)* government expenditure.

ANSWERS

46. full employment . inflation
47. government . consumers . increase
48. a decrease . will . an increase
49. decrease . MPC
50. could

51. increase . decrease . decrease
52. decrease . inflationary
53. output . unemployment
54. decrease . increase . increase

17.55 Again, these changes would have to be made in the proper amount. If they were too great,

_____ _____ would increase by too great an amount, and

_____ would result.

17.56 The arguments used to justify such policy measures to fight inflation or unemployment make good common sense in the real world. Put simply, inflation results when, at initial prices,

buyers want to purchase *(more/less)* output than can be produced and bid up prices. Unemployment results when, at initial prices, buyers want to purchase *(more/less)* output than can be produced; because the price level tends to be inflexible in a downward direction, producers *(increase/decrease)* production and employment.

17.57 Thus, when there is a threat of inflation, fiscal policy should be designed to *(increase/ decrease)* total expenditure. When faced with unemployment, the government should take action to *(increase/decrease)* total expenditure.

17.58 Changes in total expenditure can be brought about either by changes in public spending or by changes in private spending. If the decision is made to change public spending, then obviously the government can change its own expenditure directly. If it is decided to change private spending, the government can change consumption or investment expenditure indirectly by

changing _____ and _____ _____ .

17.59 Despite the fact that the use of fiscal policy to stabilize the economy makes good sense, there has been strong opposition to it on the grounds that it sometimes requires the government to have a *budget deficit*. Whenever government expenditure plus transfer payments is greater

than taxes, there is a _____ in the government's budget.

17.60 For example, if government expenditure is $60 billion, transfer payments are $30 billion, and

taxes are $70 billion, there is a budget _____ of $ _____ billion.

17.61 Suppose that initially the government's budget is balanced. That is, suppose government

expenditure plus transfer payments equals _____ . Suppose also that at the same time there is unemployment. If the government were to increase government expenditure or transfer payments or decrease taxes to eliminate unemployment, the budget *(would/would not)* be a budget deficit.

ANSWERS

55. aggregate demand . inflation
56. more . less . decrease
57. decrease . increase
58. taxes . transfer payments

59. deficit
60. deficit . 20
61. taxes . would

17.62   In this case, fiscal policy __*(increases/decreases)*__ the deficit from zero to a positive level. If initially there had been a budget deficit, then an appropriate change in government expenditure, transfer payments, or taxes would __*(increase/decrease)*__ the budget deficit to an even higher level.

17.63   In these two situations, then, fiscal policy to eliminate unemployment increases the

_____ . Is there any reason why fiscal policy should not be used, as in these two cases, when it increases the budget deficit?

17.64   One argument against using fiscal policy to eliminate unemployment if it will increase the deficit is that budget deficits cause inflation. As you know, inflation results when

_____ _____ exceeds _____ _____ in initial prices. You also know that an increase in the deficit—whether it comes about through an increase in government expenditure or transfer payments or a reduction in taxes—will __*(increase/decrease)*__ aggregate demand.

17.65   But an increase in aggregate demand brought about by an increase in the deficit __*(must/need not)*__ result in a level of aggregate demand that is greater than potential GNP in initial prices. In particular, if there is unemployment in the economy, aggregate demand initially will be __*(greater/less)*__ than potential GNP in initial prices.

17.66   In this situation, in terms of the simple model outlined in Chapters 15 and 16, the increase in aggregate demand brought about by an increase in the deficit will simply bring aggregate demand up to the level of potential GNP in initial prices. The increase in aggregate demand will result in an increase in __*(output/prices)*__ . Instead of causing inflation, the increase in the deficit will reduce _____ .

17.67   It is true, of course, that if the economy were initially at full employment without inflation, an increase in the deficit would cause _____ . In this case, the increase in the deficit would raise _____ _____ above potential GNP in initial prices.

17.68   What can be said, in summary, about the relationship between budget deficits and inflation? First, the mere fact that in a particular year there is a budget deficit *does not* by itself mean that there will be either inflation or full employment. That is, it __*(is/is not)*__ possible to have unemployment if there is a budget deficit, and it __*(is/is not)*__ necessary that there be inflation if there is a budget deficit.

ANSWERS

62. increases . increase
63. deficit
64. aggregate demand . potential GNP . increase

65. need not . less
66. output . unemployment
67. inflation . aggregate demand
68. is . is not

17.69 If there is both unemployment and a budget deficit, it would be possible to reduce unemployment by _(increasing/decreasing)_ the deficit. This could be accomplished by increasing government expenditure or transfer payments or by decreasing taxes.

17.70 If there is price stability and no unemployment along with a budget deficit, the deficit should be _(increased/decreased/unchanged)_ .

17.71 If there is both inflation and a budget deficit, the deficit should be _(increased/decreased)_ by decreasing government expenditure or transfer payments or by _____ taxes.

17.72 The budget is not restricted to being either balanced or having a deficit. It is also possible for there to be a budget *surplus*. This will occur when government expenditure plus transfer payments is _(greater/less)_ than taxes.

17.73 It is possible for there to be either inflation or unemployment when there is a budget surplus. If there is inflation with a budget surplus, the government should have had a _(larger/smaller)_ surplus to have avoided inflation. If there is unemployment with a budget surplus, the surplus should have been _(larger/smaller)_ to have avoided unemployment.

17.74 What matters is not whether there is a surplus, deficit, or budget balance, but how the actual condition of the budget compares with the ideal condition that would ensure full employment with price stability. If the actual budget differs from the ideal budget, then government expenditure, transfer payments, or taxes _(should/should not)_ be changed to attain the ideal. In _(some/all)_ situations, the ideal budget will be balanced. In others, it will show a deficit. In still others, it will show a surplus.

17.75 In order to have a balance between aggregate demand and real GNP at initial prices, it _(is/is not)_ always necessary to have a balanced budget.

17.76 Thus, budget deficits _(do/do not)_ automatically cause inflation. Therefore, fear of inflation _(is/is not)_ a legitimate reason for not using the appropriate fiscal policy when such a policy calls for a deficit.

17.77 Concern with inflation has not been the only basis for opposition to the use of _____ policy to attain full employment without inflation when rational policy requires a budget deficit. Objections to having a budget deficit are sometimes based on the belief that a large *national debt* is harmful.

ANSWERS

69. increasing
70. unchanged
71. decreased . increasing
72. less
73. larger . smaller

74. should . some
75. is not
76. do not . is not
77. fiscal

17.78   The national debt is the amount owed by the federal government to people and institutions from which it has borrowed money. When the government has a budget deficit, government expenditure plus transfer payments is _(greater/less)_ than taxes, and it is necessary for the government to borrow to make up the difference. This increases the national _____.

17.79   In Figure 17.5, the amount of the national debt is shown for the period 1929–1970. Those years in which the national debt increased must be years in which there was a budget _____ . Figure 17.5 shows that since 1929 the national debt has _(increased/decreased)_ substantially, especially during the World War II period.

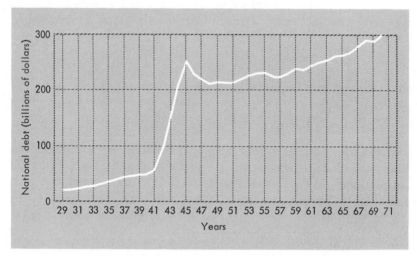

Figure 17.5 The national debt, 1929–1970 (billions of dollars)

17.80   Is it harmful to have a large national debt? Many believe that it is and make the following argument:
"If a businessman continues to spend more than his income, he will eventually be in financial trouble. Some day, his debt will reach a level that is beyond his means to repay, and he will be forced into bankruptcy. Not only will the businessman be out of business but his creditors will be left holding worthless debt. If the national debt becomes too great, the result will be a bankrupt government and impoverished bondholders. If a businessman must live within his means, so must the government." This argument implies that if the national debt becomes too large, the government _(will/will not)_ be able to repay the holders of government bonds. It also implies that the government _(should/should not)_ be run like a business.

ANSWERS

78. greater . debt   80. will not . should
79. deficit . increased

17.81 Both of these implications are incorrect, however. First, the government has very special powers that ensure its ability to repay loans. These powers are the authority to tax and the authority to create new money. That is, the government _(will/will not)_ be able to pay back its debt because it can always obtain the necessary money by collecting _____ or by creating new _____ .

17.82 A business has neither of these powers, and for this reason the amount it can safely borrow depends on the income it can earn. Government borrowing, however, is not limited by the size of government earnings because the government has the authority to _____ and to create new _____ .

17.83 Second, the government should not be run like a business. Its objectives _(are/are not)_ to make as large a profit as possible, _(not/but)_ to perform certain services for the people it represents. Many useful services performed by the government, such as carrying out justice or conducting foreign policy, _(are/are not)_ profit-making activities.

17.84 It is generally accepted that the government should take action to prevent unemployment and inflation that would otherwise occur. If this sometimes requires running a budget deficit, the government _(should/should not)_ be prevented from doing so just because that runs contrary to normal business financial practice.

17.85 There is another reason that people have been opposed to policy actions that increase the national debt. The following argument is frequently made:
"Suppose the government makes an expenditure and pays for it by borrowing money instead of collecting taxes. Then, the present generation will obtain the benefits of that expenditure without having to pay for it. When the debt must be repaid, the government will have to collect taxes, with the result that a future generation will have to pay for the expenditure of the present generation."
This argument states that when government expenditure is financed by issuing debt instead of collecting taxes, the burden of paying for it is borne by _(the present/a future)_ generation.

17.86 To evaluate this argument, consider the real economic cost (that is, opportunity cost) of any government expenditure. It is the private output (for example, automobiles, factories, and so on) that could have been produced with the _____ used to produce the output purchased by the government, that is, the opportunity cost. Consequently, in deciding whether to make any additional expenditure, the government should evaluate the benefits to society to determine whether they exceed this cost.

ANSWERS
81. will . taxes . money
82. tax . money
83. are not . but . are not
84. should not
85. a future
86. resources

17.87   Suppose that a given additional expenditure is considered worth undertaking. Then, the question arises as to how it should be financed. Should the government increase taxes or should it borrow to obtain the money to make its purchases? The answer to this question depends in part on whether the economy is at full employment. If it is at full employment, the government can obtain more goods only if private purchases of goods *(increase/decrease)* by the same amount. If GNP is equal to its potential, an increase in one type of expenditure (for example, government) can occur only if there is a _____ in some other type (for example, consumption or investment).

17.88   If there is unemployment, however, it is possible to increase government purchases without reducing real consumption or investment expenditure because the output purchased by the government could be produced with the otherwise _____ resources.

17.89   In the case in which there is full employment, if the government wants to avoid inflation, it must choose a method of financing its expenditure that *(increases/decreases)* private expenditure by the same amount. One way to do this would be to raise taxes, which would reduce disposable income and thereby reduce _____ expenditure. In this way, *(a future/the present)* generation would pay for the government expenditure by foregoing some consumption.

17.90   In the case in which there is unemployment, it would be possible and desirable to increase government expenditure without reducing private expenditure. The result, according to our model, would be a decrease in *(unemployment/inflation)* without any _____. If there were many unemployed resources, it would *not* be appropriate to finance the expenditure with taxes because to do so would restrain private _____ expenditure.

17.91   If the expenditure were financed by borrowing, the multiplier effect of an autonomous increase in expenditure could cause *(an increase/a decrease)* in consumption expenditure. If the resulting total aggregate demand did not exceed potential GNP, the consequences would be all to the good: total output, government expenditure, and private expenditure would all _____, unemployment would _____, and there would be no excess aggregate demand to cause inflation.

17.92   If we can assume that in the absence of the additional government expenditure the unemployed resources would have remained idle, then in a sense neither the present nor a future generation would have to pay for the output purchased by the government. It would be produced by _____ that would otherwise be wasted in _____.

ANSWERS

87. decrease . decrease
88. unemployed
89. decreases . consumption . the present

90. unemployment . inflation . consumption or investment
91. an increase . increase . decrease
92. resources . unemployment

17.93 Thus, we can see that when there is full employment, it makes sense to avoid inflation by financing additional government expenditure through _____ . And, when there is unemployment, it is appropriate for the government to pay for additional purchases by borrowing and consequently reduce _____ .

17.94 But what about the government debt that is accumulated when the government finances its expenditure by borrowing? Does it not place a burden on future generations? Clearly, in the example we presented above, the answer is no. In that case, the output purchased by the government did not replace output of private capital goods. Because the capital stock was not made lower than it otherwise would have been, the goods and services available for future consumers were not diminished. Instead, the output purchased by government was produced by resources that would otherwise have been _____ . Consequently, in this case, the government expenditure *(does/does not)* diminish the resources that will be left to future generations and does not impose a burden on future generations.

17.95 If and when it appears desirable to pay off the government debt, future tax payers will contribute the money to buy back the government bonds from future bondholders. This will be a transfer from the American people to the American people and will not involve any loss of _____ for the U.S. economy, although there would be some redistribution of wealth.

17.96 You have seen in this chapter how _____ policy can be used to stabilize the economy. Sometimes sound policy will involve a budget deficit. Other times, it may require a budget surplus. Neither course of action taken in appropriate circumstances will serve to impoverish future generations, but can substantially benefit the present generation by helping to assure full employment without inflation.

REVIEW QUESTIONS

17.1 In the United States in 1961, there was high unemployment; in 1968 there was full employment. In both years, the government increased expenditure for goods and services. With respect to the increase in government expenditure, which of the following is correct?

a. It is more likely that the expenditure would be possible without a sacrifice of private goods in the year of high unemployment.

b. It is more likely that the expenditure would be possible without a sacrifice of private goods in the year of full employment.

c. The expenditure is likely to influence prices more than real output in the year of high unemployment.

d. The expenditure is likely to influence real output more than prices in the year of full employment.

ANSWERS

93. taxes . unemployment
94. unemployed . does not
95. resources (output)
96. fiscal

When an economy is operating at full employment, an increase in the flow of goods and services to one group of purchasers (for example, government) is possible only if the flow of goods and services to all other groups of purchasers (consumers and firms) is reduced. When unemployed resources exist, however, increased spending by one group can, through the multiplier process, lead to additional expenditure by others, the employment of idle resources, and a larger total flow of goods and services. In other words, a decrease in unemployment occurs that leads to a higher national output. For this reason, when sufficient resources are idle, additional government expenditure does not cause a sacrifice of private goods. On the contrary, it causes an increase in the flow of private goods and services as well as an increase in government output. The correct response is a.

17.2   A government has estimated the difference between its actual and full employment national income to be $2 billion and has decided to increase its expenditure on domestically produced goods by that amount, but to keep tax rates and interest rates unchanged.

Assuming the government wants to get to full employment with as little inflation as possible and also assuming that consumers spend only part of increases in their income,

a. this policy is not sufficiently expansionary.
b. this policy is about right.

c. this policy is too expansionary.
d. which of the above is correct cannot be determined from the above information.

The multiplier process is that process by which, given unemployed resources, an exogenous increase in expenditure will generate or induce a second round of new expenditure, which in turn will induce a third round, and so on. If the economy is operating at full employment, however (or if full employment is reached before the multiplier process is complete), the increase in aggregate demand will generate higher prices, not additional output. Thus, the $2 billion increase in government expenditure is too expansionary. If, for example, the value of the multiplier is 5, an increase in government expenditure, *ceteris paribus*, of $400,000 million will induce an additional $1.6 billion expenditure, which is just the amount of total additional output required to yield full employment without excess aggregate demand. The correct response is c.

17.3   There is considerable unemployment in the economy. The government is proposing to finance a $800 million increase in expenditure for goods and services with a $800 million increase in income taxes. If other things were unchanged, and if consumers always spend 90 percent of their after-tax income such a scheme would:

a. raise national income.
b. leave national income unchanged.

c. lower national income by $800 million.
d. lower national income by $720 million.

Initially, the government expenditure increase of $800 million would be only partially offset by a $720 million decrease in consumption expenditure (90 percent of the $800 million tax increase). As a result, the proposed changes in government expenditure and taxes would cause an exogenous increase in expenditure of $80 million, which would induce further increase in expenditure and national income of $720 million, that is, the total increase in national income would be $800 million. Thus, the expansionary effect of the increase in government expenditure outweighs the deflationary effect of the increase in taxes. The correct response is a.

17.4 Which of the following would be likely to result if the government increased its spending without increasing its tax receipts during a period of full employment?

a. inflation and a decrease in the national debt

b. inflation and an increase in the national debt

c. recession and a decrease in the national debt

d. recession and an increase in the national debt

At full employment, an increase in real expenditure by the government would be possible if there was a corresponding decrease in real expenditure by consumers and/or firms. If no corresponding decrease took place and given capacity is fixed, an attempt by the government to increase real expenditure would lead to excess aggregate demand and a rise in the price level. In addition, this increase in money expenditure by the government, holding tax receipts constant, will cause an increase in the national debt. The correct response is b.

Case 17

DOES AMERICAN CAPITALISM NEED WAR SPENDING TO AVOID UNEMPLOYMENT?

Many domestic and foreign critics of American capitalism argue that it is dominated by militarism, and that, indeed, continuous massive "defense" spending is required to avoid depression and mass unemployment. Are these critics right?

Table 17.a summarizes proposed U.S. defense spending for 1972. The $75 billion total would be 7 percent of the estimated $1.1 trillion GNP for that year. It supported uniformed forces of 2.6 million people and provided civilian jobs (mainly in private industries) supplying aircraft, weapons, equipment, and construction for probably 4 to 5 million workers.

Suppose, happily, that peace descends on us, and it becomes possible to cut defense spending in half—a huge cut of about $40 billion. Could the U.S. economy maintain prosperity and high employment without the $40 billion of military spending? Or is American capitalism, in fact, dependent on a huge military budget for jobs and prosperity?

SUGGESTIONS FOR ANALYSIS

Aggregate demand and government fiscal policy are the keys to the answer. Consider first the direct effects of the cut in defense spending on aggregate demand and employment and then the offsetting effects of a government fiscal policy aimed at maintaining prosperity and high employment.

A cut of $40 billion in government spending on goods and services would directly reduce aggregate demand by about 3 percent (GNP = roughly $1.2 trillion), plus perhaps another $40 billion because of the multiplier effect (if the multiplier is, say, 2). The effect might be to raise unemployment by 3 to 4 million, including discharged armed service personnel. This would raise the unemployment rate by about 3 percent, enough to generate a substantial recession, though far short of a massive depression like the 1930s. But, if the multiplier were larger or if resulting uncertainty and pessimism induced cuts in private investment, the problem could be worse. So far, the critic's case looks good.

But the government would not be expected to sit by and do nothing to offset the undesirable effects of the defense spending cut. There are two obvious alternatives—cut taxes when military

Table 17.a

U.S. DEFENSE SPENDING, 1972[1]

	(Billion dollars)
Military personnel	$20.1
Operation and maintenance of equipment	20.2
Procurement of aircraft, weapons, supplies, etc.	17.9
Research and development	7.5
Military construction	2.0
Housing, allowances, etc.	3.6
Retirement benefits	3.7
	$75.0

[1] Estimates from President's Budget Message.

spending drops, or replace military with civilian-type government spending on needed goods and services, or some combination of both.

Suppose the government cuts taxes by $40 billion to match the spending cut. This would obviously increase the public's disposable income by just the cut in government spending and, at first glance, might seem just enough stimulus to private spending to offset the drop in government spending. But not quite. Consumer spending, assuming the public's MPC to remain constant, would rise by less than $40 billion because people would save some of their increased disposable income. To assure $40 billion of new consumer spending to fully offset the defense cut, the government would need to reduce taxes by somewhat more than $40 billion, precisely how much more depending on the public's MPC.

But the main lesson is clear. By cutting taxes, the government can stimulate private spending to fully offset the deflationary effects of the defense cut. The defense cut need cause no unemployment or drop in real GNP if government fiscal policy is managed wisely. Instead of spending our money on military pay and weapons, we as a nation can now spend it on swimming pools, automobiles, and health services, or whatever else we want most. Our scarce resources, happily, can be

allocated away from military use to meeting civilian wants.

Government fiscal policy has another obvious alternative. Instead of cutting taxes, Congress could increase government nonmilitary spending by $40 billion—on education, public health, urban renewal, aid to the poor, or any other high-priority civilian needs. Meeting our "new national priorities" on health, the environment, education, rebuilding our cities, and the like will require vastly more than $40 billion annually. There is no problem finding high-priority civilian projects on which to increase government spending to offset deflationary effects of the arms cutback. Thus, government spending would be redirected but unchanged in amount and contribution to aggregate demand.

Which is better—tax cuts or increased government spending on nonmilitary projects? Your answer will depend on your preference—on whether you believe society's productive resources are best allocated through the private marketplace in response to consumer demands or through government taxation and publicly directed spending. We face this choice whether or not there is a cut in defense spending. Here, the point to see is that wise fiscal policy, using whichever approach the public prefers, or some combination of the two, can readily see to it that aggregate demand is kept at the desired level to avoid depression and unemployment, however much defense spending is cut. Indeed, such a development is devoutly to be desired, for we could then have the freed resources for more of the civilian goods and services we want, either individually or through government action.

In emphasizing the powers of fiscal policy, we have abstracted from all the transitional problems of shifting workers and other productive resources from war to civilian production. Although the big picture outlined above is correct, the problems of shifting jobs may be highly disruptive to some workers, businesses, and localities. For example, over half of all employment in the aircraft industry is tied to military contracts; how do those workers, those companies, and those localities shift to producing recreational products or better housing if that is what consumers across the nation want when their taxes are cut? Clearly, a fast, large cut in defense spending would throw many out of jobs, and it might take months, or even years, for some to shift to the new jobs created by shifting demands. Government help in providing job in-

formation, retraining, moving allowances, and the like, could help, and a *gradual* shiftover from military to civilian spending would ease transition problems. As a practical matter, such huge cutbacks as we have postulated are extremely unlikely on short notice. The transitional problems could be painful for many, especially older workers, but they do not change the basic fiscal analysis above. And we do have evidence that the U.S. economy can make a large transition fairly effectively. Between 1945 and 1946, defense expenditure decreased by $59 billion, from 34 to only 7 percent of GNP. Despite this massive cutback, unemployment rose only from an abnormally low 1.9 percent to a normal full employment rate of 3.9 percent.

One final note is needed. As we shall see in the following chapters, the government has another major weapon in its arsenal against depression and unemployment. This is monetary policy—control over the amount of money the public has and over interest rates. Monetary policy can be used to help fiscal policy keep aggregate demand at the desired level.

18

Investment Expenditure, the Rate of Interest, and Money

18.1 Just as the government can carry out fiscal policies that lead to changes in private consumption expenditure, it can also influence investment expenditure. Although consumption expenditure is made to satisfy consumers' wants directly, investment expenditure is made to earn a profit. When a business makes investment expenditure, it hopes to increase its capacity to produce and sell output and thereby earn a _____ . Unless it is expected that an expenditure for a particular capital good (for example, a new machine or building) would yield a

_____ , that expenditure will not be made.

18.2 In order to be profitable, the capital good investment must return enough money after all other expenses to more than cover the cost of buying the capital good. For example, if an oil well costs $100,000 to construct and run and yields only $90,000 worth of oil before it runs dry, it _(would/would not)_ be profitable to make that expenditure. If it yielded $105,000 worth of

oil, there would be a return over cost of $_____ .

18.3 The return over cost of an investment is usually calculated in the same way as for a savings account or government bond. For example, a government bond that costs $18.25 and yields $25.00 after eight years is usually described as a bond that has a *rate of interest* of 4 percent per year. That is, if you invest $18.25 and earn 4 percent in interest per year, after eight years

your original investment plus the _____ will be worth $_____ .

18.4 A similar concept can be applied to investment in capital goods. In this case, the average annual return over cost is called the *rate of return*. The yearly percentage return over cost

ANSWERS

1. profit . profit
2. would not . 5,000

3. interest . 25.00
4. rate . return . 5

earned by an investment is the _____ of _____ . For the oil well, if it costs $100,000 and yields $105,000 after one year and nothing thereafter, it is an investment with a rate of return of _____ percent per year.

18.5 In order to be worth buying, a capital good must return more than just its purchase price. It must also return as much as any other asset in which the money could have been invested.

That is, it is not sufficient that an investment have a positive _____ of

_____ . It must have a rate of return that is as high as the rate that can be earned on any other asset. Otherwise, it _(would/would not)_ be better to buy the other asset.

18.6 For example, suppose the oil well has a rate of return of 5 percent per year. This means that it _(does/does not)_ have a large enough return to cover its original cost. But this _(does/does not)_ indicate by itself whether the investment is worth making.

18.7 Suppose that you could earn 6 percent per year in interest on a savings deposit in your bank. This means that after one year an initial deposit of $100,000 would be worth

$_____ . Clearly, with this opportunity available, you _(would/would not)_ invest in the oil well.

18.8 In general, businesses have the alternative of investing in capital goods or investing in financial assets such as government bonds or bank accounts. A business will find it profitable to invest

in any capital good that yields a higher _____ of _____ than the rate of interest that can be earned on financial assets, making allowances for differences in risk.

18.9 The lower the rate of interest is, the _(more/less)_ investment expenditure will be worth making, other things remaining equal.

18.10 Thus, a major factor in determining the level of investment expenditure is the _____

of _____ against which the rate of return is compared in deciding whether any investment expenditure is worth making.

18.11 The greater the rate of interest, the _(greater/smaller)_ will be the amount of investment expenditure worth making, other things remaining equal.

18.12 This relationship between the rate of interest and investment is shown in terms of a rate of return function in Figure 18.1. In this diagram, both the rate of interest and the rate of return

ANSWERS

5. rate . return . would
6. does . does not
7. 106,000 . would not
8. rate . return

9. more
10. rate . interest
11. smaller
12. vertical . horizontal

are measured along the _____ axis, and investment expenditure is measured along

the _____ axis.

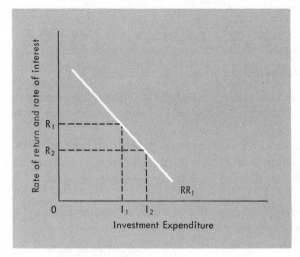

Figure 18.1
The rate of return function

18.13 Curve RR is an example of the _____ of _____ function. This
function shows, for different levels of investment expenditure, the rate of return on an extra
dollar of investment expenditure. Curve RR, for example, shows that if investment expendi-

ture were $0I_1$, the _____ of _____ on an extra dollar of investment

would be _____ .

18.14 As can be seen in Figure 18.1, the rate of return function slopes _(upward/downward)_ from
left to right. Thus, the greater the amount of investment expenditure, the _(higher/lower)_
the rate of return that can be earned on the last dollar of investment expenditure.

18.15 Suppose you were to rank all possible investment expenditures in decreasing order in terms of
the rate of return on each. That is, put first those investment expenditures that will yield a
rate of return of 20 percent or more, then those yielding 15 percent or more, then those of 10
percent or more, and so on. Then, you can see that the lower the rate of return, the
(greater/smaller) the amount of investment expenditure included. Conversely, the more

that is invested, the _____ the rate of return that is earned on the last dollar of investment expenditure.

18.16 Profit-motivated businessmen will ordinarily undertake _(first/last)_ those investment projects
promising the highest rates of return. A few investments will promise a high rate of return,

ANSWERS

13. rate . return . rate . return . $0R_1$ 15. greater . lower
14. downward . lower   16. first . $0R_2$

more will promise lower rates of return. Thus, if you plot on a graph all investment opportunities against the rates of return they promise, the rate of return function must be downward sloping to the right. For curve RR, with investment expenditure of $0I_2$, the rate of return on

an extra dollar of investment will be _____ .

18.17 From the rate of return function, it is possible to tell how much investment expenditure businessmen would want to make at different rates of interest. As long as the rate of return on an investment project is _(higher/lower)_ than the rate of interest, it will be worth undertaking. Investment expenditure will be made up to the point where _(no/some)_ projects will remain that have a rate of return higher than the rate of interest. At this point, the rate of return will be _(greater than/equal to/less than)_ the rate of interest.

18.18 In Figure 18.1, for example, given the rate of return function RR, if the rate of interest were $0R_1$, businesses would want to make no more and no less investment expenditure than

_____ . At the lower rate of interest $0R_2$, investment expenditure would be the

(greater/smaller) amount _____ .

18.19 Thus, in terms of the aggregate demand and supply model, a change in the rate of interest will

cause an _____ change in investment expenditure. As you have seen, like any other autonomous change in investment expenditure, it will appear as a _(shift in/ movement along)_ the investment function.

18.20 Because a change in the rate of interest will cause a shift in the investment function, it will also

cause a shift in the _____ _____ curve. As a result, a change in aggregate demand due to a change in the rate of interest _(can/cannot)_ be expected to have an impact similar to autonomous changes in aggregate demand caused by other factors.

18.21 Specifically, an increase in the rate of interest will cause an autonomous _(increase/decrease)_ in investment expenditure and aggregate demand. Unless there were an inflationary gap to begin with, the increase in the interest rate would have the effect of _(increasing/decreasing)_ unemployment. If there were an inflationary gap to begin with, the increase in the interest rate would _(widen/narrow)_ the inflationary gap.

18.22 A reduction in the rate of interest, of course, will have the opposite effect. It will cause _(an increase/a decrease)_ in aggregate demand and will tend to _(widen/narrow)_ the output gap or _(widen/narrow)_ the inflationary gap, depending on the situation.

ANSWERS

17. higher . no . equal to
18. $0I_1$. greater . $0I_2$
19. autonomous . shift in

20. aggregate demand . can
21. decrease . increasing . narrow
22. an increase . narrow . widen

18.23   A change in the rate of interest can also cause an autonomous change in consumption expenditure. You will recall from Chapter 13 that certain expenditures, such as purchases of automobiles, furniture, and so on, made by households are in large part _____ expenditures but are counted as _____ expenditures in the GNP.

18.24   Considerations similar to those that underly the investment decisions of businesses influence the expenditure by households for consumers' durable goods. When considering the purchase of an automobile, for example, it will make sense to buy only if the benefit derived from the car is _(greater/less)_ than the _____ of the car. Also, the benefit must be enough greater than the cost to cover the _____ that can be earned by buying a financial asset like a bond or a savings account.

18.25   Consequently, the higher the rate of interest, the _(higher/lower)_ will be expenditure for consumers' durable goods and the _(higher/lower)_ will be aggregate demand. A change in the rate of interest can affect aggregate demand by causing changes in both _____ and _____ expenditure.

18.26   The reason for analyzing the effect of a change in the rate of interest is not only that it will have an important effect on the economy but also that government policy can change the rate of interest. Thus, by taking appropriate action to change the rate of interest, the _____ can change the level of aggregate demand to move the economy toward full employment without inflation.

18.27   In order to understand how the government can influence the rate of interest, it is necessary to understand how the rate of interest is determined in a market economy. You will recall that interest is the payment, over and above repayment of the amount borrowed, that _(borrowers/lenders)_ must make to _(borrowers/lenders)_ .

18.28   The percentage of an amount borrowed for a year that must be paid in interest is called the _____ of interest. This means that the rate of interest is the number of cents that must be paid for borrowing one dollar for a year. Just as the number of cents per loaf is the price of bread, the rate of interest is the _____ of borrowing money for a year.

18.29   For example, if you were to borrow $100 for two years, the rate of interest would indicate how much you would have to pay each year for the use of that money. If the rate of interest

ANSWERS

23. investment . consumption
24. greater . cost . interest
25. lower . lower . consumption . investment (either order)

26. government
27. borrowers . lenders
28. rate . price
29. 8 . 16 . price

were 8 percent, you would have to pay _____ cents per dollar each year. Your

total interest for two years would be $_____ . In this example, the 8 percent rate

of interest is the _____ of borrowing money for a year.

18.30 Just as there are markets in which goods and services can be bought and sold, there is a market in which money can be borrowed and loaned. This market is called the money market. If you were to borrow money from a bank, for example, you would be making a transaction in the

_____ _____ . The price you would have to pay is the _____

of _____ .

18.31 In the United States economy, there are actually many types of loans. For example, there are mortgages, corporate bonds, personal loans, and many others. These differ in terms of the purpose for which the money is borrowed, type of security offered the lender, the time for which the loan is made, and so on. In general, just as different cuts of meat have different

prices, different types of loans will have different prices or _____ of

_____ . Thus, if you were to look in the financial section of the newspaper for the current rate of interest, you would find _(just one rate/many rates)_ of interest.

18.32 Although a study of differences among types of loans is very important for some purposes, it is not essential for an understanding of how rates of interest are determined or how government policy can change investment expenditure by influencing the money market. To simplify, therefore, it will be assumed here that there is only one kind of loan and, therefore, only one rate of interest. In other words, the following discussion will _(explain/ignore)_ differences among types of loans and rates of interest because those differences _(are/are not)_ important to an understanding of how government policy can influence investment expenditure through the money market.

18.33 When a loan is made, a "note," or promise to pay, which obligates the borrower to pay the

lender the amount borrowed plus _____ , is sold to the lender in the money market. This note is sometimes called a security. For example, when a business borrows

money to build a factory, it sells a _____ that commits it to repay the loan with

interest. When a bank makes a loan, it _(buys/sells)_ a note, or _____ . (Such a security is often called a *bond*.)

18.34 If you own a security that was previously issued by a borrower, it is often possible to sell it in the money market. If you need money for some purpose, you can obtain it either by issuing

ANSWERS

30. money market . rate . interest
31. rates . interest . many rates
32. ignore . are not

33. interest . security . buys . security
34. security . security . securities

and selling a new _____ or by selling an existing _____ that you own.

Thus, the money market is a market in which both new and previously issued _____ are bought and sold. (Sometimes existing securities cannot be sold again in the money market. Promissory notes given to banks in return for bank loans are an example of nonmarketable securities. Bonds are usually marketable securities.)

18.35   Securities are sold to obtain _____ . Usually, new securities are issued to enable the borrower to spend _(more/less)_ than his current income for goods and services. For example, when a family buys a house, the cost of the house is usually more than the family's yearly income. By selling a new _____ , that is, by borrowing money, it is possible to obtain the money necessary to buy the house. (This type of security is usually called a *mortgage*.)

18.36   To take another example, you will recall that when the government runs a budget _____ , it must borrow money by issuing and selling _____ in the money market.

18.37   A person, business, or government who has issued securities that are still outstanding is called a *debtor*. At any point in time, the amount owed by a _____ will not be simply the amount borrowed in the current period. Rather, it will be the total amount of securities issued by the _____ that have not yet been repaid.

18.38   For example, in 1971 the federal government's budget deficit was $23 billion, which means that during 1970 it had to sell, in addition to any new securities issued to replace existing securities that came due during the year, $_____ billion worth of securities. At the end of 1971, the total outstanding debt of the federal government was $23 billion _(larger/smaller)_ than it was at the end of 1969. The total outstanding debt at the end of 1971, $424 billion, was much larger than $23 billion because it included _(all/no)_ securities issued in previous years that had not yet been repaid.

18.39   Similarly, for persons and business, any time money is borrowed to spend more for goods and services than is available from current income, new _____ must be issued and sold, and the total outstanding debt must _(increase/decrease)_ .

18.40   For every debtor who has securities outstanding, there must be a creditor who owns those securities. For example, if you owned a security that had been issued by the American Telephone and Telegraph Corporation, you would be a _____ , and AT&T would be a _____ .

ANSWERS

35. money . more . security	38. 23 . larger . all
36. deficit . securities	39. securities . increase
37. debtor . debtor	40. creditor . debtor

18.41   In the same way, every security is both an asset and a liability at the same time. To creditors, securities are _____ , and to debtors, they are _____ .

18.42   How do creditors obtain the funds to acquire securities? You will recall from Chapter 13 that, for the economy as a whole, income must be equal to expenditure. As has just been discussed, however, income and expenditure _(must/need not)_ be equal for every individual consumer, business, or government.

18.43   Although it _(is/is not)_ possible for total expenditure to be different from total income for the economy as a whole, this _(is/is not)_ possible for an individual consumer, business, or government, by their selling _____ in the money market.

18.44   But, because total income must equal total expenditure, for every borrower who spends more than his income there must be a _____ who spends _(more/less)_ than his income. This is reflected in the fact that every time a security is sold by someone, it must be _____ by someone else.

18.45   Creditors, then, are consumers, businesses, or governments who have spent _(more/less)_ on goods and services than they have received in income and have accumulated financial _(assets/liabilities)_ .

18.46   At the same time, debtors are consumers, businesses, or governments who have spent _(more/less)_ on goods and services than they have received in income and have accumulated financial _(assets/liabilities)_ .

18.47   The assets of _____ and the liabilities of _____ are the same financial securities. They are the means by which those who save part of their income make it available to those who want to spend more than their income.

18.48   Securities, however, are not the only financial asset that creditors can hold. It is also possible to hold wealth in the form of money. That is, creditors have a choice between holding their financial assets in the form of _____ or _____ (or both).

18.49   Obviously, given their total wealth, the more securities creditors hold, the _(more/less)_ money they will be able to hold. Thus, given his wealth, if a creditor wants to increase his holdings of securities, he must reduce his holdings of _____ .

ANSWERS

41. assets . liabilities
42. need not
43. is not . is . securities
44. lender . less . bought
45. less . assets

46. more . liabilities
47. creditors . debtors
48. securities . money (either order)
49. less . money

18.50   Money, like a security, is an asset. Unlike a security, however, money does not earn interest. Why is anyone willing to hold money, which yields no interest, when it is possible to hold

_____ , which do yield interest? There are two basic reasons why asset holders are

willing to give up _____ by holding money instead of securities.

18.51   It has already been noted that money is an _____ . In Chapter 14, it was noted that money is whatever is generally accepted in payment for goods and services. Money, then,

is an _____ that is a generally accepted means for making _____ .

18.52   Because money is the usual means of payment, if a person holds only securities, it will be necessary for him to sell a security to obtain money each time he wants to purchase a real commodity. This would not cause any problem if securities could be sold at any time and without cost. Then, it would be possible to earn as _(much/little)_ interest as possible from your financial assets _(without/but not without)_ interfering with your shopping needs.

18.53   Unfortunately, securities cannot be sold at any time. In the evening and on week-ends, it would be difficult to sell a security, and therefore it _(would/would not)_ be difficult to do any desired shopping. Also, it is not costless to sell securities. There are brokers' fees, visits and phone calls to your broker, and the time required to make such arrangements. Thus, in order to earn the maximum interest from your securities by holding only securities, it _(is/is not)_ necessary to incur certain costs connected with selling securities when money is needed to make purchases.

18.54   It is possible to avoid these selling costs by holding some _____ . In fact, most

persons and businesses do hold money just to avoid these selling _____ . Thus, one reason for holding money is to meet transactions needs for money without having to pay the unwanted costs of selling securities each time you want to buy a commodity. Holding money for this reason is called the *transactions demand* for money.

18.55   If there were no costs of time, effort, or money associated with selling securities, there would

be no _____ demand for money. Because there are such costs, and most people

consider some of them not worth paying, there is a _____ _____ for money.

18.56   A second reason for holding money stems from the fact that the market value of securities can change over time. Money, on the other hand, will always have a fixed value in dollar terms.

ANSWERS

50. securities . interest	54. money . costs
51. asset . asset . payment	55. transactions . transactions demand
52. much . without	56. securities . money
53. would . is	

That is, the dollar value of _____ can change over time, but the dollar value of _____ remains fixed.

18.57 Compared to money, securities are riskier financial assets because the amount that a security will sell for in the money market fluctuates over time as the eagerness of others to buy it changes. A dollar is always a dollar, but a security for which you paid $100 may be worth only $90 next month. If you hold securities instead of money, you earn more _____ on your holdings, but you also must accept greater _(risk/safety)_ .

18.58 Most asset holders choose to hold at least part of their wealth in the form of money in order to avoid the _(risk/interest)_ that comes with holding securities. That is, most people hold money as a precaution against the possibility of a _(rise/fall)_ in the market value of securities.

18.59 Many people hold money for precautionary purposes—to make sure that at least part of their wealth is not lost due to declines in the value of securities in the money market. If some people did not consider the _(safety/risk)_ gained from holding some of their wealth in money to outweigh the _____ lost from not holding all their financial assets in securities, they would not hold money for _____ purposes.

18.60 In addition to holding money for precautionary purposes, people hold money for speculative purposes. If an asset holder became convinced that the market value of securities was going to fall, he obviously _(would/would not)_ want to hold securities and would prefer to hold _____ instead. That is, asset holders will want to hold money for speculative purposes if they expect the market value of securities to _(rise/fall)_ .

18.61 The holding of money for precautionary and speculative purposes is called the *asset demand* for money. Holding money to facilitate the purchase of goods and services is called the _____ demand. And holding money for precautionary or speculative reasons is called the _____ demand.

18.62 The two basic reasons for holding money, then, are:

(1) to avoid the selling costs to obtain money to make purchases when desired, which gives rise to the _____ demand, and

(2) to avoid the risk attached to holding securities or an expectation that the market value of securities will fall, which give rise to the _____ demand.

ANSWERS

57. interest . risk
58. risk . fall
59. safety . interest . precautionary

60. would not . money . fall
61. transactions . asset
62. transactions . asset

18.63   These reasons explain why asset holders are willing to forego some of the_____ that could be earned if they held only securities and no money.

18.64   How much money will the public be willing to hold? The riskiness and costs of selling securities make asset holders willing to give up some _____ . How much risk and selling costs asset holders will avoid by holding money will depend on how much _____ they must give up to do so.

18.65   If interest rates are high, they must give up *(a lot of/little)* interest to hold money and avoid a given amount of risk and selling costs. When interest rates are high, therefore, asset holders can be expected to hold *(more/less)* money than when interest rates are low, other things being equal.

18.66   When interest rates are relatively low, asset holders will hold *(more/less)* money because they have to give up less _____ to avoid the risk and selling costs that come with holding securities.

18.67   This can be seen in Figure 18.2, where line L is the demand curve for money. This demand curve shows the quantity of money that asset holders will want to hold at different rates of interest. Because at high interest rates it is necessary to give up a relatively large amount of

_____ to avoid the _____ and _____ _____ from holding securities, asset holders will want to hold *(more/less)* money than at low interest rates. For this reason, the demand curve for money slopes *(upward/downward)* from left to right.

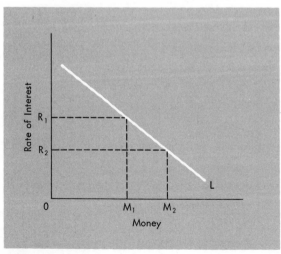

Figure 18.2
The demand for money

ANSWERS

63. interest
64. interest . interest
65. a lot of . less

66. more . interest
67. interest . risk . selling costs . less . downward

18.68 For example, at the rate of interest OR_1, asset holders want to hold an amount of money equal

to _____ . At the rate of interest OR_2, they will want to hold more of their

financial assets in _____ and less in _____ . In this case, the quantity

of money demanded will be _____ .

18.69 What are the conditions under which the money market is in equilibrium? Equilibrium exists when there is no tendency for changes in any of the relevant variables, such as the quantities of money demanded and supplied and the rate of interest. For example, if forces exist that tend

to raise the rate of interest, the money market cannot be in _____ . Only when all

the variables in a market "come to rest" can there be _____ .

18.70 In any market, the basic condition for equilibrium is equality between the quantities demanded and supplied. This means, in the case of the money market, that asset holders are willing to

hold just the available amounts of _____ and _____ .

18.71 Why is the equality of demand and supply for both money and securities a condition for

_____ in the money market? Suppose, for example, that at a given rate of interest the demand for money is less than the supply. This means that asset holders are holding more

of their financial assets in the form of _____ than they wish to. (Remember that here the question under consideration is how total financial assets are to be divided between money and securities.)

18.72 Because in our simple model the only alternative financial asset is securities, when the demand for money is less than the supply this also means that asset holders wish that some of their

assets that take the form of _____ were _____ instead. Thus, to say that there is an excess demand for money is equivalent to saying that there is an excess

_____ of securities.

18.73 In this situation, some asset holders will try to adjust their holdings by using the excess holdings

of _____ to buy _____ from other asset holders. In order to induce them to sell their securities, these buyers must offer to pay more for the securities than they were worth initially.

18.74 Suppose that a typical security was issued in the amount of $100 at an interest rate of 4 per-

cent. This means that the holder would receive $_____ in interest per year.

ANSWERS

68. $0M_1$. money . securities . $0M_2$
69. equilibrium . equilibrium
70. money . securities (either order)
71. equilibrium . money

72. money . securities . supply
73. money . securities
74. 4 . 4 . lower . 4 . 120

Suppose that someone were to buy that security from its holder for $120. The second owner would still get $_____ per year in interest from the debtor, which means that he would earn a _(higher/lower)_ rate of interest because he paid more for the security. The second owner would earn $_____ per year on a financial investment of

$_____ .

18.75 Thus, when asset holders bid up the value of securities in the money market, they also bid _(up/down)_ the rate of interest. When there is an excess supply of money, asset holders, in trying to acquire securities with their excess money holdings, will _(increase/decrease)_ the market value of securities and drive _(up/down)_ the interest rate.

18.76 This makes common sense when you consider new securities issues. When asset holders at the initial rate of interest would like to hold less money and more securities than they have, they are likely to offer a _(higher/lower)_ rate of interest to debtors to induce them to supply them with more securities. Thus, an excess supply of money, which means an excess demand for securities, will result in a _(rise/fall)_ in the rate of interest. (Remember again that here the only question being considered is how total financial assets are to be divided between money and securities.)

18.77 Because the demand for money curve slopes _(downward/upward)_ from left to right, at a lower interest rate there will be a _(larger/smaller)_ quantity of money demanded. Thus, if there is an excess supply of money, the rate of interest will _(rise/fall)_ , and the quantity of money demanded will _(increase/decrease)_ .

18.78 The rate of interest will continue to fall until the resulting increase in demand _(doubles/eliminates)_ the excess supply. At this point, equilibrium will be attained in the

_____ market. The reverse, of course, holds true when there is an excess demand for money. In this case, asset holders will try to sell unwanted securities and bid their value in the market _(up/down)_ and the rate of interest _(up/down)_ until equilibrium is established.

18.79 This can be seen in terms of Figure 18.3, in which line L is the demand curve for money and line M shows the supply of money. The fact that M is shown as a _(horizontal/vertical)_ line implies that the amount of money outstanding _(does/does not)_ change when the rate of interest changes.

18.80 If the rate of interest were OR_1 in Figure 18.3, the amount of money demanded would be

_____ , which is _(greater/less)_ than the amount of money supplied. At this rate

ANSWERS

75. down . increase . down
76. lower . fall
77. downward . larger . fall . increase

78. eliminates . money . down . up
79. vertical . does not
80. $0M_1$. greater . will not . rise

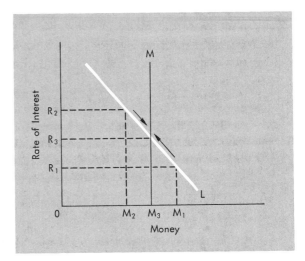

Figure 18.3
The supply and demand for money

of interest, the money market _(will/will not)_ be in equilibrium, and the rate of interest will
tend to _(rise/fall)_ .

18.81 At the rate of interest OR_2, there will be an excess _(supply of/demand for)_ money, and the
rate of interest will tend to _(rise/fall)_ .

18.82 Only if the rate of interest is _____ will the money market be in _____.
That is, at a rate of interest of OR_3, the amount of money supplied and demanded
 (will/will not) be equal and there will be _(a/no)_ tendency for the rate of interest to
change.

18.83 At the same rate of interest, OR_3, the supply and demand for securities must also be equal.
When the quantities of money supplied and demanded are equal, it means that asset holders are
not trying to use their money holdings to acquire more securities than are in existence nor are
they trying to convert any of their securities into money. That is, when the amounts of money

supplied and demanded are equal, the money market is in _____ because the

supply and demand for _____ are also equal and there is no tendency for the rate
of interest to change. Thus, in our model, by analyzing the supply and demand curves for
money, it is possible to identify the rate of interest.

ANSWERS
81. supply of . fall
82. OR_3 . equilibrium . will . no
83. equilibrium . securities

18.84 You have now seen how the rate of interest is determined in the economy. The rate that will prevail in the money market is the rate by which the quantities of money _____ and _____ are equal. Only at that rate will the money market be in _____ .

18.85 In summary, money is held for two basic reasons. One is to avoid the cost of converting securities to money whenever a purchase of real commodity is made. Holding money for this reason is called the _____ demand for money. The other is to avoid some of the risk that comes with holding securities or to avoid losses if you expect the market value of securities to fall. Holding money because it is safer than securities is called the _____ demand for money.

18.86 The rate of _____ will adjust to make the quantity of money demanded equal to the quantity _____ . The higher the rate of interest, the _(higher/lower)_ will be investment expenditure and, consequently, aggregate demand and the _(higher/lower)_ will be the equilibrium level of real GNP.

REVIEW QUESTIONS

18.1 Which of the following types of people is most likely to suffer from an unexpected rise in . interest rates? Persons whose assets consist entirely of:

a. demand deposits   c. gold
b. currency   d. long-term bonds

If the going rate of interest were 6 percent, you would be able to buy a bond that promised to pay $106 at the end of one year for $100. Conversely, in a perfect market, you would be able

ANSWERS

84. supplied . demanded (either order) . equilibrium   86. interest . supplied . lower . lower
85. transactions . asset

to sell such a bond for $100. If, however, after you had purchased this bond for $100, the rate of interest were to rise to 8 percent, you would no longer be able to sell your bond for $100. At the price of $100, this bond will only return 6 percent, and anyone with $100 can buy a bond that will now pay $108 at the end of the year. You would be able to sell this bond for approximately $98.15 because only at this lower price would a promise to pay $106 in one year yield a rate of return of 8 percent. Persons holding bonds, therefore, suffer a capital loss when interest rates unexpectedly rise because the value of bonds and interest rates are inversely related. Holders of the other assets will be unaffected by the interest rate change. The correct response is d.

18.2 Which of the following are rational explanations why a person might hold part of his wealth in the form of money even though money does not yield any interest?

1. to avoid the costs of selling securities each time he wants to purchase a good or service
2. to avoid the risk of changes in the value of securities due to interest rate changes

    a. 1 only   c. both 1 and 2
    b. 2 only   d. neither 1 nor 2

A person's wealth can be held in different forms. If we imagine the typical wealth owner confronted with the choice of holding money or securities or some combination of the two, how will he decide to invest his wealth? Will he invest it all in securities to maximize his interest income? If our wealth owner will be making purchases of goods and services from time to time, he might find that the brokerage and time costs involved in converting securities into cash at the time of expenditure would outweigh the interest earned. In that event, he would want to hold some cash for transactions purposes. If our investor disliked uncertainty about the value of his assets, he might like to give up some interest income by holding part of his wealth in the form of cash, the value of which will not fluctuate as interest rates rise and fall. The correct response is c.

18.3 Which of the following explains why a decrease in the quantity of money will result in a rise in the rate of interest?

1. The quantity of money demanded decreases as the rate of interest increases.
2. The demand curve for money slopes downward from left to right.
3. The quantity of securities demanded increases as the rate of interest increases.

    a. 1 only   c. 1 and 2 only
    b. 2 only   d. 1, 2, and 3

When interest rates are relatively low, asset holders will want to hold more money and less securities because they have to give up less interest to avoid the risk and selling costs that come with holding securities. All three of the statements express this idea. Because of this inverse relationship between the quantity of money demanded and the rate of interest, it is only at a higher rate of interest that the excess demand for money (created by the decrease in the supply of money) will be eliminated. The correct response is d.

18.4   "The more money there is in the economy, the more people spend. The more people spend, the higher the national income. Therefore, the greater the supply of money, the better off people are."

Which of the following is true?

a. The statement is incorrect because more money in the economy does not usually lead to more spending.

b. The statement is incorrect because real income is limited by the economy's capacity to produce.

c. The statement is correct because an increase in spending can lead to an increase in income.

d. The statement is correct because the amount of money in the economy determines how well off people are.

Although it is true, given unemployed resources, that an increase in the money supply can stimulate aggregate demand and thus increase real national output and living standards, it does not follow that people always will be better off, the greater the money supply. Classic cases of too much money causing rampant inflation and economic collapse are not unknown. Thus, although an increase in the money supply is one of the weapons of monetary policy used to stimulate the economy in a recession, the upper limit to the real output of a nation is determined by the nation's productive resources. The correct response is b.

Case 18

THE RATE OF INTEREST AND INVESTMENT IN RESIDENTIAL HOUSING

One frequently debated issue is whether the relationship expected in theory between the rate of interest and investment expenditure holds up in fact. As it was developed in this chapter, the theory suggests that, other things remaining equal, the amount of new investment will be inversely related to the rate of interest. Because an investment will be worth undertaking if the expected rate of return exceeds the rate of interest, the lower the rate of interest, other factors the same, the more investment expenditure can be expected to be made.

One difficulty encountered when trying to verify the validity of the theory by comparing it with events in the real world is that it is practically impossible to find a circumstance in which other factors remain the same. When confronted with data from the real world in which other factors are also changing, the economist must try to identify and measure these other factors and try to account for their interference with the relationship under consideration.

In the case of the relationship between the rate of interest and investment expenditure, one of these other factors is what investing firms expect about the long-run demand for their products. Obviously, the more optimistic firms' sales expectations are, the higher their rate of return function, and the more investment expenditure they would make for any given rate of interest. Unfortunately, this factor is practically impossible to measure, and for most business firms expectations are likely to vary considerably from year to year. But fortunately there is one type of investment, residential construction, for which long-run expectations about future returns are likely to be very stable. The expected returns to a home owner on his investment are not likely to fluctuate markedly because the demand for housing services, which depends primarily on population and per capita income, cannot be expected to be very volatile.

This latter point suggests that it is probably necessary to take into account the size of GNP as a factor influencing residential construction. Obviously, the larger the population and the higher its income, the more investment in new houses there is likely to be.

Table 18.a shows for 1961-1970 the mortgage

Table 18.a

RESIDENTIAL CONSTRUCTION, THE MORTGAGE RATE, AND GNP, 1961-1970

	(1) *Residential construction (billions of dollars, 1958 prices)*	*(2)* *Mortgage rate (percent)*	*(3)* *GNP (billions of dollars, 1958 prices)*
1961	21.6	5.8	497
1962	23.8	5.6	530
1963	24.8	5.5	551
1964	24.2	5.5	581
1965	23.8	5.5	618
1966	21.3	6.3	658
1967	20.4	6.6	675
1968	23.3	7.1	707
1969	23.3	8.2	727
1970	20.6	9.1	724

rate, residential construction, and GNP. On the basis of this evidence, what is your conclusion about the validity of the theory presented in this chapter? Does a lower rate of interest, other factors such as GNP held constant, lead to a higher level of investment expenditure?

SUGGESTIONS FOR ANALYSIS

The first problem to be solved before relating the rate of interest to residential construction is how to account for growth in the size of the economy between 1961 and 1970. The simplest way to do this is to consider residential construction as a proportion of GNP. By relating this new variable to the rate of interest, you will automatically take into account the effect of the level of GNP on the level of residential construction. Figure 18-a shows the two variables plotted on different scales.

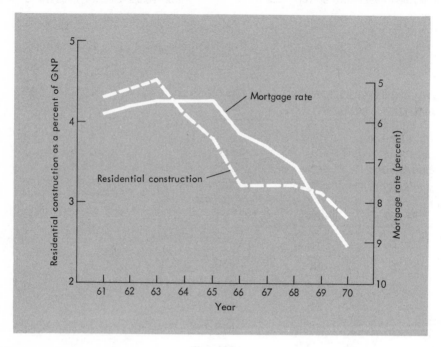

Figure 18-a

The mortgage rate is plotted on an *inverse* scale, so the fact that the residential construction line and the mortgage rate line move roughly together indicates that there is an inverse relationship between the two variables, as the theory suggests.

The same information is recorded in a different way in Figure 18-b. Here, the mortgage rate is plotted on the vertical axis, and residential construction as a proportion of GNP, on the horizontal axis. The downward slope of the scatter of points indicates once again an inverse relationship. Although a definitive conclusion must await a more rigorous econometric analysis, these data do appear to confirm the theory spelled out in the chapter.

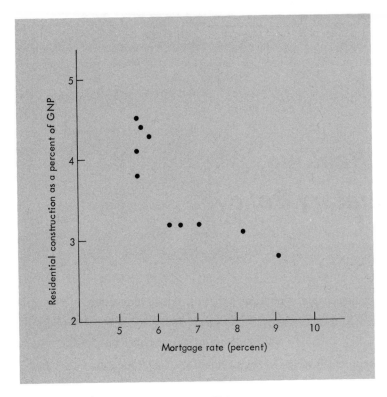

Figure 18.b

19

Money, Banking, and Monetary Policy

19.1 In the preceding chapter, you learned that the rate of interest depends in part on the supply of money, but what determines the supply of money? Money is the generally accepted means

of _____ . In the United States, currency and checks drawn on bank deposits are

generally accepted as means of payment and are, therefore, called _____ .

19.2 When you go to the store, it is possible to purchase goods and services either by exchanging

_____ for them or by writing a check against your bank deposit. Because currency and bank deposits can generally be used to purchase commodities, they are called

_____ .

19.3 Currency and bank deposits are _____ because they are generally accepted as

means of _____ . To the holders of currency and bank deposits, they are
(assets/liabilities) .

19.4 Consider currency first. If you look at a five dollar bill, for example, you will see that it is a Federal Reserve Note. This is because it is issued by the Federal Reserve, which is the central, or government, bank in the United States. Just as ordinary persons issue securities, the central

bank issues Federal Reserve Notes. For this reason, currency, or _____

_____ Notes, are _(assets/liabilities)_ of the Federal Reserve.

ANSWERS

1. payment . money
2. currency . money

3. money . payment . assets
4. Federal Reserve . liabilities

334

19.5 Federal Reserve Notes are a very special liability because by law they can be used to settle any debt. This is indicated on the Federal Reserve Note where it says, "This note is legal tender for all debts public and private." That is, currency is accepted as a means of payment because by law it _(can/must)_ be accepted as such. Thus, even though it is a _____ of the Federal Reserve, the only way a holder of currency will be repaid is with other Federal Reserve Notes. Of course, because currency _(must/may)_ be accepted as means of payment in the United States, there is no reason to ask for other money in exchange.

19.6 Bank deposits are similar to currency. Although, currency is the liability of the _____ _____ , which is the central bank, a bank deposit is the liability of commercial banks. If you have a bank deposit, that means that _(you owe the bank/the bank owes you)_ the amount deposited.

19.7 Persons usually hold bank deposits to avoid the risk of loss or theft of currency and because bank checks are a convenient means of payment. They are willing to hold bank deposits instead of currency because a check written on a bank deposit, like currency, _(is/is not)_ generally accepted as a means of payment. Unlike currency, however, there is no law that requires a person to accept a check written on a bank deposit. But if you can show that you have a bank deposit, your check will usually be accepted as a means of payment because everyone knows that the _____ will convert the check into currency without delay if this is desired.

19.8 Thus, bank deposits are _____ because they are generally accepted as a means of payment. Bank deposits are the _(assets/liabilities)_ of commercial banks, which are willing and able to convert the deposits into _____ without delay.

19.9 How does money come into existence? Through a complicated procedure, which is not important for this discussion, the Federal Reserve may issue currency when it buys securities in the money market. When it buys securities, the Federal Reserve may pay for them in effect by issuing currency, or _____ _____ _____ , which by law are means of payment. These, of course, become _(assets/liabilities)_ of their holder and are _(assets/liabilities)_ of the Federal Reserve.

19.10 For example, suppose that the Federal Reserve's total asset holdings consisted of $100 billion in securities that had been purchased in the money market and paid for with Federal Reserve Notes. If that were the case, the balance sheet of the Federal Reserve, which shows its assets and liabilities, would look like this:

Assets	Liabilities
Securities . . . $100 billion	Federal Reserve Notes . . . $100 billion

ANSWERS
5. must . liability . must
6. Federal Reserve . the bank owes you
7. is . bank
8. money . liabilities . currency
9. Federal Reserve Notes . assets . liabilities
10. assets . liabilities . 100 . assets

That is, the $100 billion in securities would be the _____ , and the $100 billion in

currency would be the _____ of the Federal Reserve. It would also mean that the

amount of currency circulating in the economy would be $_____ billion. That is,

all the liabilities of the Federal Reserve would be held as _____ by consumers,
businesses, and other government agencies.

19.11   If the Federal Reserve decided to purchase $10 billion more in securities with new issues of
Federal Reserve Notes, its balance sheet, after this purchase, would appear as follows (fill in
the amounts):

Assets	Liabilities
Securities . . . $_____ billion	Federal Reserve Notes . . . $_____ billion

Now the public's asset holdings would include $10 billion more in *(currency/securities)*
and $10 billion less in *(currency/securities)* .

19.12   Thus, currency comes into existence when the Federal Reserve purchases _____

from the public in the money market and pays for them with _____

_____ _____ .

19.13   Bank deposits come into existence in much the same way. The most familiar way is when
someone deposits currency in the bank and gets a bank deposit in return. In this case, one form

of _____ is being exchanged for another. When a bank exchanges bank deposits
for currency, money *(is/is not)* created. Nonbank asset holders are simply exchanging one

kind of _____ for another.

19.14   Bank deposits, however, can be created in another way. When the bank makes a loan (that is,

buys a _____), it usually gives the lender a new bank deposit. That is, when banks

buy securities, they usually pay for them with _____ _____ .

19.15   Thus, bank deposits are created when they are issued in return for either _____ or

_____ . As a result, the balance sheet of banks appears as follows (fill in the
blank):

Assets	Liabilities
Federal Reserve Notes	_____
Securities	

ANSWERS

11. 110 . 110 . currency . securities   14. security . bank deposits
12. securities . Federal Reserve Notes   15. currency . securities (either order) . deposits
13. money . is not . money

19.16 You will recall that earlier it was noted that because total income must equal total expenditure, for every borrower who spends more than his income there must be a _____ who spends _(more/less)_ than his income.

19.17 If securities were the only financial asset that existed, the assets that these lenders accumulated with their unspent income would be the _____ that borrowers issue to spend more than their income. That is, if securities were the only type of financial asset, the financial assets of _(creditors/debtors)_ would be the financial liabilities of _(creditors/debtors)_ .

19.18 Assuming for the moment that securities are the only type of financial asset, suppose that there were $500 billion in outstanding securities. If you were to look at the financial entries in the balance sheets for all nonbank debtors and all nonbank creditors, all the outstanding securities would appear on the _____ side for the debtors and on the _____ side for the creditors, as follows:

Debtors		Creditors	
Assets	Liabilities	Assets	Liabilities
	Securities		Securities
	. . . $500 billion		. . . $500 billion

19.19 As has been indicated previously, however, securities _(are/are not)_ the only type of financial asset that can be accumulated with unspent income. Creditors also have the option of holding their financial assets in the form of _____ .

19.20 Any income not spent for real commodities results in an increase in creditors' holdings of financial assets, whether in the form of money or securities. If nothing is done with the unspent income, it accumulates as _____ . The alternative, of course, is to purchase _____ .

19.21 Also, for any period, because total income and total expenditure must be equal, the amount of income not spent for real commodities by creditors just matches the excess of expenditure over income of debtors. That is, for any period, the increase in _(assets/liabilities)_ of creditors must equal the increase in _(assets/liabilities)_ of debtors.

19.22 The increase in assets of creditors is, in general, partly _____ and partly _____ . The increase in liabilities of debtors, however, is composed entirely of _____ .

19.23   As a result, all the outstanding securities must be equal to the holdings of money and securities by creditors. Thus, the amount of securities held by creditors must be   *(more/less)*   than the total amount of securities outstanding.

19.24   That is, if creditors hold part of their financial assets in the form of money, they *(can/cannot)* hold all the outstanding liabilities, or securities, issued by debtors. Who then holds the securities that are not held by creditors?

19.25   The answer to this question can be found in the explanation of how money is created. You will recall that money is created when either the Federal Reserve or commercial banks buy

_____ . Thus, for every dollar of money held by creditors, the Federal Reserve and

the commercial banks hold a dollar of _____ . That is, the securities not held by

creditors are held by the _____ _____ and _____

_____ .

19.26   The Federal Reserve and the commercial banks, then, act as financial intermediaries between creditors and debtors. The part of creditors' assets held as money appears as liabilities for the

financial _____ . These liabilities are matched exactly by the securities held by the

_____ _____ because, in the act of purchasing securities, the financial intermediaries created the money in existence.

19.27   Previously, the financial entries in the balance sheets of creditors and debtors were considered in the case in which securities were the only type of financial asset. In that case, all existing securities appeared as   *(assets/liabilities)*   for creditors and   *(assets/liabilities)*   for debtors.

19.28   Now, in the more general case with both money and securities as financial assets, suppose that there were $500 billion in outstanding securities and $200 billion in money. If you were to look at the financial entries in the balance sheets of creditors, debtors, and financial inter-

mediaries, you would find that money would appear on the assets side for _____

and on the liabilities side for _____ _____ .

19.29   Because money is created when financial intermediaries purchase _____ , there will

be $_____ billion in securities held as assets by financial intermediaries to balance the money, or liabilities, they have issued.

ANSWERS

23. less

24. cannot

25. securities . securities . Federal Reserve .
      commercial banks

26. intermediaries . financial intermediaries

27. assets . liabilities

28. creditors . financial intermediaries

29. securities . 200

19.30   Thus, in the general case in which there are two types of financial assets (money and securities), part of the existing securities will appear on the assets side of the balance sheet of creditors and on the assets side of _____ _____ . All the securities will still be on the liabilities side of the balance sheet of _____ .

19.31   In this example, the balance sheets would appear as follows (fill in the missing figures):

Debtors		Creditors	
Assets	*Liabilities*	*Assets*	*Liabilities*
	Securities ... $500 billion	Securities ... $____ billion Money (currency and bank deposits) ... $200 billion	

Financial Intermediaries
(Federal Reserve and Commercial Banks)

Assets	*Liabilities*
Securities ... $____ billion	Money (currency and bank deposits) ... $____ billion

19.32   Thus, creditors lend to debtors directly when they acquire the _____ issued by debtors. In effect, creditors can also lend indirectly by accumulating the liabilities of _____ _____ , which in turn make loans to debtors.

19.33   Money is created whenever a financial intermediary purchases securities and pays for them with their liabilities. The two kinds of money, currency and bank deposits, are the liabilities of the _____ _____ and _____ _____ . These institutions are called financial intermediaries because they hold _____ (the liabilities of debtors), while creditors hold _____ (the liabilities of financial intermediaries).

19.34   Creditors, therefore, lend to debtors directly by holding _____ , and indirectly by holding _____ , which enables financial intermediaries to hold securities.

ANSWERS

30. financial intermediaries . debtors
31. 300 . 200 . 200
32. securities . financial intermediaries
33. Federal Reserve . commercial banks (either order) . securities
34. securities . money

19.35   The more securities financial intermediaries buy, the greater the supply of _____ .
And the greater the supply of money, the lower the _____ of _____ .

19.36   Because a purchase of securities by financial intermediaries will _(raise/lower)_ the rate of
interest, it will lead to _(an increase/a decrease)_ in investment expenditure and, consequently,
an increase in _____ _____ .

19.37   The money supply is composed of _____ and bank _____ , which are
the liabilities of the Federal Reserve and commercial banks. The money supply increases whenever the Federal Reserve or commercial banks buy securities, because they pay for them with
_____ or bank _____ .

19.38   A change in the money supply will affect the _____ rate because the amount of
money consumers and businesses are willing to hold increases as the interest rate _(increases/
decreases)_ .

19.39   Suppose that the money market is in equilibrium, which means that at the existing interest rate
the quantities of money supplied and demanded are _____ . Then, for example,
if the money supply is increased, at the initial interest rate, the quantity of money demanded
is _(greater/less)_ than the quantity supplied.

19.40   At that interest rate, consumers and businesses would not be satisfied with their situation and
would try to eliminate the excess supply of money by buying securities (or, as we shall see later,
other assets). This would tend to drive _(up/down)_ the value of securities and drive
(up/down) the interest rate, until the quantity of money demanded _(increased/decreased)_
enough to match the quantity supplied.

19.41   Changes in the money supply and the resulting changes in the interest rate will have an effect
on _____ expenditure (including, of course, investment type expenditure by
households, such as purchases of consumers durable goods). As the interest rate decreases, for
example, more investment projects will be worth undertaking, and firms will _(increase/
decrease)_ investment expenditure.

19.42   The autonomous changes in investment expenditure that result from changes in the interest rate
lead to autonomous changes in _____ demand. As we saw in Chapter 16, these
changes in aggregate demand will have a multiplier effect on real GNP.

ANSWERS

35. money . rate . interest
36. lower . an increase . aggregate demand
37. currency . deposits . currency
   . deposits
38. interest . decreases

39. equal . less
40. up . down . increased
41. investment . increase
42. aggregate

19.43 You are now in a position to see how the government can influence the rate of interest. As you know, when the Federal Reserve buys securities from the public, in effect, it issues

_____ in order to pay for them. Suppose that the money market is initially in equilibrium. This means that the rate of interest is at a level where the quantities of money

_____ and _____ are equal. Suppose now that the Federal Reserve buys more (existing) securities. The effect of this action will be to *(increase/decrease)* the supply of money and *(increase/decrease)* the rate of interest.

19.44 Similarly, if the Federal Reserve decided to sell some of its holdings of securities in the money market, it would give securities to asset holders in return for outstanding Federal Reserve liabilities, which is _____ . As a result, the supply of _____ would decrease and the supply of _____ not held by the Federal Reserve would increase. The effect of this change would be to *(increase/decrease)* the rate of interest.

19.45 Thus, through buying and selling of existing _____ in the money market, the Federal Reserve can change the rate of interest. Such action is called open market operations. If the Federal Reserve wants to raise the rate of interest, it can do so by carrying out

_____ _____ operations in the form of *(buying/selling)* securities.

19.46 Selling securities to *(increase/decrease)* the supply of money and thereby *(increasing/ decreasing)* the rate of interest is an example of _____ _____

_____ .

19.47 When considering the effect of open market operations, remember that a sale of securities by the Federal Reserve to the public *(increases/decreases)* the supply of securities held by the public and decreases the money they have. As a result, an open market sale by the Federal Reserve drives the rate of interest *(up/down)* . And an open market purchase drives the rate of interest *(up/down)* .

19.48 This can be seen in a diagram showing the supply and demand for money. In Figure 19.1, L and M_1 are the initial demand and supply curves. The rate of interest determined by these two curves is _____ .

ANSWERS

43. money (currency) . supplied . demanded (either order) . increase . decrease
44. money (currency) . money . securities . increase
45. securities . open market . selling
46. decrease . increasing . open market operations
47. increases . up . down
48. $0R_1$

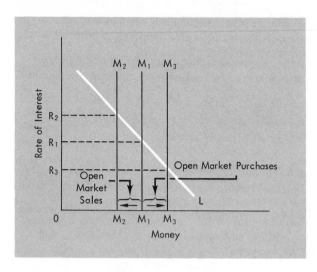

Figure 19.1
Open market operations

19.49   If the Federal Reserve makes open market sales of securities, the supply curve of money will
shift from M_1 to ___(M₂/M₃)___ . At the initial rate of interest, the market would not be in

_____ , and the rate of interest would rise until it reached a level of

_____ . That is, the market value of securities would be driven __(up/down)__
by Federal Reserve open market sales.

19.50   Open market purchases would have the opposite effect because the Federal Reserve would be
paying money to consumers and firms for their securities. In this case, the money supply
would shift from M_1 to _____ , and the rate of interest would shift from OR_1 to

_____ .

19.51   Federal Reserve open market sales to and purchases from the public are not the only way in
which the money supply and the rate of interest can be changed. Because the Federal Reserve
is the government agency that regulates the banking system, it can also take action that encourages commercial banks to purchase or sell securities and thereby increase or decrease the

supply of _____ and raise or lower the _____ of _____ .
(Remember that when a bank makes a loan it is buying a _____ . Similarly, when
a bank decreases its loans, it is _____ securities.)

19.52 One Federal Reserve regulation that commercial banks must follow is the reserve requirement. This is a requirement that a certain proportion of their total assets must be held as reserves in the form of Federal Reserve Notes or other liabilities of the Federal Reserve. That is, a percentage of banks' total assets must be held as _____ in the form of Federal Reserve liabilities.

19.53 The main liability of the Federal Reserve, other than Federal Reserve Notes, is commercial bank deposits in the Federal Reserve. Thus, the _____ requirement can be met by commercial bank holdings of Federal Reserve Notes or commercial bank _____ in the Federal Reserve.

19.54 Whether a commercial bank holds reserves in the form of Federal Reserve Notes or deposits in the Federal Reserve is a matter of convenience. Either way, it makes no difference to the amount of securities banks can hold because both Federal Reserve liabilities can be used to meet commercial bank _____ _____ .

19.55 If commercial banks had total assets of $200 billion and faced a reserve requirement of 20 percent, their balance sheet might look like this:

Assets		Liabilities	
Reserves–Federal Reserve Notes and deposits in the Federal Reserve	$ 40 billion	Bank deposits	$200 billion
Securities	160 billion		

If the commercial banks were in this position, they _(could/could not)_ buy more securities and create more money because their reserves would then _(fall below/rise above)_ the 20 percent reserve requirement.

19.56 Suppose now that the Federal Reserve lowered the reserve requirement to 10 percent. Then the banks would have $40 billion in reserves when they needed only $_____ billion. With excess reserves, the banks _(could/could not)_ increase their holdings of securities until the excess reserves were eliminated. (Remember again that increasing their holdings of securities often takes the form of _(more/fewer)_ loans.)

19.57 With reserves of $40 billion, the banks could increase their total assets until their required reserves were $_____ billion. With a reserve requirement of 10 percent, they could increase their total assets to $_____ billion. Thus, they could increase their

ANSWERS
52. reserves
53. reserve . deposits
54. reserve requirements

55. could not . fall below
56. 20 . could . more
57. 40 . 400 . 200

holdings of securities by $_____ and pay for them with new bank deposits of an equal amount.

19.58 It is possible, therefore, for the Federal Reserve to induce commercial banks to increase the

money supply by reducing the _____ requirement.

19.59 If the Federal Reserve were to raise the reserve requirement, commercial banks would be forced to *(increase/decrease)* their holdings of securities, (that is, their loans and investments), which would thereby *(increase/decrease)* the money supply.

19.60 Changing the money supply by a given amount through changes in the reserve requirement will have substantially the same effect as a change in the money supply brought about by open market operations. In both instances, an increase in the money supply will drive the rate of interest *(up/down)* , and a decrease will drive the rate of interest *(up/down)* .

19.61 Because commercial banks are required to hold reserves equal to only a fraction of their deposits, the effect of open market operations can be greater than indicated previously. Suppose that the Federal Reserve purchases $10 billion of securities from the public. If $5 billion of the currency created to pay for those securities is deposited in commercial banks, this will *(increase/decrease)* the reserves of commercial banks. If the banks did nothing other than accept the deposit of $5 billion, there would be no further change in the money supply. The

public would simply have changed $5 billion of money in the form of _____ into

$5 billion in the form of _____ _____ .

19.62 This, however, is likely to stimulate the banks to make new loans (that is, buy more securities). The deposit of currency will have increased their total assets by $5 billion and their total

reserves by $_____ billion. If the reserve requirement is 20 percent of total assets,

however, the increase in the amount of reserves required will be only $_____ billion.

19.63 Thus, the banks' actual reserves will have increased by $_____ billion, while the

amount required by the Federal Reserve will have increased by only $_____ billion. If the banks initially had no excess reserves, a deposit of $5 billion in currency would

leave them with $_____ billion in excess reserves.

ANSWERS

58. reserve
59. decrease . decrease
60. down . up

61. increase . currency . bank deposits
62. 5 . 1
63. 5 . 1 . 4

19.64   With excess reserves, the banks will be able to acquire more _____ on which they can earn interest. By making more loans to debtors, usually by giving them bank deposits, the commercial banks will acquire new _____ and at the same time create more

_____ .

19.65   The deposit in commercial banks of part of the money created by Federal Reserve open market purchases from the public makes possible further increases in the money supply because it gives the commercial bank excess _____ . When banks have excess reserves, they can acquire more _____ and create more _____ in the form of bank deposits.

19.66   To repeat an example used earlier, if commercial banks had total assets of $200 billion and faced a reserve requirement of 20 percent, their balance sheet might look like this:

Assets		Liabilities	
Reserves–Federal Reserve Notes and deposits in the Federal Reserve	$ 40 billion	Bank deposits	$200 billion
Securities	$160 billion		

In this situation, there would be no excess _____ , and the banks would be unable to purchase more _____ .

19.67   Suppose the Federal Reserve made open market purchases amounting to $10 billion, and $5 billion of the resulting increase in currency was deposited in commercial banks. At first, the banks would find themselves in the following new position:

Assets		Liabilities	
Reserves–Federal Reserve Notes and deposits in the Federal Reserve	$_____ billion	Bank deposits	$_____ billion
Securities	$160 billion		

19.68   In this situation, actual reserves would be $_____ billion, but required reserves would be only $_____ billion. This means that the banks could expand their holdings of _____ .

19.69 Banks could buy securities, paying for them with new deposits, until the actual and required

_____ were equal, that is, until there were no _____ reserves.

19.70 Given their reserves of $45 billion and a reserve requirement of 20 percent, the banks could expand until deposits reached a level of $_____ billion. The final position for the banks would look like this:

	Assets		Liabilities
Reserves ...	$ 45 billion		Bank deposits ... $_____ billion
Securities ...	$_____ billion		

The initial increase in deposits of $5 billion has led the banks to expand deposits by an

additional $_____ billion, so that together deposits increased by $_____ billion.

19.71 Taking into account the response of the commercial banks, what has been the total effect of the Federal Reserve open market purchases of $10 billion? The money supply has increased by

the $5 billion held by consumers and businesses in the form of _____ , plus the increase in bank deposits of $_____ billion that resulted when consumers and businesses deposited the other $5 billion of the currency issued by the Federal Reserve.

19.72 The total increase in bank deposits will be a multiple of the amount initially deposited. You can see that, with a reserve requirement of 20 percent, an increase in reserves of $1 will permit

an increase in total assets of $_____ . Of this total increase in assets,

$_____ will be the increase in securities.

19.73 Thus, open market purchases by the Federal Reserve will lead to an increase in the money supply that is _(greater/smaller)_ than the increase in currency. The extra money will be created when some of the new currency is deposited in commercial banks, providing the banks

with excess _____ and making it possible for them to buy more _____ . When the commercial banks buy more securities, they will create new bank deposits, which

constitutes a further increase in the supply of _____ .

19.74 The same multiple effect could result if the Federal Reserve purchased securities directly from the banks. For example, an open market purchase of $5 billion would reduce banks' holdings

of _____ and increase banks' holdings of _____ either in the form of

ANSWERS

69. reserves . excess
70. 225 . 180 . 225 . 20 . 25
71. currency . 25

72. 5 . 4
73. greater . reserves . securities . money
74. securities . reserves . excess

Federal Reserve Notes or commercial bank deposits in the Federal Reserve. This would create

_____ reserves and permit a multiple expansion of bank security holdings and bank deposits.

19.75 Another, less important way in which the Federal Reserve can influence the amount of bank deposits in existence is by lending reserves to the commercial banks. This allows banks to meet their reserve requirement by borrowing _____ from the Federal Reserve.

19.76 The price banks must pay for these loans is called the discount rate. It is called this because the loans are made in an amount from which the interest is deducted, or discounted. By changing the _____ rate, the Federal Reserve can make it more or less expensive to borrow reserves. An increase in the _____ rate will encourage banks in debt to the Federal Reserve to reduce this debt. To do so, they must sell _____ , which reduces the _____ supply.

19.77 A reduction in the _____ rate will make it less expensive to borrow reserves. This is likely to result in the _(purchase/sale)_ of securities and _(an increase/a decrease)_ in bank deposits by banks who are willing to borrow reserves at the lower discount rate.

19.78 Of these three policy actions—open _____ operations, changes in _____ requirements, and changes in the _____ rate—open market operations are by far the most important.

19.79 You are now in a position to trace the effects of monetary policy on the economy as a whole. This can be done in terms of Figure 19.2, which has four diagrams. Suppose the economy to be initially in equilibrium, with a money supply curve of M_1 and a rate of interest _____ , as shown in (i), and an aggregate demand curve of AD_1 and a real GNP of _____ , as shown in (iv).

19.80 In (ii), the rate of return function RR shows the investment expenditure that would be made at different rates of _____ , given the level of real GNP 0Q. Thus, at the rate of interest $0R_1$, given a real GNP of 0Q, investment expenditure will be _____ .

ANSWERS

75. reserves
76. discount . discount . securities . money
77. discount . purchase . an increase
78. market . reserve . discount
79. $0R_1$. 0Q
80. interest . $0I_1$

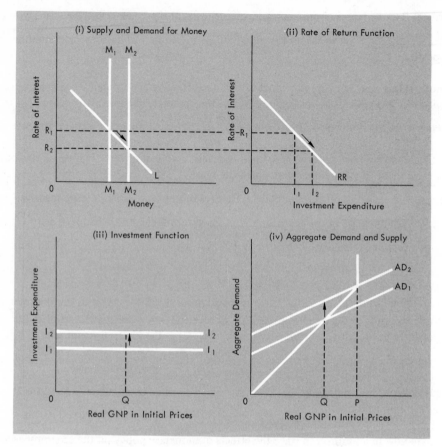

Figure 19.2 Monetary policy

19.81 In (iii), the investment function shows the investment expenditure (including investment type expenditure made by households) that would be made at different levels of _____ _____ , given the rate of interest $0R_1$. Thus, at a real GNP of $0Q$, given the rate of interest $0R_1$, investment expenditure will be _____ . Of course, the amount of $0I_1$ in (ii) and the amount of $0I_1$ in (iii) are equal.

19.82 Suppose now that the government tries to increase aggregate demand by using monetary policy and increases the money supply from $0M_1$ to $0M_2$. In (i), this will have the effect of _(increasing/decreasing)_ the rate of interest to _____ .

ANSWERS

81. real GNP . $0I_1$ 82. decreasing . $0R_2$

19.83 The decline in the rate of interest will result, as can be seen in (ii), in a movement along the rate of return schedule and _(an increase/a decrease)_ in investment expenditure. The level of investment expenditure at the new rate of interest will be _____ .

19.84 The increase in investment expenditure due to a decrease in the rate of interest will appear as a _(shift in/movement along)_ the investment function in (iii). At the lower rate of interest, the investment function will be in the _(higher/lower)_ position of I_2. At the new rate of interest, with the original level of real GNP 0Q, investment expenditure will be _____ .

19.85 The upward shift in the investment function will have the effect of shifting the aggregate demand curve in (iv) from AD_1 to AD_2. This will have a multiplier effect on real GNP, which will _(increase/decrease)_ from 0Q to _____ .

19.86 With the new money supply of $0M_2$, then, the economy _(will/will not)_ have full employment without inflation. In this situation, then, the increase in the money supply from $0M_1$ to $0M_2$ _(was/was not)_ the appropriate action for the Federal Reserve to have taken.

19.87 In our analysis, we have concentrated on the effects of changes in the money supply affecting _____ expenditures through changes in the rate of _____ . You will remember from Chapter 18 that changes in the rate of interest can also affect consumption expenditure. For example, at a lower rate of interest, the cost to consumers of buying ("investing in") automobiles will be lower, and, as a result, expenditure will be _(higher/lower)_ .

19.88 Another way of looking at this is that when the Federal Reserve or banks buy securities from households, the households may use the money received to replace the securities given up with other assets, for example, consumer durables such as houses, automobiles, or clothing. Either way, the effect of increasing the money supply through buying securities is to _____ aggregate demand.

19.89 Some economists believe that open market operations to increase the money supply mainly reduces the interest rate on securities and thus only indirectly increases private investment and aggregate demand. Others believe the increased money supply will lead to both increased investment and increased consumption expenditures, as people have more money than they were previously satisfied to hold. Whatever the outcome of this dispute, the Federal Reserve can increase aggregate private demand by _____ securities.

ANSWERS

83. increase . $0I_2$

84. shift in . higher . $0I_2$

85. increase . 0P

86. will . was

87. investment . interest . higher

88. increase

89. buying

19.90   Thus, the government has at least two types of policy that can be used to fight unemployment or inflation. It can change taxes or government expenditure to influence aggregate demand, which would be _____ policy, or it can take action that leads to a change in the money supply, which would be _____ policy.

REVIEW QUESTIONS

19.1   An economy is at full employment and the price level is relatively stable. Many people, however, have protested that the government's policy of promoting rapid economic growth places too much emphasis on future consumption and too little on present consumption.
   Which of the following could satisfy the protestors' wishes without causing more inflation or more unemployment?

1. a reduction in income taxes
2. an increase in interest rates
3. an increase in government expenditure

   a. 1 taken by itself   c. 1 and 2 taken together
   b. 2 taken by itself   d. 1 and 3 taken together

At full employment, an increase in consumption expenditure would be possible only if there were a corresponding decrease in real government and/or investment expenditure. Thus, if consumers wish to increase present consumption at the expense of future consumption, resources will have to be diverted from the production of investment goods to the production of consumption goods. The reduced investment would make future consumption lower than it otherwise would be but would make possible higher present consumption. Of the policies given, a reduction in income taxes would generate an increase in consumption expenditure, and an increase in interest rates would be appropriate to reduce investment expenditure. Both responses a and d would be inflationary and response b would lead to higher unemployment. The correct response is c.

19.2   The economy is at full employment. Over the next decade, with existing government policies, the rates of inflation and unemployment should remain unchanged and the rate of growth in output should be 3 percent per year. To increase the rate of growth over the next decade, but also without increasing inflation or unemployment, which of the following policies should the government adopt?

1. encourage businesses to invest more
2. encourage households to save a higher proportion of their income
3. encourage households to consume a higher proportion of their income

   a. 1 only   c. 1 and 2 taken together
   b. 2 only   d. 1 and 3 taken together

ANSWERS
   90. fiscal .   monetary

Given the assumption, an increase in the growth rate would be possible only if the productive capacity of the economy were increased at a rate greater than that which would be generated by existing policies. Productive capacity (capital stock) is increased when net investment takes place. Thus, to increase the growth rate, it is necessary that businesses invest more than they otherwise would have. However, because the economy is at full employment, if businesses attempt to invest more without consumers spending less and saving more, inflation will result. Therefore, in order to increase the share of output going to investment it is necessary for the government to encourage an increase in investment. To avoid inflation, however, it is also necessary to encourage households to save more. In other words, to avoid both inflation and unemployment and also to achieve the higher growth rate, the additional planned investment would have to be matched exactly by additional planned saving. The correct response is c.

19.3   In 1931, the United States economy suffered from a very high unemployment rate. Interest rates were at an all-time low, prices were falling, and gold reserves were declining. Which, if any, of the following policies would have been appropriate to reduce unemployment and why?

1. Decreasing the money supply because this would cause prices to fall and thereby aggregate demand to increase.
2. Increasing interest rates because this would stimulate saving and thereby increase investment and aggregate demand.
3. Increasing income taxes because this would permit an increase in social security payments and thereby increase consumption and aggregate demand. (Assume all consumers spent 90 percent of their income).

   a. 1 only
   b. 2 and 3 only
   c. 3 only
   d. neither 1 nor 2 nor 3

Each of the responses a, b, and c contains a fallacy. Although each one recognizes that what the United States economy required in 1931 was an increase in aggregate demand, none of the suggested policies would have led to such an increase. A decrease in the money supply, an increase in interest, and an increase in taxes all would have reduced aggregate demand, thereby aggravating the situation. The correct response is d.

19.4   If a market economy were operating at full employment which, if either, of the following two changes would have to take place for national output to increase?

1. an increase in productive capacity
2. an increase in total expenditure

   a. 1 only
   b. 2 only
   c. both 1 and 2
   d. neither 1 nor 2

If an economy were operating at full employment, an increase in output would only be possible if productive capacity were to increase. An increase in productive capacity, however, is not sufficient to guarantee that national output will increase. If aggregate demand is insufficient to purchase all output the economy is capable of producing, actual output will be less than potential output, and unemployment will result. Thus, an increase in total expenditure and an increase in productive capacity are both necessary to guarantee an increase in national output when the economy is operating at full employment. The correct response is c.

Case 19

MONETARY VS FISCAL POLICY

In recent years, one issue that has been hotly debated is whether the government should rely primarily on fiscal policy or monetary policy to regulate aggregate demand. In this controversy, three positions have been taken: The "Extreme Keynesian" (or fiscal policy) position that when it is needed most monetary policy will be ineffective and only fiscal policy will work; the "Extreme Monetarist" (or monetary policy) position that fiscal policy will not work and only the supply of money matters in determining the level of aggregate demand; and the "Orthodox," or "Reasonable Man," position, which says that both monetary and fiscal policy can be effective. The following provides a brief summary of each of these positions:

THE EXTREME KEYNESIAN

There are two reasons why monetary policy will not work effectively. First, in some circumstances an increase in the quantity of money will not reduce the rate of interest very much because the demand-for-money curve will be nearly horizontal. This is likely to occur when interest rates are very low, as they are during recessions and depressions, because at low rates of interest most wealth holders will expect interest rates to rise. That is, they will expect to earn capital losses from holding securities that will wipe out the interest income they might earn. As a result, when the Federal Reserve buys securities in the open market in an attempt to reduce the interest rate and increase aggregate demand, it will find that people will be happy to unload securities at the going price. In this event, the purchase of securities by the Federal Reserve will not bid up security prices and, consequently, will not reduce the rate of interest. Second, even were the Federal Reserve able to change the interest rate, it would not have much effect on aggregate demand because investment expenditure is not very responsive to interest rate changes. That is, the rate of return function is nearly vertical. For these reasons, we must rely on fiscal policy to stabilize the economy. Fiscal

policy directly affects aggregate demand, and hence output and employment.

THE EXTREME MONETARIST

(1) More money directly increases consumption as well as investment spending. If households receive more money (say, through transfer payments), they will spend some of the money on consumer goods, as well as on securities (which is what Keynesian economics assumes they will do exclusively). Thus, more money will directly increase consumer spending, as well as increasing investment spending through reducing interest rates (raising security prices). The economy's demand-for-money curve is seldom, if ever, horizontal; in most cases it is more nearly vertical.
(2) Moreover, expansionary fiscal policy is generally self-defeating unless the deficit is financed by creating new money—in which case it is monetary policy that matters. If the government spends more, this clearly increases aggregate demand. But if taxes are raised to obtain the funds, this largely offsets the expansionary effect by reducing private spending. If the funds are raised by borrowing from households and businesses (not from the banks), this raises interest rates and "crowds out" private borrowers, leading to a fall in private investment that offsets the increased government spending. For these reasons, we must rely on monetary policy to stabilize the economy.

THE REASONABLE MAN

Both monetary and fiscal policy can be used to stabilize the economy. In the real world, the demand for money is neither vertical nor horizontal and the rate of return function is not vertical. Consequently, a change in the money supply will change the rate of interest, investment and consumption expenditure, and aggregate demand. At the same time, an expansionary fiscal policy will not be fully offset by a decline in investment expenditure due to a rise in the rate of interest. As long as the demand for money slopes downward, an increase in the demand for money resulting from a higher GNP will be offset by the decline in demand due to a rise in the rate of interest, and it will be possible to have equality between the supply of and demand for money at a higher level of GNP. Because both policy instruments will work, which one is used should be determined by other considerations. The combination of monetary and fiscal actions that meets our stabilization goals and also achieves other policy objectives is the best policy package.

What are the sources of disagreement among our three stereotype debaters? Which is correct?

SUGGESTIONS FOR ANALYSIS

In assessing the three arguments presented above, it is important to note that they disagree mainly over empirical evidence, not over theory. Most economists accept a basic theoretical framework similar to that developed in this and preceding chapters. What they do disagree about are the facts of the case, namely the shapes of the demand for money and rate of return curves. If the de-

mand for money is vertical, only monetary policy will work. If the demand for money curve is horizontal, or if the rate of return function is vertical, only fiscal policy will work. The issue can be decided only by finding out whether either of these situations prevails in the real world.

One main reason that there is disagreement on this issue is that it is impossible to identify periods in U.S. economic history when the only autonomous changes were either fiscal or monetary policy actions. Proponents point to various periods to bolster their cases—the Keynesians to the mid-1930s, the Monetarists to the 1968 tax increase—but in each of these periods the evidence is not clear cut. Perhaps the most persuasive evidence is the result of econometric work that estimates from historical evidence the shape of the demand for money curve and the sensitivity of investment and consumption spending to changes in the rate of interest. The results of these studies support the orthodox position. This explains why the argument of our Reasonable Man is accepted by the great majority of economists and—as you may have detected—coincides with the view implicitly expressed in this and preceding chapters.

20

Problems in Stabilizing a Dynamic Economy

20.1 In Chapters 15 and 16, a simple model was used to explain how the level of _____

_____ relative to potential GNP determines whether there will be unemployment, inflation, or full employment without inflation. In Chapters 17 through 19, you learned how the government can influence aggregate demand through _____ and

_____ policy to help avoid unemployment or inflation.

20.2 The ideas developed in these chapters are basically simple ideas. Given the widely accepted goals of full employment and average price stability, your reaction may very well be that it

should be simple to avoid both _____ and _____ by applying these ideas to actual policy. But, as you know, the American economy has had periods of unemployment, periods of inflation, and periods of both.

20.3 This record does not necessarily indicate, however, that the theories presented in the preceding chapters are incorrect. In fact, many economists argue that much of the unemployment and inflation of the past resulted because the government did not use the policies suggested by these theories. These economists feel that had their theories been followed, much of this unemployment and inflation _(would/would not)_ have been avoided.

20.4 There has, however, been a growing acceptance of the basic ideas presented in this book by government policy makers. For example, after a period of high unemployment from 1958-1963, the government followed these ideas and both decreased taxes and increased the money supply to reduce unemployment. The subsequent reduction of the unemployment rate from 5.5 percent in 1963 to 4.0 percent by the end of 1965 suggests that the kind of fiscal and monetary policy suggested by economic theory _(can/cannot)_ work.

ANSWERS

1. aggregate demand . fiscal . monetary   3. would
2. unemployment . inflation (either order)   4. can

20.5   But even if there were complete acceptance of these ideas, several factors that were excluded from the simplified discussion of the preceding chapters may make it difficult to make the correct policy decisions. That is, the real world is __*(more/less)*__ complicated than it appears in the models analyzed in the preceding chapters, and real-life complications can make it __*(more/less)*__ difficult to choose the right policies than seems apparent at first.

20.6   One complication that policy makers must take into account is the continuous growth of the American economy. Most of the previous analysis was concerned with how policy is aimed at

equating aggregate demand and a given _____ _____ in initial prices. But, because population increases result in growth of the labor force, because investment expenditure results in growth of the stock of capital goods, and because technological change results in increased productivity of the economy's resources, potential GNP __*(remains/ does not remain)*__ constant.

20.7   Because continuous growth in the quantity and productivity of resources means continuous growth of potential GNP, in order to achieve full employment without inflation it is necessary

to have continuous growth of _____ _____ .

20.8   This means, of course, that the level of aggregate demand that was adequate in achieving those goals last year will be too __*(great/small)*__ this year. Therefore, unless policy makers take into account the growth in potential GNP, policy that was successful last year will result in __*(inflation/unemployment)*__ this year.

20.9   Keeping track of the growth in potential GNP is not the only difficulty that arises from the dynamic, changing nature of the economy. Nor is it the most serious difficulty. Because the growth in the quantity and productivity of resources takes place at a fairly steady rate, it __*(is/is not)*__ possible to forecast relatively accurately future growth in potential GNP from what has happened to potential GNP in the recent past. Unfortunately, this is not always true of other variables that are important to policy makers.

20.10   If the goal is to have full employment without inflation, you know from the simple model that it is necessary to have growth in aggregate demand, matching the growth in potential GNP. But what changes this will require in the policy variables—such as taxes, government expenditure, or the money supply—depend on what autonomous changes there will be in consumption and investment expenditure independent of government action. That is, if other factors will cause a change in aggregate demand, the government __*(must/need not)*__ know what they will be before it can properly decide what actions to undertake. In other words, to make the right policy decisions, the government must be able to forecast __*(only/not only)*__ how its actions will change aggregate demand but __*(not/also)*__ how other factors will change aggregate demand.

ANSWERS

5. more . more
6. potential GNP . does not remain
7. aggregate demand

8. small . unemployment
9. is
10. must . not only . also

20.11   For example, suppose that this year aggregate demand was at just the right level to achieve full employment without inflation. Suppose also that the government accurately forecasts a growth in potential GNP of 4 percent between this year and next. Economic theory tells you that to keep the economy at full employment without inflation aggregate demand must grow by

_____ percent between this year and next. If it grows more than that, the result

would be _____ . If it grows less than that, the result would be _____ .

20.12   In this situation, it matters _(little/a great deal)_ how much private expenditure will change as a result of factors other than government policy. It also is of considerable importance how

accurately the government can _____ this change.

20.13   For example, suppose consumers and businesses expected many commodities to become scarce and increased their expenditure enough to raise aggregate demand by 5 percent in the absence of any change in government policy. If this were the case, the correct policy would be to use

fiscal and monetary policy to _(increase/decrease)_ aggregate demand by _____
percent from what it would otherwise be.

20.14   In this example, if the government was unable to forecast accurately the autonomous increase in private expenditure and used fiscal and monetary policy to increase aggregate demand by 4 percent in addition to the unforseen autonomous increase in demand, the result would be

_____ . A situation similar to this occurred in 1951 when consumers and businesses reacted to the start of the Korean War by stockpiling many commodities. This unanticipated increase in aggregate demand resulted in a 7 percent increase in the price level (GNP deflator).

20.15   To take another example, discoveries of new products lead businesses to acquire the capital goods necessary to produce them. Suppose that this year fewer discoveries than normal are made. With a given rate of interest, businesses _(would/would not)_ find as many profitable investment opportunities as in the past, and, other things equal, investment expenditure would _(increase/decrease)_ .

20.16   Suppose the decrease in investment expenditure were enough, in the absence of other changes, to cause an autonomous decrease in aggregate demand of 6 percent. Again supposing potential GNP were to increase by 4 percent this year, fiscal and monetary policy should be used to add

to aggregate demand an autonomous increase of _____ percent: _____

percent to offset the decline in investment expenditure and _____ percent to match the growth in potential GNP.

ANSWERS

11. 4 . inflation . unemployment	14. inflation
12. a great deal . forecast	15. would not . decrease
13. decrease . 1	16. 10 . 6 . 4

20.17 If the decline in investment expenditure were not forecast by the government, and fiscal and monetary policy were used to increase aggregate demand by only enough to match the growth in potential GNP, the result would be _____ .

20.18 Most recessions, as well as the Great Depression of the 1930s, have resulted primarily from a decline in investment expenditure that was not sufficiently offset by increases in other types of expenditure to keep aggregate demand from falling below potential GNP in initial prices. This means, of course, that the appropriate fiscal and monetary policies __*(were/were not)*__ used. One explanation is that until recently these modern theories were not generally recognized, and at other times the government __*(was/was not)*__ willing to use the policies suggested by modern economic theory. But, even if the government had always been willing to adopt rational policies, in order to decide on the right course of action, it would still have been necessary to

_____ correctly the changes in investment expenditure brought about by other factors.

20.19 Thus, it may be difficult to choose the right policy because it may be difficult to _____ accurately what changes in aggregate demand will occur because of changes in expectations, in the rate of discovery of new products, the impact of international developments, and other such factors.

20.20 Because it may often be impossible to forecast changes in aggregate demand due to other factors, the government may find out about the change only after unemployment or inflation has occurred. In this situation, fiscal and monetary policy __*(can/cannot)*__ be used to prevent the problem, but they __*(can/cannot)*__ be used to alleviate it.

20.21 You have seen that fiscal and monetary policy must be continuously adjusted to avoid unemployment or inflation. Fiscal and monetary policy must be adjusted not only to keep aggregate demand growing along with _____ _____ but also to offset changes in _____ _____ due to other factors.

20.22 In order to choose the "right" policy, it is necessary to _____ correctly both changes in potential GNP and changes in aggregate demand due to other factors. Changes in potential GNP are relatively __*(easy/difficult)*__ to forecast accurately because the quantity and productivity of resources grow at a relatively steady rate. Changes in aggregate demand due to other factors, however, do not occur in a regular fashion and are relatively __*(easy/difficult)*__ to forecast accurately.

ANSWERS

17. unemployment
18. were not . was not . forecast
19. forecast

20. cannot . can
21. potential GNP . aggregate demand
22. forecast . easy . difficult

20.23   When the government does not forecast changes in aggregate demand correctly, it __(will/ will not)__ be able to determine what is the right policy in time to avoid inflation or unemployment.

20.24   In addition to the time lag involved in identifying the nature and size of the problem, a considerable length of time may be required by Congress or other government policy makers to decide exactly what policies should be undertaken and to put the policies into effect. Suppose the government were to be caught by surprise by a rise in the unemployment rate from 4 percent to 7 percent in just a few months. Before a tax cut, for example, could be put into effect, the President must make a proposal to Congress, there must be hearings on the proposal, and a bill must be written and enacted into law. Because all this takes _____ to be done, an immediate application of economic theory to fiscal policy is practically __(possible/impossible)__ even when the exact nature of the problem is known.

20.25   The example of the large tax cut of 1964 gives an indication of the time it can take for the government to act. The decision to propose a tax cut was made by President Kennedy in the summer of 1962 after almost two years of persuading by his economic advisers, but it took until February 1964 for the tax cut to be passed and to go into effect. The cost of the delay was that the unemployment rate remained __(higher/lower)__ for a __(longer/shorter)__ period of time than would otherwise have been the case.

20.26   A more recent example is the tax increase that President Johnson proposed in January 1967, again after a year's persuading by economists, when inflation threatened, and that was not passed until mid-1968, after inflation was in full swing. The purpose of the tax increase was to __(increase/decrease)__ aggregate demand to stop _____ . Because of the delay in being enacted, it was too little and too late to prevent inflation.

20.27   Because of the delays that necessarily result from the nature of the political process, many economists have urged that arrangements be made to put specific policies into effect automatically once the problem is recognized. Such an arrangement would have the advantage of helping eliminate unemployment or inflation __(more/less)__ quickly.

20.28   Actually, there are some policies that are automatically put into effect when unemployment or inflation occurs. For example, when unemployment increases, the payment of unemployment compensation to workers without jobs __(increases/decreases)__ . Unemployment compensation is an example of a __(government expenditure/transfer payment)__ that increases automatically when unemployment increases.

ANSWERS

23. will not
24. time . impossible
25. higher . longer

26. decrease . inflation
27. more
28. increases . transfer payment

20.29   As with any other transfer payment, an increase in unemployment compensation results in _(an increase/a decrease)_ in aggregate demand. As a result, the decline in aggregate demand, relative to potential GNP in initial prices, that caused unemployment would be _(deepened/ offset)_ to some extent by the unemployment compensation program.

20.30   Arrangements that put policies into effect automatically are called *built-in stabilizers*. The unemployment compensation program is an example of a _____ _____ because when unemployment increases it automatically increases _(government expenditure/ transfer payments)_ .

20.31   Another example of a built-in stabilizer is the federal income tax structure. Because the amount of income taxes collected by the government depends on the size of the national income, whenever income increases, income tax receipts _(increase/decrease)_ . As a result, when there is inflation, income in current prices increases and tax receipts _(increase/decrease)_ . When there is a recession and income falls, tax receipts _(increase/decrease)_ .

20.32   In each case, given the goal of full employment with no inflation, the changes in tax receipts that result automatically when inflation or recession occurs is in the _(right/wrong)_ direction. That is, the tax structure tends to stabilize the economy because it results in tax _(increases/ decreases)_ when there is inflation and tax _(increases/decreases)_ when there is unemployment.

20.33   Both the unemployment compensation program and the tax structure are examples of _____ _____ because they automatically change transfer payments and tax receipts in the right direction when the economy deviates from full employment without inflation. Unfortunately, however, the built-in stabilizers are not sufficient to prevent unemployment or inflation from occurring, but serve only as a partial offset to the changes in _____ _____ that cause the problem.

20.34   Thus, despite the existence of built-in stabilizers, additional government policies are required to help achieve the goals to full employment and _____ stability. Two time lags posing problems for policy makers are: (a) the time lag involved in identifying the problem, and (b) the time taken to put the appropriate policy into operation. Many economists have urged that an arrangement be made by which it would be possible, immediately upon identification of a problem, to generate the appropriate fiscal stimulus or restraint. The purpose of this arrangement would be to avoid the time lag connected with _(identification of the problem/the decision-making process)_ .

ANSWERS

29. an increase . offset
30. built-in stabilizer . transfer payments
31. increase . increase . decrease

32. right . increases . decreases
33. built-in stabilizers . aggregate demand
34. price . the decision-making process

20.35 Still a third time-lag exists for policy makers. Once a policy is undertaken, it takes time for it to affect aggregate demand, income, and employment. That is, the full response of aggregate demand to a particular fiscal or monetary policy change ordinarily _(will/will not)_ take place immediately.

20.36 For example, an increase in the money supply may reduce the rate of interest, but this may not lead to _(an increase/a decrease)_ in investment expenditure until a substantial period of time has elapsed.

20.37 To take another example, a decrease in income taxes will increase disposable income, but it may take a considerable length of time before the full _(increase/decrease)_ in consumption ex-

penditure will be made by consumers. Consumers take _____ to readjust their spending levels and the multiplier process takes time to work itself out.

20.38 The uncertain time lag between undertaking a policy and its full effect on aggregate demand makes it _(more/less)_ difficult for policy makers to time their actions properly. This lag makes it necessary for the government to forecast changes in the economy _(further/less far)_ ahead than would otherwise be the case.

20.39 In summary, you have seen how three types of _____ lags make it difficult to

apply the basic ideas analyzed in preceding chapters. These lags stem from the _____ required (a) to identify the problem, (b) to decide what action to take, and (c) for any policy action to have its full effect.

20.40 The difficulties involved in putting theory into practice to eliminate unemployment or inflation are not limited to time lags involved with fiscal and monetary policy. You will recall that in the preceding chapters it was assumed that as long as there was an output gap, the price level _(would/would not)_ rise. Or, put the other way around, it was assumed that the price level

would rise only when there was an _____ gap.

20.41 In the real world, this is not strictly true. If you examine Figures 20.1 and 20.2, you will observe that there have been periods when the unemployment rate was above 4 percent and the rate of inflation was greater than 2 percent. That is, in the real world both unemployment and inflation _(can/cannot)_ exist at the same time.

ANSWERS

35. will not
36. an increase
37. increase . time
38. more . further

39. time . time
40. would not . inflationary
41. can

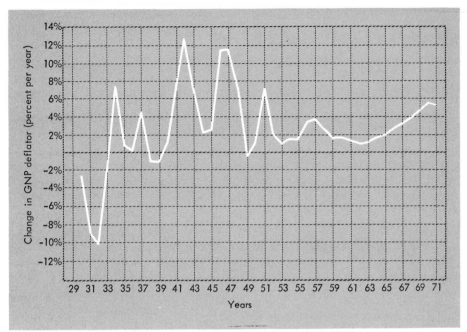

FIGURE 20.1 Change in GNP deflator, 1930-1971

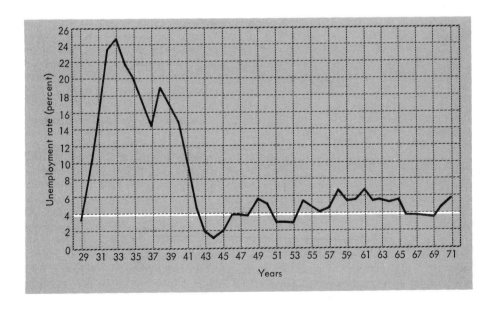

FIGURE 20.2 Unemployment rate, 1929-1971

20.42   This fact does not destroy the usefulness of the conclusions reached in the preceding chapters. It still remains true that excess aggregate demand will cause _____ and insufficient aggregate demand will cause _____ .

20.43   What was assumed away for the sake of simplicity in the preceding chapters was that sometimes inflation can result from factors other than excess _____ _____ . In fact, there _(can/cannot)_ be both inflation and unemployment at the same time.

20.44   To understand one reason that inflation can occur at less than full employment, consider a typical firm. If this firm is in an industry with many competitors, the price it charges for its product must be in line with the market price. Otherwise, it _(would/would not)_ be very difficult to sell much of its output. But if the firm is in a market with only a few competitors and it produces a product that is not exactly the same as any of its competitors', the firm will have considerably _(more/less)_ independence when setting its price.

20.45   As we saw in Chapter 11, in the United States many markets are characterized by only limited competition, with the result that many firms have _(considerable/practically no)_ leeway in setting their prices.

20.46   Although it is very difficult to prove, many economists believe that firms in markets with limited competition customarily set their prices to cover costs plus a percentage margin of profit. For example, if costs are 80 cents per unit and a firm charges $1 per unit, it is setting its price to cover _____ plus a profit margin equal to _____ percent of the price.

20.47   If firms actually do set prices this way, whenever there is a rise in costs per unit of output there will also be a rise in _____ . Thus, a factor that can cause inflation, even when there is unemployment, is a _(rise/fall)_ in _____ per unit of output.

20.48   Why might unit costs rise during a period of unemployment? One situation in which unit costs might rise is when firms are expanding their rate of production very rapidly. That is, a firm may be able to expand its rate of production without a rise in unit costs if the expansion is spread out over a _(long/short)_ period of time. But if it tries to expand its rate of production quickly, its unit costs are likely to _(rise/fall)_ .

20.49   A rapid increase in the rate of production may lead to _(increasing/decreasing)_ unit costs because firms may have to pay higher prices for materials to get them delivered promptly. Or it

ANSWERS

42. inflation . unemployment
43. aggregate demand . can
44. would . more
45. considerable

46. costs . 20
47. prices . rise . costs
48. long . rise

may not be able to find the best combination of labor skills immediately and must settle for second best. If firms set prices to cover costs plus a _____ margin, the increase in unit costs will lead to _____ increases.

20.50 Thus, if the economy is moving toward full employment very rapidly, many firms in the economy will be increasing their rate of production *(rapidly/gradually)* . As a result, many firms will incur *(higher/lower)* unit costs and will *(raise/lower)* prices to preserve their desired profit margins.

20.51 Look back to Figures 20.1 and 20.2, which show changes in the price level and the unemployment rate. In 1934, for example, even though the unemployment rate was very *(high/low)* , it fell sharply, and real GNP rose by 9 percent. At the same time, there was a fairly *(high/low)* rate of inflation, almost 8 percent.

20.52 Another reason that costs might rise when there is unemployment is that wages for many workers are not determined in highly competitive markets. As a result, it is possible for wages to rise even though there is an excess supply of labor. For example, suppose that there is an unemployment rate of 6 percent. If the labor market were highly competitive, you would expect wage rates to *(rise/fall)* . But, many wage rates are determined in collective bargaining between unions and employers, and unions may push wage rates up even though there is unemployment.

20.53 An increase in wage rates does not by itself necessarily raise unit costs, however. Technical change, which tends to increase the productivity of workers each year, must also be taken into account. For example, if labor productivity were to increase by 3 percent between this year and next, it would mean that the same amount of output could be produced next year with 3 percent *(more/fewer)* workers. If wages were to remain constant between this year and next, the labor cost per unit of output would *(rise/fall/remain the same)* .

20.54 This can be seen in Table 20.1. In this example, next year it will require *(more/fewer)* men to produce 1,000 units of output because labor _____ will have increased.

20.55 An increase in labor productivity from 10.0 to 10.3 units of output per man will reduce the labor required to produce 1,000 units from _____ to _____ men. As a result, if the annual wage paid to a man is $1,000 in each year, the total labor cost will fall from $_____ to $_____ .

ANSWERS

49. increasing . profit . price
50. rapidly . higher . raise
51. high . high
52. fall

53. fewer . fall
54. fewer . productivity
55. 100 . 97 . 100,000 . 97,000

Table 20.1

LABOR PRODUCTIVITY INCREASES AND UNIT LABOR COSTS

	This year	*Next year*
Output	1,000	1,000
Labor productivity (output per man)	10.0	10.3
Labor requirements (men)	100	97
Wage rate (dollars per man)	$1,000	$1,000
Total labor costs	$100,000	$97,000
Labor costs/unit of output	$_____	$_____

20.56 It is possible now to calculate unit labor costs in each year. This year, total labor costs were $100,000, and next year they will be $97,000. With output equal to 1,000 in both years, the

labor cost per unit of output will decline from $_____ to $_____,

which is a drop of _____ percent. (You can enter these unit costs in the table.)

20.57 Thus, if labor productivity rises and wage rates remain unchanged, unit labor costs will _(rise/ fall)_. Put another way, if labor productivity rises, it _(will/will not)_ be possible to raise wages without increasing unit labor costs.

20.58 In fact, as long as wage rate increases do not exceed labor productivity increases, unit labor costs _(will/will not)_ rise. If the wage rate increase exceeds the productivity increase, how-

ever, _____ labor costs will _(rise/fall)_.

20.59 In the example given above, because labor _____ rose by 3 percent, it would have

been possible to increase the wage rate by _____ percent without raising

_____ _____ costs.

20.60 A wage rate increase will result in higher unit labor costs only if they exceed the increases in

_____ _____. If wage rates increased by 4 percent when labor pro-

ductivity increased by only 3 percent, those firms that set prices to cover costs plus a required

profit margin will raise their _____.

ANSWERS

56. 100 . 97 . 3   59. productivity . 3 . unit labor
57. fall . will   60. labor productivity . prices
58. will not . unit . rise

20.61 Thus, even if there is no excess aggregate demand, if collective bargaining results in wage rate increases that are greater than labor _____ increases, the result is likely to be a _(rise/fall)_ in the price level. The 1970-1971 period provides a case in point. During this period, the rate of productivity increase was well below average, about 1½ percent per year, while the rate of increase in wages was about 6 percent per year. This implied an increase in unit labor costs of _____ percent per year.

20.62 If wage rate increases just match labor productivity increases, inflation can result if firms try to increase their profit margins by raising prices. As indicated previously, because many firms operate in markets in which they have few competitors, they _(do/do not)_ have considerable control over the prices that prevail in those markets. Therefore, it is sometimes possible for these firms to change their profit margins by changing their _____ .

20.63 Thus, it is possible for inflation to result, even if there is no excess aggregate demand, because the markets for many types of labor and for many products _(are/are not)_ highly competitive. If unions manage to obtain wage increases in excess of labor _____ increases, the result can be _____ . Or if firms try to use their control over market prices to increase their _____ margins, the result can be _____ . In addition, earlier you learned that when output is increasing rapidly, it may result in rising _____ costs, and the result can be _____ .

20.64 Inflation that results from these factors is often called *cost-push inflation*. This term is used to distinguish it from inflation that is due to excess aggregate demand, which is called *demand-pull inflation*. The difference between these two is that _____ inflation is caused by too great a level of expenditure, and _____ inflation is caused by rising costs of production.

20.65 Although it is possible for cost-push inflation to occur at any time, it is more likely to occur when the economy is at or near full employment, when the strong market positions of firms and unions tempt them to make inflationary adjustments in profits and wages. Thus, when the economy approaches full employment, _____ inflation is likely to occur even if there is no excess aggregate demand.

20.66 One situation in which costs are likely to rise even if there is unemployment is when people expect inflation to occur in the future. Suppose, for example, that labor and management in an

ANSWERS
61. productivity . rise . 4½
62. do . prices
63. are not . productivity . inflation . profit . inflation . unit . inflation
64. demand-pull . cost-push
65. cost-push
66. higher . rise

industry are bargaining over a three-year wage contract. If workers expect prices to rise over the period of the contract, they would require a *(higher/lower)* wage settlement to achieve a given real income increase than if they expected no price change. As a result, negotiated wage increases are likely to be larger when prices are expected to *(rise/fall)* .

20.67   Because people are likely to expect inflation when they have recently experienced it, cost-push inflation frequently follows a period of demand-pull inflation. That is, if in one period prices rose, people are likely to expect prices to *(continue to rise/stop rising)* . The expectation of future inflation will lead workers and other income earners to demand *(higher/lower)* compensation than they would otherwise, thereby raising costs and, ultimately, prices.

20.68   Thus, a demand-pull inflation, by affecting people's expectations, causes _____ -

_____ inflation to occur in subsequent periods. The Nixon Administration be-lieved that this was a major factor in the inflation of 1969-1971. During the 1966-1968 period, the substantial growth in aggregate demand due to the Vietnam military build-up reduced un-employment below 4 percent unemployment and drove the rate of inflation to over 4 percent

per year. This was clearly a case of _____ - _____ inflation.

20.69   During the period 1969-mid-1971, unemployment rose well above the 4 percent mark. Despite the elimination of the *(output/inflationary)* gap, however, the rate of inflation remained above 4 percent. Government economists believed that the inflation due to excess aggregate demand in the 1966-1968 period led people to expect continued *(inflation/unemployment)* , and that this in turn led to abnormally *(high/low)* demands for wage increases, with re-sulting higher costs and prices. This would clearly be a case of *(demand-pull/cost-push)* inflation.

20.70   Another reason it may be difficult to achieve both full employment and average price stability at the same time is that not all markets will have the same supply and demand conditions. For example, suppose that the government through its fiscal and monetary policy adjusts aggregate demand to just the right level, as suggested by the analysis in terms of the simple model of the

preceding chapters. This means that _____ _____ is just equal to

_____ _____ in initial prices. If this model were an exact duplicate of the real world, the economy *(would/would not)* experience both full employment and average price stability.

20.71   In the real world, however, there are many commodities and many markets. Even if aggregate demand were at the "right" level in terms of this model it would generally not be true that at

ANSWERS

67. continue to rise . higher
68. cost-push . demand-pull
69. inflationary . inflation . high .
    cost-push

70. aggregate demand . potential GNP . would
71. rise . downward

initial prices the amounts demanded and supplied would be equal in all markets. In some markets, at initial prices there would be excess demand, and prices would tend to __*(rise/fall)*__ . In other markets, at initial prices there would be excess supply, and, therefore, __*(upward/ downward)*__ pressure on prices.

20.72 If all markets functioned perfectly it would be expected that prices in all markets __*(would/ would not)*__ adjust—some upward and some downward—to their new equilibrium levels. The upward and downward movements in individual prices would cancel each other out, __*(leaving/causing)*__ the average price level __*(unchanged/to rise)*__ .

20.73 But as you will recall, many markets do not function perfectly. As a result, many individual prices tend to be __*(flexible/rigid)*__ in a downward direction. Thus, in many of the markets that have excess supply, prices will not _____ as might be expected.

20.74 At the same time, even in imperfect markets, prices do tend to _____ in response to excess demand. Thus, in a situation in which some markets have excess supply and others excess demand, the expected price __*(increases/decreases)*__ would be forthcoming, but the expected price __*(increases/decreases)*__ would not.

20.75 When aggregate demand is at the "right" level, some markets will be characterized by excess supply and others by excess demand at initial prices. Because not all markets function perfectly in this situation, the price increases in the markets with excess demand __*(will/will not)*__ be offset by decreases in markets with excess supply, and consequently, the average price level will

_____ .

20.76 Thus, even with the theoretically correct level of aggregate demand, because of market imperfections there can be __*(no/some)*__ inflation. In those markets where prices do not fall in response to excess supply, firms will __*(increase/decrease)*__ output and employment. This will occur because when demand falls consumers are not willing to purchase all the commodities that suppliers are willing to produce. Thus, not only will there be some inflation in this situation but there will also be some _____ .

20.77 When the economy is far from full employment, there will be few, if any, markets where there is excess __*(supply/demand)*__ , and many markets where there is excess _____ . In that situation, the average price level __*(will/will not)*__ rise rapidly.

ANSWERS

72. would . leaving . unchanged
73. rigid . fall
74. rise . increases . decreases

75. will not . rise
76. some . decrease . unemployment
77. demand . supply . will not

20.78 The closer the economy is to full employment, the more markets there will be that are characterized by excess _(supply/demand)_ . Consequently, the closer the economy is to full employment, the _(more/fewer)_ markets there will be in which prices will rise. That is, the

lower the unemployment rate, the higher the rate of _____ .

20.79 Earlier, you learned that the closer to full employment, the more costs and prices are likely to
rise in markets where there is _(perfect/imperfect)_ competition. Now you have learned that
because prices rise in markets where there is excess demand, _(and also/but do not)_ fall in

markets where there is excess _____ , the closer the economy is to full employ-

ment, the higher the rate of _____ . This can be true even when there is no excess
aggregate demand.

20.80 This phenomenon of the rate of inflation increasing even when there is no excess aggregate demand is represented in Figure 20.3. The rate of _____ is measured along the verti-

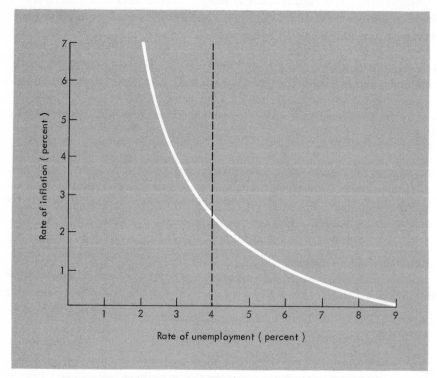

Figure 20.3   Example of trade-off between unemployment and inflation

ANSWERS

78. demand . more . inflation   80. inflation . unemployment . high
79. imperfect . but do not . supply .
    inflation

cal axis, and the rate of _____ along the horizontal axis. The curve that slopes downward from left to right shows that at low rates of unemployment the rate of inflation tends to be _(high/low)_ .

20.81 This curve shows the trade-off between unemployment and inflation from which government policy makers must choose when deciding monetary and fiscal policy. Should they, for example, stimulate aggregate demand so as to maintain low unemployment and thereby accept a relatively _(high/low)_ rate of inflation, or should they restrain aggregate demand in order to avoid inflation and thereby accept a relatively _(high/low)_ rate of unemployment?

20.82 The existence of a trade-off between unemployment and inflation poses a dilemma for policy makers. It makes it difficult to use fiscal and monetary policy to avoid both inflation and unemployment at the same time. If fiscal and monetary policy are used to keep the economy at full employment, some _____ is likely to occur. If they are used to keep aggregate demand so low that no inflation will occur, then some _____ will result.

20.83 Faced with this dilemma, the government must choose between two evils. It must decide where along the inflation-unemployment trade-off curve it should aim for. That is, it must decide whether it is worse to be near full employment with some _____ or to have price stability with some _____ .

20.84 The decision as to what point policy makers should aim for cannot be decided on the basis of economic analysis alone. The people who are hurt most by inflation and the people who are hurt most by unemployment _(are/are not)_ in general the same people. Any decision about which policy to choose will involve dividing the costs of inflation and unemployment among different people in some way. Such a decision is more _(economic/political)_ than _(economic/political)_ in nature. Consequently, there is no objective or scientific right or wrong decision. Which decision you would support would depend on your point of view.

20.85 In an attempt to avoid facing the dilemma of choosing between evils, economists and political leaders have advocated a variety of policy actions to accompany monetary and fiscal policy. Such policies can be thought of as shifting the trade-off in Figure 20.3 to the _(left/right)_ . One action would be wage and price controls. Another would be voluntary wage-price and price restraint according to the wage-price guideposts. Both of these are discussed in the case at the end of this chapter.

20.86 A longer-run solution that has been advocated by some and regarded as impractical by others is the attempt to make markets more efficient and more competitive through antitrust and

ANSWERS
81. high . high
82. inflation . unemployment
83. inflation . unemployment
84. are not . political . economic
85. left
86. cost-push . unemployment

other government policies, such as improved retraining facilities, employment exchanges, and job information. Whether or not they would work, such proposals are designed to make labor more mobile and prices more responsive to supply and demand conditions. They are intended to eliminate _____ - _____ inflation and the downward rigidity of wages and prices when there is _(unemployment/full employment)_ .

20.87   Whether any such actions are taken to deal with the unemployment-inflation trade-off, it is clear that monetary and fiscal policy _(can/cannot)_ be used to control aggregate demand and thereby help avoid or eliminate unemployment or demand-pull inflation. But as long as a trade-off exists, monetary and fiscal policy _(can/cannot)_ be expected to eliminate completely both unemployment and inflation.

REVIEW QUESTIONS

20.1   Last year, output per worker in the carpet industry was 3 percent higher than the year before. The union, through collective bargaining, was able to obtain a 3 percent increase in wages. If nonlabor costs per unit of output remained the same, by how much would it be necessary to raise the price of carpets to keep profit per unit of output from falling?

a. more than 3 percent   c. less than 3 percent, but more than 0 percent
b. 3 percent   d. 0 percent

Assuming that all of last year's higher output of carpets was sold at the previous year's prices, total revenue would have risen by 3 percent, the productivity increase. Thus, all costs, that is, wages, interest and profit, could have risen by 3 percent, and the previous year's relative factor returns would have remained unaltered. Because wages are less than 100 percent of factor returns, and because nonlabor costs per unit of output remained unchanged, the 3 percent gain in productivity made possible a 3 percent gain in wages and a 3 percent increase in profit without a price increase. Using a numerical example could clarify this point and help avoid a common error. The correct response is d.

20.2   If this year the economy is at full employment with a rate of inflation as expected for a fully employed economy and if there are no autonomous changes in aggregate demand, then it is likely that next year there will be:

a. full employment with reasonable price   c. full employment with more inflation, since
    stability, since aggregate demand and   the growth in potential GNP will induce
    consequently GNP will remain un-   greater consumption and aggregate demand.
    changed.   d. unemployment with more inflation, since
b. higher unemployment with less in-   the fact that the economy was at full em-
    flation, since the usual increase in   ployment this year will result in greater
    potential GNP can be expected to re-   demands for wage increases.
    main unchanged.

ANSWERS
    87. can . cannot

If there are no autonomous increases in aggregate demand, actual GNP can be expected to remain unchanged. Potential GNP can be expected, as usual, to increase from this year to the next as a result of this year's investment in new capital goods and this year's growth in the labor force. Consequently, a gap between actual and potential GNP can be expected to develop. This output gap would mean higher unemployment, which in turn, because of the downward slope in the Phillips curve, would mean less inflation. The correct answer is b.

20.3 Which of the following will be true when inflation occurs, even though the economy is below full employment?

1. Aggregate demand exceeds potential GNP.
2. Increases in wages or other income payments exceed factor productivity increases.
3. Monetary and fiscal policy cannot achieve price stability without worsening the unemployment problem.

   a. 1 and 2 only
   b. 1 and 3 only

   c. 2 and 3 only
   d. 1, 2, and 3

When the economy is below full employment, aggregate demand is below potential GNP by definition. Therefore, statement 1 cannot be true. Inflation occurs because of rising unit costs when the economy is below full unemployment. It must be true that the price of some factor of production must be rising faster than the productivity of that factor. And, if monetary and fiscal policy were used to reduce aggregate demand in an attempt to fight inflation, the result would have to be a widening gap between actual and potential GNP and a worsening of the unemployment problem. The correct response is c.

20.4 In response to expansionary monetary and fiscal policy, national income has risen to an all-time high, unemployment has fallen to its lowest level in three years, and the rate of inflation, though somewhat higher than in recent years, is only slightly above the historical average. A leading economist has proposed that for the coming year the government reduce income taxes or increase its spending. What can be inferred about the economist's policy objectives?

   a. He seeks lower unemployment even at the expense of a higher rate of inflation.
   b. He seeks a lower inflation rate even at the expense of higher unemployment.

   c. He seeks lower unemployment and lower interest rates.
   d. He seeks higher unemployment and higher interest rates.

As aggregate demand has expanded relative to aggregate supply, the difference between actual and potential output has diminished—we know this because the level of unemployment has fallen. If aggregate demand were increased at a faster rate, the unemployment rate would become even lower. It is expected, however, that the rate of inflation, which has risen somewhat as unemployment has fallen, would increase even more at still lower unemployment levels. The economist obviously feels that the marginal benefit from the lower unemployment exceeds the marginal cost of higher inflation. The correct response is a.

Case 20

COST-PUSH INFLATION, GUIDEPOSTS, PHASE ONE, AND PHASE TWO

Monetary and fiscal policy makers, in their pursuit of price stability and full employment, have had to face the fact that it seems impossible to have zero unemployment and zero inflation. As was discussed in this chapter, it appears that if the government relies exclusively on monetary and fiscal policy, it is faced with a trade-off between unemployment and inflation. A gain on one front can be expected only at the expense of a loss on the other.

During the Kennedy-Johnson Administrations, an attempt was made to alter this trade-off to permit reductions in unemployment without significant increases in inflation by establishing guideposts for noninflationary wage-price behavior. Although compliance to the guideposts was voluntary, the government hoped to bring about cooperation through public pressure on large firms and unions. The guideposts to be followed had the following provisions:

(1) The rate of increase in wages for any industry should equal the national average percentage increase in labor productivity.

(2) The rate of increase in prices for any industry should equal the rate of increase in wages minus the rate of increase in productivity for that industry.

If the guideposts were followed in all industries for both wages and prices, those industries with above average productivity increases would have price cuts, industries with below average productivity increases would have price hikes, but on average there would be no change in the price level. Those industries with above average productivity gains would be able to expand output and stimulate demand for their additional output by cutting prices. The reverse would occur in low productivity growth industries. This pattern follows what we would expect to observe in the long-run if all industries were competitive. This means that if the guideposts were generally complied

with, they would permit growth of output to full employment levels without inflation, but they would not interfere with efficient patterns of resource allocation. Although the guideposts seemed to work reasonably well from 1962 through 1965—the unemployment rate fell from 7 to 4½ percent while the rate of increase in the GNP deflator rose from 1.1 percent to only 1.9 percent—it failed miserably in 1967 and 1968 if for no other reason than that the Vietnam build-up resulted in an excess aggregate demand situation. With an inflationary gap, the guideposts could not be expected to work because they were designed to avoid the price increases that might occur during periods of insufficient aggregate demand. Clearly, the guideposts would be useful only as a complement to, not as a substitute for, sound monetary and fiscal policy, the absence of which was apparent in 1967-1968.

During the 1968 election campaign, soon-to-be President Nixon argued vigorously against the guideposts, labeling the policy an improper interference in the workings of the free enterprise system, and indicated that he would allow firms the freedom to make their own price decisions. Upon being elected, Nixon announced his (now abandoned) "economic game plan" for dealing with inflation, which was to reduce aggregate demand and move down the trade-off to a point at which inflation was lower, even though this would require accepting a higher unemployment rate. What Nixon was unable to foresee and what caused him to adopt a new strategy in mid-1971 was that as unemployment rose, so would the rate of inflation.

Two factors are believed to have caused this perverse phenomenon. First, the rapid rise in prices was considered to be in part a lagged response to the inflationary gap that existed from mid-1967 to mid-1969. This could well have been due to the formation of inflationary expectations that led to demands for wage increases far in excess of productivity gains. Second, imbalances in labor markets due to changes in the composition of the labor force—a shortage of certain skilled workers and a surplus of less-skilled workers, mainly older women and teenagers—and changes in the composition of industrial demand created excess demands and large wage gains in some sectors and excess supplies and increased unemployment in others.

Whatever the cause, President Nixon felt compelled to take action. On August 15, 1971, he announced Phase I of his new strategy, a three-month freeze for all wages and prices. Although clearly an interim policy, it gave the President and his advisers time to come up with a more viable long term plan. Moreover, he hoped it would serve to break the upward spiral of inflationary expectations. In November of the same year, the freeze gave way to Phase II, the establishment of special boards (a Pay Board and a Price Commission) that were given the authority to limit price and wage increases. The goal of the Administration was to reduce overall annual wage and price increases to 5½ and 2½ percent respectively by the end of 1972, that is, in time for the next Presidential election.

The Pay Board adopted as its overriding guideline the provision that "permissible annual pay increases would be those normally considered supportable by productivity improvement and cost-of-living trends." The initial standard for new contracts and adjustments was set at 5½ percent and was meant to apply to employees in all industries.

The Price Commission's regulations also imposed a ceiling on the firm's overall ratio of profit to sales; profits could not be a higher ratio to sales than the average of the best two of the last three years. Price increases would be permitted to cover wage increases that did not exceed the Pay Board's basic standard, but would not be permitted to increase profit margins above the ceiling ratio, and prices had to be reduced if profits exceeded the ceiling. By contrast, the earlier guideposts focused entirely on wages and prices.

How would you compare Phase II with the Kennedy-Johnson guideposts? Are Nixon's criticism's of the guideposts applicable to Phase II? How would you assess Phase II as a stabilization policy?

SUGGESTIONS FOR ANALYSIS

In terms of their basic objectives—reasonable wage and price stability—Phase II and the guideposts are similar. Both seek to keep wage increases in all industries in line with nationwide average productivity increases and both allow individual firms and industries to raise prices in proportion to increases in unit costs. One major difference is that Phase II recognizes explicitly the practical impossibility of restricting average price increases to 0 percent per year and has built into its structure an allowance for an overall rate of inflation of 2½ percent per year, at least for 1972. Another significant difference is that Phase II has the force of law behind it. Whereas the guideposts were intended merely to bring public pressure on large business and labor organizations to act in the public interest when making wage and price decisions, the Pay Board and Price Commission, on paper at least, have the authority to force firms and unions to conform to Phase II guidelines. Whether they have the political "muscle" to win out over dissident private parties remains to be seen, but there can be no doubt that the ultimate threat of court action is bound to have a greater effect than are public and private requests for compliance to voluntary guideposts.

To the extent that in their rulings on individual cases the Pay Board and Price Commission adhere to their general guidelines, the operation of Phase II will be broadly similar to the guideposts' goals as to both the distribution of income and the allocation of resources. Under both policies, the rate of increase in wages is expected to exceed the rate of increase in prices only by the rate of increase in average labor productivity (output per worker). If real wage increases rise in proportion to productivity and total output, real profits will rise at the same percentage rate, and the shares of wages and profits in the national income will remain unchanged. Suppose, for example, that productivity increases by 3 percent per year, wages go up by 5½ percent, and prices increase by 2½ percent. In this case, for a given amount of capital and labor, total money income, wage income, and profit income will all increase by 5½ percent, and real wages and real profits by 3 percent.

With respect to resource allocation, both the guideposts and Phase II allow considerable flexibility for shifts in the pattern of output in accordance with changing technology and consumer preferences. Under the guideposts, in industries with above average productivity gains, prices should fall relative to the average, and sales should increase. In technically less-progressive industries, prices would rise relative to the average, and sales would decrease. These relative price and resource allocation changes can be obtained only if relative increases are allowed in those industries with low productivity gains and relative price decreases in industries with above average productivity gains. Note that this would not likely be achieved if wage increases in each industry were set equal to productivity increases *in that industry*, rather than to the nationwide average productivity increase that the guideposts required. Under the individual industry productivity guide, unit costs would remain unchanged in all industries, and there would be no room for relative price changes without drastically altering the industrial pattern of profit margins. Phase II has vacillated over which productivity figures to use.

Phase II's limitation on profits *per se*, although politically attractive, has predictably caused serious resource use problems. In early 1972, as the economy recovered from the preceding recession, profits rose rapidly for most firms even without price increases. This happens in most recoveries as business operating rates improve; profits nosedive in recessions while wages stay up or continue to rise, but then profits rise faster than wages in recoveries. Assume that you were a profit-maximizing businessman in 1972 with your profits clearly rising above the level permitted by Phase II. What would you do? Possibly you would cut your selling prices, as the Price Commission

hoped. But another alternative, which would also keep profits within the Phase II limit, would be to increase your spending (costs) on advertising, painting your buildings, hiring more staff assistants, and the like, all things that are good to do, especially if you are just going to have to give customers the money anyhow through lower prices as an alternative. Instead of the desired antiinflationary result, the profit ceiling could readily induce more "wasteful" use of resources. In devising public policies, careful attention to incentive effects is well worthwhile.

Undoubtedly, Phase II will have its problems. How well it overcomes these problems will depend on the wisdom and good luck of the regulatory boards. Perhaps the greatest strength of Phase II in dealing with the inflation problem—and on this point it clearly dominates the guideposts—is that it provides the government with authority to make its decisions about wages and prices stick. But the effectiveness of any such policy depends basically on public acceptance, and undoubtedly considerable pressure will be put on Pay Board and Price Commission members to make exceptions to general policy. Only if widespread public support can be maintained and these pressures can be resisted, can Phase II be expected to achieve its stabilization objectives without interfering unduly with the patterns of income distribution and resource allocation.

Last, most economists emphasize that no set of guideposts or mandatory wage-price controls can be expected to withstand large inflationary excess demand pressures more than temporarily. Such direct controls offer promise only where excess demand is limited or absent, except possibly in periods of national emergency such as wars.

21

International Trade

21.1 So far in this book, we have analyzed the functioning of the economy without taking into account any economic relationships with other countries. In other words, we have been concerned with the allocation of resources, the distribution of income, unemployment, and inflation in the context of the ___(domestic/international)___ economy, and we have ignored any effect arising from the export and import of goods, that is, we have ignored internationally traded goods.

21.2 As Table 21.1 makes clear, although over the past decade exports and imports have ___(increased/decreased)___ both in value and as a percent of GNP, the overwhelming proportion of output produced in the U.S. was sold ___(at home/abroad)___ , and about 95 percent of the output bought in the U.S. was produced ___(at home/abroad)___ .

Table 21.1

U.S. EXPORTS AND IMPORTS, 1960-1970

	1960	1965	1970
Exports (billions of dollars)	27	39	62
Imports (billions of dollars)	23	32	59
Exports as a percentage of GNP	5.4	5.7	6.4
Imports as a percentage of GNP	4.6	4.7	6.0

21.3 The fact that U.S. exports and imports are only small proportions of U.S. GNP should not lead you to believe that international trade is unimportant. First, as Table 21.2 makes clear, exports and imports constitute much *(larger/smaller)* shares of GNP for many other countries throughout the world. Second, as Table 21.2 also makes clear, a *(large/small)* proportion of international trade for these other countries takes place with the United States. That is, even though U.S. exports and imports are *(large/small)* relative to U.S. GNP, they constitute *(larger/smaller)* percentages of the international trade of other countries for whom a more substantial portion of GNP is produced or consumed abroad.

Table 21.2

EXPORTS AND IMPORTS FOR SELECTED COUNTRIES, 1965

	Exports		*Imports*	
	% of GNP	*% to U.S.*	*% of GNP*	*% from U.S.*
Japan	11	30	10	25
United Kingdom	18	10	19	12
Venezuela	30	37	22	45

21.4 For example, even though the U.S. imported only about *(5/15)* percent of its GNP, its imports amounted to _____ percent of Japan's exports and _____ percent of Venezuela's exports.

21.5 But it is not just because international trade is very important to other countries that you should study international trade. It is important for you to know why U.S. trade with other countries is only a small proportion of GNP, whether it would be desirable to expand or contract imports and/or exports, and what policies the government should adopt with regard to foreign trade. Obviously, to answer any of these questions correctly you need to understand the causes and effects of international trade. Just as we have seen that individuals can

_____ utility or satisfaction by exchanging goods, so, too, will nations become better off through international trade.

21.6 The first point to understand about international trade is that trade between two individuals or groups in different countries is basically no different from trade between two individual or groups within one country. That is, if it is mutually advantageous for two people to exchange goods, there is *(an/no)* incentive for trade to take place *(unless/even when)* the two people live in different countries.

21.7 Under what circumstances will it be advantageous for two people to trade goods? You will recall that in Chapter 9 an example was given in which one person had only nuts and another had only fish. Because of this unbalanced distribution of the two goods, the two individuals'

ANSWERS

4. 5 . 30 . 37
5. increase

6. an . even when
7. different . lower

opinions about the value of an additional nut relative to an additional fish were __*(different/ the same)*__ . That is, in terms of utility, the person who had only fish considered the marginal utility of fish relative to the marginal utility of nuts to be much __*(higher/lower)*__ than did the other person.

21.8 Because their relative marginal utilities were different, these two people found that it would be possible to increase _____ utility by exchanging some of their goods. That is, each person could gain in total utility by giving up some of the good for which his _____ utility was relatively __*(high/low)*__ in exchange for the good for which his _____ utility was relatively _____ . If these two persons lived on different islands or in different countries, there would be no difference in how they would gain from trade.

21.9 Of course, it is not necessary for two persons each to have a good that the other does not have for there to be possible gains from trade. All that is required for trade to be beneficial to both is that the relative _____ utilities be different. Suppose, for example, that a brother and a sister are each given a box of chocolate cherries and a box of bubble gum. Suppose that they each like both goods but that the brother's preferences are biased toward gum and the sister's toward chocolate so that with the amounts they have, their respective marginal utilities are as shown in Table 21.3. It is clear from this table that if the brother were to trade one chocolate cherry for one of his sister's pieces of gum, his total utility would __*(increase/ decrease)*__ by _____ while his sister's total utility would _____ by _____ .

Table 21.3

MARGINAL UTILITIES OF GUM AND CHERRIES

	Gum	*Cherries*
Brother	4	2
Sister	3	4

21.10 We have shown that given whatever amounts of goods different people have, whether they live in one country or another, if their relative marginal valuations of goods are __*(the same/ different)*__ , there are possible gains from _____ . We will now consider how differing capabilities of producing goods will influence trade.

ANSWERS

8. total . marginal . low . marginal . high
9. marginal . increase . 2 . increase . 1
10. different . trade

21.11   Suppose you and I both are capable of producing food and clothing, and that we both have the same preferences. Suppose that we each produce the same amount of food and clothing and do not trade with each other with the result that our marginal utilities for each good are as given in Table 21.4. It is clear that with the amounts of each good that we presently produce, there _(are/are no)_ possible gains from trade because our relative marginal utilities are _(different/ the same)_ .

Table 21.4

MARGINAL UTILITIES OF FOOD AND CLOTHING

	Food	Clothing
You	3	2
I	3	2

21.12   But what if we take into account possible differences in our abilities to produce food and clothing? Suppose, for example, it turns out that we have different capabilities of producing food and clothing perhaps because you are a better weaver of cloth or because I have land better suited to growing food. Suppose that because of these differences our marginal costs of producing food and clothing are as shown in Table 21.5. According to Table 21.5 it will cost

me _____ times as much to produce an extra suit of clothes as it will cost me to produce an extra basket of food, whereas for you the marginal cost of producing suits is

_____ times as much as the marginal cost of producing food.

21.13   If all of your resources are being used to produce food and cloth, then it would be

possible to increase the output of one commodity only by _____ the output of the other. Consequently, if you were to increase your production of clothes by one unit you

would have to reduce your production of _____ by enough to free sufficient resources to produce the clothes.

Table 21.5

MARGINAL COSTS OF PRODUCING FOOD AND CLOTHING

	Marginal cost of producing	
	a suit of clothes	a basket of food
For you	8	4
For me	6	2

ANSWERS

11. are no . the same   13. decreasing . food . 8 . 4 . 2
12. 3 . 2

Because your marginal cost of producing clothes is _____ , you will need 8 units of resources to produce an extra suit. Because your marginal cost of producing food is

_____ , you will free 4 units of resources by producing 1 fewer basket of food. In order to free enough resources to produce an extra suit of clothes, therefore, you will need to

reduce your production of food by _____ baskets.

21.14   Because my marginal cost of clothes is _____ , if I were to reduce my production

of clothes by 1 unit, I would free _____ units of resources, which would enable

me to produce _____ more baskets of food.

21.15   If you were to produce 1 more unit of clothes and I were to produce 1 unit fewer of clothes, our total production of clothes would   *(increase/decrease/remain unchanged)* , but our total

food production would _____ . Your production of food would fall by 2 baskets,

while my production of food would rise by _____ baskets.

21.16   Because total output has gone up through the change in resource allocation, it is obviously possible to make both of us better off. The total output of clothes has remained unchanged,

but the total output of food has _____ even though the same quantities of resources are being used. But, as you will see, you and I must have the opportunity to trade food and clothes to reap the potential benefits from the reallocation of resources.

21.17   Without trade, but with the new allocation of resources, you would have 2 fewer baskets of food and 1 more suit. I would have 3 more baskets of food and 1 less suit. This is shown below.

	Additional baskets of food	*Additional suits of clothes*
You	−2	+1
I	+3	−1
Total	+1	0

Without trade, the fact that total output has _____ does not guarantee that either of us is better off under the new arrangement. You might not want an extra suit of clothes if it means giving up 2 baskets of food; and I   *(must/might not)*   want an extra 3 baskets of food if it means giving up a suit.

21.18   Suppose, however, that I offered you 2½ baskets of food for the extra suit you could produce by reallocating your resources. In that case, you could reduce your production of food

ANSWERS

14. 6 . 6 . 3
15. remain unchanged . increase . 3
16. increased

17. increased . might not
18. 2 . better . ½

by _____ baskets, increase your production of clothes by 1 suit, and then trade the suit to me for 2½ baskets of food. You would clearly be __(better/worse)__ off than before because your clothes consumption would be unchanged but your food consumption would be increased by _____ basket.

21.19 It is clear then that in these circumstances you can gain by reorganizing your production and trading with me, but can I gain also? If I reduced my production of clothes by 1 suit, I would increase my production of food by _____ baskets. My trading 2½ baskets of food to you for a suit means my consumption of clothes would __(increase/decrease/ stay the same)__ , but my consumption of food would increase by _____ basket.

21.20 What this example demonstrates is that when two people have different relative _____ costs of producing goods, they can both become better off. They can both __(increase/decrease)__ their consumption by changing the allocation of resources (and, consequently, the composition of output produced by each) and then by _____ with each other.

21.21 Two persons can gain from trading whenever there are differences in the *relative* marginal costs of producing two goods. If you look again at Table 21.5, you will see that in our initial situation I was able to produce an extra unit of either good at __(higher/lower)__ cost than you were. But even though I could produce an extra unit of either good more cheaply than you, the opportunity for me to gain by trading with you __(did/did not)__ exist.

21.22 In this example, I could produce clothing at three-fourth's the cost that you could, but I could produce food at only _____ the cost that you could. In other words, although I had an *absolute advantage* in producing both goods, I had a *comparative advantage* in producing __(food/clothing)__ .

21.23 The principles that were demonstrated in these simple examples apply equally well to the real world. That is, they explain why trade takes place between individuals within one country, and they also explain why _____ takes place between _____ in different countries.

21.24 One main difference between our simple examples and the real world is that in our examples we imagined two individuals exchanging goods with each other, whereas in the real world people usually sell one good for money and use money to buy other goods. This difference results from the fact that in the real world trade takes place in a more complicated fashion, typically

ANSWERS

19. 3 . stay the same . ½
20. marginal . increase . trading
21. lower . did

22. half . food
23. trade . individuals
24. the same

involving many people rather than just two. But whether trade takes the form of an exchange of goods between two people or many purchases and sales of goods by many people, _(the same/different)_ principles apply.

21.25 To summarize: Trade will take place whenever there are differences among consumers in the relative marginal _____ of two goods, or whenever there are differences among producers in the relative marginal _____ of two goods.

21.26 You might ask why trade would take place between two countries when there are probably plenty of opportunities for trade within each country. The answer is that trading within a country _(rules out/does not rule out)_ the possibility of obtaining further gains by trading between countries. There is nothing about trades of oranges for clothing between Californians and New Yorkers that eliminates the desirability of trades of computers for perfume between Americans and Frenchmen.

21.27 In fact, when you think about the reasons for trade—that is, differences in relative _____ utilities and _____ costs—one might expect there to be greater differences between countries where there are likely to be large differences in attitudes, climate, resource endowments, and so on. We might ask, then, why there is not more trade between countries.

21.28 One factor that limits the extent of international trade is the fact that most countries discourage imports from other countries by imposing *tariffs*. A tariff is a tax on an imported good. Anyone buying an imported good will have to pay the cost of producing the good plus the _____ . Thus, whenever there is a tariff on a good, the _____ of the good will be greater than the _____ of producing the good.

21.29 Imagine the following hypothetical, but fairly realistic, situation involving the United States and Japan. If the two countries did not trade with each other (or with any other countries), and there were perfect competition within each country, you would expect the output of any two goods in each country to expand to the point where the ratio of the _____ costs would be equal to the ratio of the _____ utilities. But, in the absence of trade between the two countries, these ratios _(would/would not)_ necessarily be the same in the two countries.

21.30 Suppose that the prices that prevailed in the absence of trade would be as shown in Table 21.6. It is clear from looking at the price ratios in the two countries that cloth has the lower relative

ANSWERS

25. utilities . costs
26. does not rule out
27. marginal . marginal

28. tariff . price . cost
29. marginal . marginal . would not
30. Japan . prices . can

price in _(the U.S./Japan)_ . We would expect the price of wheat to be relatively lower in the U.S. because U.S. resources (abundant fertile land and ample heavy machinery) are relatively better suited to growing crops while Japanese resources (including a large supply of manual workers) are better suited to manufacturing cloth. It is also clear that as long as there

is a difference in the relative _____ in the two countries (which reflect differences in the relative marginal utilities and costs between the two countries), there _(can/cannot)_ be gains from trade.

Table 21.6

PRICES OF WHEAT AND CLOTH IN THE U.S.
IN THE ABSENCE OF TRADE
(HYPOTHETICAL)

	Wheat (price per bushel)	Cloth (price per yard)
U.S. (dollars)	4	3
Japan (yen)	500	200

21.31 How would trade actually take place? In order to buy goods in Japan, Americans would have to obtain the Japanese currency, yen. Similarly, in order for Japanese to buy goods in the

U.S., they would have to obtain _____ . Suppose that the American and Japanese governments each agreed to buy and sell its own currency in return for the other at a fixed exchange rate of 1 dollar per 100 yen. (In the next chapter you will learn more about the exchange rate). This would mean that if you wanted to buy a bushel of wheat in Japan, you

would take _____ dollars and buy _____ yen from the Japanese government, which you would then use to buy the bushel of wheat.

21.32 With the official exchange rate of _____ dollar per _____ yen, it would be possible to determine from Table 21.6 which product is cheaper in which country.

In terms of dollars, for example, the price of U.S. wheat is _____ dollars, while

Japanese wheat is _____ dollars. At the same time, the price of U.S. cloth is

_____ dollars, while Japanese cloth costs _____ dollars.

21.33 At the initial prices and with an exchange rate of 1 dollar per 100 yen, Americans would

tend to import _____ from Japan and export _____ to Japan because Japanese cloth has a _(higher/lower)_ price and Japanese wheat has a _(higher/lower)_ price.

ANSWERS

31. dollars . 5 . 500   33. cloth . wheat . lower . higher
32. 1 . 100 . 4 . 5 . 3 . 2

21.34 In the absence of any restrictions on trade between the two countries, how much trade would you expect there to be? Obviously, as long as the price of Japanese cloth was less than U.S. cloth, American buyers would tend to buy _(more/less)_ U.S. cloth and _(more/less)_ Japanese cloth. Similarly, Japanese buyers would continue to shift their purchases of wheat

from Japanese to U.S. sources as long as the _____ of Japanese wheat was greater than the price of U.S. wheat.

21.35 But, what would happen to the prices of cloth and wheat in each country as the outputs of

wheat expanded and cloth contracted in _____ , and as the outputs of cloth

expanded and wheat contracted in _____ ? Obviously, this would depend on the forces of supply and demand if we assume competitive markets.

21.36 Because the demand for U.S. wheat has _(increased/decreased)_ as a result of trade with Japan, you should expect the price of wheat in the U.S. to _(rise/fall)_ . Similarly, because the opening up of trade with Japan has resulted in _(an increase/a decrease)_ in the demand for U.S. cloth, you would expect the price of cloth in the U.S. to _(rise/fall)_ .

21.37 These changes in prices in the U.S. reflect, of course, the underlying changes in the marginal costs of production. As output in the wheat industry is expanded, the marginal cost of wheat can be expected to _(rise/fall)_ . (If you forget why, you should reread Chapters 5 and 6.)

Also, as U.S. cloth production declines, the marginal _____ of cloth should be expected to _(rise/fall)_ .

21.38 At the same time, the marginal utilities of wheat and cloth can be expected to change. As the price of wheat rises and the price of cloth falls in the U.S., consumers can be expected to

change their consumption pattern in favor of _____ and at the expense of

_____ . And as the amount of wheat consumed relative to cloth _(increases/ decreases)_ , the marginal utility of wheat relative to the marginal utility of cloth can be expected to _(increase/decrease)_ . (If you forget why, you should reread Chapter 3.)

21.39 So, the change in relative prices in the U.S. reflects the changes in the relative _____

costs and relative marginal _____ . At the same time, changes in relative prices, marginal costs, and marginal utilities will occur in Japan. But, in Japan, the changes will be in the _(same/opposite)_ direction, because there the output of cloth will be increasing and the output of wheat will be decreasing.

ANSWERS

34. less . more . price
35. the U.S. . Japan
36. increased . rise . a decrease . fall

37. rise . cost . fall
38. cloth . wheat . decreases . increase
39. marginal . utilities . opposite

21.40   What this means is that U.S. exports of wheat will cause the price of wheat to rise in

_____ and fall in _____ . U.S. exports of wheat and cloth will expand to the levels at which the price of wheat will be the same in both countries. At this point, there will be _(an/no)_ incentive for the Japanese to increase the level of their imports from the U.S.

21.41   The opposite will happen with respect to cloth. The price will rise in Japan and fall in the U.S. until it is _(equal/unequal)_ in both countries, at which point there will be no incentive for U.S. buyers to expand further their _(imports/exports)_ of cloth. To facilitate a clear understanding, we have made certain simplifying assumptions in our analysis. One assumption has been that there are no transportation costs. In the real world, trade will take place up to the

point at which price differentials are equal to _____ costs.

21.42   Suppose now that instead of allowing free trade, the U.S. government imposed a tariff on imported cloth of 50 percent. In that event, U.S. buyers of cloth would have to pay the

price of Japanese cloth plus the _____ . Because the Japanese price of cloth is

200 yen, the price in terms of dollars would be $ _____ , and the tariff would be

$ _____ .

21.43   Because, with the 50 percent tariff, the U.S. buyer would have to pay $ _____ to obtain a yard of Japanese cloth, and because the price of U.S. cloth is $3, there _(would/ would not)_ be an incentive for U.S. buyers of cloth to import from Japan. That is, the tariff would act as a barrier to trade.

21.44   It is possible to imagine the Japanese government imposing a tariff that discouraged Japanese buyers from importing any wheat from the U.S. Because the U.S. price of wheat is $4 and the Japanese price is 500 yen, and because the exchange rate is 1 dollar per 100 yen, a tariff

of _____ percent would eliminate any competitive advantage of U.S. wheat growers.

21.45   What would happen if the tariffs imposed were not sufficient to entirely eliminate the incentive to trade? Then, of course, trade would take place, as before, up to the point where

the U.S. price of _____ rose enough to preclude any further increase in Japanese

imports and where the Japanese price of _____ rose enough to discourage any further rise in U.S. imports.

ANSWERS

40. the U.S. . Japan . no	43. 3 . would not
41. equal . imports . transportation	44. 25
42. tariff . 2 . 1	45. wheat . cloth

21.46 But, with the tariff, the amount of trade that would occur would be _(greater/smaller)_ . This is because with the tariff the price increases necessary to eliminate any incentive to import would be _(greater/smaller)_ .

21.47 For example, without any U.S. import duty (tariff) on cloth, U.S. imports would rise until the Japanese price of cloth, in terms of dollars, was _(less than/equal to/greater than)_ the U.S. price. With a tariff, however, U.S. imports will rise to the level where the Japanese price plus

the _____ was equal to the U.S. price.

21.48 Now, you might ask: If trade can make people in both countries better off, why would any government want to restrict trade by imposing tariffs? The answer is that although international trade can make some people better off in both countries and can even increase the average real income in both countries, it is not likely to make every individual in both countries better off. In fact, it is likely to make some persons in both countries worse off. That is, the gains from international trade _(are/are not)_ likely to be shared evenly.

21.49 In terms of our example, the effect of international trade would be very different for wheat producers and cloth producers in the United States. It is true that both would benefit by being able to buy cloth at a _(higher/lower)_ price. But although U.S. wheat producers found that the demand for their product was _(increasing/decreasing)_ , U.S. cloth producers would be confronted by a _(growing/declining)_ market for their product.

21.50 As a consequence, producers in the wheat industry would earn _(higher/lower)_ profits while cloth manufacturers would experience a _(rise/decline)_ in profit. Similarly, employees in the U.S. wheat industry would find expanded job opportunities while workers in U.S. textile mills might expect higher unemployment. The fact that international trade would raise the

incomes of those in the U.S. _____ industry by more than it would reduce the

incomes of those in the U.S. _____ industry can be expected to provide little consolation to those whose incomes would fall.

21.51 The reason for tariffs is now clear. Those who would be adversely affected by imports would argue vigorously for tariffs, and, as the record shows, governments _(are/are not)_ likely to listen to them. Unfortunately, Ralph Nader not withstanding, there is little effective lobbying for the consumer. For example, you frequently hear arguments to protect textile workers from foreign competition, but you seldom hear arguments for lower-priced but equally good Japanese underwear that would benefit the American consumer.

ANSWERS

46. smaller . smaller
47. equal to . tariff
48. are not

49. lower . increasing . declining
50. higher . decline . wheat . cloth
51. are

21.52   This raises the question as to whether it is good or bad policy for governments to impose tariffs to discourage imports. It is clear that increased trade will __(increase/decrease)__ the average real income in both countries. But it is also clear that it will alter the income distribution in favor of those in __(import/export)__ industries and against those in __(import/export)__ industries.

21.53   In the absence of any other policy changes, a decision to maintain tariffs is a decision to do without an increase in average real income, in order to protect the incomes of workers and employees in __(import/export)__ industries. A decision to eliminate tariffs is a decision to sacrifice incomes of those in import industries in order to bring about an increase in

_____ real income.

21.54   But the possibility remains that through other policy measures, it would be possible to obtain the gains from trade without the adverse changes in income distribution. If this were the case, it would be clearly desirable to __(eliminate/maintain)__ tariffs. Such policies, to accompany a gradual reduction of tariffs, might include job retraining programs for workers displaced by imports and income guarantees for a period of years for those suffering a loss in income due to tariff reductions. Such a program would help workers in __(import/export)__ industries and facilitate the flow of resources to __(import/export)__ industries.

REVIEW QUESTIONS

21.1   Two countries, X and Y, can produce only wheat and cloth according to the following schedule.

Commodity	Marginal Costs of Production	
	Country X	Country Y
a unit of wheat	1 man-day	2 man-days
a unit of cloth	3 man-days	4 man-days

Assuming no other production costs, transportation costs, or trading restrictions, which of the following is true?

a. Country X will export wheat and import cloth.

b. Country X will export both wheat and cloth.

c. Country X will neither import nor export wheat or cloth.

d. The pattern of trade cannot be determined from the above information.

Compared to country Y, country X can produce a unit of wheat and also a unit of cloth with

ANSWERS

52. increase . export . import   54. eliminate . import . export
53. import . average

fewer resources. Thus, country X has an absolute advantage in the production of both commodities. Country X, however, requires three times more man-days to produce cloth compared with wheat, but country Y requires only twice the number of man-days to produce cloth compared with wheat. Therefore, because country X has a comparative advantage in wheat production, and country Y has a comparative advantage in cloth production, country X will export wheat and import cloth. The correct response is a.

21.2 Which of the following would make possible higher living standards throughout the world?

1. an increase in the skills of the labor force in each country
2. an increase in the stock of capital goods in each country
3. an increase in protective tariffs in each country

   a. 1 only   c. 1 and 3 only
   b. 1 and 2 only   d. 1, 2, and 3

A higher world standard of living means a higher per capita gross world product. This could occur in a variety of ways. For example, the same world output and a lower population or a lower world output with a disproportionately lower population. Assuming a given world population, however, a higher output would be required to increase living standards. Higher output comes about with an increase in the quantity and/or quality of the factors of production or by a more efficient allocation of these factors. Although an increase in a protective tariff could benefit one country, a universal increase in protective tariffs would lead to a less efficient allocation of world resources and, consequently, a decrease in world output. Both an increase in worker skills and an increase in capital goods would increase output. The correct response is b.

21.3 Suppose that diplomatic initiatives by the United States led to the opening of extensive trade with the Soviet Union. Which of the following best describes the effects this would have on the United States?

a. Incomes in export industries would rise, but not by as much as incomes in import-competing industries would fall.
b. Incomes in import-competing industries might fall, but not by as much as incomes in export industries would rise.
c. Per capita income would rise as long as incomes in both export- and import-competing industries would rise.
d. Incomes in both export- and import-competing industries could either rise or fall.

The effect of opening trade with the Soviet Union would be to increase per capita income in both countries because it would expand the opportunities for consumers in each country to consume combinations of goods that are more in accord with their preferences, and it would also permit each country to specialize in the production of those goods for which it has a comparative advantage. Although there would definitely be an increase in U.S. national income, not all workers and employers would share evenly in this increase. It is likely, at least in the short-run, that those in import-competing industries would face a decline in income. This decline would not be as great, however, as the increase in incomes in export industries. The correct response is b.

21.4   Which, if any, of the following would result if all restrictions to trade were removed?

1. higher average living standards
2. lower living standards for some persons

     a. 1 only
     b. 2 only

     c. both 1 and 2
     d. neither 1 nor 2

The increase in world trade, by permitting more efficient resource allocation, would lead to higher world income and an higher average living standard. It would even be possible as a result to make everyone better off if appropriate income redistribution schemes were adopted. But, even though the average would rise, some people could experience a decline in income and a lowering of living standards. The correct response is c.

Case 21

IMPORT QUOTAS FOR STEEL?

Arguments for protection from foreign competition for domestic producers have been made since the beginning of the industrial revolution. The major points made in support of protection seem to change little. The following statement appeared in the Wall Street Journal.[1] It is a plea by an American steel executive for quotas to limit the importation of steel into the United States.

If steel is an important basis of our growing economy, and if its availability is essential to our national defense—which it certainly is—then the question which all of us must face is: How much of the vitality of the domestic industry are we willing to see dissipated by imports? And the next question is whether we are willing to face up to the fact that steel's problems are not of its own making, and therefore not soluble solely by its own efforts. The world of trade which steel must confront is anything but a world of free trade.

By this time there must be a general public awareness of steel import trends. In 1957 only a little over a million tons of steel were imported. Their impact was limited in terms of product and geography. Since then world steel capacity has grown by leaps and bounds—much more than have world markets for steel. Thus the pressure

is on to sell the surplus; and this country offers the greatest market and the easiest entry.

In 1968 steel imports into the U.S. probably reached about 18 million tons, and they now affect all categories of products and all geographical areas within our domestic market. True, 1968 was affected by a strike threat; but history indicates that once buyers have broken down their natural reluctance to seek foreign sources for some of their steel needs, they are not again so reluctant. They continue to buy foreign in subsequent years, even when the pressures are not so intense.

Why do steel users in the United States buy foreign steel? By and large, the answer is quite simple; it is a matter of price, most often a price of $25 to $45 a ton lower than domestic prices.

And the quality of imports is no deterrent. While the American steel industry still sets the quality standards for the world, it is nevertheless true that due to the help which was provided by the U.S. to the steel industries of Europe and Japan in the postwar period, and due to the fact that steel technology in this day of rapid intercontinental communications is increasingly worldwide, the product of the Europeans and the Japanese is quite acceptable in all markets of the world.

Why then—if quality is comparable—don't we just cut the price and solve the problem? Price difference is basically cost difference because most of price is cost. Profits in the

[1] R. Heath Lary, "Import Quotas for Steel?" *Wall Street Journal* Jan. 8, 1969.

domestic steel industry have steadily declined, and cuts in prices of such proportions as $25 to $45 per ton on all products would invite financial disaster to the industry, its employees, and stockholders.

The critics of the domestic steel industry often argue, and I am sure they would like to believe, that the problem is caused by a lack of research on the part of the domestic steel industry, and by its alleged backwardness in terms of technology and managerial skill. They argue therefore that heavy investment in research and in new facilities is all that is needed to produce a level of efficiency which will bring about a full solution of the problem, without the need for any form of limitation upon the invasion of our markets by foreign sources.

We in the domestic steel industry devoutly wish that the problem could be defined in these terms, for then it would be one which we could solve by our own efforts. Unfortunately, it has different dimensions.

The domestic steel industry is not backward in technology. Its companies undoubtedly spend far more on research than those of any other steel-producing nation in the world.

It is not a less efficient industry. Even the domestic industry's most difficult competitor, i.e., Japan, used some 17 man-hours per ton of product in 1966, compared with 13 in the U.S.

If hourly labor costs in the various steel-producing nations were relatively equal, domestic steel producers would suffer no disadvantages whatever, based on relative levels of technology and relative efficiencies of facilities. In fact, on this ground alone, they would have the edge.

Unfortunately, however, steel labor costs are not the same everywhere. They are, in fact, greatly different. In the Japanese steel industry, for example, employment cost per hour is only about one-quarter of that in the U.S. To equalize this kind of cost advantage on the basis of an improvement in efficiency would require that U.S. steelmakers discover a technological forward leap which could reduce their 13 man-hours a ton down to approximately 4 man-hours a ton.

Such an accomplishement is today unforeseeable on the basis of technology now known or even dreamed of, anywhere. Further, this labor cost differential seems to be growing despite higher percentage increases in employment costs abroad, because our base costs were so much higher to start with.

This difference in labor standards is important not only in the production of steel in existing facilities, but it is important to the development and installation of new facilities. Thus, according to the Oriental Economist for July 1968, the Japanese take comfort from the knowledge that their labor cost differential enables them to put new facilities in place in Japan for approximately one-third of the cost to American steelmakers. They thus foresee the ability to maintain or improve the relative technological position which they have vis-a-vis the U.S. in the years ahead, in the absence of some radical change in comparative wage and construction costs as between the two economies, not now foreseeable.

This then is one of the problems: That relative parity of technology has been reached in the principal steel-producing nations of the world, considerably ahead of relative parity in labor standards.

Governmental monetary and fiscal policies in recent years have been all-important influences in producing and tolerating inflationary trends in this country of such order as continually to aggravate this problem. And, the fact is that there will be no satisfactory solution to the import problems of the steel industry or of other industries until there is a constructive and a continuing reversal of these past governmental policies toward inflation.

A second part of the steel import problem grows out of the assortment of subsidies, non-tariff barriers (including the impact of border taxes and value-added tax schemes) by which other governments effectively give protection to the steel industries within their own markets, and at the same time provide assistance to their steel industries when they move into external markets, the most important of which is ours.

. . . it has been encouraging to note that many responsible voices in Washington have given increasing recognition to the growing relative importance of the nontariff barriers, and particularly to the unfairness to U.S. producers which results from them.

The fact of the matter is that while Japan and members of the Common Market talk glowingly of free trade, their own economies are loaded with devices which tend to give their own producers a strong advantage. And they continue to show every intention of pursuing their foreign policies and their trade policies with the single purpose of giving first support to their own respective economies. They are first and foremost pragmatists. Thereafter, they are very vocal free trade theorists, mainly when it seems to their advantage to be so. Some "retaliation" against their protective devices could very well serve as leverage to move reality closer to theory.

A third point to be mentioned in connection with the steel problem is that just as in the case of their agriculture, most other nations take a very paternalistic view toward their own steel industries. A great part of the steel industry in the rest of the world is either government-owned or under various forms of government direction or control. The result is steel industries whose export marketing and pricing policies are more often keyed to reacting to government pressures, be they those directed in support of full-employment programs or in support of acquisition of foreign exchange, than to the force of competition in a free market.

Now, despite a growing recognition of these various factors which make the competition presented by other steel-producing nations of the world anything but equal and free competition, and despite the recognition of a need to bring about a change in such factors if American manufacturers are to have a reasonable chance in world trade, no one seriously expects that there can be an early equalization of trade opportunities. Nor does anyone point to the possibility that there may be a reversal of past cost-push and demand-pull inflationary trends of sufficient magnitude in the near future to benefit the competitive posture of industries such as steel, which are not competitively inefficient, but which cannot be expected to develop a margin of efficiency over other nations sufficiently great to compensate for the wide disparity in their respective labor standards.

What then is to happen meanwhile? Unless the domestic steel industry can participate proportionately in the growth of the domestic steel market, it is unlikely that our domestic steel producers will have either the ability or the desire to continue to invest record-breaking sums in new facilities and in steel research in the U.S. Certainly the declining profit results offer little basis for investing further if other opportunities offer higher rewards. As the Senate Finance Committee report on "Steel Imports" states: "Unless output increases by at least 2 to 2.5 million tons annually . . . the industry cannot expect to improve its stance in competition with foreign imports."

This would mean that the domestic steel industry could only drift further into a less competitive posture in the world than it now is.

By placing an even greater reliance upon foreign sources for its most vital metal, the U.S. would be risking both its national security and the basis for a sound and continuing growth of its economy. An adequate, continuing and immediately available source of domestic steel is something the U.S. cannot afford to be without.

This is not a case in which adjustment assistance might be useful in helping producers to shift into some other form of business activity. The U.S. needs its domestic steel industry. And it needs to take steps to prevent it from being further distressed during the time period in which other actions may be under way to attempt to bring about a greater evidence of fair competition in the world steel market.

We know of no other effective and prompt means of achieving the needed help other than some reasonable and effective form of limitation upon the access of foreign steel producers to the domestic steel market—the most effective form of which would be quota legislation.

We know of no other major steel-producing nation in the world whose policies toward trade in steel are sufficiently free that they could have any justifiable objection to practical steps which might be taken by the U.S. to assist its steel industry in this fashion.

In short, as long as we do not yet have a world of free trade in steel, we must face the world as it is rather than as we wish it were. Thus we should and we must move in tactical and practical ways wherever, as in the case of steel, there is a critical problem—even if so doing may offend long-term theory in which all of us, including those of us in steel, still believe.

Although Lary's article appeared in 1969, many of the arguments he used then are espoused today not only by steel executives but also by management and labor leaders in American industries ranging from steel to shoes, from transportation equipment to textiles, from ships to sealing wax.

How valid are Lary's arguments? If you were a congressman, how would you vote on this issue? Would you limit imports of foreign steel by quotas or higher tariffs? Are quotas or tariffs essential because of the cheaper labor in Japan and other nations? Who would benefit from a more protective quota? Who would lose? Is a large steel industry essential to the survival and health of the U.S. economy?

SUGGESTIONS FOR ANALYSIS

Nations engage in international trade because trade can increase the well-being of each nation as we saw in the "you and I" example above. However, in the real world, removal or reduction of barriers to free trade invariably makes some people worse off while it helps others. The importation of German automobiles, Italian shoes, and Scotch whiskey usually means a switch from U.S.-produced to foreign-produced autos, shoes, and liquor. Consumers buy the foreign-produced goods because they thereby get more satisfaction per dollar spent. However, this switch to foreign products could obviously reduce job opportunities in the U.S. industries and real income of workers and stockholders in the displaced American industries. Of course, you should recognize that a shift in purely domestic demand from one product to another would similarly hurt those who lost their jobs and markets. Consumers are constantly shifting their patterns of purchase, partly because their demands shift and partly because the prices and products offered by different sellers vary. To adjust to these shifts is often painful to producers, but such change is the essence of our free society.

Should we prohibit consumers from having access to cheaper foreign steel (or other products) in order to protect U.S. steelworkers' jobs and U.S. stockholders' profits? The law of comparative advantage (the basic cause for specialization and exchange) says no. Perhaps the national defense argument justifies our supporting a steel industry that cannot meet foreign competition. But leaving that argument aside, clearly American consumers are better off by having foreign steel come in if it is cheaper, and foreign steel producers obtain U.S. dollars with which to buy other American products that we can sell cheaply. Both nations gain from specializing on the things they produce most efficiently and exchanging, as in the chapter's example. This is the law of comparative advantage at work. More wanted goods are produced in total, and both nations are better off with free trade. In America, there might be fewer jobs in steel, but there would be more in our relatively more efficient industries (for example, office equipment and agriculture) whose export sales would rise as foreigners spent their newly acquired dollars.

But some Americans, here in the steel industry, are clearly hurt by free trade if they are now protected against foreign competition, or benefited if new barriers are set up against steel imports. If we want cheap steel but also want to ease their adjustment to free trade in steel, there are numerous ways to help U.S. steelworkers without penalizing all U.S. steel users. We could have the government provide information on alternative jobs, free retraining, moving allowances, and the like. Conceivably, temporary subsidies could be granted the U.S. steel companies themselves. How far we want to go in easing the adjustment problems of presently protected industries if we move further toward free trade will depend on how strong we think their case for compensation is on grounds of equity and efficiency.

Would the average American standard of living (say GNP per capita) be raised or lowered if we opened all our markets to free trade? The answer is raised, even though workers abroad now receive lower wages then American workers. First, remember that when we buy more from abroad, we can thereby sell more abroad. Opening our markets to free trade may mean fewer jobs in some industries, but it will mean correspondingly more in export industries. Remember, from Chapters 17–19, that by using stabilizing monetary and fiscal policy we can keep aggregate demand at a roughly full employment level, so we can substantially avoid general unemployment.

Second, average U.S. wages (incomes) will be higher after the adjustment to a free trade pattern than with trade restrictions. Remember that wages are basically determined by workers' productivity. Each worker's wage will be highest when he works where his productivity is highest— in the most efficient industry, which can best meet the test of the market without protection. Under free trade, U.S. workers will shift to those industries where our comparative advantage is greatest (that is, where their marginal productivity is highest) away from industries with a lower comparative advantage (where their marginal productivities are lower). The total number of jobs is no different in the long-run under free trade or protection, but the allocation of resources is more efficient under free trade, so average incomes can be higher.

One last point. Just because foreign wages are low does not necessarily mean that foreign unit labor costs are lower per unit produced. Although U.S. wages are the highest in the world, so is U.S. productivity, reflecting our huge capital accumulation, technological advance, and worker education and skills. Thus, over all U.S. firms compete very effectively in international markets. U.S. merchandise exports in 1971 were $43 billion, and U.S. exports of goods and services have exceeded imports in twenty-four of the last twenty-five years.

22

The Balance of Payments

22.1 When a buyer in the United States wants to make a purchase in another country, he must first buy some of the currency of that country. Similarly, when a foreigner wants to buy something in the U.S., he must first buy _____ .

22.2 The market in which people buy and sell different national currencies is called the *foreign exchange* market. For example, if an English importer wants to buy a computer in the United States, he will first have to buy _____ in the _____ _____ market. Of course, at the same time he will be *(buying/selling)* pounds (the British currency) in the foreign exchange market.

22.3 Like any other market, the foreign exchange market is subject to the forces of supply and demand. That is, if the demand for a currency increases, we can expect the _____ of that currency in terms of other currencies to increase. Similarly, when the supply of currency increases, we can expect the _____ of that currency to _____ .

22.4 For example, suppose there were only two currencies: the U.S. dollar and the British pound. The price of the dollar is the number of pounds you must pay to buy it. And the price of the pound is the number of _____ you must pay for it. These prices are called *exchange rates*. In 1971, prior to Nixon's new economic policy, the exchange rate between dollars and pounds was $2.40 to the pound. That is, the price of a pound was $2.40 dollars and the price of a dollar was about _____ -tenths of a pound.

ANSWERS

1. dollars
2. dollars . foreign exchange . selling

3. price . price . decrease
4. dollars . 4

22.5 What determines the supply of and demand for dollars? Clearly, the number of dollars that

people want to sell in exchange for pounds is the _____ , and the number of

dollars people want to buy with pounds is the _____ . Because people will want
dollars to buy goods in the U.S., the greater the amount of goods foreigners want to buy from
the U.S., the greater the *(supply of/demand for)* dollars. And the greater the quantity of

foreign imports Americans want to buy, the greater the _____ _____
dollars.

22.6 How will the quantity of dollars supplied and demanded change as the exchange rate changes?
Consider what is likely to happen if the price of dollars increases. This means that foreigners
are going to have to pay *(more/fewer)* pounds to obtain a dollar and, consequently, in
terms of pounds American goods will be *(more/less)* expensive. Because a higher price for
U.S. goods means fewer will be bought, a higher price for dollars will mean a *(larger/smaller)*
demand for dollars.

22.7 A higher price for dollars also means that Americans can obtain *(more/fewer)* pounds with
a dollar. This means that British goods will be *(more/less)* expensive in terms of dollars, and
Americans will want to import *(more/fewer)* British goods. As long as the elasticity of demand for British goods is greater than one, that is, as long as the dollar price times quantity
bought increases when the dollar price falls, the supply of dollars will *(increase/decrease)* .

22.8 The supply (SS) and demand (DD) curves for dollars are shown in Figure 22.1. These show
that as the value of the dollar increases in terms of pounds, the quantity supplied

(increases/decreases) and the quantity demanded _____ . Where the two curves

intersect, the quantities supplied and demanded will be _____ .

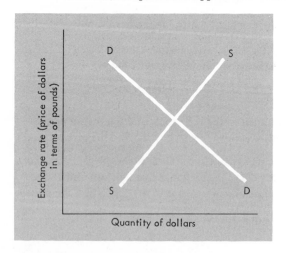

Figure 22.1
The supply and demand for dollars

22.9   As long as there is a free market for foreign exchange, we can expect the _____ rates to adjust to the level where the quantities supplied and demanded are _____ . When there is a free market for foreign exchange, we say that there are *flexible exchange rates.*

22.10   In the real world, we do not have a system of flexible _____ rates. That is, the exchange rates (the _____ of currencies) are not allowed to adjust to levels where the quantities supplied and demanded would be equal. In the real world (with a few exceptions), we have a *fixed exchange rate system.*

22.11   Under a fixed exchange rate system, the governments of the various currencies agree to buy or sell sufficient quantities of their currencies to keep the exchange rate at an agreed-upon value. In terms of Figure 22.2, the free market equilibrium exchange rate is _____ . But suppose the U.S. government intends to keep the exchange rate at p_1 instead. At p_1, the quantity demanded exceeds the quantity supplied by the amount _____ . In order to keep the price from moving from p_1 to p_3, the U.S. government would have to _(buy/sell)_ dollars in the amount _____ in exchange for pounds.

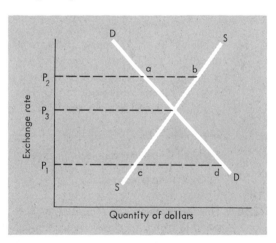

Figure 22.2
The supply and demand for dollars

22.12   What if the U.S. government had wanted to fix the exchange rate of p_2? At that price, the quantity demanded would be _(greater/smaller)_ than the quantity supplied by the amount _____ . In order to prevent the exchange rate from falling to the free market equilibrium of _____ , the government would have to _(buy/sell)_ dollars and pay for them with pounds.

ANSWERS

9. exchange . equal
10. exchange . prices

11. p_3 . cd . sell . cd
12. smaller . ab . p_3 . buy

22.13   Notice that whenever there is an excess demand for dollars, the U.S. government can satisfy the demand for dollars at the fixed exchange rate without any trouble. This is because

through borrowing or taxing it can always obtain enough _____ to sell in the foreign exchange market. But, when there is an excess supply of dollars at the fixed exchange rate, the government will only be able to maintain that exchange rate if it has ample *reserves*

of _____ . If it does not have ample _____ of pounds, it will not be

able to buy enough dollars to eliminate the excess _____ at the fixed exchange rate.

22.14   If the U.S. government ran out of reserves, there would be at least two possible ways to eliminate the excess supply of dollars. One would be to borrow pounds from the British government and use those pounds to purchase the excess supply of dollars. The other

would be to persuade the British government to buy the _____ to eliminate the excess supply. Obviously, limits exist to both of the above. As we shall see later, foreign governments will be unwilling to lend to the U.S. or accumulate dollars indefinitely if there is an excess supply of dollars year after year. And it is highly unlikely that a nation would loan money to another nation forever or be prepared to purchase another nation's currency *ad infinitum.*

22.15   In the real world, of course, there are many currencies and many exchange rates. But the market for each currency operates just like the market for dollars we have described. There is one special currency, however, that is not the national currency of any country, namely *gold.* For many years prior to 1971, the United States agreed to exchange gold for dollars at a fixed price of $35 per ounce. That is, the U.S. agreed to fix the exchange rate between

_____ and _____ . In order to do that, it had to stand ready to

buy gold whenever there was an excess _____ of gold at that price and to sell

gold whenever there was an excess _____ at that price.

22.16   This arrangement also obligated the U.S. government to exchange gold for dollars whenever asked to by a foreign government, which might, for example, have acquired dollars in the process of maintaining the fixed exchange rate between its currency and the dollar. In order for the fixed exchange rate between the dollar and gold to be maintained, the U.S.

had to have ample _____ of gold, so that it could stand ready to sell gold whenever

there was an excess _____ for gold at the price of $35 per ounce.

ANSWERS

13. dollars . pounds . reserves . supply   15. dollars . gold . supply . demand
14. dollars   16. reserves . demand

22.17 Throughout most of the post-World War II period, because the U.S. had huge reserves of gold and because it stood ready to convert dollars into gold, other countries regarded gold and dollars as near perfect substitutes. They held either gold or dollars interchangeably as reserves because they considered their values to be fixed and stable. Consequently, dollars were valuable as reserves because a country could always use them to buy its own currency when

it was in excess _____ . If a country held reserves in the form of some "weaker" currency, that is, a currency whose price might change, this country would take the risk that that currency would not have its full value when the time came to use it. Thus, dollars and

gold were held around the world as _____ because there was little uncertainty about their value.

22.18 After 1958, however, the dollar began to be in excess supply, and the United States

maintained its fixed price in terms of gold by buying _____ and paying for them

with _____ . As a result, its gold reserves _(increased/decreased)_ . Between 1958 and 1971, U.S. gold holdings fell from $27 billion to $13 billion. The continued excess

_____ of the dollar and the continued decline in U.S. _____ reserves led to a chain of events that will be discussed in the case for this chapter. At this point, it will be useful to consider the *balance of payments*, which is the record of international transactions between one country and the rest of the world.

22.19 By studying a nation's balance of payments, it is possible to discover whether its currency is in

excess supply or demand and what factors are causing that condition. The U.S. _____

of _____ shows the quantities of dollars supplied and demanded as a result of all international transactions involving the United States. All items that added to the supply of dollars are recorded with a minus (–) sign, and all items that added to the demand for dollars enter with a plus (+) sign. Consequently, you would expect to see the entry for exports have

a _____ sign and the entry for imports have a _____ sign.

22.20 If the U.S. had $40 billion in exports and $40 billion in imports and no other international transactions, its balance of payments would look like this (fill in the numbers):

Exports	_____
Imports	_____
Balance	0

Because the quantities of dollars supplied and demanded _(were/were not)_ equal the government _(did/did not)_ have to make any official transactions to preserve the fixed value of the dollar.

ANSWERS

17. supply . reserves
18. dollars . gold . decreased . supply . gold

19. balance . payments . plus . minus
20. +40 . –40 . were . did not

22.21 But what if there were $40 billion in exports and $30 billion in imports and no other private international transactions? In this case, there would be an excess _(demand for/supply of)_ dollars, and in order to maintain the value of the dollar at the agreed upon rate the U.S. government would have to sell _(dollars/gold)_ , or in other words buy _(dollars/gold)_ .

22.22 In this case, the balance of payments would look like this (fill in the numbers):

Exports	_____
Imports	_____
Changes in reserves	_____
Balance	0

Notice that when the U.S. adds to its reserves it enters the balance of payments with a

_____ sign because when the U.S. buys reserves, just as when it buys goods, it

adds to the _____ of dollars.

22.23 Notice also that because the balance of payments includes official transactions undertaken to offset an excess demand or supply of dollars resulting from regular transactions, the balance is

always equal to _____ . That is, because official transactions that are taken to equate supply and demand for dollars at the fixed exchange rate are included, the balance of payments _(always/never)_ balances.

22.24 If the balance of payments always balances, what is meant by the balance of payments *deficit* or *surplus*? Whenever the government must take action in the form of buying or selling dollars in order to maintain the value of the dollar at its fixed rate of exchange, there is a balance of

payments _____ or _____ . When there is an excess supply of dollars so that the government has to _(buy/sell)_ dollars, there is a balance of payments deficit. Conversely, a balance of payments surplus occurs when there is an excess _(supply of/demand for_ dollars and the government has to _(buy/sell)_ dollars.

22.25 A balance of payments deficit then is equal to the excess _____ of dollars that results from normal international transactions. When there is a deficit in the balance of payments, it is necessary for the government to carry out special transactions in the form of _(purchases/sales)_ of dollars in order to maintain the fixed exchange rate.

22.26 Whenever there is a balance of payments deficit, because the government _(buyes/sells)_ dollars and _(pays/gets paid)_ for the dollars with reserves, the U.S. will _(gain/lose)_ reserves. Similarly, when there is a balance of payments surplus, the U.S. will _(increase/decrease)_ its holdings of reserves.

ANSWERS

21. demand for . dollars . gold
22. +40 . –30 . –10 . minus . supply
23. 0 . always

24. deficit . surplus (either order) . buy . demand for . sell
25. supply . purchases
26. buys . pays . lose . increase

22.27   There is an exception to this point. We said earlier that when there is an excess supply of dollars, it would be possible to maintain the value of the dollar without the U.S. government buying dollars if it could get someone else to buy the dollars. During the late 1960s, when the U.S. had a large balance of payment deficit, it was able to maintain the value of the dollar

without very large losses of _____ by getting foreign governments to agree to *(buy/sell)* dollars. For example, when the U.S. was running a balance of payments deficit with Japan, Japan agreed to accumulate the excess supply of dollars temporarily rather than have the U.S. use its diminishing gold reserves to purchase dollars.

22.28   To summarize: The U.S. balance of payments records the quantities of _____ supplied and demanded arising out of all international transactions involving Americans. Whenever there is an excess supply or demand resulting from normal transactions, the government must undertake (or persuade someone else to undertake) special transactions to stabilize the exchange rate at its agreed-upon level. When there is an excess supply of dollars,

we say there is a balance of payments _____ , and the government must *(buy/sell)* dollars and will *(gain/lose)* reserves.

22.29   When there is an excess demand for dollars, we say there is a balance of payments

_____ , and the government must _____ dollars and will

_____ reserves.

22.30   If you look at the official U.S. balance of payments for 1970 in Table 22.1, you will find that there are many more items on it than just exports, imports, and changes in reserves. First, you should notice that the balance of payments is divided into a *current account* and a *capital account*. The current account shows all transactions that do not result in the addition to or subtraction from U.S. claims on resources abroad. All transactions that affect the amount of U.S. claims on resources abroad are shown in the capital account. Into which account would you put each of the following items?

U.S. purchase of sweaters from Scotland	*(current/capital)*
U.S. purchase of a factory in France	*(current/capital)*
French purchase of a U.S. government bond	*(current/capital)*
Donations by Americans to the International Red Cross	*(current/capital)*
Purchase of food in Vietnam for U.S. servicemen	*(current/capital)*

22.31   The current account of the U.S. balance of payments is shown in Table 22.2. You will

recall that items that add to the demand for dollars are shown with a _____

ANSWERS

27. reserves . buy
28. dollars . deficit . buy . lose
29. surplus . sell . gain

30. current . capital . capital . current . current
31. plus . minus . dollars . exports . imports
    (either order)

Table 22.1

U.S. BALANCE OF PAYMENTS, 1970

(billions of dollars)

	Current account	
1.	Exports	+42.0
2.	Imports	−39.9
3.	Net military purchases	− 3.4
4.	Net investment income	+ 6.2
5.	Net travel and transportation	− 2.0
6.	Other services	+ 0.6
7.	Unilateral transfers	− 3.1
	Balance on current account	+ 0.4

	Capital account	
8.	U.S. Government net long-term loans	− 2.0
9.	Private net nonliquid loans and investments	− 2.0
10.	Allocations of special drawing rights	+ 0.9
11.	Errors and omissions	− 1.1
12.	Private net liquid loans and investments	− 6.0
13.	Net loans by foreign official agencies to the U.S.	+ 7.3
14.	Changes in U.S. official reserves	+ 2.5
	Balance on capital account	− 0.4
	Overall balance	0

sign, and items that add to the supply of _____ are shown with a _____ sign. You can see that the two largest items in the current account were _____ and _____ .

22.32 To deepen your understanding of the balance of payments, let us consider each of the other items in the current account. Item 3, net military purchases, represents military purchases from foreign countries including the expenses incurred from maintaining U.S. troups abroad minus the sale of military equipment to foreigners. The entry of −3.4 indicates that the U.S. _(bought/sold)_ more military goods abroad than it _(bought/sold)_ because the minus sign represents an addition to the _(supply of/demand for)_ dollars.

ANSWERS
    32. bought . sold . supply of

Table 22.2

U.S. BALANCE OF PAYMENTS, CURRENT ACCOUNT, 1970

(billions of dollars)

1. Exports	+42.0
2. Imports	−39.9
3. Net military purchases	− 3.4
4. Net investment income	+ 6.2
5. Net travel and transportation	− 2.0
6. Other services	+ 0.6
7. Unilateral transfers	− 3.1
Current account balance	+ 0.4

22.33 Item 4, net investment income, represents the income paid to Americans from foreign assets (for example, dividends paid to American stock holders of an Arabian oil company) minus the income paid to foreigners from U.S. assets (for example, interest paid to a German depositer in a U.S. savings bank). Because the entry for this item is +6.2, it added to the *(supply of/demand for)* dollars, which means that U.S. investment income from abroad was *(greater/less)* than foreign income from the U.S. (If you have trouble understanding this one, ask yourself if you earned, let us say, pounds from a British investment and converted those pounds to dollars, would that have added to the supply of or demand for dollars. Clearly, it would have added to the *(supply/demand)* .)

22.34 Item 5, net travel and transportation, shows the amount spent abroad for these items by Americans less the amount spent in the U.S. by foreigners. Because the entry is _____, this item added to the *(supply of/demand for)* dollars, which means that Americans spend *(more/less)* on travel and transportation abroad than foreigners spent on these services in the U.S.

22.35 Item 6, other services, includes the purchases of such items as shipping insurance and brokerage services from foreigners by Americans less the purchase of these services from Americans by foreigners. The entry of _____ indicates that we *(sold/bought)* more of these services *(to/from)* foreigners than we *(sold to/bought from)* them.

ANSWERS

33. demand for . greater . demand
34. −2.0 . supply of . more

35. +0.6 . sold . to . bought from

22.36   The last item in the current account, unilateral transfers, shows the effect on the balance of payments of all gifts and grants to foreigners by Americans less foreigners' gifts and grants to

the U.S. The fact that this item is entered with a _____ sign means that on balance we were net _(givers/receivers)_ of gifts and grants by an amount equal to $3.1 billion.

22.37   The balance on current account for 1970 was _____ . This shows that, adding up all the additions to the supply of and demand for dollars of the various items in the current account, there was an excess _(supply of/demand for)_ dollars of $0.4 billion. That is, there was a _(surplus/deficit)_ on current accout.

22.38   Before you can say whether there was a surplus or deficit in the overall balance of payments,

it is also necessary to know what happened on the _____ account. Table 22.3 shows the capital account separately for the U.S. in 1970.

22.39   In analyzing the capital account, it is essential to understand that when someone in the U.S. buys a foreign asset it is just like an import in terms of its effect on the balance of payments. Thus, for example, when an American business buys a foreign factory or an American bank

buys a foreign bond, it will enter the balance of payments account with a _____ sign because it adds to the _(supply of/demand for)_ dollars in the same way that _(imports/exports)_ do.

Table 22.3

U.S. BALANCE OF PAYMENTS, CAPITAL ACCOUNT 1970

(billions of dollars)

8. U.S. Government net long-term loans	− 2.0
9. Private net nonliquid loans and investments	− 2.0
10. Allocations of special drawing rights	+ 0.9
11. Errors and omissions	− 1.1
12. Private net liquid loans and investments	− 6.0
13. Net loans by foreign official agencies to the U.S.	+ 7.3
14. Changes in U.S. official reserves	+ 2.5
Balance on capital account	− 0.4

22.40   Also, when a foreigner buys a U.S. asset, the transaction will enter the balance of payments

with a _____ sign. For example, if a Frenchman buys stock in an American

ANSWERS

36. minus . givers
37. +0.4 . demand for . surplus
38. capital

39. minus . supply of . imports
40. plus . dollars . demand for

company, he will have to first buy _____ . Consequently, he will be adding to the _(supply of/demand for)_ dollars.

22.41 Let us consider each of the items in the capital account. The first item is U.S. government long-term loans to foreigners. Remember, a new loan is like an _(import/export)_ because the government is really buying an IOU of a foreigner. The entry of -2.0 indicates that new loans by the U.S. government added to the _(supply of/demand for)_ dollars.

22.42 Private net nonliquid loans and investments represents U.S. new investments abroad (including real assets, like new oil wells, and financial assets, like Japanese bonds) minus foreign new investments in the U.S. Because this item was recorded as -2.0 in the balance of payments, it must have been that Americans bought _(more/fewer)_ new assets abroad than foreigners bought in the U.S.

22.43 Item 10 in the balance of payments, allocations of special drawing rights (SDR's), reflect the effort of the International Monetary Fund to create more international reserves as a substitute for gold. The IMF bought from each country some of its currency in exchange for SDR's, a new type of international currency, sometimes called "paper gold." From the point of view of the U.S. balance of payments, this allocation of SDR's adds to the _(supply of/demand for)_ dollars and, consequently, is recorded with a _____ sign.

22.44 Errors and omissions (item 11) includes all unrecorded transactions, many of which may be illegal. When an American deposits money in an unnumbered Swiss bank account (that is, imports an IOU from the bank), it shows up in errors and omissions with a _____ sign because he adds to the _(supply of/demand for)_ dollars.

22.45 The next item, private net liquid loans and investments, consists mostly of bank accounts. The recording of -6.0 reflects the increase in American's deposits in foreign banks, and so on, minus the increase in foreigner's deposits in U.S. banks, and so on. It indicates that Americans deposited _(more/less)_ abroad than foreigners deposited in the U.S. because the minus sign indicates a net _(import/export)_ of the IOU's of _(U.S./foreign)_ banks.

22.46 Item 13 in the U.S. balance of payments reflects the assistance of foreign governments in stabilizing the value of the dollar. Instead of forcing the U.S. to sell reserves in order to eliminate the excess supply of _____ resulting from normal transactions, these foreign government agencies agreed to buy the dollars and either exchange them for U.S. government IOU's or deposit them in U.S. banks. Either way, these actions constitute a loan to the U.S. and enter the balance of payments with a _____ sign.

ANSWERS

41. import . supply of
42. more
43. demand for . plus

44. minus . supply of
45. more . import . foreign
46. dollars . plus

22.47 The last item in the capital account is the change in U.S. reserves. This, of course, represents the sale or purchase of reserves necessary to maintain the fixed rate of exchange. A sale of gold or other reserves is recorded on the balance of payments like any other *(export/import)* . That is, a sale adds to the *(supply of/demand for)* dollars and enters with a _____ sign. In 1970, this item was +2.5, which means that the U.S. *(gained/lost)* reserves in that year.

22.48 The balance on capital account for 1970 was –0.4, which just offset the balance on current account, which it must by definition. Whenever there is a surplus on current account and a deficit on capital account, it means that the amount the U.S. is selling of goods and services and earning in income abroad is *(greater/less)* than it is spending abroad, and it is using the difference to *(buy/sell)* more foreign assets. (Remember, a negative sign on capital account represents the purchase of some type of foreign asset whether it be real capital, a bank account, or somebody's IOU.)

22.49 So, if you want to know whether the U.S. is increasing or decreasing its net foreign assets (that is, adding to its net claims against foreigners), you can look either at the balance on current account or the balance on capital account. If the current account balance is positive,

the capital account balance will be _____ , and you will know that U.S. net foreign assets *(increased/decreased)* .

22.50 Notice, however, that it is possible for the U.S. to add to its net foreign assets and at the same time have a balance of payments deficit. These are two different concepts and are not to be confused. The balance of payments deficit, remember, is the amount by which the supply of dollars *(exceeds/falls short of)* the demand for dollars as a result of normal transactions. That is, it is the amount of special transactions that must be made to eliminate this excess supply of dollars. It is found by adding together item 13 (net loans by foreign official agencies to the U.S.) and item 14 (change in U.S. official reserves). In 1970,

together these amounted to $ _____ billion, which was an unusually high deficit. At the same time, of course, the U.S. was increasing its net claims on foreigners by

$ _____ billion. The balance of payments deficit counts only some items on the capital account, but our net investment abroad includes all items.

22.51 By this time, you may have wondered why we have a fixed exchange rate system when it creates the problem of having always to undertake special transactions to preserve the fixed exchange rate. Why not, in other words, allow exchange rates to adjust to where the quantities supplied and demanded for each currency are equal. The two extreme alternatives then are: (1) a _____ exchange rate system, which requires the government to buy or sell

ANSWERS

47. export . demand for . plus . lost   50. exceeds . 9.8 . 0.4
48. greater . buy   51. fixed . flexible
49. negative . increased

reserves to eliminate any excess supply of or demand for its currency; and (2) a _____ exchange rate system in which the exchange rates adjust to bring about equality of the quantities supplied and demanded for each currency.

22.52 In deciding among these and any other alternative international monetary arrangements, a more fundamental question must be answered first: What are the purposes of any such arrangement? The generally agreed-upon answer to this question is that the best international monetary system is the one that does the best job of encouraging the free flow of goods and services between countries. That is, the goal of the system should be to encourage international exchange of goods, services, and resources. The reasons for encouraging trade, you will recall, were spelled out in Chapter 21, the main one being that trade between countries results in a

more efficient allocation of _____ and increases world per capita income.

22.53 The main reason that many people believe that a fixed exchange rate system will do a better

job of promoting _____ between countries is that under such a system importers

and exporters will not have to worry about whether the _____ _____ will rise and fall. The fear is that under a flexible exchange rate system the exchange rate would fluctuate a great deal, thereby causing the prices of foreign goods to fluctuate a great deal and making imports appear to be a good buy one day and a bad buy the next.

22.54 Actually, very little is known about how a flexible exchange rate system would operate because it has not been tried extensively for very many years. But the government officials of most of

the major trading nations believe a fixed _____ _____ system to be superior, and that is the system we are likely to have for a good many years. As you know, however, this system creates problems for these governments.

22.55 One of these problems is sometimes called the *liquidity problem*. Under a fixed exchange rate system, some countries will undoubtedly have a deficit in their balance of payments. That is, normal transactions will result in an excess _(supply of/demand for)_ their currencies. This will require the governments of these countries to _(buy/sell)_ their currencies (that is, to _(buy/sell)_ reserves) if the fixed exchange rate is to be preserved.

22.56 In order for this to be done by each country when it has a balance of payments

_____ , it is necessary for each country to have an ample supply of

_____ . In the past when gold was the main form of international reserves, the supply depended largely on gold discoveries. Many felt that there was not a sufficient growth in the supply to fully satisfy the needs of governments for reserves to finance their balance

ANSWERS

52. resources
53. trade . exchange rate
54. exchange rate

55. supply of . buy . sell
56. deficit . reserves . deficits

of payments _____ . It was for this reason that SDR's (item 10 in the capital account) were created.

22.57   But even if there were ample reserves in the international monetary system, there would still be what is called the *adjustment problem.* The adjustment problem arises whenever a country's fixed exchange rate is persistently above or below the equilibrium rate. When the former occurs, the country will always have a balance of payments _(deficit/surplus)_ . In this circumstance, the currency is said to be *overvalued.* When a country has an _____ currency, it will tend to have a continuing balance of payments _____ .

22.58   No matter how much reserves a country has, it cannot continue to run a deficit forever. As the deficit continues, the country will _(gain/lose)_ reserves and eventually will run out of _____ . Before that happens, it will have to eliminate its balance of payments deficit. This is the _____ problem.

22.59   There are a number of actions a government might take to eliminate its balance of payment deficit. One would be to reduce its domestic price level relative to foreign price levels by having a _(higher/lower)_ rate of inflation than other countries. With a lower rate of _____ , its price level will fall relative to foreign price levels and its goods will become cheaper relative to foreign goods. This would result in an increase in _(exports/imports)_ and a decrease in _(exports/imports)_ and a reduction in the balance of payments _____ .

22.60   An alternative policy would be for the deficit country to increase its rate of interest. This would make it _(more/less)_ attractive for foreigners to make loans to that country and _(reduce/add to)_ the incentive for citizens to invest in bonds and other securities abroad. By increasing foreign investment at home and reducing its citizens' investment abroad, it would be possible to reduce the payments _____ .

22.61   A major difficulty with either of these policies is that they might interfere with the country's domestic economic objectives regarding full employment. Reducing aggregate demand to reduce the rate of inflation or raising interest rates to attract foreign capital is likely to result in a _(rise/fall)_ in unemployment. Thus, to use either of these policies would involve sacrificing the goal of _____ _____ in order to reduce the balance of payments _____ .

ANSWERS

57. deficit . overvalued . deficit
58. lose . reserves . adjustment
59. lower . inflation . exports . imports . deficit

60. more . reduce . deficit
61. rise . full employment . deficit

22.62 Because of the costs of these policies, they are rarely pushed to the limit, although some economists explain in part the failure of government to fight the Great Depression vigorously at its inception on the Federal Reserve's preoccupation with the balance of payments deficit. Also, a number of recent British recessions have been blamed on the government's attempt to solve its balance of payments problems by reducing aggregate demand. But, if these policies cannot be actively used to solve a balance of payments problem, other measures must be adopted. Unfortunately, many countries faced with balance of payments difficulties have adopted policies (such as tariffs, quotas, controls on capital movements, and so on) that *(encourage/restrict)* trade. The difficulty with such policies is that they compromise the objective that the fixed exchange rate system was set up to achieve, namely, the encouragement of international _____ .

22.63 Often when a currency is overvalued, because of the difficulty of solving the _____ problem any other way, it becomes necessary to change the exchange rate. To eliminate a chronic balance of payments deficit, a country should *(raise/lower)* the price of its currency relative to other currencies. This is called *depreciation* of the currency. When a currency depreciates, its price *(rises/falls)* relative to other currencies, thereby making that country's exports *(more/less)* attractive and imports from abroad *(more/less)* attractive.

22.64 In 1971, there was a general realignment of the fixed exchange rates. The dollar, which had been repeatedly in excess supply, was *(depreciated/appreciated)* relative to most European currencies and the Japanese yen. At the same time, there was a *devaluation* of the dollar relative to gold. That is, in addition to its changed price relative to other currencies, the dollar also changed relative to _____ . The official price of gold rose from $35 to $37.80 per ounce. Although this received a good deal of attention in the newspapers, in terms of solving the adjustment problem, the _____ of the dollar in terms of gold was not at all important. What did matter was the _____ of the dollar relative to other countries' currencies. This is particularly true, as you will see in Case 22, since the U.S. no longer will exchange gold for dollars. Previously, the U.S. guaranteed convertibility of dollars into gold. Now that there is no longer convertibility, the price of dollars in terms of gold has no direct bearing on the adjustment problem.

22.65 Actually, the devaluation of the dollar in terms of gold had the effect of helping to solve the liquidity problem. In terms of dollars, it had the effect of *(increasing/decreasing)* the value of gold reserves. In other words, the devaluation of the dollar served to *(increase/decrease)* the amount of reserves for those countries who held _____ as part of their reserves.

ANSWERS

62. restrict . trade

63. adjustment . lower . falls . more . less

64. depreciated . gold . devaluation . depreciation

65. increasing . increase . gold

22.66   In conclusion, it should be noted that despite the many drawbacks of our fixed exchange rate system and the many international financial crises that have occurred in recent years, the record of trade liberalization and the growth of international trade since its establishment after World War II suggests that it has not failed completely to achieve its purpose.

REVIEW QUESTIONS

Questions 1 and 2 are based on the following information:

One year, under a system of flexible exchange rates, one pound sterling was exchanging for 2.4 United States dollars. The following year, the rate of exchange was one pound for 2.8 dollars.

22.1   Which of the following is likely to have caused this change?

a. an increase in British interest rates

b. an increase in United States interest rates

c. a rise in the British inflation rate

d. a rise in the United States unemployment rate

In terms of pounds, a change from $2.4/£1 to $2.8/£1 is a fall in the price of dollars. Under a system of flexible exchange rates, such a decrease in price would be caused by excess supply of dollars at the original price. Of the choices listed, only a rise in British interest rates would cause a flow of dollars into Britain that would, *ceteris paribus*, generate such an excess supply. (An alternative way of thinking about this question is in terms of a dollar base, in which case the change from $2.4/£1 to $2.8/£1 is a rise in the price of pounds. Excess demand for pounds would cause such a rise. Once again, of the choices listed, only a rise in British interest rates would cause an increase in the demand for pounds.) The reason that a rise in British interest rates would increase the supply of dollars (and the demand for pounds) is that it would encourage Americans to buy more British securities (that is, lend more to British borrowers). To do so, they would have to sell dollars and buy pounds. All the other alternatives would tend to increase the demand for dollars and the supply of pounds. The correct response is a.

22.2   What would be the immediate effect of this change in the exchange rate between dollars and pounds?

a. United States goods would become more expensive for British consumers.

b. United States goods would become less expensive for British consumers.

c. United States goods would become neither more nor less expensive for British consumers.

d. British goods would become less expensive for United States consumers.

A dollar in the United States still buys the same basket of goods in the United States. One pound sterling, however, now exchanges for 2.8 dollars instead of 2.4 dollars, that is, one pound sterling can now purchase more United States goods than before. United States goods have become less expensive for British consumers just as British goods have become more expensive for United States consumers. The correct response is b.

22.3   Is the analysis in the following statement correct or incorrect, and why?

"This year our imports of goods and services will exceed our exports of goods and services by $4 billion. At the same time, capital investment abroad by United States residents will exceed foreign capital investment in the United States by $6 billion. Consequently, there will be a net inflow of gold and foreign exchange in the absence of any other foreign transactions."

a. Correct, because the inflow from foreign capital investment exceeds the outflow from the balance of trade.

b. Incorrect, because whenever imports of goods and services exceed exports of goods and services, a country will have a balance of payments problem.

c. Correct, because the net foreign capital investment will increase British assets abroad by $6 billion, which exceeds the deficit in the balance of trade.

d. Incorrect, because the deficit in the balance of trade plus the foreign capital investment will cause an outflow of gold and foreign exchange.

In any year, when the value of a country's imports exceeds the value of its exports, a deficit in the country's current account balance will be recorded and, in the absence of any offsetting items, will lead to an outflow of gold and/or foreign exchange. Similarly, if United States residents invest more abroad than foreign residents invest in the United States, in the absence of a current account surplus, there will be an outflow of gold and/or foreign exchange. Because both items mentioned would lead to an outflow of reserves, the analysis in the statement is incorrect. The correct response is d.

22.4   Suppose a drastic decline in the national income of all other countries led to a decline in this country's exports. Also suppose that in response to this the U.S. government increased the interest rate from 6 percent to 10 percent but made no other change in policy. What could be inferred about the U.S. government's attitude towards the change in economic conditions that would have resulted from the decline in foreign income? The government was:

a. more concerned about the rising inflation than the deteriorating balance of payments.

b. more concerned about the deteriorating balance of payments than the rising unemployment rate.

c. more concerned about the deteriorating balance of payments than the rising inflation.

d. more concerned about the rising unemployment rate than the deteriorating balance of payments.

A decline in foreign national income leading to a decline in this country's exports would, *ceteris paribus*, reduce aggregate demand, increase unemployment, and reduce the rate of inflation. In addition, because a decline in the inflow of foreign exchange would result, the balance of payments deficit would increase. The increase in the interest rate, while attracting foreign funds and thereby offsetting the increase in the payments deficit, would reduce aggregate demand and consequently would cause an increase in unemployment. This policy, therefore, will offset the deterioration in the balance of payments caused by the decrease in exports at the expense of higher unemployment. Thus, option d is ruled out. Because the initial decline in exports would tend to reduce rather than increase the rate of inflation, neither a nor c could be correct inferences. The correct response is b.

Case 22

THE 1971 REALIGNMENT OF EXCHANGE RATES

Ever since the late 1950s the United States has been confronted with balance of payments deficits. In some years, it has been able to run a surplus through the adoption of special measures; but year in, year out, the threat to the dollar persisted, and in 1970 and early 1971 the deficit increased sharply, prompting President Nixon to take dramatic steps to solve the problem on a more permanent basis. The record of the continuing balance of payments deficit and declining U.S. reserve position is shown in Table 22.a.

Let us briefly review what action was taken by the President and what changes in the international monetary system occurred as a result. On August 15, 1971, Nixon made three announcements: (1) The United States would no longer buy or sell gold on the international market. (2) The United States would impose a 10 percent tariff surcharge on most imports (that is, would increase all tariffs by 10 percent). (3) The U.S. would no longer act to fix the price of the dollar relative to other currencies (that is, the price of the dollar would be determined by the forces of supply and demand). The first of these actions was stated to be permanent and the last two to be temporary until international agreements on

new tariff levels and new fixed exchange rates could be achieved. In response to the President's initiative, the Finance Ministers of the 10 leading trading countries began negotiations to seek agreement on these issues. In December of 1971, it was decided that the dollar would be devalued in terms of gold by 8 percent and depreciated in terms of other leading currencies by differing amounts depending on the amounts of excess supplies of dollars in terms of each of these currencies (see Table 22.b). At the same time, the United States agreed to eliminate the 10 percent tariff surcharge that had been imposed in August.

How would you assess the soundness of these changes? Were they really necessary? Will they benefit the United States? Will they benefit the world?

SUGGESTIONS FOR ANALYSIS

In trying to evaluate the chain of events that occurred in 1971, it is helpful to understand what factors brought on the crisis and what alternative courses of action were open to the government to bring about a long-term correction of the imbalance in our international payments

Table 22.a
U.S. BALANCE OF PAYMENTS, 1961–1971
(billions of dollars)

	Balance on current account	Balance of payments deficit	Decrease in official reserve assets
1965	4.3	– 1.3	1.2
1966	2.4	.2	0.6
1967	2.1	– 3.4	0.1
1968	– .4	1.6	–0.9
1969	– .9	2.7	–1.2
1970	.4	– 9.8	2.5
1971 (1st half)	–1.0	–22.5	2.7

Table 22.b

CHANGES IN EXCHANGE RATES

	Amount bought with one U.S. dollar	
	May 1971	*December 1971*
Japanese yen	357.0	308.0
German marks	3.63	3.22
French francs	5.51	5.12
British pounds	.41	.38
Swiss francs	4.29	3.85

position. As was indicated above, the crisis was brought on by a sharp increase in the U.S. balance of payments deficit after more than a decade of declines in reserves due to repeated deficits. A deficit, you will recall from the chapter, is the amount of excess supply of a nation's currency arising out of normal international transactions. Under a fixed exchange rate system, this requires the government to eliminate the excess supply to prevent the exchange rate from falling by selling reserves (that is, by purchasing the excess supply of dollars) or by getting other governments to agree to acquire dollars, or both. When a country has repeated deficits, it will continue to lose reserves and must face the prospect of running out of reserves unless the deficits can be eliminated.

This day of reckoning may arise sooner than later if international investors anticipate an eventual change in the exchange rate. If speculators expect, let us say, a decline in the price of the dollar, they will want to sell dollars at the current rate and buy them back when the price is lower, thereby earning a capital gain. But this overflow of dollars adds to the excess supply and worsens the situation. In large part, the sharp increase in the payments deficit in 1970–1971 was due to the actions of speculators as they became convinced that the then current price of the dollar was too high and would have to be reduced in the near future.

One reason that speculators became convinced

that the U.S. payments deficit would not improve without a change to the price of the dollar was the deterioration in the balance on current account. Prior to 1968, the U.S. current account balance had usually been positive. That is, the excess of exports over imports had usually been sufficient to compensate for the sizable outflow of dollars due to private gifts and government grants to foreigners. Previously, the U.S. deficit had been caused by the substantial amount of U.S. investment abroad due to relatively high rates of return to foreign investment. Remember, although it is true that an outflow of capital adds to our net claims on foreigners, it also adds to our balance of payments deficit. (During the Johnson administration an interest equalization tax—a tax on income earned on financial investments abroad—that was designed to reduce the outflow of capital was imposed.) Once the current account surplus evaporated, it seemed to many speculators highly probable that the exchange rate would fall.

In the crisis situation, Nixon's bold announcement ending convertibility of the dollar into gold and "floating" the dollar with respect to other currencies put the U.S. in a strong position. Prior to this announcement, foreign governments repeatedly put pressure on the U.S. to correct its balance of payments deficit by reducing its inflation, increasing its productivity, and other internal measures that were difficult or undesirable from a domestic point of view. These other governments (and, until then, the U.S. government) did not favor a change in the price of the dollar on the grounds that this would prove to be too much of a disruption to the international monetary system. But with Nixon's statement, other countries were put in the position of having to finance the U.S. deficit (that is, if they wanted to preserve the fixed exchange rates, they would have to acquire the excess supply of dollars), or allow the dollar price to fall in response to the forces of supply and demand. In either event, the deficit problem would be alleviated as far as the U.S. was concerned. If foreign governments wanted the existing exchange rates to be preserved, they would have the headache of dealing with the U.S. deficit. If the exchange rate were allowed to fall, the U.S. deficit would decline as U.S. goods would become cheaper abroad and foreign goods more expensive at home.

The final resolution of the crisis came with the establishment of a new set of fixed exchange rates that would certainly result in an improvement in the U.S. balance of payments position. The difficulty with this decision is that it is practically impossible to tell whether the new exchange rates are the "right" ones or whether they will result in one or another or several countries having to deal with continued deficits. It is this difficulty of finding a set of rates that will prove to be correct for all countries for a long period of time that makes many economists sympathetic to a flexible exchange rate system.

Such a system would have the advantage of allowing the exchange rate to adjust continuously, thereby eliminating as a matter for public policy the adjustment problem. These economists feel that any costs to importers and exporters that might result from uncertainty about exchange rates under a flexible exchange rate system would be less damaging than the disruptions caused by recurring crises under a fixed exchange rate system. Although there is considerable merit to this argument, there does not seem to be sufficient empirical evidence to permit a clear-cut choice as to which system would operate more effectively. Until the trading world becomes either sufficiently innovative or sufficiently desperate to experiment with a flexible exchange rate system, it appears we will be operating under a fixed exchange rate system. Hopefully, those fixed exchange rates will approximate long-run equilibrium exchange rates.

One encouraging outcome of the 1971 negotiations both for the world and the United States was the move toward freer trade. One of the fears that arose from the imposition of the 10 percent tariff surcharge was that other countries would retaliate by raising their tariffs. In the end, however, the United States was able to win an array of trade concessions from Japan and the promise of concessions from Canada and common market countries, all designed to expand foreign trade.

23

Poverty:
Analysis and Policy

This chapter is a case study—of poverty in America. It is similar to the short cases following each of the preceding chapters in that it states a problem, suggests the relevant analytical concepts and approaches, and asks you to solve the problem —what to do about poverty. But it is far more complex, with far more real-world details, than the end-of-chapter cases. By now you have the micro- and macroeconomic tools to make your own judgments on complex real-world problems that require use of both, and the problem of poverty presents an excellent opportunity to apply the economic theory you have learned. For poverty illustrates the intricate intermix of micro- and macro-economics in the world about us, as well as the close interactions among economic, social and political issues in our society. The first two sections define the problem—what is poverty, and why are the poor poor? Then the question is, what are the best policies to use if we want to lessen or eliminate poverty? A range of policies is presented, most of them suggested by the analysis used in defining the problem. Your job is to decide, all things considered, what, if anything, should be done, and who should do it?

WHAT IS POVERTY?

Poverty is as old as man. America is rich, and by the standards of most of the world poverty has been virtually eliminated here. In terms of per capita incomes, our "poor" in New York live as well as does the average worker in Leningrad or Mexico City. The visitor from India or the Congo would see nothing that even approaches the poverty that the mass of his people take for granted. Even by our own standards, today less than 15 percent of our people live in poverty. But even in the "affluent society" of modern America, there is an economic underworld of poverty.

There is no one accepted definition of poverty. Perhaps the most widely used definition today is that suggested by the Social Security Administration and widely used by the government in compiling its statistics. This definition says that, as of 1970, any urban four-person family receiving less than $3,970 was considered poor. For rural families, this figure is reduced by 30 percent. For larger or smaller families, the figure is adjusted appropriately; for individuals living alone, the poverty line was about $1,900 as of 1970. Note that under this definition, the "poverty" level will change each year if the cost of purchasing the prescribed market basket of food and other goods and services changes. Thus, over the 1960s, there was substantial inflation, and the poverty income level for urban families rose from about $3,200 to nearly $4,000.

These poverty-line figures were based on an extensive analysis of the living standards of

people under different circumstances in the
United States during the 1960s. Technically,
the figure for each year is arrived at by finding
the cost of a reasonable, but very moderate, diet,
and multiplying this amount by 3; this ratio is
based on analysis of a large number of budgets
of low-income families. Obviously, this approach
is arbitrary, and the figures arrived at each year
provide nothing more than a working definition
of poverty.[1]

What is considered poverty changes with the
times, and some people say we just define poverty
so that there will always be some. They argue
that there is only a poverty problem in the eyes
of the do-gooders. Twenty years ago, the median
money of all families was about $4,000 (in 1970
prices), the present poverty level. Then, $2,000
was widely considered the poverty level, and
nearly half of all families would have fallen below
the poverty level we now use. Economic growth
has steadily pushed most families above the
minimal levels that seemed reasonable a generation
or two ago. But our aspirations have risen with
rising incomes.

The above picture is substantially accurate,
but statistics can be misleading. Some observers
argue that using money income as a test over-
states the magnitude of the problem. The poor
southern farmer with an annual income of $2,000
and six children eats better off the land than the
arithmetic would suggest. Some poor families,
especially the elderly, have accumulated assets,
and draw on them to supplement their current
incomes. Thus, their actual consumption is well
above the incomes they report. As a college student, you are probably another example. In many
ways, consumption would be a better measure of
poverty than is current money income, and such
a measure might show an appreciable number of
the "poor" families better off than they seem.
Clearly, families whose incomes drop temporarily
may appear very poor by the income test, but
they may maintain their consumption standards
while waiting for a return to normal incomes. But

with all these reservations, most of those who are
poor by the income test above are poor by
modern American standards.

If we accept the government's definition of
poverty, how many poor are there now in the
United States? In 1970, the median family income in the United States was about $9,900;
that is, half of all families received more than
that amount and half less. In that same year,
about 27 million people (13 percent of the total
population) were "poor" by the standard government test. About 7 million families had money
incomes below $3,900; their median income was
about $2,400, and over 1 million of the families
were raising four or more children on that
income. About 5 million people living alone
had incomes below $1,900. These are the poor.

WHO ARE THE POOR?

In 1962, Michael Harrington wrote a book, *The
Other America,* that touched the conscience of
many Americans. The other America, Harrington
wrote, is the world of the poor in the midst of
plenty—a world of desolation, of hopelessness,
of bitterness and resentment, of slums, of
discrimination. It is the world of blacks and
Puerto Ricans living in the great city slums; of
old men and women living alone in rented tenement rooms; of poor southern farmers living in
ramshackle huts without plumbing; of fatherless
families whose mothers struggle to support their
children; of failures and rejects for a dozen other
reasons.

To understand poverty, Harrington argued,
we must add sociology to economics. The poor,
he wrote, live in a subculture of their own. Most
of them feel—with apathy or resentment—that no
one cares. It is a world whose inhabitants are
isolated from the mainstream of American life
and alienated from its values. It is a world whose
occupants are literally concerned with day-to-day
survival, whose minor illness is a major tragedy,
where fatback and cheap greens are a standard
diet. Last, it is a world turned in on itself in its
values and its habits, a world in which the poverty
of the parents is visited upon the children.

Each year, many families move up from the
ranks of the poor, and some families slide down

[1]For a full description of Social Security Administration procedures and historical data, see U.S. Department of Commerce, *Poverty in the United States*
(*Current Population Reports*, Series P-60), December 31,
1969.

below the imaginary line. But the great bulk of the poor stay poor.

To understand the problem of poverty, you must recognize that the poor differ widely. Five groups loom large.

Negroes. Although only 1.6 million of the 7 million poor families are nonwhite, over 30 percent of all Negro families are poor. Some 8 million of the 27 million poor persons in 1970 were Negroes. Many poor Negro families live in the rural South; over 60 percent of Negro farmers are in the poverty group. But increasingly, they have moved to the northern city slums. Those who live in the cities have incomes 30 percent below whites with comparable education. In the city slums, over half of Negro youths are high school dropouts. The breakdown of the Negro family in the city slum is a critical part of the problem of Negro poverty. Over half of all poor Negroes live in family units headed by females. Other minority groups are also poor, but their numbers are far less than the Negroes involved.

Farmers. Over 20 percent of all farm families are poor, about twice the urban rate. Rural poverty is concentrated in the South. A substantial portion of poor southern farmers are the Negroes mentioned above. Government aids to agriculture provide virtually no help to poor farmers; the money goes largely to the big, well-capitalized farmers.

Old people. Old age brings poverty about as often as it brings adequate retirement. About 1.3 million families in which the husband is over sixty-five are poor; this is about 18 percent of all such families, and it accounts for about 25 percent of all poor families. In addition, nearly half of all old people living alone have incomes below $1,900. Social security does not help much. The average benefit is only a little over $1,000 a year, and only half of the nation's aged poor receive social security retirement payments.

Fatherless families. Nearly 40 percent of all women left alone to provide for their children are poor; for nonwhites the figure is nearly 60 percent. Fatherless families are common in the low-income groups, and the woman who has to earn her family's living must either leave her children alone (which she often does in the poverty groups) or find someone to look after them. She faces many lost workdays and consequently job instability. The breakdown of the family is near the core of the difficult social problems of the city slums. Probably not one out of three black children in poor families who now reaches age eighteen has lived all his life with both his parents. Nationwide, the number of children on public "welfare" has risen from less than 1 million to over 7 million since 1950, with most of the increase during the 1960s, a decade of growing prosperity and falling unemployment. In New York City alone, over 1 million mothers and children were on welfare in 1970, out of a total population of under 8 million.

Others. About one-third of all poor families do not fit into any of the groups above. They live in depressed areas; they have poor motivation; they have low intelligence; most have had little education; there is little demand for the jobs they can do. By the test of the market, they are failures, the rejects of our modern economy.

One generalization applies to all these groups. Most come from poor families and have been poor all their lives.

WHY ARE THEY POOR?

There are many reasons why the poor are poor. The theory of the preceding chapters should help you in straightening out the causes of poverty. Before reading on, try to answer the question for yourself: What does the preceding analysis suggest as to why the poor are poor?

Inadequate aggregate demand. When there is a recession, unemployment raises the proportion of the population below the poverty line. Conversely, prosperity brings more jobs, especially for marginal members of the labor force who are last to be taken on. A major depression is a catastrophe for the poor.

But only a small fraction (perhaps 10 percent) of the poor even in the recession year of 1970 were "unemployed," as measured by the unemployment statistics. Most unemployed are only temporarily out of work and find other jobs in a few weeks, or months at most. Thus, their annual incomes are above the poverty level. Over half the poor were simply out of the labor market; children were the largest group. Many of the poor were elderly people, past their working years. Many in the slums, especially Negroes, had given up looking for work. Others were not in the labor force for a variety of other reasons. Rising aggregate demand and falling unemployment help to lessen poverty, but they give jobs and higher incomes only to those who have a service to sell. The best estimates suggest that reduction of the overall unemployment rate from 4 percent to 3 percent would reduce the population below the poverty line by only about 1 percentage point.

It is important to recognize these facts. But the indirect effects of prosperity are more important than this figure suggests in lessening barriers against minority groups as labor markets tighten, in providing more on-the-job training for marginal workers, in providing partial employment for the elderly, and in other indirect ways. Recession can be an important direct and indirect cause of poverty.

Low productivity. The message of Chapter 12 was that individuals' incomes depend primarily on the marginal productivity of their labor and the capital they own. If this is correct, given a reasonable level of aggregate demand, poor people in the labor market are by and large poor because their marginal productivity is low. They are poor because they are not worth more to employers in a profit-motivated economy. Or, if they are elderly, they are poor now because they did not adequately plan ahead or did not have an adequate life income to provide a reasonable retirement income through savings.

This is a harsh conclusion, and, as we shall see in a moment, one that is only partially correct. But it has a strong core of truth. Over 60 percent of all poor families are headed by an individual with less than an eighth-grade education; only 20 percent by individuals who completed high school. Many old people, even though seeking work, can offer only limited services in the market. Women attempting to support their children inescapably lose more time than others. Many of the adult poor have no skills, or obsolete ones.

Market imperfections and discrimination. If there is effective competition among employers, this competition will bid the wages of each worker up to the value of his marginal product. And the value of his marginal product will be highest where he makes the greatest contribution to the production of goods and services that consumers want to buy. Conversely, if there are market imperfections that prevent workers from finding employment where their productivity is highest, or that prevent effective competition from forcing wages up to that level, society's resources would not be most efficiently allocated, and workers would not earn the maximum incomes they could obtain in a competitive economy.

In fact, inability, apathy, and ignorance of job openings are generally characteristic of the poor. Poor Southern farmers, both Negro and white, appear to be highly immobile except for the young. In Appalachia, there has been a massive exodus of population, but again almost entirely of young people. Thus, the poor, especially those middle-aged and beyond, tend to not know about job opportunities, nor to be willing or able to move if this information is available. To move is expensive and uncertain. The subculture of the poor has little contact with the formal processes of employment exchanges and the information and mobility devices available to the middle classes. Even in the cities, many poor have little contact with the job market of the middle classes.

Moreover, there are many market imperfections on the buying side of labor. There are areas where employers do not compete effectively for some types of labor, especially when labor tends to be immobile in those areas. As we saw in Chapter 12, a monopsonist can sometimes get by with paying them less than their marginal productivity.

A major market imperfection and a major cause of poverty for nonwhites is discrimination— in education, jobs, access to medical care, on nearly every score. If employers, rationally or irrationally, refuse to bid for Negro workers on the same basis as they bid for white workers, it is to be expected that Negro incomes will be lower at the same jobs. In fact, Negro incomes average 30 to 35 percent lower than those for whites of the same years of education, areas of residence, and sex. Just how much of nonwhite poverty is accounted for by discrimination is sharply debated by the experts. Some estimates suggest about $15 billion, but this is only a very rough approximation.[2]

Progress against discrimination was made in the 1960s, but there is disagreement over how much. Nearly 40 percent of all black families received over $8,000 in 1970, compared to only 15 percent in 1960 (in constant 1970 dollars); but only 23 percent of black families earned more than the median family income in both years. For northern black families headed by a male aged 25 to 34, incomes in 1970 were 95 percent those of comparable whites. The Negro unemployment rate declined sharply over the decade as the economy grew and aggregate demand rose, though it remained nearly twice that for whites. The number of black "professional and technical" employees more than doubled during the 1960s, compared to a 40 percent increase for whites. Progress in reducing economic discrimination against nonwhites has been substantial, but the problem is still a massive one.

Absence from the labor force. Nearly 60 percent of all poor families are headed by individuals who are not in the labor force. Many of these are elderly people, but many others are discouraged youths and mothers of fatherless families who have given up looking for work. Thus, the problems of poverty, family instability, and insecurity in old age are inseparably intertwined. Others are out of the labor force for a variety of reasons—ill health, lack of motivation, family circumstances, or simply because they have given up hope of finding a job. "Welfare" has helped both to break up poor families (because until recently no aid could be given to a family headed by a male of working age) and to keep people out of jobs (because any earnings would lead to a dollar-for-dollar reduction in welfare benefits). Unless rising aggregate demand,

[2]See, for example, J. Kain, *Race and Poverty* (Englewood Cliffs, N.J.: Prentice-Hall, Inc., 1969); and L. Thurow, *Poverty and Discrimination* (Washington, D.C.: The Brookings Institution, 1969), especially Chaps. 7 and 9.

lessened discrimination, improved welfare practices, or improved information and mobility were to pull some of these individuals back into the labor force, no improvement in economic conditions or in the workings of the market could help alleviate their poverty. Over 40 percent of all poor people are children below working age.

The vicious circle of poverty. Beyond these economic causes, most observers add a socio-economic analysis. Poverty breeds poverty, in a vicious circle. A poor individual or family has a high probability of staying poor. The poor live largely in slums or in backward rural areas. Their children do not learn to read, to write, even to speak well. They grow up to apathy or resentment, and they go to poor schools with other poor children. They lag far behind children in middle-class schools, and their drop-out rate is high—not surprisingly, for there is little in their culture to make them care about education. When the poor are sick, they stay sick longer because they have inadequate medical care. Thus, they find it harder to keep jobs. Broken homes are common. Often there is little motivation or hope to rise from the vicious circle of poverty, either for the young or for adults.

POLICIES AGAINST POVERTY

How serious is poverty? Do the poor deserve higher incomes? Should they receive help even if they don't work, or their productivity is low? If so, how much help, and how should it be provided? Can we help the poor without hurting somebody else? Who should pay, if there is a real cost to raising living standards for the poor? The following sections outline a variety of policies that have been suggested to reduce poverty in this country. Consider each one carefully—and come up with your own anti-poverty program! Suggestion: remember the basic causes of poverty laid out above, and the following concepts which may be helpful—aggregate demand and the avoidance of wasteful unemployment; economic growth through increasing productivity; scarcity and the need to economize; economic incentives; economic efficiency in the allocation of resources; marginal productivity and the determination of incomes;

consumer welfare and freedom in spending incomes; market imperfections and barriers to the efficient allocation of resources; and the broad issue of equity vs. efficiency as social goals.

Maintaining high employment. Macro-economic theory tells us that we need not have depressions and mass unemployment if we maintain aggregate demand at roughly the level needed to buy the full employment output of the economy. It tells us that poverty, because of unemployment, is a preventable waste, although keeping aggregate demand just on the right stable path is a difficult task indeed. Difficult though it may be, maintaining a prosperous economy at approximately full employment is a first, and vital, step against poverty.

The importance of this point is illustrated by what happened to the number of poor in 1970, when we suffered our first recession in a decade. Over the entire decade of the 1960s, the number of poor had steadily declined, from about 40 million people in 1960 to 23 million in 1969. The recession of 1970, even though it was mild by historical standards, reduced per capita real income for the first time in the decade, and the number of poor people in the economy rose to about 27 million. Although unemployment does not usually account directly for many of the poor, it can do so in a serious recession. And it is important to remember that unless real output and the total number of jobs grow steadily, unemployment and related poverty will grow as the total labor force seeking work expands year after year.

Accelerating economic growth. Over the long-run, faster growth in output per capita provides a fundamental approach to the erosion of poverty. This is shown dramatically by Figure 23·1. Over the past two decades, economic growth has reduced poverty by some-what over 1 percent a year. If the rate of the 1960s could be maintained (remember that the decade included a cyclical upswing from a slack economy in the early 1960s), poverty as it is now defined would be entirely eliminated in less than ten years. But important as rapid growth is, the nearer poverty approaches zero, the harder it will be to make further gains. The remaining poor will be increasingly those insulated from labor markets—the aged, the disabled, what some have called the "hard core poor."

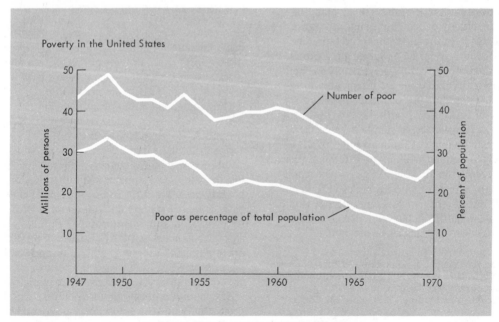

Figure 23.1 Poverty in the United States

Improving the productivity of the poor.
Probably the most basic reason for low incomes is
the low productivity of the poor, except for
children and the aged. Investment in human
beings increases their productivity, just as does
investment in nonhuman wealth. For many reasons, society's investment in the poor falls far
short of its investment in most individuals who
rise above poverty. The poor live in slums, in
squalor. They receive short and poor education.
They get little job training in schools or on the
job because they so often find no employment.
They receive inadequate medical care. If we
want to raise the productivity of many of the
poor, more investment through education and
training to raise their productive capacity is the
first prescription of the preceding economic
analysis.

Improving labor markets. Many of the poor
are effectively isolated from jobs by lack of
information, immobility, and inertia. This is
especially true of the rural poor in the South.
But it is also true in the slums of the great
cities, where for thousands of unskilled and
poorly educated teenagers and adults there is
no practical channel into the jobs that are
opening up elsewhere in the economy, even in
the same city. To say that individuals with
proper motivation would seek out the jobs that
may be open elsewhere is not much of an answer
for the Puerto Rican or Negro teenager in Harlem
or in the backwoods of Alabama.

Better job training programs, employment
exchanges, guidance and counseling services, and
the like could help those who suffer merely from
inadequate information or are immobile because
of financial difficulties. Better information,
better education, and better training programs
for both youth and adults make sense both to
fight poverty and to improve the efficiency of
our economic system. More subsidized day-care
nurseries for poor working mothers could both
improve their economic productivity and get
under-privileged youngsters off to a better
educational start.

Many economists blame unions and the government itself for important job barriers. Many craft
unions have *de facto* barriers against nonwhites
for apprenticeships and union membership and

limit memberships for whites as well, thus in
effect blocking them from higher paying jobs.
And the federal minimum wage law of $1.60 per
hour as of 1970, however admirable its purpose,
surely shuts many low productivity workers out
of jobs that might be there at lower wage rates
for such workers, especially poorly educated,
poverty-group teenagers.

Lessening discrimination. For nonwhites,
reduction in discrimination is essential to long-
run economic progress. Barriers to current jobs
must be reduced, and better educational
opportunities can improve minority groups'
chances to break out of the vicious circle of
poverty.

Debate over steps to eliminate racial discrimination far transcends issues of how best to
reduce poverty. The answers are at least as
much political and social as they are economic.
Both government and private steps have made
some headway in recent years, but it is only a
beginning. The public sector has a better record
than the private one; the ratio of blacks to total
government employees far exceeds the comparable
ratio in private business. Discrimination in education and housing poses even deeper problems,
which are probably basic to the meaningful
establishment of economic equality of opportunity. Reduction of discrimination is essential
to long-run economic progress for minorities,
and makes economic sense; it would raise the real
income of both whites and blacks if gains
from using resources more efficiently were
distributed to both groups. But economic
measures alone will fall far short of solving the
problem.

Money-income redistribution. To close the
gap between all present below-poverty incomes
and 1970 $3,900-per-family and $1,900-per-
individual poverty levels would require about
$10 billion. Direct money grants of about $10
billion would be only about 1 percent of GNP.
Assuming 3 percent per capita annual growth in
total real income, if the non-poor 85 percent of
the population would forego a small fraction of
that growth for a few years, this poverty gap
could be filled. This solution to the poverty
problem looks simple. And indeed some redis-

tribution of income toward the lower groups has been occurring. The government annually redistributes, through taxing and spending, a large amount of income. Table 23.1 shows the general shift toward less income inequality over the past half century.

Table 23.1

FAMILY INCOME SHARES, 1929–1969

	Percent of Total Income Received			
	1929	*1950*	*1960*	*1969*
Lowest fifth	13.0	{ 4.5	4.8	5.6
Second fifth		{ 12.0	11.7	12.3
Third fifth	14.0	17.4	17.4	17.6
Fourth fifth	19.0	23.5	23.6	23.4
Top fifth	54.0	42.6	42.6	41.0
All families	100.0	100.0	100.0	100.0

Some economists argue that direct income transfers (gifts) are the best attack on the poverty problem. It would have the virtue of letting us see the actual cost of the program. In addition, it would give recipients of aid freedom to spend their incomes as they wish, in contrast to programs that force them to take aid through food stamps, housing subsidies, medical assistance, education, and the like. (Remember the analysis of the "food stamp" program from Chapter 3, in comparing money grants with grants-in-kind.)

But fighting poverty by this approach would not raise society's total real income; it would merely redistribute what we now produce without using the productive potential of many poor. Moreover, such direct cash grants to all the poor might raise serious problems on the incentive front, because individuals now earning more than the poverty level might prefer to take direct subsidies and avoid work. Thus, the actual cost of such a direct subsidy approach to the poverty problem would probably be substantially larger than the $10 billion indicated. At the extreme, if everyone in the poverty range who now works stopped, the total cost would obviously go up

sharply and total GNP might even drop temporarily. But it would still be a small percentage of GNP.

"Welfare," or "relief," is the name generally applied to cash transfer payments by the government to the poor, as well as to such direct aid-in-kind as food stamps. Welfare has been the main form of direct government aid to the poor, and it has grown rapidly. In 1955, about 6 million people received welfare, totalling about $3 billion. By 1971, the total was over 16 million recipients and over $14 billion, with about half the money provided by the federal government and half by state and local governments.

The current welfare system just about everyone agrees, is a mess. It has four big failings. 1) It excludes a lot of the poor people because if there is an adult male in the family, even though he earns nothing or less than the poverty level, the family is not eligible for welfare. It also tends to break up families because welfare payments can only be received by families with no father present who is able to work, so fathers tend to leave their families so the families can get welfare payments. Thus, only about half the poor receive any welfare payments. At the same time, many perfectly able people honestly or dishonestly live off welfare instead of looking for work. 2) The welfare system until recently in effect imposed a 100 percent marginal tax rate on any welfare family earnings, because welfare payments were reduced by the full amount of any earnings from work. This is a direct incentive not to work. This effective welfare tax rate has now been reduced to 67 percent, but it still has the same general effects. 3) Benefits have been very unequal because they have been set by the individual states. They varied from $39 to $263 per person per month in 1970, with the very low benefit payments in the deep South. (4) Costs of administering the complex system have used up a substantial part of the funds allocated to helping the poor.

The "negative income tax." Recently, a novel proposal to reform the welfare system has been advanced simultaneously by Milton Friedman, an adviser to Barry Goldwater and President Nixon, and James Tobin, an adviser to President Kennedy. It is to substitute a "negative income tax" for part or all of the present welfare system—to combine compassion with incentives by first guaranteeing everyone a basic minimum income (a negative income tax for the poor instead of the positive income tax which we now pay if we are rich), and second, permitting him to keep, say, half of all the earnings in addition, up to some moderate income level when he would slide over to a regular taxpayer status. It should be easy to see how it flows directly from the economic analysis of the present chapter. It is widely favored by economists of a variety of political persuasions, because it does rest so directly on basic economic analysis of the situation.

As you saw in Case 12, President Nixon in 1969 proposed a new "Family Assistance Plan" to replace the present welfare system, incorporating a substantial part of the negative income tax proposal. Congress turned the proposal down, for a variety of reasons, including some strictly political ones, but President Nixon resubmitted it in 1971. One can argue over the details of the Nixon plan and of the negative income tax, but it is hard to escape the basic economic analysis which underlies both of them.

Table 23.2
FEDERAL AID TO THE POOR, 1971

(In billions)

Education	$ 2.7
Employment assistance	2.3
Health assistance	6.4
Direct income assistance	17.8
Other	3.7
	$32.9

How much aid?   All this leaves unanswered one big question—how much aid should be given to the poor, through income transfers or other measures. Table 23.2 summarizes *federal* aid to the poor in 1971. Some of the figures are rough estimates (for example, the amount of special educational aid that goes to help the poor), but the order of magnitude is right. Note that this table excludes most of the huge social security

system, whose $30 billion annual payments go mainly to people who are above the poverty level. In addition to the total shown in Table 23.2, state and local governments spend directly perhaps another $8 billion, bringing the total payments up to around $40 billion.

Is this too much? Whatever the exact amount should be, who should pay the costs? The answers to these questions depend in considerable part on your notions of equity, of fairness in the distribution of income. But they depend also on some issues of incentive—incentives for the poor to work, and incentives for those in higher income groups who have to give up some of their earnings to help the poor. At what point do the social benefits of additional assistance no longer outweigh the social costs?

For some people, this simply depends on ethical standards—how equally *should* income and consumption be distributed, or what minimum income level should be established for everyone, whether he works or not? For others, it's a straight economic cost-benefit comparison. How much will the "richer" 85 percent of the population above the poverty level gain by spending the money to get the other 15 percent out of poverty —through producing a more stable sociopolitical environment, through checking when decay associated with poverty, and through increasing the poor's abilities to support themselves in the future? Is altruism or economic self-interest the dominant force for most Americans to spend money to reduce poverty? For you? What politics you favor may depend heavily on your answer.

CONCLUSION

One purpose of this chapter is to provide information about an important social problem—poverty. But an even more important one is to show you how the economic analysis you have learned can help you understand such big social problems and make up your own mind about what are appropriate private or governmental measures to deal with the problems. Just looking at "the facts" does not get you very far with complex economic problems, unless you have some analytical framework to help you ask what the relevant facts are and to understand the facts when you find them. Look at the central economic concepts you have used in this chapter: scarcity and the need to economize; economic efficiency in the allocation of resources; economic incentives; marginal productivity and the determination of incomes; consumer welfare and freedom in the allocation of incomes; aggregate demand and the avoidance of unemployment; economic growth through increasing productivity and efficient use of resources; market imperfections as barriers to the efficient allocation of resources. These analytical concepts can not give you easy answers to tough social problems, but they can help you significantly in analyzing the problems. Without them, you are likely to be sidetracked, to miss the essentials, and to end up relying mainly on emotion or the latest newspaper story rather than on reasoned judgments of your own.

24

Does The American Economy Need Radical Change?

It is time for a look back at the whole American economy—at what it is and how well it meets the standards we can reasonably set for it. Each previous chapter has focused on a particular part of the economy or a particular problem. The goal of this chapter is to provide a concluding overview—a look at the "big picture" to provide perspective. A useful way to do this may be to examine some of the major "radical" criticisms which have recently been levelled at the economy, by those who want drastic changes in the existing system and those who would like to replace it completely with a communist state.

Nearly everyone objects to something about the American economy and the way it works, even people who think that over all it is a very good system indeed. The preceding chapters have examined a number of widely-heard criticisms—of poverty, monopoly, unemployment, inflation, pollution. How serious these problems are is a matter of dispute, but nearly all supporters of the American "capitalist" system (as we shall call it, although it is in fact a very mixed system) agree that it is far from perfect in the way it operates on a practical day-to-day basis. On the other hand, most Americans clearly think that something like the present American system is better than the alternatives we know about—and that it has, on the whole, done very well for the American people, even though it ought to be patched up here and there.

But some radical critics, including at least some college students, say the failings of the U.S. economy are far deeper and more basic than this. They contend that only drastic, radical changes can make it perform acceptably. Some, mainly Marxists, challenge the whole concept of an individual-initiative, market directed economy, and would replace it with some type of planned system. The next two sections summarize these radical criticisms of the American economy. The final part of the chapter analyzes the criticisms, with the primary objective of helping you see what the central issues are so you can make up your own mind on them, and on where we ought to be steering the American economy.

MARX AND RADICAL CRITICISM

The historical roots of modern radical economic criticism lie largely in Karl Marx. Marx, writing about a hundred years ago, developed an elaborate set of theories about the working of capitalist economic systems and the course of history. To look at his ideas closely would take a whole book, but the central ideas can be summarized briefly (and over-simplistically) as follows:

1. All history can be interpreted primarily in terms of economic issues and conflicts.
2. Value is created only by labor, and the labor time socially necessary for the production of any commodity will determine its value (price).

3. Capitalists (employers) do not pay workers the full value of the goods they produce. They take the "surplus value" above what they pay workers for themselves as profits and interest on their capital, using this surplus to support their own rich living and further accumulation of capital. Indeed, the capitalist class, which is the dominant class, will force the wages of the working class down to a subsistence level, and the "surplus value" seized by capitalists will become ever larger as workers produce more but are continually ground down to a subsistence existence.

4. The operations of any economy can be understood best in terms of a class struggle—between capitalists and workers, oppressors and oppressed, the rich and the poor. The capitalists, who exploit the workers by seizing the surplus value created by the workers, also dominate governments. "The State," Marx wrote, "is nothing but the organized collective power of the possessing classes."

5. Out of this class struggle will emerge, eventually, the end of capitalism and the beginning of a communist society. The class struggle will develop "contradictions" in the capitalist system. Most important, unemployment and human misery will increase as the capitalists seize more and more surplus value and accumulate more capital, while the poor are increasingly unable to purchase the growing production of the capitalist society. A "reserve army of the unemployed" will develop, in increasingly violent depressions. Capital will be increasingly monopolized by a few huge firms, which will lead to "finance capitalism," in which capitalists reach abroad for new opportunities to oppress workers in other nations and to further develop their own capital hoards. But in the end, the class struggle will bring the whole capitalist accumulation to a halt, because the oppressed workers will finally rise up in revolt, overthrow the capitalists, and establish a socialist or communist system.

History has proven Marx wrong on some of his major points. In the Western capitalist societies, the working class has not been ground down to subsistence levels; on the contrary, living standards for the masses have risen spectacularly over the last hundred years under capitalism. Modern monetary and fiscal policy appear to have provided the answer to a reasonably stable, growing capitalist economy. There is certainly a concentration of capital in the hands of the rich, but it is not clear that this inequality of wealth and power is any greater than it was under the precapitalist conditions or in many noncapitalist societies today, for example in some of the less developed nations. Although monopoly is a serious problem for many capitalist societies, it is not clear in America, for example, that the degree of monopoly has changed significantly over the last fifty to seventy-five years. Certainly, the violent overthrow of capitalism by the workers that Marx predicted looks to be a long way distant in the American economy today. Workers may complain about some of the issues Marx raised, but they vote Democrat or Republican, not Communist, in the elections. And perhaps most significant of all, there are regular elections in which workers and others are free to vote for the individuals and policies they prefer in the Western capitalist democracies at which Marx sneered.

Economists also point to basic flaws in Marx's economic theory—particularly in his "labor theory of value," which argued that all value is created by labor and that all prices will be proportionate to labor input. Clearly this is wrong; prices are determined by the forces of supply and demand in markets, as was explained in the preceding chapters. How will the labor theory of value explain the high price of a perfect pearl picked up with little labor by a beachwalker? The argument that capital is not itself productive is equally fallacious; yet it was on this proposition that Marx declared interest, profits, and other returns to capital to be useless and improper.

But many of Marx's ideas have refused to die. His modern interpreters have changed his ideas substantially, and V. I. Lenin, the founder of the modern Russian economy, spelled out in far more detail than Marx a pattern for an operating communist society. It is against the background of these ideas that modern radicals mount their charges against today's capitalist economies, even though they pay little attention to many aspects of Marx's writings and openly disavow some of his arguments.

MODERN RADICAL CRITICISM

A recent book by three young radical economists from Harvard, *The Capitalist System: A Radical Analysis of American Society,* is reasonably typical of the arguments of modern radicals.[1] The authors organize their book around a big question: "What's wrong in America?" They have the following answer: inequality, alienation, racism, sexism, irrationality, and imperialism, and they spell out at length the bad things (as they see them) about modern American society on these various scores. This list makes it clear that the criticism of modern radicals goes far beyond what we usually think of as economics, and far beyond topics with which this book has dealt. Indeed, it is difficult for most observers of the American scene to take very seriously the radical allegations that inequality, alienation, racism, sexism, irrationality, and imperialism are peculiar to modern capitalism. Poverty, for example, is surely greater in the noncapitalist systems than in the Western industrialized economies that the radicals say epitomize capitalism. Alienation seems to be a widespread problem in all industrialized societies, and apparently in a lot of nonindustrialized ones as well. Racism and sexism are hardly limited to capitalist societies; racial discrimination is common in noncapitalist as well as capitalist nations, and the lot of women is far more menial in most "less developed" economies than in the Western democracies. Pollution and urban crowding, examples of what the authors mean by irrationality, are openly acknowledged by the Russians as serious problems for them, and the worst pollution in the world is to be found in the "less developed" economies where modern sanitation methods have not arrived

[1] R. Edwards, M. Reich, and T. Weisskopf, *The Capitalist System: A Radical Analysis of American Society* (Englewood Cliffs, N.J.: Prentice-Hall, 1971).

at all. Imperialism has been the mark of nationalist states, capitalist and communist, as far as history goes. This is not to say that the problems are not serious ones; many people feel they are indeed. But it is doubtful that they are significantly related to capitalism as distinct from other forms of economic organization, or that they are *economic* in more than a very partial sense.

At the risk of over-simplification, the modern radical *economic* criticisms of the American economy can be grouped under five major headings. Let us state the criticisms first, and analyze their validity later.

Inequality—concentration of income and power. Under capitalism, the radicals charge, vast wealth and power are concentrated in the hands of a few. These rich capitalists, who dominate the great corporations that in turn dominate economic life, systematically manipulate and oppress the masses. This enormous inequality in the distribution of income, wealth, and both economic and political power is fundamental to modern capitalism, and will bring about its downfall.

Income, wealth, and economic power are all highly concentrated, the radicals argue. The richest 5 percent of families receive about 15 percent of the total income; the richest fifth of all families receive 41 percent. This gives them great purchasing power in the market to bid goods and services away from poorer families. The concentration of wealth is even more extreme. The top 1 percent of all families own over 20 percent of all private wealth in the nation. Moreover, their ownership of corporate stocks, which gives them control of the giant corporations is much more concentrated than this. Although there has been some reduction in the degree of inequality of income and wealth since the 1920s, it seems likely that the economy is moving back toward greater inequality again. Tables 24.1 and 24.2 present estimates of the inequality in the distribution of income and wealth since 1929.

The hundred largest manufacturing corporations, controlled almost completely by the few rich capitalists, account for over 40 percent of total industrial sales in the United States in 1970. General Motors' annual sales were nearly $25

Table 24.1

**FAMILY INCOME DISTRIBUTION IN
THE UNITED STATES, 1929–70***

	Percent of Total Income Received			
	1929	*1950*	*1960*	*1969*
Poorest fifth	3.5	4.5	4.8	5.7
Second fifth	9.0	12.0	11.7	12.4
Third fifth	13.8	17.4	17.4	17.7
Fourth fifth	19.3	23.5	23.6	23.7
Richest fifth	54.4	42.6	42.6	40.6
Total:	100.0	100.0	100.0	100.0
Richest 5 percent	30.0	17.0	16.8	14.7

*Source: U.S. Census Bureau

Table 24.2

**ESTIMATED WEALTH OWNED BY TOP 1
PERCENT OF ADULT POPULATION***

	Percent
1929	32
1939	28
1949	19
1956	25
1962	22**

* Source: R. Lampman, *The Share of Top Wealth-Holders in National Wealth* (National Bureau of Economic Research, 1962), p. 209. Estimates are based on estate tax returns filed in the years shown are very rough.

**Estimated by Federal Reserve Board from detailed field survey. May not be comparable with earlier figures from estates.

billion, larger than the entire gross national product of most of the world's nations. Together, the top 10 manufacturing corporations accounted for 14 percent of total industrial sales in the United States, totaling $100 billion. The power of these corporate giants over the nation's economy is enormous. Through them, the capitalist ruling class manipulates and oppresses the masses of workers and consumers, who have little to say about what goes on in the economy.

Moreover, this same capitalist ruling class controls the government as well as the economy. The great corporations can readily buy votes and control the policies adopted by our government, especially policies relating to themselves and to their special interests. Marx was right: the state is essentially a vehicle through which the ruling class maintains control over the masses.

This concentration of capital in the hands of the few has no economic or moral justification. The rich have attained their capital largely by seizing the "surplus value" created by the workers. Fundamentally, it is only labor that is productive. But even if machines and other capital goods owned by the capitalists are in themselves physically productive, they represent no sacrifice or abstinence on the part of their rich owners. They represent, instead, the work and sweat of the masses who labored to produce them. The "savings" of the rich capitalists thus give them no moral claim on the fruits of their capital. This capital should be seized by the state and returned to the workers. It could be equally productive, if it has any productivity, and its fruits could be distributed to all the workers, instead of being seized by the ruling capitalist class.

Reliance on markets. Capitalism relies primarily on markets to organize society. Market forces substantially decide what shall be produced, what prices shall be charged, and who shall get society's production. But in fact, the radical critics say, these markets are largely manipulated by the huge corporations for the benefits of the capitalist oppressors. Adam Smith's "invisible hand" has little relevance in modern capitalist societies. His argument that consumer sovereignty will prevail—that consumers' dollar votes will determine what is produced—has been swept away by two major developments. First, consumers no longer have a chance to decide what shall be produced. The great corporations decide what to produce and then sell it to consumers through advertising and other Madison Avenue demand-creation activities. Second, society is no longer characterized by millions of small businesses competing actively so that prices are driven down to the lowest possible cost of production for the consumer. Instead, the few corporate giants dominate the markets and set prices high to insure huge profits for the capitalists, while forcing consumers to buy shoddy and often useless goods. Big business monopoly, not competition, is the basic fact of modern economic life. Thus, markets become merely tools of the capitalist class to seize surplus value from the workers through huge profits, and to assure that workers buy the things on which capitalists can make the largest profit.

Competition rather than cooperation. To many radicals, competition is immoral, cooperation is good. Although Marx found in competition and the capitalist state an impressively productive arrangement, many modern radicals believe that it would be a "better" society if we all cooperated rather than competed. Excessive pressure of competition drives man on an unhappy treadmill. His main goals are to get enough to live on and to get ahead of his neighbors. The speed-up of the impersonal factory assembly line characterizes modern capitalism. Little wonder that alienation increasingly characterizes our working classes. The good life would stress cooperation among men, not competition.

Quantity rather than quality of life. The drive for economic growth—ever more GNP— dominates modern capitalism. Economic growth has become the *raison d'etre* of life. More output, not a better quality of life, has come to dominate all. Capitalism blindly rushes ahead, producing more and more of things that people want less and less, while the air is fouled, streets are dirty, rats race through the slums, and social tensions mount everywhere. Capitalism is so profit-oriented and growth-dominated that our social priorities are completely twisted. Quantity is all, quality of life is nothing.

Imperialism. As finance capitalism has seized more and more power, the radicals say, the huge corporations and their capitalist masters have found it increasingly difficult to satiate their urge for profits within their own nations. Thus they have increasingly turned abroad for profits to the so-called less-developed economies, where natural resources and cheap labor abound. In these helpless nations, they exploit the workers at starvation wages and exploit the natural resources to feed their huge productive facilities at home.

Dominating their national governments, the capitalists dictate foreign policies that send troops to seize lesser nations where this seems necessary to protect American investments abroad. Indeed, in recent decades growth in international markets has become essential to the continued growth and well-being of the huge multinational corporations that now dominate the Western capitalist system. War and exploitation of the lesser nations is the result. The military-industrial complex, through which the huge corporations assure continued heavy military spending at home and military activities abroad, is the machinery that assures profits for these corporations. Their monopoly powers at home can be extended to nations abroad only with the help of their governments, and international imperialism is the result. Huge profits from exploitation of the helpless less-developed countries, especially in Southeast Asia, thus explain our nationalist aggression in such countries and increasingly provide the foundation on which U.S. domestic prosperity must rest. For without those raw materials and profits, the American economy could not maintain its wastefully high production and consumption levels.

ANALYSIS

Are the radicals right? Is the modern American economy a mess? Are income and power unacceptably concentrated in the hands of a few? Do we misguidedly rely on impersonal markets rather than human direction to run our economy, on competition rather than cooperation to motivate work and production of the things we want? Does our prosperity depend on imperialist exploitation of the less-developed nations? Answering these questions can provide an overview of how well the U.S. economy does work and how far short it may fall.

To analyze thoroughly all the radical criticisms of the modern American economy would take another book bigger than this one. But the concepts and analysis you have learned thus far can help substantially in understanding the issues involved and in making your own judgments on them.

In considering these criticisms, it is important to keep separate three different issues. First, the differences between radicals and more conventional defenders of American capitalism reduce partly to differences in *values or ethics*. The radicals say that cooperating is *morally* better than competing; the defenders say it is not, and that competition is better for us because it gets our resources used more efficiently. If the radical critics say that is irrelevant because competition is bad *per se*, economic analysis cannot convince them or settle the argument, although it can throw a good deal of light on the economic consequences of using competition versus cooperation. Similarly, some people believe that an unequal distribution of incomes is ethically bad, no matter what economic benefits may come from using personal gain as a stimulus to efficient production and distribution of desired goods. Economic analysis cannot say that one man's ethics are better than another's, but it can tell us a good deal about why people get the incomes they do and the consequences that would probably follow from drastic changes toward more or less equality. Thus, it is essential to be clear when you are making judgments based on ethics or values *per se*, and when on economic analysis of the consequences of different systems.

Second, different conclusions may reflect *differences in analysis* of the results produced by communism and capitalism. On this score, clear thinking and careful analysis should help to settle some issues. If we want to make incomes more equal, is a minimum wage law an efficient device? Will rent ceilings on slum housing succeed in transferring income from greedy capitalist landlords to poor tenants, or will the result be primarily a reduction in the supply of future housing for low-income families? More generally, will reliance on markets give a more efficient allocation of resources than would reliance on government controls and centralized planning?

Third, some disputes arise because people do not bother to look at the facts or disagree over *what the facts are*. Disputes about facts can usually be settled, or at least partially settled, by looking at data. There is no use shouting at one another about such issues; the sensible approach is simply to go look at the data and find out who is right and who is wrong. For example, what share of the total gross national product is produced by the 100 largest corporations? Is it true that incomes are more unequally

distributed in American capitalism than in non-capitalist countries? Do the poor under American capitalism have higher living standards than the poor in the USSR and Communist China?

Bearing in mind these three different kinds of issues, it is useful to analyze radical charges against American capitalism by asking four big questions.

How shall the economy be organized—markets vs. bureaucracy? Radical economists (sometimes called "The New Left") object strongly to capitalism's reliance on *markets* to organize economic activity. Markets are cold, impersonal, nonhuman ways of making decisions as to what is to be produced, how production is to be organized, and who is to get the output. More basically, the radicals deny that consumers really control what is produced. First, big corporations decide what will make the largest profits, not what consumers want, and consumers must buy what is produced. Second, corporations manipulate consumer "wants" through advertising. Third, even if markets do reflect consumer wants, they reflect mainly the wants of the rich, not of the poor masses. Thus, markets are nothing but devices by which the rich capitalists impose their wishes on the poor.

Suppose we agree that our goal is to organize production so that the desires of individuals in society are met, insofar as is possible with the existing productive resources. The fundamental issue is, then, what is the best way to achieve this goal? The preceding chapters suggest that markets are indeed a powerful device for achieving the goal, *if* consumer spending does reflect consumer wants, and *if* there is active competition in markets. Consider the three radical challenges in the preceding paragraph.

Do big businesses disregard consumer wants and simply produce what will bring them the largest profits? The most elementary analysis shows the flaw in this argument. If consumers do not want the products enough to buy them, obviously producer profits are going to be nonexistent. All economists agree that substantial monopoly power exists in some markets, but even the oligopolist's or monopolist's power is sharply limited by consumer demands and potential competition. Increased competition may clearly make capitalism serve consumers better. But it is easy to overstate the degree of monopoly in modern America. The statistic above that the hundred largest corporations account for 40 percent of sales in the United States certainly makes it sound like a valid charge. But a closer look at the statistics shows that it is only 40 percent of *manufacturing*, or industrial sales. Manufacturing in turn accounts for only about 25 percent of the total gross national product. The enormously important, rapidly growing, sectors of services (retailing and wholesaling, travel, lesiure, medical services, and the like) are largely dominated by small firms, nor have large firms been growing relatively in these areas. Thus, for the economy as a whole, the statistic quoted above gives a highly misleading impression of the degree of concentration for the whole economy. Moreover, change has a way of under-cutting monopoly powers in the dynamic American economy. Twenty-five years ago, aluminum was a classic case of virtually pure monopoly; today there are at least half-a-dozen major firms in the industry, with bitter competition and low rates of return on investment. Vacuum tubes for radios and electronic instruments have been virtually replaced by transistors. So it goes for a vast number of the products in the oligopolized sectors of the economy. Not least, government antitrust laws present an ever-present threat to big firms that try to expand their share of the markets, gobble up small competitors, and exercise monopoly powers over prices and output.

How about the second critism: are consumer "wants" dictated by sellers through advertising, so we all "want" what big businesses want us to want? Partly, the answer depends on some facts. Case 4 above laid out the facts and some of the issues. It is clear that advertising does influence consumer demands; but it is also clear that advertising serves useful informational purposes, that it is a tiny fraction of sales for most goods and services, and that the extreme radical charges that consumer demands are completely manipulated by rich capitalists are grossly overstated.

Third, none of this refutes the radical argument that markets respond to dollar demands and

hence respond more to the rich man than to the poor man. Even in purely competitive markets, with no manipulation of consumer demand, economic efficiency would still mean that different people would receive goods in proportion to the dollars they spend. Here, we are back at the value judgments versus economic analysis dilemma. The market system will pay out wages and salaries roughly in proportion to people's marginal productivities—to how much each person contributes to producing what others will buy. To some, this seems an equitable way to distribute incomes and buying power. To others, the resulting inequalities of income seem highly inequitable; they believe that equality of income, or "to each according to his needs," is the only equitable system. Both agree that capitalism also provides incomes to owners of capital; wealthy people get incomes in proportion to their own marginal productivities and those of their capital, a proper result under the market system if capital as well as human resources is to be allocated efficiently to producing what individuals want to buy. The critics conversely argue that capital has no productivity *per se*, or that even if it does, the returns ought to go to all the people ("the workers") rather than to rich individuals who have "seized the surplus value created by the workers."

If you believe that inequality of income is ethically wrong, you will presumably want to change the existing U.S. allocation of income. More details are provided in the next section—but clearly you can have *both* the market system *and* more equal incomes by redistributing income through the public sector (taxing the rich to subsidize the poor) and then leaving the free market to respond to the spending of these post-transfer incomes. A good communist, of course, would simply seize the capital of the rich and take the proceeds for the benefit of "the workers," presumably through the government.

The main alternative to markets is government control over the allocation of resources. But the same radicals who dislike reliance on markets to organize society are often bitterly critical of centralized *political* power as a means of making economic decisions. They argue that the same rich capitalists who dominate markets dominate the government. Moreover, even in a less capitalist system (like the USSR, which some extreme radicals say is now really more capitalist than communist), government bureaucracy, rather than "the workers," often exercises centralized power over what shall be produced and who shall get it.

It is not clear whether such critics fear centralized bureaucratic power or reliance on markets more. But it should be obvious from the economics you now know that these parallel criticisms should pose a real dilemma for the critics. If we do not rely on decentralized markets and also do not rely on centralized control and planning, how *will* the economy be organized? Who *will* make the decisions as to what shall be produced, how it shall be produced, what resources shall be used, and who shall get the output? Most supporters of modern capitalism argue that the case for the market system is precisely that it assures a highly decentralized system of decision-making, with widely dispersed economic power. Over 200 million different individuals with different views and different judgments "vote" on what ought to be done and how, and the market compromises the varying demands and preferences. Many modern capitalists fear central planning and government direction of economic activity, as do many communists, just because it would involve dramatic concentration of economic power in the hands of the central government planners.

If the radical critics deny both reliance on the market and central planning and control, what is their answer? None is obvious. Many, who have not faced the problems of how complex economies operate, call for a return to communal living and communal decision-making—a sort of return to Walden Pond, or at least to Skinner's Walden II utopia. But while this might work for a few hundred people on an island, or for some small community, to dream that it can operate effectively for a complex industrialized society of over 200 million people is a dream indeed—unless we are willing to return to a primitive standard of living, something like that of our ancestors two centuries or so ago. The attempts of communist societies to avoid reliance on both concentrated central planning and markets in complex societies

have failed consistently thus far. The USSR is the classic case in which individual freedom has been drastically limited and central planners have exercised far-reaching power over production and distribution decisions, in spite of Marxian doctrine that the state should "wither away." Recent Russian moves toward profit incentives and greater use of markets to guide production reflect growing difficulties in centrally planning an enormously complex economy. The other communist nations of eastern Europe have all had central economic dictatorships to a substantial degree, although like the Russians they started out with Marxian socialist ideals. Communist China is often cited as a counter-example, but it is far from clear that the Chinese masses really have much say over what is to be produced; political power is highly concentrated, as in the other communist nations. In any case, the Chinese standard of living is so low, and the levels of production so primitive, that the Chinese experience to date has little direct relevance for the organization of the advanced, industrialized Western economies.

It is striking that it is precisely those economies that have begun with the strongest communist ideals where the degree of political and economic democracy seems to be smallest. Conversely, the Western capitalist democracies seem, in fact, to have a higher degree of dispersed individual power over the political and economic processes, however imperfectly these Western capitalist economies may meet the ideals of a perfect market system. To make up your own mind on the radical challenge, consider the way the U.S. economy operates as you have studied it in the preceding twenty-three chapters. Then figure for yourself how all these decisions would be made and how an economy could operate more effectively without markets. Would you as a typical individual have more economic and political freedom and influence under a market or centrally planned system? Under which would your standard of living be higher?

Inequality, ethics, and incentives. Both critics and capitalist supporters agree that income and wealth are unequally distributed in the modern American economy; some facts were presented in Tables 24.1 and 24.2 . Radical critics believe this degree of inequality is indefensible and symptomatic of the basic unfairness of modern capitalism. Capitalist defenders differ widely as to what distribution of income is ethically most just—but most agree that the existing distribution reflects to a considerable extent different marginal contributions to the general welfare, and that the incentive of higher incomes is an important one if we want people to produce the goods and services demanded by others in the market.

If you do not care how income is distributed, or if you think people should be rewarded according to their contribution to total output, you will probably want to rely heavily on individual initiative and self-interest to induce individuals to work and take risks in meeting market demands. But if your value judgments prefer a more equal distribution of income, and you also want economic efficiency, you face a dilemma. How far can a society equalize incomes without destroying people's incentives to work hard, innovate, and take risks in producing the goods and services others want?

American capitalism already alters market-determined incomes substantially—through progressive taxes and heavy government transfer payment and services for lower and middle income groups. (See Cases 3 and 12 and Chapter 23.) But, although the great mass of Americans are in the comfortable middle income classes, big after-tax income inequalities remain. In contrast, the radical critic says, "from each according to his ability, to each according to his needs." He contends, explicitly or implicitly, either that scarcity is no longer a problem or that the common good will serve as a better incentive to efficient, well-directed production than will self-interest and income differentials. Thus, he sees no problem in taking away the existing capitalist incentive of earning more to provide more and better goods and services for yourself and your family.

Supporters of modern capitalism say this may be a nice ideal, but it simply does not correspond to the facts. First, to say that scarcity is no longer a problem, in America and in the world, is ridiculous if we let people judge for themselves.

Radical critics may say that Americans *should* not want more, but the empirical evidence is clear that they do. They take jobs rather than leisure, and they buy more goods and services with the higher incomes. You may not approve of inside plumbing, air conditioning, nice clothes, comfortable houses, and the like, but millions upon millions of Americans work long and hard for higher incomes to buy them. Even if we completely equalized incomes (temporarily neglecting the problem of incentives), the average family income of about $9,000 would still be well below what you, as a typical college graduate soon, would probably consider a decent minimum for yourself and your family. And the great bulk of the world's population lives in what we consider abject poverty—about two-thirds of all people have per capita *annual* incomes of $300 or less.

If we recognize the need to increase world production in order to raise living standards, the incentives to work, innovate, and take risks become a central problem for any society, capitalist or communist. History suggests that individual and family self-interest has been a powerful motive in modern and ancient times. "Command" economies, like feudalism and modern dictatorships, have attempted to solve the problem by force, but their success has generally been short-lived and in any case the approach is contrary to today's widespread belief in democracy and individual freedom. If the individual is to have considerable freedom, some system of incentives and rewards seems essential.

If we look at nations around the world today, it is striking that all of those with the highest living standards rely heavily on individual initiative and rewards in the market place for high productivity. For example, in 1970, gross national product per capita in the United States was about $5,000; in the Western European capitalist democracies from $1,800 to $3,500; in the USSR perhaps $1,800-$2,000; in India and Communist China, which together include some 40 percent of all living human beings, about $110-$120 per capita. The figures are rough, but close enough to make the general picture clear. Many capitalist supporters argue that the huge per capita income differentials between the Western capitalist democracies and the rest of the world are attributable in large part to the different types of economic systems in the different nations. Most economists give some weight to this argument but point to many other factors as well. In any case, the problem of effective incentive for work, innovation, and risk-taking is desparately important for the less-developed nations, where inequality is also far greater than in the Western capitalist nations.

Just why the Western European and North American market-directed, capitalist nations have such high per capita incomes compared to the rest of the world is a complex issue. But the general point looms large—the total production of a nation is the critical determinant of the living standard of its people, poor and rich. A wealthy nation will provide higher living standards even for its poor than the poor nations can for their middle and upper classes. Increased efficiency and total production are the major goals if a nation wishes to raise its standard of living. Comparatively speaking, little can be accomplished by redistributing income if the total income to be distributed is small, as in most of the less-developed nations. The "poor" of the Western capitalist nations are rich, and rapidly becoming richer, compared to the middle class and poor masses of the less developed economies.

Quantity vs. quality in economic life. Growth in GNP has become a national fetish in American capitalism, the radicals charge. More and more goods and services, rather than a better quality of life, dominate our thinking. This drive for more produces unhappy lives and alienated people. It produces dirty streets, slums, fouled rivers, and smoky air, while we grind out more unwanted and unneeded physical goods, is the charge.

Some supporters of modern capitalism agree. Others reply that the charges are grossly overstated. Some issues can be readily sorted out.

First, anyone who knows anything about GNP knows that it was never intended to be a measure of the general welfare, and that it includes only those goods and services that are produced and sold through the markets. (See Case 13.) Thus, thoughtful defenders of the capitalist system agree with critics that merely increasing the GNP

without reference to other factors would be a nonsense undertaking. GNP does not put any price on leisure or on other nonmarket activities. It does not take into account the composition of goods and services produced. It neglects pollution and the like. *But*, it is easy to go too far the other way. Currently produced goods and services *are* the foundation of the economic standard of living of the people of any nation. And although GNP is a very imperfect measure of total economic welfare, in a crude sense more goods and services mean higher consumption and higher investment levels for any nation. It is striking that only the rich nations can afford to be critical of growth as a national goal; the rest of the world's nations understandably hold economic growth to be their number one objective. They are desperately poor and they desperately need more goods and services for consumption and for investment.

It is important to remember that economic growth (increasing GNP per capita) does not *necessarily* imply more pollution, more wasted resources, or more of the other undesirable elements that the critics allege are the inescapable by-products of growth. We can devote our growing economic capacity to producing more electrical power or cleaner steel, to producing Beethoven quartets or beefsteak. The choice as to *how* to use the growing productive capacity is ours. Indeed, it is only rich nations that can consider using significant parts of their total production to pay for clean air, clean water, and the other amenities that are increasingly sought in modern America. The less-developed nations, for example, have such a need for steel that they cannot afford to use the extra resources required to produce steel cleanly. Only in the United States and other rich nations can we afford to think of making steel in ways that keep the nearby air clean. Pollution (more broadly, negative externalities in production) is nothing unique to capitalism. The Russians complain as bitterly about pollution as we do, and are as hard-put to doing something about it as we are. They, like us and everyone else, confront the fact that cleaning up air and water is an expensive undertaking, and that with limited resources, more devoted to antipollution measures means less than for something else.

Any understanding defender of the capitalist

market system will agree immediately that the market will not function satisfactorily where substantial negative externalities exist, in pollution, for example. In such cases, only private production costs will be included in the price of the final product, the price will be too low, and too much of the product will be produced. If we want the market to operate effectively where large externalities exist, we must find ways of internalizing those externalities—of including in the cost of producing the product its full social cost, not merely the private accounting costs that firms normally include in their prices. (See Case 10.) The problem is the same if the system is centrally planned, for example, the USSR. There, society must rely on the central planners to take the externalities into account, but in a market system we must rely on our government to levy taxes and other charges or to set pollution limits for producers if we want cleaner air and water. The central issue turns out not to be one of capitalism versus communism, but of what society's goals are and of finding efficient ways to accomplish those goals. We can have whatever balance we choose between quantity and quality of economic life, but we must choose. More of one in most instances necessarily implies less of the other.

Imperialism. Imperialism, the radicals charge, is the foundation of modern international capitalism. Huge corporations are exhausting the profit possibilities within their own national boundaries and are increasingly turning to international markets, especially to the less-developed nations where they can exploit the people and the natural resources. Partly, the charge is an economic one, that multinational corporations enrich themselves by exploiting the poor nations; partly, it is political, that the giant corporations lead their national governments into wars and military-political oppression of the poor nations to support the economic objectives of American corporations. The issues here are complex ones, and this brief book has given you only the elements necessary to analyze some of the *economic* issues. But we can go some distance with the tools you now have.

Some of the issues are factual. The claims of some radical critics are clearly overstated. The notion that the prosperity of America rests on the exploitation of the underdeveloped nations, particularly those in Southeast Asia, is patently false if one looks at the data. In 1970, total earnings of all U.S. corporations in the so-called developing countries were $3.7 billion, about 4 percent of total U.S. corporate profits in that year. Their total earnings in all of Southeast Asia (excluding India and the Philippines) in 1970 were $247 million, or about one-half of 1 percent of total U.S. profits. To argue that the profits made in the developing nations were the foundation of all U.S. corporate prosperity can hardly be taken seriously by anyone who looks at the facts. Even if we assume that U.S. corporations at home were primary beneficiaries of Vietnam war expenditures on goods and services, the picture is little changed. All such U.S. expenditures totaled less than $10 billion, producing profits of at most around 1–2 percent of total corporate profits.

The argument that American capitalist prosperity depends fundamentally on the raw materials obtained from the developing nations similarly will not stand careful examination. Total merchandise imports from all of Latin America, Asia, and Africa (excluding Japan) were $12 billion in 1970. This is compared with the total U.S. gross national product of just under $1 trillion, or about 1 percent of the total GNP. Although some of these imports of raw materials were very important to particular industries, it is obvious that the prosperity of the American capitalist system can hardly depend fundamentally on the import of 1 percent of its total production from the developing nations all over the world, much less from any one particular sector of the developing nations, such as Southeast Asia, which provided only a small fraction of the $12 billion total.

There is no doubt that foreign markets are important to many American businesses. This is especially true of Western Europe, Canada, and Japan, our biggest customers by far. Markets in the developing nations are important to some firms. However, the facts need to be kept in perspective in considering the allegations as to the dominant role of imperialism in relation to the American economy.

Chapters 21 and 22 developed the fundamental principles of comparative advantage and gain from trade in international as well as domestic exchange. The same principle holds for international investment. If each country specializes in doing what it does best, and all exchange, total production of wanted goods and services will be maximized and each of the participating countries will gain as a result, compared to a situation where each tries to be self-sufficient. Similarly, if American investors judge they can obtain higher returns, taking risk into account, in foreign nations than at home, they will presumably gain by making foreign investments. Similarly, if foreign nations invite these investments because they will help provide production there, jobs for nationals, and markets for their raw materials, presumably the foreign nations do so because they believe they will have a net gain from the transaction. Thus, international investment, when both nations and the business involved act voluntarily, presumably redounds to the benefit of both. This is not to say that the gains from trade and investment will be equally distributed between the two nations involved; often they are not. But unless each nation felt that it would gain, it is hard to see why each would enter into the transaction. Thus, the common radical argument that American investment worsens the plight of the developing nations in which the investment takes place is hard to accept.

Analyze an extreme case. Even if American corporations brought home to America all their profits each year, the developing nation involved would be better off than without the U.S. investment there—it would have more and/or higher-paying jobs for its workers. The fact that foreign workers chose to accept employment with American firms there suggests that, whatever the wages involved, they felt they were better off in those jobs than having no job at all or working in some other less-attractive job. If foreigners buy products produced there by American corporations, presumably they judge that is a better use of their incomes than any other available alternative. Clearly, the developing nation would have been still better off had the United States companies or government simply given them the capital that was invested in the country. But that

does not alter the central proposition that both countries, and the individuals and businesses in both countries, will presumably gain from international trade and investment if each enters into the exchange voluntarily.

Strikingly, it is the U.S. radicals who demand that we stop plundering the developing nations of their natural resources to support our high standard of living. By contrast, developing nations' governments generally plead with the United States and U.S. companies to buy *more* of their mineral and raw materials; they criticize the United States bitterly when we raise tariffs or impose quotas on U.S. purchases from the developing nations. And understandably so. For most developing nations, sale of their minerals and other products is the most effective means they have of obtaining the foreign exchange they need to buy food, materials, and capital goods abroad that they need to raise their own standard of living.

Much of the emotional content of the imperialism argument centers on war and international political activities. This book on economics gives you no basis for judging such military and political arguments. But you should be able to see some of the central issues, both factual and analytical, on the economic side of the debate.

CONCLUSION

The purpose of this concluding chapter has been to summarize some of the main radical criticisms of modern American capitalism, and, more important, to suggest how the analytical concepts and theory you have learned can help you reach your own conclusions about the validity of such charges. Although your tools give you only the beginnings of a complete analysis, they do suggest a fundamental framework around which thinking can be organized in judging such issues.

In considering possible alternatives to the U.S. economic system, it is important to realize that in the real world there is no example of either a pure free enterprise market system or an entirely centrally planned collective system. How different economies actually operate can usefully be summarized by looking at three major functions: deciding how output is to be used and distri-

Table 24.3

Country (Approximate GNP per capita in 1970 U.S. dollars)	How are consumption decisions made?	How are production decisions made?	How are consumption and production decisions coordinated?
U.S.A. ($4,800)	Primarily individually by consumers, but about 20 percent of GNP is purchased collectively through governments.	Primarily by private owners of resources, but about 10 percent of GNP is produced by governments.	Primarily through free markets, although some prices and outputs are controlled by governments.
United Kingdom ($2,300)	A majority by individual consumers, but about a third is purchased by governments or influenced by governments through subsidies.	A majority of output is produced by private firms, but the government share of production is greater than the government share of consumption.	Primarily through free markets, but many more prices are controlled by government than in the United States.
U.S.S.R. ($1,700)	Individuals are substantially free to choose among available goods, but government largely determines what commodities are produced.	The overwhelming majority by government enterprises, but a third of agricultural output is privately produced.	Primarily through central planning for heavy industry and broad categories of output. In allocating consumer goods and labor, considerable reliance is now placed on the market mechanism.
China ($100–115)	Because of the low level of economic development in China, most consumers have a very limited selection of goods to choose from. Roughly 80 percent of the population live on agricultural communes and consume mainly the food they produce. Central planners attempt to set and enforce targets for most agricultural production. For industrial output, central planners set production goals for state-owned enterprises. A few consumer goods are distributed through markets.		

buted, deciding what goods are to be produced and how, and, finally, coordinating consumption and production decisions.

Table 24.3 summarizes how these functions are carried out in four economies. In each country, some decisions are made collectively and others individually, and every country relies to some extent on the market mechanism to coordinate these decisions. The difference between any two economies is one of degree,

and the difference changes as countries respond to economic problems. In the United States, for example, the share of output collectively purchased through government has increased substantially over the last half century, as externalities and public goods became more important. By contrast, the Soviet Union has placed greater reliance on the market system to make its allocation decisions, as the Soviet economy became larger and decision-making more complex. Although these two economies remain far apart in their economic organization, they appear to be moving closer together on these scores. The practical advantages in terms of economic efficiency of mixing different types of economic organization keeps individual countries from operating according to an ideologically pure extreme. The lesson of history may well be that different combinations of economic institutions best serve the objectives of societies under different conditions.

In comparing capitalism and communism, a favorite trick of advocates on each side is to compare the actual operations of the opposing system, with all of its practical shortcomings, with the ideal operation of the system they favor. Communist critics, thus, generally point to the American economy in operation with all of its day-to-day practical shortcomings— monopoly, inflation, unemployment, and the like. By comparison, they suggest that communism can avoid all these shortcomings, and point out how communism might ideally operate. It is easy to point to practical shortcomings in the U.S. economy and to infer from that that communism with central political planning would be a much better way of letting individuals decide what should be produced, how it should be produced, and who should get it in an economy. Capitalists are often no more fair in their criticism of communist systems in operation. But if we are to examine the day-to-day frailties of one system, we should do the same for the other. The market has its weaknesses in meeting the demands of millions of different consumers—but so does central planning, the main practical alternative. Or you may want to compare an idealized market system against an idealized textbook picture of democratic socialism. But comparing one idealized system with the real world operations of the other is unlikely to provide a very enlightening basis for intelligent judgments on the real merits of the competing systems.

Index